Short-Term Macroeconomic Policy in Latin America

NATIONAL BUREAU OF ECONOMIC RESEARCH

Edited by
Jere Behrman
James A. Hanson

Short-Term Macroeconomic Policy in Latin America

Other Conference Series No. 14

Published for the National Bureau of Economic Research Inc.
by
Ballinger Publishing Company,
Cambridge, Mass.
A Subsidiary of Harper & Row Publishers, Inc.

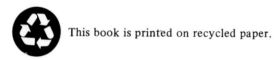
International Standard Book Number: 0-88410-489-3

Library of Congress Catalog Card Number: 78-24053

Printed in the United States of America

Library of Congress Cataloging in Publication Data

Main entry under title:
Short-term macroeconomic policy in Latin America.

   Proceedings of a conference jointly sponsored by the Latin American Institute for Economic and Social Planning, Ministerio de Planificación y Política
Económica de Panamá, and the National Bureau of Economic Research, held in
Isla Contadora, Panama, Oct. 31-Nov. 2, 1975.
   1. Latin America—Economic policy—Congresses. 2. Latin America—Economic
conditions—Mathematical models—Congresses. I. Behrman, Jere, R. II. Hanson,
James A. III. National Bureau of Economic Research. IV. Latin American Institute for Economic and Social Planning. V. Panama. Ministerio de Planificación y
Política Económica.

HC125.S49	330.9'8'003	78-24053
ISBN 0-88410-489-3		

Relation of the National Bureau Directors to Publications Reporting Conference Proceedings

Since the present volume is a record of conference proceedings, it has been exempted from the rules governing submission of manuscripts to, and critical review by, the Board of Directors of the National Bureau.

*(Resolution adopted July 6, 1948,
as revised November 21, 1949,
and April 20, 1968)*

Prefatory Note

This volume contains some of the papers presented at the Conference on Planning and Short-Term Macroeconomic Policy in Latin America, held in Isla Contadora, Panama on October 31 through November 2, 1975. The conference was sponsored by the National Bureau of Economic Research, Instituto Latinoamericano de Planificación Económica y Social (ILPES), and Ministerio de Planificación y Política Económica de Panamá. We are grateful to the IBM Corporation for its financial support for this conference and to the members of the Program Committee, James Hanson, Jere Behrman, M. Ishaq (Ned) Nadiri, and Nicolás Ardito Barletta. We wish to thank the staff members of the Panamanian Ministry of Planning responsible for making local arrangements for the conference.

Martin Feldstein, President
National Bureau of Economic Research

Contents

ix

List of Figures

List of Tables

JERE
BEHRMAN
JAMES A.
HANSON

Editors' Introduction
to
Short-Term
Macroeconomic
Policy in
Latin America

In 1974 and 1975 the Latin American economies experienced particularly severe stagflation. Many of the Central American and Caribbean countries suffered from double digit inflation, which normally is confined to the southern cone of South America, while in that region Chile and Argentina suffered from hyperinflation, abnormal even for them, of over 30 percent per month. Brazilians, Colombians, and Peruvians saw the rate of inflation double or triple. At the same time growth rates generally fell substantially below those obtained during the previous long period of prosperity, urban unemployment increased, and it became difficult, if not impossible, to absorb the rapidly growing labor force in productive employment.

As a result, the Panamanian Ministry of Planning and Economic Policy, the Latin American Institute for Economic and Social Planning (ILPES), and the National Bureau of Economic Research decided to hold a conference to reexamine short-run macroeconomic policy as applied to the Latin American economies. The objectives of this reexamination were: 1) to evaluate the usefulness to Latin

American planners of recent work on short-run forecasting techniques, particularly econometric models, to improve the planner's ability to participate in short-run policymaking and thus increase the weight given to developmental goals in day-to-day policymaking; 2) to reassess short-run constraints on policymaking, often crucial in determining the success of development plans, particularly in light of the prevailing Latin American version of stagflation; and 3) to consider the impact of conventional monetary and fiscal policy in the Latin American institutional framework and to examine some less conventional policies.

The conference on short-term macro policy in Latin America was held in November 1975 at Isla Contadora in Panama. This volume represents a selection of papers presented at that conference.

The first paper, by the coeditors, suggests some essential modifications that must be made in prototype, developed country econometric models before they are suitable for Latin American. Examples are taken from recent theoretical and econometric work and from the Behrman Chilean and the Behrman-Vargas Panamanian models.

First, particular attention must be paid to the wage-price-output nexus. The possibility of surplus labor, of disguised unemployment, and of poor unemployment figures should be taken into account. In inflationary economies various hypotheses regarding price and wage formation must be explored.

Second, the foreign sector cannot be treated cursorily, since it is of crucial importance in most developing economies. For example, early development plans tended to emphasize import substitution, treating exports as fixed and using an overvalued exchange rate and tariffs as policy instruments. Most recent work shows that major and minor exports respond significantly to price incentives. Thus, exports represented another avenue for growth which might have been exploited by alternative policies, in particular, maintaining more realistic exchange rates.

A third important and somewhat neglected interrelationship is the link between the government budget, monetary policy, and the balance of payments. Ambitious government spending programs must be financed, but limited taxing capacity and small local capital markets make this difficult, leaving either foreign borrowing or monetary emission as alternatives. These may have unintended and undesirable effects on the balance of payments. The structuralist school has also pointed out reverse linkages running from poor export performance and slow agricultural growth to rapid monetary expansion. Thus, neglect of this interrelationship leads to an overstatement of the available policy options, and returns us to the wage-price-output nexus mentioned earlier.

These problems are far from settled issues in developed country models. Indeed, they are increasingly becoming the subject of intense study in the Phillips curve-rational expectations debate, the monetary theory of the balance of payments literature, and the criticisms of passive or interest rate targeted monetary policy. Further study of developing countries can help resolve these issues as well as provide specific answers for Latin American policymakers.

The two economy-wide econometric models included in this volume not only meet the three objectives of the conference but also shed some light on the issues raised by the coeditors. The Behrman-Vargas study of Panama is the first medium sized, quarterly econometric model of a developing country and involved construction of quarterly output series as well as econometric estimation. The model tracks the major variables within the sample period, indicating the potential usefulness of similar exercises in other countries if reasonably good quarterly data can be obtained within a relevant time horizon. In general, agricultural production and exports seem responsive to price variables. Policy simulations provide slight support for the effectiveness of fiscal policy as exports move inversely to government spending, indicating supply bottlenecks. Even less support is found with the model for the effectiveness of monetary policy, as measured by variations in agricultural credit. Service exports, represented by net income from the Canal Zone, have a much larger multiplier.

These results seem to support a monetary model of the balance of payments, but the authors warn that the linkages yielding this result are not clear. They are particularly concerned with improving the specification of the capital account of the balance of payments, where the possible interest inelasticity of foreign loans casts some doubt on the applicability of fiscal policy results to large budget deficits. Moreover, the authors also point out that (unspecified) inventory variations, not imports, are used to close the model residually in the face of demand shocks, which also may not be a correct interpretation for large policy changes.

The Duran-Solis model of Nicaragua is less ambitious, being essentially an experiment in using a model of minimum complexity, based on GNP, domestic credit, and a few other variables, to track the economy. Domestic credit has a strong, positive effect on private investment and consumption, but a strong negative effect on the balance of payments, through imports and capital flows, reflecting a monetary approach to the balance of payments. The success of the exercise and the model's usefulness in illustrating the effects of exogenous shocks indicate that this approach may be fruitful for other countries.

The ability to track within sample data is only one measure of a model's effectiveness; perhaps its ability to forecast is even more important. However, most econometric models of developing countries are of recent origin and based on annual data. Thus, there is little data with which to evaluate their forecasting performance. An exception is Abel Beltran del Rio's Wharton-Mexico model; his paper provides a useful evaluation along these lines. As with other Wharton models, forecasting is done through a mixture of econometrics and expert opinion. The paper shows that there is some improvement in accuracy as the forecast horizon shortens; the use of expert opinion also reduced forecast errors. However, the paper also highlights the difficulty of forecasting when the government is a major source of expert opinion as well as an output consumer. According to Beltran del Rio the two areas that exhibited the worst errors in prediction—primary production and the trade balance—suffered from forecasts that shaded toward government predictions.

The following papers by Brodersohn, Barro, and Fernandez deal specifically with the wage-price-output nexus and, indirectly, with the effectiveness of monetary policy in the larger Latin American economies. Brodersohn estimates a traditional Phillips curve relation for Argentina and finds no significant relationship between the rate of wage change and unemployment, particularly when fairly rapid and full adjustment to inflation is taken into account. (Over 90 percent of the adjustment to errors in expectations occurs within one year and the coefficient of adaptive inflationary expectations does not differ significantly from one.) Changes in strike activity are also important in explaining wage inflation.

Brodersohn concludes that aggregate demand policies acting through changes in unemployment will not affect wage inflation, although policies that act on expectations will be important. He supports this conclusion by referring to the significant effect of the wage-price control policies of Campora-Peron-Gelbard period and of the budgetary restraint of the Ongania-Krieger Vasena period. However, the former case is a short period at the end of the time series, which preceded a major upsurge in inflation. In the latter case it is difficult to separate the usual effect of reduced aggregate demand on inflation and thereby on expectations from a direct effect on expectations.

Barro's and Fernandez's papers deal with the outprice-price nexus rather than the traditional Phillips curve. Both papers concentrate on the effectiveness of monetary policy and posit a link between money and prices and prices and output. Both papers also posit the rational expectations hypothesis that only unexpected changes in money-prices will affect output. Barro uses a simple autoregressive process to predict money, and thus, as he points out, it is difficult to separate the rational expectations hypothesis from one in which actual money growth has lagged effects. The Fernandez paper allows for more complex monetary process, involving past inflation as well as past monetary growth, by using Box Jenkins ARIMA estimates. Both he and Barro find relatively short autoregressive processes. They also experiment with other variables to predict monetary growth with little additional effect, except in Barro's study of Mexico.

Both papers find that unexpected changes in monetary policy are relatively ineffective. Most, if not all, (unexpected) monetary growth (80-90 percent) seems to lead to price changes; there is only a small feedback to higher output. This supports Lucas's hypothesis that response to nominal shocks should be less when such shocks are frequent.

Barro finds a significant effect only in the case of Mexico, where there is some doubt about the independence of money—the terms of trade, effective exchange rate, and U.S. variables are important variables in both equations. Barro's paper predicts 1974 and 1975 output reasonably accurately. Insignificant coefficients are the rule for Colombia and Brazil, though here the monetary processes are not well specified. Fernandez's paper also finds nearly insignificant co-efficients for Brazil (quarterly data). He obtains small coefficients for Argentina, though here the data refer only to industrial output, there being no quarterly information on total output. Fenandez's simulations of cuts in money growth in Argentina produce periods of stagflation—prices rising and output falling—such as those that lead to claims that the "old" remedies don't work. However his model is one in which only the "old" remedies will work, with some lag.

Wachter's paper is also concerned with monetary policy, but with its formulation rather than its effectiveness. She tests a quasi structuralist model in which reductions in agricultural supply lead to rapid increases in relative prices of agriculture (because of rapidly clearing markets) and would cause urban unemployment in the face of down-wardly rigid industrial prices, except for "passive" monetary policy on the part of the authorities. Using quarterly data Wachter finds a significant effect of agricultural prices on the Chilean CPI—other prices do not grow more slowly when agricultural prices rise—and some evidence of money reacting to past price changes, thus supporting the structuralist view. However, these effects are less pronounced in annual data.

The papers by Siri and Borts and Hanson deal with the foreign sector and its effect on the domestic economy. Siri presents a model that determines output in five Central American countries based on their major exports and intraregional trade. In general he finds significant responses to prices, in some cases with a lag, supporting the view of exports mentioned above. The multiplier effects of major exports range from 1.5 (Costa Rica) to about 1 (Guatemala). This is similar to Behrman and Vargas's Panamanian results for services exports. The model tracks each country's output reasonably well, indicating these countries' dependence on foreign markets. The significant and different time trends in the export supply equations of each country indicate much work remains to be done in explaining export supply.

The Borts-Hanson paper also is concerned with the foreign sector, but concentrates on its interrelationships with monetary and output growth. The paper uses a home goods–flow variant of the monetary model of the balance of payments. Changes in (flow) monetary emission produce changes in relative prices so that households feel they have more income since they do not "notice" the loss of reserves. Thus *all* of the extra monetary emission does not "leak" out and monetary policy has some effect on output. However, a flow loss in reserves does occur and thus eventually the flow emission has to be reversed or the effective exchange rate changed. The possibility of a (small) effect on output is consistent with Behrman's and Barro's results and seems borne out in the paper's empirical work on Panama. Panamanian prices do not move proportionately to import prices and domestic credit is shown to have small but significant effects on prices and output.

The final paper in the volume is Schydlowsky's study of excess capacity and policies to reduce it. Casual empiricism suggests there is plenty of idle capacity in Latin American manufacturing, but Schydlowsky shows just how prevalent it is and suggests reasons for its occurrence—implicit and explicit second shift premia, high user cost, and overvalued exchange rates, among others. He argues that changes in these policies could yield significant benefits in terms of additional output, employment, and improved balance of payments positions.

The papers in this volume represent a good sampling of work on Latin American macro problems and policies. They indicate that econometric forecasting is a useful exercise for Latin American countries, even if undertaken at a minimum level. They also point up the importance of exports to growth and the strong influence of price variables and effective exchange rates on exports.

The papers generally provide little support for the effectiveness of monetary policy. In small, open economies such as Panama there seems to be a large spillover into the balance of payments, while in closed, inflationary economies such as Brazil and Argentina the analyses seem to indicate that prices (and wages) react swiftly to changes in monetary growth with output only briefly affected. In medium sized economies such as Mexico there is a greater effect; but here the balance of payments again presents a constraint. Fiscal policy seems somewhat more effective in raising output, although its interrelationship with monetary policy and foreign loans may provide a constraint on its use. Nonconventional macro policies, such as removing constraints to high utilization rates, may be a more promising method of affecting output in the long as well as short run.

We wish to thank the sponsors that made this useful and provocative conference possible: the Latin American Institute for Economic and Social Planning, the Panamanian Ministry of Planning and Political Economy, and the National Bureau of Economic Research (as part of its Latin American Workshop Series). We hope that readers will find this conference volume helpful in understanding the current state of analysis of important short-run macroeconomic policy issues in Latin America and elsewhere in the developing world.

1

JERE BEHRMAN
and
JAMES A.
HANSON

The Use of Econometric Models in Developing Countries*

1. INTRODUCTION

National-income-determination models and stabilization have not been the major concern of either empirical or theoretical macroeconomic analysis in the developing economies. For example, a recent survey of the state of the art regarding the use of economywide models for less developed countries (LDCs), Blitzer, et al. (1975), does not even include a chapter on macroeconomic income-determination models.

Instead, the dominant frameworks for macroeconomic policy analysis and policy recommendations have been provided by Harrod-Domar aggregate-growth models, static and dynamic linear-programming models, and Chenery-Strout two-gap models.[1] These

*This paper draws on Behrman, "Econometric Modeling of National Income Determination in Latin America, with Special Reference to the Chilean Experience," presented at the Seminar on *Use of Econometric Models in Latin America*, sponsored by The Center of Economic and Demographic Studies of El Colegio de México and the National Bureau of Economic Research, held in Mexico City on November 27–29, 1974.

models generally include assumptions that: (i) the degree of capacity utilization, the rate of inflation, and the level of aggregate demand are unimportant considerations; (ii) that the financial constraints on government and central bank behavior (and, thus, the entire fiscal-monetary-income-international policy-inflation nexus) can be ignored; (iii) short-run flexibility is limited by low elasticities of substitution and short-run unresponsiveness to price; (iv) (at least for the programming models on which the greatest resources have been expended) the most interesting question is "what *could* happen if socially optimal readjustment of the economy occurred in response to policy changes," rather than "what *would* happen if the independent economic units which make up the economy followed their traditional behavioral patterns in response to such changes."[2] The resulting models usually include only real phenomena and are characterized by supply bottlenecks resulting from foreign exchange or capital constraints.

Such an emphasis reflects two widely held views: (1) Growth is a relatively more important economic objective (and stabilization less important) in the developing countries than in the developed countries. (2) Income-determination models involving demand as well as supply are of limited value for developing economies.[3]

Some exceptions to the predominant view have long existed. The participants in the "structuralist-monetarist" controversy in Latin America, for example, accorded significant importance to inflation and stabilization policies in the development process.[4]

These exceptions have been increasing in number. The recognition by such authors as Schydlowsky (Chapter 9, this volume) and Behrman (1973b) of considerable underutilized capacity, particularly in cyclical downturns, has increased interest in using national-income-determination models for stabilization purposes. Numerous partial equilibrium econometric estimates have been made that imply significantly nonzero elasticities of substitution and significant responses to prices in both capacity utilization and capacity creation decisions.[5] Even the strongest advocates of supply-oriented capital and foreign-exchange-constrained analysis seem to be having second thoughts about the importance of short-run factors and stabilization problems. For example, throughout the above-cited survey by Blitzer, et al. (1975), there are frequent references to the need to consider short-run features (e.g., prices responses, capacity utilization determination, aggregate-demand-related policies).

Recently, because of this growing interest in stabilization and other short-run problems, a large number of Keynesian-based national-income-determination models have been constructed and utilized for the developing economies.[6]

A basic problem with the construction and use of these models for policymaking purposes in developing economies is the general lack of accurate, up-to-date information (e.g., quarterly information on output and its components and sectoral or cyclical indicators that are available with a short time lag). This is a gap that at present forces policymakers to act on incorrect or dated information.[7] It also means that income-determination models of developing countries are annual rather than quarterly. However, in the developed countries econometric models have been "most successful" in predicting output in the next quarter or six months; over a nine or twelve-month period simple trends are often as good.[8] Thus improvement in modeling may require an investment in improving the data base, an investment that has the additional payoff of providing more accurate and up-to-date information to policymakers.[9]

There remains the more philosophical question of our present ability to forecast and affect in predictable ways the very short run with corresponding effects on the long run. However, political pressures force governments to accept some advice and take some action in the very short run, often to the detriment of the long run. Therefore, it is probably best for economists to offer advice on the short run and on short-run–long-run tradeoffs while specifying the fragile nature of such advice.

A second problem results from a simplistic transfer of aggregate demand models of developed economies with little or no adjustment for the special conditions in the developing countries. As a result, there are numerous shortcomings in such models' specifications, shortcomings that, while they may also exist in developed country applications, are perhaps less important in that context. For example: (1) National income is determined by aggregate demand in a Keynesian fashion with no testing for the existence of possible constraints due to the stocks of capital or labor, the supply of foreign exchange, or supply limitations imposed by quantitative restrictions.[10] (2) Underemployed or surplus labor and dualism in the labor market are not explicitly incorporated. (3) Aggregation is so great that there is no possibility of capturing the impact of policies on relative prices, even though economists like Hansen (1973b) have maintained that policies in developing nations are primarily reflected in altered relative prices and Wachter (Chapter 8, this volume) has demonstrated, econometrically, the structuralist proposition that differing speeds of adjustment of relative prices (plus passive money) may result in inflation. The possible importance of intersectoral flows, moreover, is lost by the high level of aggregation. On the other hand, data problems are often cited as preventing disaggregation to any significant level, and there remains the question of whether disaggregated models provide more accurate projections of the aggregate variables, and to what extent such models divert attention from more global problems, such as the financial-monetary-international policy-income nexus. (4) Potential policy variables are often overlooked. For example, it is often assumed that an overvalued exchange rate will be maintained through a continuance of exchange control although this is obviously a policy that is subject to change. (5) The significance of the foreign sector as a source of noncompetitive, intermediate imports, of capital goods, of government finance, and of household money and nonmonetary asset holdings is not well presented. (6) The importance—owing to fragmented and poorly functioning capital markets—of direct flows and retained earnings in the real investment process is not explored. (7) The degree of endogeneity of fiscal, monetary, and international variables and their interrelation in poorly functioning capital markets is ignored with the result that policy options are overstated. (8) There is little attempt to integrate the short-run income-determination model with long-run development models. In particular, although plant and equipment decisions are well treated, no attempt is made to study human capital formation, despite the growing evidence for its significance in development. The role of social overhead capital, long emphasized by such leading development economists as Rosenstein-Rodan (1961), also is not explored.[11] (9) There is a tendency to ignore economywide disequilibrium.[12]

At the same time as interest in and use of income-determination–stabilization models for the LDCs has been growing, controversies have emerged over the specification of such models in the developed economies. In the past decade, critics have claimed that deficiencies in the theoretical structure, deficiencies that may be related to points 1 to 9 above, make any analysis of stabilization policies based on such models suspect. Recently, however, some convergence seems to have occurred, at least regarding the nature of the issues. Ando (1974), Blinder and Solow (1973), and Hansen (1973a) and others have attempted to adjust the IS-LM model to explore these controversies. However, less agreement has been obtained on the significance of Lucas's (1976) point that systematic attempts to use an estimated model for policymaking purposes alters the parameters of the system and thus the responses to policy.

Given some convergence on the nature of stabilization issues in the developed countries and given the increasing preoccupation with stabilization problems in the developing countries, the time seems ripe to reexamine the applicability of modern stabilization analysis to the special situations of the developing countries.

The strategy pursued in this chapter is to examine briefly each of the components of recent econometric models used in developed economies. Then the chapter considers how these models need to be altered for analysis of stabilization in developing economies. Models of Chile and Panama are considered as examples incorporating these alterations.

The prototype model for the developed economies uses as a starting point the combination of the features of the closed economy model of Ando (1974) and the analysis of international capital movements of Branson (1974). These models are somewhat complex in order to incorporate a number of features discussed in recent controversies. Solution by differentiation does not lead to simple elegant expressions. For an understanding of such models beyond the explanation provided below, the reader is referred to the papers by Ando and Branson.

Regarding the two developing country models, Behrman's (1976b) Chilean study is an annual macroeconomic model for the period 1945-1965. It is a nine-sector model with capacity creation, capacity utilization, export, import, and price and wage determination relations for each sector involving 172 endogenous variables. Consumption–savings decisions are estimated for households and nonprofit institutions, business, and the government. Many aspects of government fiscal and monetary policies are endogenous. Its specification attempts to overcome the nine shortcomings listed above, which are frequently encountered in Keynesian-based national-income-determination models for developing economies. Less explicit reference is made to Behrman and Vargas's (Chapter 2, this volume) trimestral model of Panama. Though less complex than the Chilean study this model still includes 97 endogenous variables describing production, prices, and wages in three broad sectors—exports, other traded and nontraded goods—which in turn are subdivided into eight producing sectors. Final demand components are also estimated separately.

Finally, before considering the appropriate modifications of the developed country model, two caveats are in order. First, the developing countries are far from homogeneous. For almost any relevant feature the range across countries is enormous. In what follows below, therefore, the suggested modifications reflect characteristics not necessarily common to all developing countries but at least to a significant number of them. Second, a separate paper, if not a book, could be written on data problems. In this chapter some allusions are made to these problems, but they are not treated systematically so that the chapter can be kept to a manageable length.

2. COMPONENTS OF NATIONAL-
INCOME-DETERMINATION MODELS

Table 1–1 presents the prototype model for the developed economies that is used as a starting point for the discussion of this section. Each of the major components of that model will be examined in turn with a focus on altering them for analysis of stabilization issues in developing countries.

2.1 Labor Market, Labor Supply, and
Determination of Prices and Wages

2.1.A The Developed Country Model: Equations (1) through (4) describe the labor market and the determination of prices and wages in a representative econometric model of developed economies.

Equation (1) depicts the short-run relationship between output and the required man-hours to satisfy demand. It is assumed that at any point in time the economy has a collection of machines whose labor-output ratios were determined by the technology and the expected relative prices at the time of each machine's manufacture. Given the current relative prices, machines (and the labor associated with them) are used in descending order of efficiency until the demanded (= desired) output is produced. New machines may contain different technology based on expected relative prices. Thus producers' durable equipment takes the form of putty-clay.

Equation (2) gives the unemployment rate as a function of man-hours and population characteristics. It incorporates into one expression the determination of hours worked per person and the response of labor force size to employment conditions and to demographic features of the population.

Equation (3) is a Phillips curve relation for the determination of the rate of change of wages as a function of the unemployment rate and price expectations. It may be considered a reduced form equation of underlying supply and demand relations in the labor market. Lucas (1973) argues that this relation may depend upon government policy and provides some evidence to that effect.

Equation (4) determines the price level of output under the hypothesis of a (possibly lagged) markup on minimized average cost. The price level should vary proportionally with the money wage level and reciprocally with long-run productivity. The markup factor is μ. Since the markup may vary in the short run with the utilization of capacity, the unemployment rate is also included in the function.

Table 1-1. Prototype Macroeconomic Model for Developed Economies

I. Labor Market, Supply Price, and Wages
    Demand for Labor
$$E = E(Z) \tag{1}$$

Supply of Labor and the Definition of Unemployment Rate

$$u = u(E, N) \tag{2}$$

Determination of Money Wage Level

$$\frac{\dot{W}}{W} = W\left(u, \ L\left[\left(\frac{\dot{P}}{P}\right)_{-1}\right]\right) \tag{3}$$

Determination of Real Wage Rate and Price Level

$$P = Wf\left(L\left[\frac{E}{Z}\right], \mu, u\right) \tag{4}$$

II. Product Market and Aggregate Demand
    Definition of Net National Product
$$Z = C + I + G + X - IM \tag{5}$$

Consumption Function

$$C = C(Y, A) \tag{6}$$

Investment Function

$$I = I(Z, r_k, \tau) \tag{7}$$

Government Expenditure

$$G = G_{ex} + G_{end}(Y, N, r_k) \tag{8}$$

Import Function

$$IM = IM(ER, P, Y) \tag{9}$$

Export Function

$$X = X(ER, P) \tag{10}$$

III. Financial Markets and Assets
    Demand for Real Assets
$$V = A \cdot f^V(r_k^h, r_b^r, r_s^h, Y) \tag{11}$$

Demand for Bonds

$$B/P = A \cdot f^B(r_k^h, r_b^r, r_s^h, Y) \tag{12}$$

Table 1-1.   continued

Demand for Foreign Securities

$$\frac{S \cdot ER}{P} = A \cdot f^S(r_k^h, r_b^r, r_s^h, Y) \tag{13}$$

Demand for Money

$$M/P = A \cdot f^M(r_k^h, r_b^r, r_s^h, Y) \tag{14}$$

Definition of Net Worth

$$A = V + \frac{M + B + S \cdot ER}{P} \tag{15}$$

Relation between Holding Rate and Capitalization Rate

$$r_k^h = r_k - \frac{r_k^e - r_k}{r_k} \tag{16}$$

Relation between Real and Nominal Short-Term Interest Rates

$$r_b^r = r_b - \frac{P^e - P}{P} \tag{17}$$

Relation between Holding and International Rate for Foreign Securities

$$r_s^h = r_s + \frac{ER^e - ER}{ER} \tag{18}$$

Generation of Expected Rate of Change of r_k

$$\frac{r_k^e - r_k}{r_k} = F^k\left(L\left[\frac{\dot{r}_k}{r_k}\right]\right) \tag{19}$$

Generation of Expected Rate of Change of Prices

$$\frac{P^e - P}{P} = F^P\left(L\left[\frac{\dot{P}}{P}\right]\right) \tag{20}$$

Generation of Expected Rate of Change of Exchange Rate

$$\frac{ER^e - ER}{ER} = F^{ER}\left(L\left[\frac{\dot{ER}}{ER}\right]\right) \tag{21}$$

Expected Income from Capital

$$\pi^e = F^\pi\left(\pi, P \cdot L\left[\left(\frac{\pi}{P}\right)_{-1}\right]\right) \tag{22}$$

Table 1-1. continued

Market Value of Capital

$$P \cdot V = \frac{\pi^e}{r_k} \tag{23}$$

IV. Identities and Miscellaneous Relations
Definition of Disposable Income

$$P \cdot Y = P \cdot Z + r_b \cdot B - P \cdot T + r_s \cdot S \cdot ER \tag{24}$$

Definition of Savings

$$d(P \cdot A) = P \cdot Y - P \cdot C \pm d^*(P \cdot V) \tag{25}$$

Definition of Income from Capital

$$\pi = P \cdot Z - W \cdot E - \tau_c (P \cdot Z - W \cdot E) \tag{26}$$

Capital Gains on Existing Capital

$$d^*(P \cdot V) = d(P \cdot V) - P \cdot I \tag{27}$$

Balance of Payments Surplus

$$H = P \cdot X - P \cdot IM + r_s \cdot S \cdot ER - d(S \cdot ER) \tag{28}$$

Tax Function

$$P \cdot T = T(P \cdot Z + r_b \cdot B + r_s \cdot S \cdot ER, \pi, \tau) \tag{29}$$

Government Budget Constraint

$$dM + dB = P \cdot G - P \cdot T + r_b \cdot B \tag{30}$$

V. Variable Definitions

A :   Net Worth of Consumers

B :   Government Debt Held by Private Sector

C :   Consumption in Constant Currency

$d^*(PV)$: Real Capital Gain on Existing Real Assets in Current Currency

E :   Employment in Man-Hours

ER :   Exchange Rate in Domestic Currency per Unit of Foreign Currency

ER^e :   Expected Exchange Rate in Domestic Currency per Unit of Foreign Currency

G :   Total Government Expenditures in Constant Currency

Table 1–1. continued

G_{ex}:	Exogenous Government Expenditures in Constant Currency
G_{end}:	Endogenous Government Expenditures in Constant Currency
H:	Surplus on Balance of Payments in Current Currency
I:	Net Investment in Constant Currency
IM:	Imports in Constant Currency
L:	Lag Operator
M:	Money Supply in Current Currency (Currency Plus Reserves)
N:	Vector Expressing Total Population and its Structure
μ:	Standard Mark-up Factor (i.e., the Ratio of Price of Output to its Minimized Cost of Production Expected to Prevail under Normal Employment Conditions)
P:	Price Level for Output
P^e:	Price Level Expected to Prevail
π:	Income from Real Assets in Current Currency
π^*:	Expected Income from Existing Real Assets in Current (not future) Currency
r_b:	Nominal Rate of Interest on Government Debt
r_b^r:	Real Rate of Interest on Government Debt
r_k:	Capitalization Rate (in real terms) Applicable to Real Assets
r_k^e:	Level of r_k Expected to Prevail
r_k^h:	Holding Rate (in real terms) Applicable to Real Assets
r_s:	Real Rate of Interest on Foreign Securities
r_s^h:	Holding Rate (in real terms) Applicable to Foreign Securities
S:	Net Foreign Securities Held by Private Sector
T:	Taxes in Constant Currency
τ:	Tax Rates (Subscript "C" refers to Corporations)
u:	Unemployment Rate
V:	Market Value of Existing Real Assets in Constant Currency
W:	Nominal Wage Rate per Man-Hour

Table 1-1. continued

X:	Exports in Constant Currency
Y:	Disposable Income in Constant Currency
Z:	Net National Product in Constant Currency

2.1.B.1 Wage and Price Determination in Dualistic Labor Markets: Most developing economies are characterized by dualism in labor and product markets. To capture the effects of long-run changes in the sectoral distribution of the labor force, as well as the short-run problems of income determination, it is necessary to include explicitly this dualism.

In a dualistic labor market there is thought to be a modern sector that is market oriented and pays wages approximately proportional to the value of the marginal product of labor. Its technology is of recent vintage and permits only limited substitution between primary factors.[13] In some countries unions are quite powerful in this sector.

The traditional sector is much less market oriented. In most countries a major component of this sector is noncommercial agriculture. For this subsector the marketed surplus often is a small part of total production and *may* be an inverse function of price. However, analysis in Behrman (1968) suggests that this response is *positive* and *quite large*. While factor substitution usually is possible, the relatively high labor-to-capital ratio often results in disguised unemployment with marginal products substantially below those in the modern sector. Because of family and communal arrangements, the income of individual laborers may be determined by tradition and related to the average rather than the marginal product.

The dominant view of the impact of this dualism on the labor market is based on the well-known model of Lewis (1954). The average share of labor in the traditional sector, plus a differential for moving costs, provides a floor for modern sector wages.[14] The average share of labor in the traditional sector is assumed to remain approximately constant over a wide range of sizes of the traditional labor force.[15] It is therefore argued that over a substantial range the supply of labor for the modern sector is quite elastic.

One way of incorporating this approach into equations (1) and (2), would be to apply them only to the modern sector (with all the included variables referring only to that sector). The traditional sector would act as one residual claimant on labor, and urban unemployment, open or disguised, as the other.[16] In practice it might be necessary to aggregate these two residuals, given the problems of defining urban unemployment and due to continual shifts in demand for "modern" goods, which affect both open unemployment and rural-urban migration in a complicated fashion.

Prima facie this approach might *seem* to lead to an approximation of a Keynesian case in the modern sector, with an "unlimited supply of labor" at a fixed wage and employment in the modern sector determined by the demand for modern sector goods. But this wage is fixed in real terms, and thus the situation is also classical in an important sense, which suggests an alternative approach.

If modern and traditional goods were good substitutes, so that we could treat them as one good, equations (1) and (2) could be said to apply to the economy and equation (3) could be replaced by an equality between (expected) real wages in the modern sector and the exogenously given, traditional labor income. Equilibrium employment and output would be unresponsive to changes in aggregate demand. Rather than wages determining the price level, as shown in equation (4), prices (as determined by equation [14], the demand for money) would tend to determine nominal wages in classical fashion.[17] These results hold in their essentials if the goods are not perfect substitutes, although in this case a shift in demand patterns could alter the distribution of employment and, if directed toward modern goods, yield some aggregate efficiencies.

The problem with this approach is that it does not cover the case of urban Keynesian unemployment, resulting from a lack of aggregate demand. For a given, fully employed labor force there is a unique allocation of labor that equates (expected) urban wages with a given, traditional labor income.[18] To consider both dualistic labor markets and Keynesian unemployment the strict equality between labor incomes in the traditional and modern sectors must be replaced by a gradual adjustment process toward equality. In that case a drop in aggregate demand, assuming also a slow adjustment of prices, would lower modern sector output, cause urban unemployment, and slow rural-urban migration out of the growing population. The average rural income might differ from the (expected) wage for a time.

Over a longer period migration and human capital would alter urban labor supply substantially, and capital-labor ratios would vary. Moreover, changes in minimum (as opposed to average) wages may depend (inversely) upon (lagged?) urban unemployment. These factors would tend to narrow the relation between measured (expected?) urban wages and the average share of labor in the traditional sector over the longer run.

The basic problem highlighted in this discussion is that equation (3) remains a reduced form of the operation of the labor market in which the underlying supply and demand relations are not well stated or perhaps even understood. The explicit statement of these relations becomes very important in explaining wages in one sector of a jointly determined two- (or more) sector model. In an explicitly two-sector model wages in the urban sector are determined by the demand for labor, which depends on nominal wages and prices of urban sector goods and the supply of labor, which in turn is dependent upon nominal wages and on prices in the *two* sectors. Far from being constant, rural supply, relative prices of rural goods, and rural incomes may all vary with employment in the urban sector.[19]

The same problem of incomplete specification exists in the equation of price determination via markup, expressed in equation (4), aside from the obvious point that short-run variations in markups (and therefore, their explanation) are much more important in countries where the industrial nonwage share reaches 40 to 50 percent of value added (see Michalopolous [1969]) and some important items in the price index are produced by government factories or closely controlled by governments. At best equation (4) could explain relative prices in a two-good model but not their absolute level.

One solution might be to treat the traditional sector rather than its labor force as a residual. The urban wage level could be related to the unemployment rate and some trend in rural incomes. The price *index* could be determined through a markup equation with a nonunitary elasticity of the price index with respect to urban wages. The difficulty with this approach is that it neglects the determinants of the intersectoral movements it is trying to model.

Perhaps the best solution would be to retain the demand-determined modern sector employment figure of equation (1) and jointly determine the unemployment rate, the wage in the modern sector, and the (residual) labor force, output, and average product in the traditional sector through a set of equations that require *relative* prices to adjust to equate demands and supplies for both traditional and modern products and long-run equality between real labor earnings in the two sectors. This approach obviously requires a division of aggregate demands between the two sectors and an additional equation to determine the *general* price level.

In the Chilean model (Behrman [1976b]) of income determination in an inflationary economy, the major determinant of the *gen-*

eral price level was the rate of change of the money supply, with its impact distributed over a number of years. As described below, this money supply was determined by other factors in the system, such as the government budget deficit. Because of the distributed lags in the price-determination process, moreover, stemming inflation is quite difficult unless expectations about future price movements can be lowered drastically.

Nonmonetary factors also affect the general price level. Cost-push factors operating through intermediate input and unit labor costs are more important in transmitting overall inflationary pressures (including those that arise from the role of expectations in the wage-bargaining process) than previous studies, such as Harberger (1963), have maintained. Real changes in per capita gross domestic product (and other indices of current activity), in labor productivities, in demands (final and intermediate) relative to sectoral capacity, and in the distribution of factoral income and of sectoral product have significant effects, as do foreign sector policies. Government minimum wages, although widely discussed in Chilean circles, do not appear to have a very significant impact on wage changes once other prices are incorporated into the wage change relations.

On the other hand, in the Panamanian case, which is probably a prototype of open economies, prices seemed to be largely determined by the world economy, plus taxes and tariffs. However, Borts and Hanson (Chapter 9, this volume) suggest the relation is not proportional, perhaps because of home goods and variations in the *effective* exchange rate or government price setting. Thus there is more scope for monetary policy than Johnson's (1973) simple, monetary model of the balance of payments allows, as discussed below. Regarding wages, the (expected) price levels are one of the most important determinants, unemployment rates and sectoral productivity seem less important, and minimum wages have almost no effect. Brodersohn (1977), Behrman (1971a), and other studies cited in Fernandez and Hanson (1977) confirm the fact that price expectations are important in Latin American wage determination, generally entering proportionately. However, Brodersohn (Chapter 7, this volume) in the Phillips curve context, and Barro (Chapter 6, this volume), Fernandez (Chapter 5, this volume), and Lucas (1973) in an alternative form provide little support for a stable relation either between wage growth and unemployment or between cyclical variations in real output and monetary fluctuations.

2.1.B.2 The Importance of the Foreign Sector: The foreign sector plays a much more important direct role in labor, production, and price relations in most developing economies (and probably in most small open developed countries) than is indicated in the model of Table 1-1. Four modifications of the counterparts of equations (1) to (4) for the modern sector need to be made to reflect the impact of the foreign sector.

(i) Some imported intermediate inputs and raw materials are critical in the production process. The elasticity of substitutions between such imports and domestic factors may be low or zero. Especially in the disequilibrium exchange rate system common for many developing economies, the constraint on production and employment may not be the putty-clay stock of machinery and equipment, but the availability of these·imported inputs. Equation (1) may require modification to reflect this possibility.

(ii) Equation (1) also needs to be modified to reflect the fact that technologies used in the modern sector are largely imported from developed countries with much different factor endowments. Very little choice may be available (or may be thought to be available) even ex ante for the capital-labor ratio of the developing countries. Therefore, the putty-clay response to expected relative prices is constrained to a choice among relatively capital-intensive technologies. What Eckaus (1955) calls the "factor proportions problem" limits the absorption of labor by the modern sector.

(iii) The discussion in section 2.1.B.1 suggests that for many developing economies equation (3) should be modified or the structural form more explicitly specified. One further modification needs to be made. In many developing economies an important and easily available index of inflationary expectations is the rate of change of the exchange rate. In addition to the history of past inflation, therefore, this variable (or some function of past values of it) should be included for such countries.

If wages respond to such factors, they may "overshoot" the devaluation-induced price rises in some industries. In that case it is possible that equation (1) does not hold because wage costs on the "last" machine needed to produce demanded output exceed the firm's income. Output is then determined by desired supply, not demand as indicated in (1), and unemployment is related to high real wages, not a lack of demand. Such an interpretation may explain the negative output effects associated with devaluation in Chile in the late 1950s (Harberger [1963]), Argentina in 1959, and Colombia in 1962.

(iv) In light of the widespread importance of consumption and intermediate and raw material imports if a variant of equation (4) is included, then it should be modified to reflect markups on imports as well as on labor costs. Changes in the international prices or in import policies, therefore, have direct effects on the domestic price level and on output, particularly in open economies such as those of the Caribbean and Central America.

2.2 Product Market and Aggregate Demand

2.2.A Developed Countries: Equation (5) is the definition of net national product. Equations (6) through (10) describe the demand for real output.

Equation (6) is the *consumption function.* Real consumption depends upon expected real disposable income (approximated by a distributed lag of actual real disposable income) and net worth in a variant of the life cycle hypothesis.

Equation (7) is the *investment function.* For the developed countries in which capital markets are well functioning so that the cost of capital is well identified, investment decisions are based on a comparison of the present value of the expected stream of income generated by the investment and the cost of investment. Simultaneous variables that enter into the investment decision, therefore, include the capitalization rate applicable to real assets and net national product in real terms. The appropriate tax rates also have a role.

Equation (8) defines total *government expenditure* as the sum of exogenous central government expenditures and endogenous local government expenditures. The latter respond fairly strongly to cyclical conditions of the economy.

Equation (9) is the *import function* and equation (10) is the *export function* for developed economies. Imports respond positively to the level of income and the domestic price level and inversely to the exchange rate (defined as the number of units of domestic currency per unit of foreign currency). Exports are assumed to respond directly to the exchange rate and inversely to the domestic price level.

2.2.B.1 Consumption in Developing Countries: For the developing economies, several hypotheses about private consumption behavior have been suggested. (i) Because of the existence of a large number of individuals at or near a subsistence income level, consumption may not be proportional to income even in the long run. If true, the high marginal propensity to consume at low income levels, *ceteris paribus*, may imply a relatively high multiplier. (ii) Retained business earnings (although not necessarily from corporations) are a relatively important source of savings. Therefore, a division between unretained and retained income of businesses might be desirable. Modigliani and Tarantelli (1975) provide some evidence that a further division between property and labor income may be less fruitful. (iii) The marginal propensity to consume out of the income generated in some sectors—especially sectors related to exports—may be higher than elsewhere in the economy. The inclusion of a separate argument in the function for income from exports might be desirable. This modification would further increase the impact of the foreign sector on stabilization. (iv) If interest rates are controlled, then a policy-oriented model would consider the direct effect of their decontrol on the rate of consumption. Controlled interest rates may also increase the substitution between foreign and domestic saving.

Finally, data problems may make it difficult to include nonmonetary assets in the measure of net worth.[20] This distortion is not as great as it would be for the developed countries because the stock of money balances represents a large percentage of privately held assets, perhaps as great as 40 percent in nominal terms.[21]

2.2.B.2 Investment in Developing Countries: For some of the more advanced developing countries, evidence exists that supports the use of the same basic formulation (e.g., Behrman [1972b] considers investment by sectors). More generally, however, substantial modifications are needed to reflect special aspects of capital markets, social overhead capital, and international considerations.

(i) Domestic capital markets in developing economies often are not well functioning. Markets are very fragmented, especially between the traditional and modern sectors. In the modern sector legal limits on nominal interest rates frequently are effective so that credit rationing occurs in bank markets. Government planning organizations also often attempt to control the allocation of physical capital by nonmarket means.

The net result is that much of the domestically financed investment does not pass through a capital market (or, at least not through "the" capital market). Instead it originates in retained earnings or in direct flows from the government. Government policy is often directed toward increasing the former source by changes in the terms of trade, by price ceilings, and foreign trade policies in favor of sectors in which investment is desired. Quite commonly industry is so favored over primary production, and import substitution or nontraditional exports are favored relative to traditional exports.

To capture these features, direct financial flows from the government and the results of quantitative allocations mechanisms need to be included in the investment function. Some success was obtained with these real credit variables in the Panamanian model. To represent the impact of policies that work through altering terms of trade, a multisector model is required.

(ii) The development literature emphasizes repeatedly the role of social overhead capital in the development process. Because of externalities and increasing returns to scale over the relevant range, Rosenstein-Rodan (1961) and others maintain that the government must increase such social overhead capital in order to induce private investment. Birnberg and Resnick (1973) show that social overhead capital was an historically important element in export growth. The role of social overhead capital in determining the stream of expected net income from investment, therefore, should be made explicit.

(iii) International considerations may enter into investment decisions in two important ways.

First, a considerable portion of the capital stock originates from direct foreign investment in the modern sectors of many developing economies. One implication of this foreign ownership is that for such investment the relevant cost of capital reflects the opportunity cost in the international capital market (modified by local tax, repatriation and earnings regulations, and expected exchange rate movements) and not in the domestic market. Another implication is that net factor payments abroad may have a stabilizing influence if they are determined as a residual. (See Reynolds [1968].)

Second, for many of the developing economies much of the machinery and equipment for investment in the modern sector is imported.[22] This point is related to the factor proportions problem referred to above because of the concentration on developing relatively capital-intensive technology in the mature economies and to the disaggregation of imports referred to below. It also means that exchange rate policy and other import policies have important roles in determining the cost of capital. Finally, it is possible that the quantity of imported capital goods may constrain real investment if the elasticity of substitution between domestic and foreign investment goods is, in fact, very low and quantitative restrictions are an important component of trade policy as in many developing countries. Behrman (1975a) provides evidence that the availability of imported machinery and equipment constrained investment in Chile.[23]

2.2.B.3 Government Expenditure in Developing Countries: For developing economies current government expenditures often (but not always) are more centralized than in developed economies such as the United States. Nevertheless, there remains a large, effectively endogenous component. The government is a relatively large employer in comparison to total modern sector employment, its wage bill makes up a substantial portion of its expenditures, and cuts in these expenditures as part of stabilization policy would be extremely risky politically in most cases.

Government expenditures also generally are affected directly by foreign sector conditions through the budget constraint. Taxes related to the foreign sector are a major source of variance in government revenues (see below). A further effect is through official capital inflows. The evidence presented by Papanek (1972, 1973) suggests (although not conclusively, see Mikesell and Zinzer [1973]) that such flows are diverted partly to current government expenditures. These inflows may also lead to local inflationary problems if they result in monetary creation instead of increased imports.

2.2.B.4 The Import Equation in Developing Countries: For most developing economies, as is noted above, imports play a critical role in the provision of noncompetitive raw materials, intermediate inputs, and machinery and equipment capital goods for the modern sector. Moreover, because many of these imports are noncompetitive and because import substitution policies often have reduced competitive imports to a low level, the price and exchange rate elasticities usually are thought to be low while measured income elasticities are high. However, for Chile estimated elasticities suggest that the 63 percent drop in the price level deflated exchange rate (between 1946 and 1973) implied *ceteris paribus* increases in imports of 57 percent for secondary consumption goods, 88 percent for transportation-related investment goods, 18 percent for intermediate goods, and 50 percent for services (Behrman [1975a] and [1976a]).

To capture the differential impact of the various types of imports on growth and stabilization as well as the differential responses to different components of income and price indices, some disaggregation is necessary.

Policies to regulate imports are widely thought to be among the most potent available to the governments of developing countries in their quest toward growth, distribution, and stabilization objectives. Among the policies often utilized are multiple exchange rate systems, tariffs, direct government imports, prior import deposits, and quantitative restrictions.[24] Clearly in a policy-oriented model these policies should be included explicitly in the import function. It should also be noted that import demand may depend on "excessive" monetary expansion in a fixed-rate regime as discussed in the Panamanian model and Borts and Hanson (Chapter 9, this volume).

Quantitative restrictions frequently are used to maintain a disequilibrium system with overvalued exchange rate(s) and excess demand for foreign exchange. Disequilibrium is allowed to persist because of the perceived negative distribution, inflationary and political effects of devaluation, and widespread convictions about inadequacies of allocation by prices. The existence of strong vested interests in the disequilibrium system (e.g., owners of factors in import substitution subsectors, the recipients of import licenses, or the government bureaucracy) also helps to perpetuate the continuance of these systems. To satisfy what appears to be substantial excess demand, perpetuated in part by the restrictions themselves,[25] controls generally are relaxed when foreign exchange becomes available from export booms or increased capital inflows. The import functions need to be modified, therefore, not only to include the above-mentioned policy tools and foreign prices, but also the availability of foreign exchange in a system of disequilibrium exchange control.

2.2.B.5 The Export Equation in Developing Countries: The correct specification of the export function, or functions, is a critical component of a stabilization model for most developing economies. Fluctuations in the value of exports from developing economies, according to the structuralists and a large number of others (e.g., Heller [1954] and Higgins [1968]), are a major source of instability for these countries. Not only do such variations directly affect total aggregate demand, but, through the government deficit they also change aggregate demand because of the dependence of government revenues on international trade revenues. Furthermore, they may alter production in the modern sector because of the low elasticity of substitution for critical, imported inputs and a short-run foreign exchange constraint. The holders of this view conclude that general fiscal and monetary policy will not be very effective in stabilization attempts. Instead emphasis must be placed on exchange rate and tax policies directly related to exports. Some observers further conclude that movement toward less dependence on the foreign sector is desirable in order to lessen its destabilizing influence.

MacBean (1966) summarizes a variety of previous work on export-based instability and suggests that the above-hypothesized strong relationship between export instability and overall instability is exaggerated. Díaz Alejandro (1977) reports substantially more variation in Colombian imports than in exports and in exports than in GDP. Mathieson and McKinnon (1974) even conclude that there is a slight indication that "outward-looking" trade policies may decrease instability. MacBean (1966) posits that two factors lie behind the lack of a strong relationship between domestic variables and export fluctuations: (i) the low value of the foreign trade multiplier in part because of repatriation of factor returns to foreign owners and because of leakages into taxes on exports and (ii) the distributed lag nature of reactions to change in exports.

Such studies challenge the once-conventional wisdom about the destabilizing influence of international markets. The issue is far from resolved, however, because of the failure of such studies to specify adequately the structure (including the lags in responses mentioned above) of the developing economies. Even the strongest doubters of the importance of international market fluctuations, moreover, grant that export variations probably are destabilizing in those cases in which exports are very concentrated in a few products.

To effectively capture the important, short-run role of exports, it seems best to divide them into two (or more) categories that differ substantially in exchange rate and tax subsidy treatment: traditional (largely primary products) and nontraditional (often industrial products).

The traditional exports are often major sources of government revenues. In addition to their "world" price, as modified by taxes, some element of market power (perhaps within the framework of international commodity agreements) may need to be represented.

Far from being taxed, many nontraditional exports may receive substantial subsidies in hopes of diversifying sources of foreign exchange and gaining entry into faster growing markets without causing a decline in "world" price. Many studies have shown a substantial positive response to changes in these subsidies and a corresponding negative response to an increasingly overvalued exchange rate. Referring once again to Chile, Behrman (1975a) and (1976a) show that the 63 percent drop in the price level deflated nominal exchange rate between 1946 and 1972 caused, *ceteris paribus*, drops in exports of 100 percent from industry, 50 percent from small- and medium-scale mining, 32 percent from agriculture, 19 percent from large-scale mining, and 13 percent for exports from services. These results also suggest that these foreign sector regimes increase *dependence* on traditional exports (i.e., those from large-scale mining) despite stated intentions to encourage diversification. The response to uncertainty in relative prices was widespread although not generally large in magnitude, implying that there was a significant, but not substantial, payoff to the sliding-peg exchange rate policy of 1965-1970 in terms of reducing balance of payments difficulties.

For Colombia various studies show that "minor" exports, that is, noncoffee, nonpetroleum exports, were extremely responsive to changes in the effective exchange rate (elasticities of two to four are reported in Díaz Alejandro [1977], Musalem [1970], and Sheahan and Clark [1972]). The system of effective devaluations initiated in 1967 is generally considered responsible for the enormous jump in the proportion of minor exports in a much higher total export figure.[26]

2.3 Financial Markets and Assets

2.3.A A Simple Model of Financial Markets in Developed Countries: The financial market for the developed economies in Table 1-1 is patterned on the extensions of Tobin's (1969) portfolio equilibrium model by Ando (1974) and Branson (1974). Equations (11) to (14) are demand functions of private sector asset holders for four imperfectly substitutable assets: equities, government bonds, foreign securities, and money. Equation (15) is the definition of the rates of return (with a fixed zero rate of interest for money) and income (with a transactions demand for money). The nominal supplies of money and bonds and the interest rate on foreign securities of a given risk are assumed to be exogenous.

All assets are gross substitutes. Domestic asset holders must hold given quantities of equities and government bonds, since these assets are not traded internationally. Domestic asset holders face an elastic supply of foreign securities at an interest rate fixed internationally. They are free to trade in money and foreign securities. Any purchase of the latter implicitly reduces domestic foreign exchange by an identical amount, and its effects on domestic money supply are completely sterilized.

Equations (16) to (18) are relations between holding and capitalization, real and nominal, and holding and international rates for the three respective nonzero return assets. Equations (19) to (22) are simple hypotheses about the formation of expectations. Equation (23) determines the market value of real assets by capitalizing the expected stream of income from *existing* assets.

Branson (1974) analyzes a similar model for developed countries. His main results are as follows. (1) The inclusion of noninternationally traded assets restores the effectiveness of monetary policy as measured by the possibility of altering rates of return on such domestic assets relative to foreign securities. (2) The relative impact of open market operations on domestic asset rates depends on which asset is the instrument of open market operations.

For the developing economies a number of changes need to be made. As discussed above, asset markets are generally fragmented, function poorly, and are relatively unimportant in channeling investible funds. Dualism is a common feature, with changes in the organized market having only limited impact on the unorganized sector. Government bond markets and private security markets both generally are quite small.

Monetary policy usually is limited in scope, especially internally. Central banks are hesitant to undertake substantial open market operations in the very narrow bond market. In some cases the Central Bank acts as a development bank, making lines of credit available to favored sectors. The nominal money supply is not only dependent upon such credit or rediscount operations but also on de facto or de jure obligations to finance the government deficit and on foreign exchange movements. Among the monetary instruments that might be included in a complete model of the financial sector are marginal and average reserve requirements, rediscount rates, prior deposits on imports, and exchange rate(s). Also important are interest rate ceilings and quantitative restrictions on internal credit and on international capital flows. The use of this latter group of policies may require that relations in the model be modified to reflect rationing due to quantitative variables. Uncertainty about future quantitative policies also may complicate the formation of expectations in equations (19) to (22).

The foreign sector impinges on the financial markets in a number of important ways. As is indicated in the previous paragraph, foreign exchange movements have substantial impact on the domestic money supply, and the major discretionary monetary operations are in the foreign sector. This discretion is probably limited to the short run, especially if the government attempts to maintain overvalued exchange rates. In particular, with fixed, effective exchange rates it may be difficult to pursue an independent monetary policy because domestic credit expansion will largely "leak out" via excessive imports and capital outflows that lead to drops in international reserves and money.[27] Rather than affecting inventories and ultimately output, imports and local holdings of foreign assets may simply increase. To be effective monetary policy may have to be linked with effective devaluation.

Foreign direct ownership or domestic capital in the modern sector often is important, and therefore equation (22) or (23) must be modified so that only the value of the domestically owned portion of the capital stock enters into domestic portfolio decisions.

In a few developing countries, such as Mexico, the interest rate in the international market may effectively create a liquidity trap for the organized monetary market. In general, however, the international interest rate does not peg the domestic rate for at least one of three reasons: (i) Quantitative restrictions on capital movements break the link between domestic and international capital markets. (ii) The existence of Bransonian internationally nontraded assets that are not perfect substitutes for internationally traded assets permits some independence in interest rate movements. (iii) Risk premiums may be dependent upon the debt-income ratio (Hanson [1974]).

While some of these features have been incorporated in various models of less developed countries, particularly the interrelation between money supply, the foreign sector, and the government deficit, this area remains one of the weak points of such models. Too little is known about the functioning of domestic capital markets to permit an adequate specification though the information accumulated through results of the OAS Capital Markets program may improve future models.

2.4. Identities and Miscellaneous Relations

Equations (24) to (28) define *disposable income, private savings, income from capital, and the balance of payments surplus*. For the developed countries these definitions are basically self-explanatory. Note that capital gains on existing assets arise because of changes in the capitalization rate or changes in the expected stream of income from these existing assets due to varying economic conditions. They do not, of course, include additions to real assets from current net investment. For the developing countries the major special problem is the evaluation of capital gains because of the narrow markets for internal equities.

Equation (29) is the tax function (net of transfers). For developed economies the major complication behind this simple representation often is the treatment of the corporation income tax. Therefore, income from capital is included as an argument in this function in addition to total personal income.

In developing economies the tax equation is more complex. (i) The traditional sector is not monetized. (ii) Within the modern sector wages represent a smaller function of output than in developed countries, making withholding difficult. (iii) Literacy is relatively low. (iv) Systematic accounting systems are not widely used. (v) The legitimacy of government revenue collection is less widely accepted and the tradition of voluntary compliance is less strong. (vi) Lack of resources, low civil service pay, and traditional social relations often make efficient and honest tax collection very difficult.

As a result, the relative importance of alternative sources of tax revenues differs from patterns in developed countries. General personal and corporation income taxes are much less important. Instead dependence is greater on import and export taxes, indirect taxes, and taxes on income generated by foreign-owned corporations. Taxes related to the foreign sector are much more significant because generally they are relatively simple to administer and more difficult to evade. This greater dependence on the foreign sector adds to the difficulties of stabilizing these economies because balance of payment considerations may conflict with the use of taxes for stabilization purposes. The more regressive nature of the tax structures with its greater dependence on indirect taxes, moreover, implies less "automatic stabilization" from the tax system than in more developed countries. Thus it might be appropriate to disaggregate the tax system (see Behrman [1976b] for example).

Equation (30) is the government budget constraint that Christ (1968) and others emphasize repeatedly. In a closed economy or in an economy with balance of payments equilibrium, this relation need not appear explicitly. The model already contains the private sector accounts and a full recording of transactions between the private and government sectors. If the private sector accounting identities are satisfied, so also must be those for the government sector, and the model is a closed system. However, as alluded to above, and as discussed in the Panamanian model, the question of the appropriate way of closing the model is important when output and demand functions are estimated separately. Models based on developed country experience seem to use inventories as the slack variable while those dealing with more open economies and fixed exchange rates tend to use the balance of payments deficit.

The model of Table 1-1 for the developed economies is presented on a very aggregative level. Actual empirical utilizations of such models often are on a more disaggregate level. The frequently encountered hypothesis that a major source of inflation in the United States and in some of the other more developed economies is the combination of sectoral shortages with short-run rigidities points to the need for at least some disaggregation.

For the developing countries, we have already discussed the need to separate the labor market. In addition, Hansen (1973b) argues that disaggregation is much more important than in developed countries since much of the direct policy impact is on relative prices. The estimation of Chilean sectoral relations (Behrman [1976b]) provides support for this claim. There is a great deal of heterogeneity across sectors in technological substitutabilities and in both the degree and the time path of behavioral responses to economic variables. Relative prices play major roles in both short-run and long-run resource allocation decisions. Both capacity utilization and capacity creation decisions respond significantly to these prices. Possibilities for substantial increases in capacity utilization and for factor substitution do exist.[28]

To ignore the role of the price system and these other characteristics when conducting analysis and giving policy presumptions, therefore, may be costly in terms of foregoing the use of some policy tools, overemphasizing the role of "key factors," and creating incentives for misallocations. And yet the dominant macroeconomic frameworks utilized for analysis of development problems for the most part assume that these factors can be ignored. For example, in the Chilean case, ODEPLAN (*Oficina de Planificación Nacional*, National Economics Planning Office) has utilized relative rigid fixed-capital-coefficient and/or foreign-exchange-saving gap models as the basis for planning and prediction.[29] On the other hand, policy tools have included price ceilings, quantitative restrictions on international trade and on credit, and multiple exchange rates at overvalued levels.

2.6 The Effects of Macroeconomic Policy in Models of Income Determination

To explain how the developed and developing country models work, as well as to obtain a qualitative simulation of the impact of policy variables, it is useful to consider two hypothetical experiments, an unexpected increase in the money supply and an increase in government spending, and trace out their effects on the major variables in the system.

In the developed country model, an increase in the stock of money, realized through the open market purchase of government bonds (equation [30]), tends to change interest rates (equation [14] and equation [16]). To the extent the cost of capital falls, it stimulates demand for investment goods (equation [7]). (We neglect the foreign sector, changes in taxes, and any possible wealth effects from a change in the ratio of money to bonds.) Demand for labor and output rise, stimulating second round demands of households, government, and investors (taxes also rise, which may have second-order effects on government bonds and private wealth). Unemployment falls (equation [1] and equation [2]) and prices rise because of the direct effect of unemployment (positive in equation [4]) and the indirect effect on wages (equation [3]) and prices (equation [4]). The extent of the price rise, relative to the rise in output, depends on the ratio (lagged?) of aggregate demand to the labor force.

An expansion of government demand, financed through bond sales, raises demand directly (equation [8]) and indirectly (equations [30] and [6]) through the second-round output–income effects. (We again neglect the foreign sector, changes in taxes, and changes in wealth.) The rise in bond sales raises interest rates and reduces investment, partially offsetting the increase in government spending. The fall in unemployment (equations [1] and [2]) has positive, direct, and indirect effects on prices (equations [3] and [4]).

In the developing country model it is difficult to separate monetary policy from government spending because there are no organized financial markets in which to buy or sell bonds.[30] Aside from the use of government spending, about the only practical way to increase the money supply is through changes in bank reserves or central bank credits. In all three cases the effects of changes in money tend to be concentrated in certain sectors and affect their second-round spending directly, owing to previous credit rationing, as compared to the more general effects of interest rate changes in developing countries. The more general effects of monetary policy in developing countries occur through such second-round spending of income recipients on local as opposed to imported goods and on local intermediate purchases by the favored industries. To the extent that the favored industries and their suppliers are close to "capacity" and fixed exchange rates are maintained, relative prices tend to change and/or imports and capital flows tend to vary, weakening the general impact of monetary policy on domestic output. In particular, in the Panamanian case, the effect of increases in nonagricultural credit or money was quite small although positive.[31] While coordinated variation in effective, exchange rates would permit greater independence in monetary policy, the necessity of their coordination with monetary policy reduces the number of completely independent instruments.

Fiscal policy in developing countries is closely related to monetary policy, again because of the narrow financial markets. Variations in government spending, financed locally through variations in bank holdings of government debt, tend to cause inverse variations in credit that "crowd out" other local credit demand and produce offsetting effects in investment. On the other hand, variations in government spending, financed through foreign borrowing that does not bid up local interest rates, have a two-pronged effect through their indirect effect on reserves and money as well as their direct effect on spending. The Panamanian model seems to indicate the "crowding out" effect or capacity constraints are quite important.

In developing economies both monetary and fiscal policy have their greatest effect on the modern sector. Their effect on the traditional sector occurs through variations in relative prices and in rural-urban migration rates. The greater the gap between (expected) wages in the city and the average labor income in the country, the smaller is the variation in relative prices and the greater is the variation in migration rates. Thus, in a special sense, the rural sector also acts as a capacity constraint that affects the division of changes in aggregate demand between price and output effects.

2.7 Conclusions: Some General Points in Income-Determination Models and Short-Term Policymaking in Developing Countries

While conditions vary substantially across countries and modeling of certain aspects of the developing countries remains rudimentary, several important general points or questions about income determination processes and countercyclical policy have appeared in our discussions.

(1) Supply variations in the traditional sector may cause cyclical variations while countercyclical policies mainly affect the modern sector. More general policy tools must be developed to affect both sectors.

(2) If the traditional sector determines the real wage for the modern sector and there is no money illusion, then the modern sector labor market is very classical. Increased aggregate demand will not raise equilibrium employment and production although they will affect these variables when urban unemployment is abnormally high. Decreases in aggregate demand will lower urban employment and slow migration. However, much research remains to be done on the determination of labor's income in the traditional sector and its relation to urban wages through migration.

(3) Changing international conditions and/or variations in government policy seem to be responsible for most of the cyclical fluctuations in developing countries, as opposed to the traditional view expressed in developed country models that investment is the key.[32] In addition to the oft-described direct and multiplier effects of changes in world prices of exports or imports, variations in world prices tend to have indirect effects through variations in international reserves and, correspondingly, the money supply. Government policy may respond to reserve losses and variations in conditions in the ex-

port and import competing industries; in addition, variations in external financing may force variations in monetary emission. Variations in prices of noncompetitive raw materials and intermediate import may cause short-run fluctuations through either supply limitations or reduction of demand in other sectors. Finally, attempts to maintain disequilibrium exchange rates may lengthen the period of adjustment to external disturbances.

Given the importance of the foreign sector in generating cyclical fluctuations, some effort should be devoted to ensuring its correct specification in the income-determination model. The various policies to reduce its impact should be closely studied and some effort made to direct stabilization policies toward it. Some attempts have been made in this direction, both on the level of individual countries and in cooperation with other countries. However, stabilization problems often are viewed as less important than objectives such as growth and distribution. If a temporary foreign exchange surplus is available because of an export boom or increased capital inflows, for example, pressures are enormous to utilize it to alleviate other problems. Only rarely do governments find it feasible to conserve such an excess for use when the next foreign exchange deficit occurs. Only when such governments are convinced that the costs to these fluctuations are large or that there are gains in other policy dimensions of increased stabilization are more resources likely to be utilized for stabilization purposes.

(4) The international capital market does not limit stabilization options in developing countries by fixing domestic interest rates.[33] This is so because of the existence of Bransonian noninternationally traded assets, because of quantitative restrictions and exchange rate variations that break the link between international and domestic markets, and because of variations in risk premiums as international debts vary relative to national product.

(5) Stabilization policies are limited by international creditors, by the lack of integrated and well-functioning financial markets, and by the offsetting response of international reserves to domestic credit expansion. The last limitation is, of course, true only under fixed exchange rates, and monetary policy would be "more independent" under flexible rates. However, exchange rate and aggregate demand policies are too often treated as independent policy investments.

(6) The partial equilibrium evidence of substantial technological and behavioral flexibilities suggests that models that assume too great rigidities (see the introduction) may distort the perceived choice set and overemphasize the importance of "key" factors. The partial equilibrium evidence of significant substitution possibilities and price

responses suggest that macropolicies might have significant impact on aggregate variables. However, general equilibrium simulations of the Chilean model and particularly the Panamanian model indicate that these policies may have much less aggregate impact than partial equilibrium analysis might suggest, owing to overall resource constraints and indirect effects (such as those transmitted through the money supply–foreign exchange–price nexus).

A great deal of the effect of macropolicies also depends on the size of and behavior within the traditional sector as well as relations between conditional and modern sectors and the ratio between aggregate demand and existing capacity, factors that are not well described in existing models.

(7) Both the partial equilibrium and the general equilibrium analyses lend support to Hansen's (1973b) emphasis on the need for disaggregation to capture relative price effects. The estimated partial equilibrium relations are quite heterogeneous across sectors in regard to technological possibilities, behavioral responses, and patterns of adjustment. The general equilibrium simulations suggest that policies may have much greater impact on the composition of aggregates than on their size, especially when the economy is near its capacity as defined by existing institutions and behavior. To what extent institutions and behavior of individuals and policymakers should be taken as given remains a special dilemma for those who would venture into the tangle of income-determination models of developing countries.

NOTES

1. Examples include Adelman and Thorbecke (1966), Blitzer, Clark, and Taylor (1975), Cabezon (1969), Chenery and Strout (1966), Clark and Foxley (1970, 1973), Eckaus and Parikh (1968), Manne (1974), UNECAFE (1960), and UNCTAD (1968).

2. "Socially optimal" is used here not to imply the incorporation of externalities, but to mean the maximization of an objective function, given constraints imposed by the model, starting and terminal conditions, and exogenous variables. Some aspects of behavioral responses are incorporated in these studies, such as the sectoral pattern of income elasticities for private consumption.

3. Rao (1952) presents an early statement of this view. Ranis (1974) gives a recent summary.

4. For good summaries of the "structuralist-monetarist" debate, see Campos (1964) and Wachter (1974).

5. Behrman (1968) summarizes many of the estimates that relate to agricultural supplies. Morawetz (1974) gives references for a number of studies of elasticities of substitution. Behrman (1971a, 1972a, 1972b, 1972c, 1973a, 1973b, 1973c, and 1976b) and Behrman and Garcia (1973) present sectoral estimates for the Chilean experience.

6. Beltrán (1974) summarizes the features of many of the Latin American models. Larry Lau (1975) has compiled a bibliography of 200 such models of which 50 relate to Latin America.

7. For example, R. French-Davis (1973) shows that the Chilean Klein-Saks stabilization program was originally thought to have failed when inflation doubled in 1958 but reestimates show the rate was approximately constant over the 1957–1958 period. While the social costs of this stability also may have been judged too high, the facts of the case were substantially different from those that went into the original evaluation.

8. See Zarnowitz (1967), for example.

9. See Behrman and Vargas (Chapter 2, this volume) for an attempt to develop and use such data bases in constructing quarterly models of developing countries.

10. See Barro and Grossman (1976) for a theoretical framework of supply as well as demand restraints that determine income for an economy that is not in general equilibrium. Howard (1976) finds support for the Barro-Grossman hypothesis regarding supply constraints in a controlled economy.

11. Many of the studies previously mentioned attempt to correct one or two of these shortcomings. Nevertheless, the list of shortcomings in any specific study generally is quite large. For example, Corbo's (1971) well-known study of Chile considers the problem of an endogenous money supply and includes supply constraints, but it does not avoid most of the other shortcomings listed in the text. Moreover in the simulations of that study, because of convergence problems, excess demand is exogenized so that there is no link between monetary and real variables or the money supply and prices.

12. See Barro and Grossman (1976) and Behrman (1976b).

13. The movement toward putty-clay considerations in the macroeconomic literature for developed economies lags substantially the emphasis on ex post fixed proportions for the modern sector of the less developed economies. Eckaus (1955) provides an early statement regarding less developed countries.

14. The discrepancy between the marginal products in the two sectors obviously leads to static inefficiencies.

15. The average share per laborer sometimes is assumed to be fixed by tradition until withdrawal of surplus labor raises the marginal product in this sector to that prevailing in the modern sector, when market behavior begins to dominate the economy (Fei and Ranis [1964]).

16. Harris and Todaro (1970) attribute a certain minimum level of urban unemployment to the existence of government or unions, which establish fixed wages. They claim that rural-urban migration occurs as long as the expected income (taking into account both the higher modern sector wage and the probability of obtaining employment) exceeds the average labor share in the traditional sector. The result is an equilibrium level of open employment or disguised unemployment in the cities, which persists as long as government or unions maintain a differential between the traditional sector's average labor share and the modern sector wage.

17. Interest rates might also enter so the model need not be completely dichotomized.

18. Suppose that production functions in both sectors are subject to constant return to scale and for simplicity that individual returns in the traditional sector are equal to the average product of labor. For given capital stocks in the two sectors there is only one labor allocation that equates the marginal product in the modern sector and the average in the traditional and "employs" all of the labor force. If unemployment in the urban sector is permitted, then a single "equilibrium" level of unemployment will be determined unless the elasticities of labor "demand" schedules in the two sectors have a very particular configuration.

19. Fei and Ranis (1964) claim that it may be difficult to use the rural surplus for development if rural labor incomes do not remain at the traditional level and prices of rural goods tend to rise. See also Hymer and Resnick (1971).

20. The theoretical question also remains as to whether privately held government bonds should be counted as private wealth. See Barro (1974).

21. See Gomez and Schlesinger (1971) for an attempt to estimate family net worth in Colombia.

22. Díaz Alejandro (1977) reports 75 percent of investment of Colombian machinery and equipment was imported in 1975.

23. If the availability of foreign capital inflows (both official and private) directly or indirectly affects investment (e.g., see Areskong [1974]) they should be included in the model as part of a reduced form of the investment equation and through spillovers of frustrated demands in the consumption-saving function. The theoretical framework for modeling such spillovers might follow Barro and Grossman (1976).

24. In some developing economies considerable smuggling exists in attempts to avoid these policies.

25. See Bruton (1969) and Musalem (1971).

26. Noncoffee exports grew from $177 million or approximately 25 percent of exports in 1966 to $671 million or 55 percent of exports in 1974 or over 28 percent per year. While Calvo and Escandón (1973) and Cabarrouy and Spillane (1974) attribute much of the growth up to 1969 or 1971 as simple maintenance of market share, one must point out that market share would not be maintained without appropriate incentives to export, that is, conversion of the world price into an appropriate local currency value.

27. Borts and Hanson (Chapter 9, this volume) discuss the extent to which this view is correct with some empirical results for the Panamanian case.

28. Estimated sectoral elasticities of substitution between capital and labor range from 0.0 to 0.9. The adjustment periods for substitution between primary factors are fairly long in several cases in which the long-run elasticities are high. For most sectors in the short and medium runs, therefore, the results provide some support for the assumption of limited flexibility that underlies Eckaus's (1955) technological explanation of the existence of under- or unemployed labor, the structuralist analysis of inflation, and the use of fixed coefficients in input-output-based models. Limited flexibility, however, is not the same as no flexibility. Some primary factor substitution apparently is always possible in response to real relative price changes.

29. For example, see Harberger and Selowsky (1966) or ODEPLAN (1970).

30. The lack of markets may reflect government attempts to sell bonds at low, fixed rates of return to banks as well as the stage of development.

31. See Behrman and Vargas (Chapter 2, this volume) and Borts and Hanson (Chapter 9, this volume).

32. But see Friedman (1965) and Okun (1970).

33. Macrotheory suggests that fiscal policy would retain its potency under fixed rates; it is only the effectiveness of monetary policy that is questioned. See Mundell (1968).

REFERENCES

Adelman, Irma, and Erik Thorbecke, eds. *The Theory and Design of Economic Development*. Baltimore: Johns Hopkins, 1966.

Ando, Albert. "Some Aspects of Stabilization Policies, the Monetarist Controversy, and the MPS Model." *International Economic Review* 15:3 (October 1974), 541–576.

Areskoug, Kaj. "Private Investment and Capital Formation in Developing Countries." (Mimeo., New York University, 1974).

Barro, Robert. "Are Government Bonds Net Wealth?" *Journal of Political Economy* 82:6 (November/December 1974), 1095–1117.

——."Money and Output in Mexico, Colombia, and Brazil." This volume.

Barro, Robert, and Herschel Grossman. *Money, Employment and Inflation*. Cambridge: Cambridge University Press, 1976.

Behrman, Jere R. *Supply Response in Underdeveloped Agriculture: A Case Study of Four Major Annual Crops in Thailand, 1937–1963*. Amsterdam: North Holland Publishing Co., 1968.

——. "The Determinants of the Annual Rates of Change of Sectoral Money Wages in a Developing Economy." *International Economic Review* 12:3 (October 1971a), 431–447.

——. "Review Article: Trade Prospects and Capital Needs of Developing Countries." *International Economic Review* 12:3 (October 1971b), 519–525.

——. "Sectoral Elasticities of Substitution between Capital and Labor in a Developing Economy: Time Series Analysis in the Case of Postwar Chile." *Econometrica* 40:2 (March 1972), 311–327.

——. "Sectoral Investment Determination in a Developing Economy." *American Economic Review* 62:5 (December 1972b), 825–841.

——. "Short-Run Flexibility in a Developing Economy: The Postwar Chilean Experience." *Journal of Political Economy* 80:2 (March-April 1972c), 292–313.

——. "Aggregative Market Response in Developing Agriculture: The Postwar Chilean Experience." in R. Eckaus and P.N. Rosenstein-Rodan, eds. *Analysis of Development Problems: Studies of the Chilean Economy*. Amsterdam: North-Holland Publishing Co., 1973a, 229–250.

——. "Cyclical Sectoral Capacity Utilization in a Developing Economy," in R. Eckaus and P.N. Rosenstein-Rodan, eds . *Analysis of Development Problems: Studies of the Chilean Economy*. Amsterdam: North-Holland Publishing Co., 1973b, 251–268.

——. "Price Determination in an Inflationary Economy: The Dynamics of Chilean Inflation Revisited," in R. Eckaus and P.N. Rosenstein-Rodan, eds. *Analysis of Development Problems: Studies of the Chilean Economy.* Amsterdam: North Holland Publishing Co., 1973c, 369–398.

——. "Modeling Stabilization Policy for the LDC's in an International Setting," in A. Ando, ed. *International Aspects of Stabilization Policy.* Proceedings of ISPE—Boston Federal Reserve Bank Conference, 1974.

——. "Foreign-Sector Regimes and Economic Development in Chile." Paper presented at the ECLA-NBER Conference, 1975c.

——. "Econometric Modeling of National Income Determination in Developing Countries, with Special Reference to the Chilean Experience." *Annals of Economic and Social Measurement* 4:4 (Fall 1975b), 461–488.

——. *Foreign Trade and Economic Development: The Chilean Experience.* New York: NBER and Columbia University Press, 1976a.

——. *Macroeconomic Policy in a Developing Country: An Econometric Investigation of the Postwar Chilean Experience.* Amsterdam: North-Holland Publishing Co., 1976b.

Behrman, J.R., and M. Jorge Garcia. "A Study of Quarterly Nominal Wage Change Determinants in an Inflationary Developing Economy," in R. Eckaus and R.N. Rosenstein-Rodan, eds. *Analysis of Development Problems: Studies of the Chilean Economy.* Amsterdam: North-Holland Publishing Co., 1973, 399–416.

Behrman, J.R., and L.R. Klein. "Economic Growth Models for the Developing Economy," in W.A. Eltis, M. Fg. Scott and N.N. Wolfe, eds. *Induction, Growth and Trade.* Oxford: Oxford University Press, 1970.

Behrman, J.R., and J.R. Vargas. "A Quarterly Econometric Model of Panamá." This volume.

Beltrán del Rio, Abel. "Statistical Regularities in Macroeconometric Models of Developing Economies." Paper presented at Seminar on Economic Models of Emerging Nations, Tel Aviv, October 1974.

Beltrán del Rio, Abel, and L.R. Klein. "Macroeconometric Model Building in Latin America: The Mexican Case," in N. Ruggles, ed. *The Role of the Computer in Economic and Social Research in Latin America.* New York: NBER and Columbia University Press, 1974.

Birnberg, Thomas, and Stephen Resnick. "A Model of Trade and Government Sectors in Colonial Economies." *American Economic Review* 63:3 (September 1973), 572–587.

Blinder, Alan, and Robert Solow. "Does Fiscal Policy Matter?" *Journal of Public Economics* 2:2 (June 1973), 319–337.

Blitzer, Charles R., Peter B. Clark, and Lance Taylor, eds. *Economy-Wide Models and Development Planning.* Oxford: Oxford University Press, 1975.

Borts, George, and James Hanson. "A Monetary Model of the Balance of Payments with Empirical application to Panamá." This volume.

Branson, William H. "Portfolio Equilibrium and Monetary Policy with Foreign and Non-Traded Assets." (Mimeo., draft for Third Paris-Dauphine Conference, 1974).

Bruton, Henry. "The Two Gap Approach to Development: Comment." *American Economic Review* 59:3 (June 1969), 439-446.

Brodersohn, Marco. "The Phillips Curve and the Conflict Between Full Employment and Price Stability in the Argentine Economy, 1964-1974." This volume.

Cabezón, Pedro. "An Evaluation of Commercial Policy in the Chilean Economy." Madison: University of Wisconsin, unpublished Ph.D. dissertation, 1969.

Caburrouy, Evaldo, and James Spillane. "La Experiencia de Colombia en Materia de Exportaciones de Manufacturas en el Período 1960-69." *Revista de Planeación* 6:1 (enero-marzo 1974), 51-86.

Calvo, Harold, and Jose Escandón. *Las Exportaciones Columbianas de Manufacturas: 1963-1971.* Bogotá: FEDESARROLLO, 1973.

Campos, Roberto de Oliveira. "Economic Development and Inflation with Special Reference to Latin America," in OECD, *Development Plans and Programmes.* Paris: OECD Development Centre, 1964, 129-37.

Chenery, Hollis B., and A. Strout. "Foreign Assistance and Economic Development." *American Economic Review* 56:3 (September 1966), 679-733.

Christ, Carl. "A Simple Macroeconomic Model with a Government Budget Restraint." *Journal of Political Economy* 76:1 (January-February 1968), 53-67.

Clark, Peter Bentley, and R. Alejandro Foxley. "Sub-Optimal Growth: The Social Cost of Make-Work Employment Policies." Paper presented at the session on "Numerical Models of Development Planning," Second World Congress of the Econometric Society, Cambridge, England, September 8-14, 1970, mimeo.

Corbo Lioi, Vittorio. "An Econometric Study of Chilean Inflation." Ph.D. dissertation, MIT, 1971. Published as *Inflation in Developing Countries: An Econometric Study of Chilean Inflation.* Amsterdam: North-Holland Publishing Co., 1974.

Díaz Alejandro, Carlos. *Foreign Trade Regimes and Economic Development: Colombia.* New York: NBER and Columbia University Press, 1977.

Eckaus, R.S. "The Factor-Proportions Problem in Underdeveloped Areas." *American Economic Review,* 1955. Reprinted in A. Agarwala and S. Singh, eds. *The Economics of Underdevelopment.* Oxford: Oxford University Press, 1958, 205-218.

Eckaus, Richard S., and Kirit S. Parikh. *Planning for Growth: Multisector Intertemporal Models Applied to India.* Cambridge, Mass.: MIT Press, 1968.

Fei, John, and Gustav Ranis. *Development of the Labor Surplus Economy.* Homewood, Ill.: Irwin Publishing Co., 1964.

Fernandez, Roque. "The Short-Run Output Inflation Tradeoff in Argentina and Brazil." This volume.

Fernandez, Roque, and James Hanson. "Los Interrelaciones del Carto Plazo entre Inflación, Producción y Empleo en América Latina." In ILPES, *Planificación del Corto Plazo: La Dinámica de los Precios, el Empleo y el Producto,* Santiago: 1977.

French-Davis, Ricardo. *Políticas Económicas en Chile, 1952-1970.* Santiago: Ediciones Nueva Universidad, Universidad Católica de Chile, 1973.

Friedman, Milton. "Monetary Policy in Developing Countries," in Paul A.

David and Melvin W. Reder, eds. *Nations and Households in Economic Growth: Essays in Honor of Moses Abramovitz.* New York: Academic Press, 1974, 265-278.

——. *The Great Contraction.* Princeton: Princeton University Press, 1965.

Gomez, Armando, and Daniel Schlesinger. *Análisis Preliminar de las Cuentas de Flujo de Fondos Financieros de la Economía Colombiana 1962-1964.* Bogotá: Banco de la República, 1971.

Hansen, Bent. "On the Effects of Fiscal and Monetary Policy: A Taxonomic Discussion." *American Economic Review* 63:3 (September 1973a), 546-71.

——. "Simulation of Fiscal, Monetary and Exchange Policy in a Primitive Economy: Afghanistan." In *Economic Structure and Development.* Amsterdam: North-Holland Publishing Co., 1973, 215-237.

Hanson, James. "Optimal International Borrowing and Lending." *American Economic Review* 64:3 (September 1974), 616-630.

Harberger, Arnold. "The Dynamics of Inflation in Chile," in Carl Christ, ed. *Measurements in Economics.* Palo Alto, Calif.: Stanford University Press, 1963.

Harberger, Arnold C., and Marcelo Selowsky. "Key Factors in the Economic Growth of Chile: An Analysis of the Sources of Past Growth and of Prospects for 1965-70." Paper presented at Conference on "The Next Decade of Latin American Economic Development," April 20-22, 1966, Cornell University, mimeo.

Harris, John R., and Michael P. Todaro. "Migration, Unemployment and Development: A Two-Sector Analysis." *American Economic Review* 60:1 (March 1970), 126-142.

Heller, Walter W. "Fiscal Policies for Underdevelopment Economies," in Haskell P. Wald, ed. *Conference on Agricultural Taxation and Economic Development.* Cambridge, Mass: International Program in Taxation, Harvard Law School, 1954.

Higgins, Benjamin. *Economic Development: Principles, Problems and Policies,* rev. ed., New York: W.W. Norton and Co., 1968.

Howard, David. "The Disequilibrium Model in the Controlled Economy: An Empirical Test of the Barro-Grossman Model." *American Economic Review* 66:5 (December 1976), 871-879.

Hymer, Stephen, and Stephen Resnick. "A Model of an Agrarian Economy." *American Economic Review* 59:4 (March 1969), 493-506.

Johnson, Harry. "The Monetary Approach to the Balance of Payments," in M. Connally and A. Swoboda, eds. *International Trade and Money.* Toronto: University of Toronto Press, 1973, pp. 206-224.

Lau, Lawrence. "A Bibliography of Macroeconomic Model of Developing Economies." Palo Alto, Calif.: Stanford University (Mimeo., 1975).

Lewis, W. Arthur. "Economic Development with Unlimited Supplies of Labor." *The Manchester School* 22:1 (May 1954), 139-191.

Lucas, Robert. "Some International Evidence on Output-Inflation Trade-offs." *American Economic Review* 63:3 (June 1973), 326-34.

——. "Econometric Policy Evaluation: A Critique," in Karl Brunner and Allan Meltzer, eds. *The Phillips Curve and Labor Markets.* Amsterdam: North-Holland Publishing Co., 1976.

MacBean, Alasdair I. *Export Instability and Economic Development.* Cambridge, Mass.: Harvard University Press, 1966.

Manne, Alan. "Multi-Sector Models for Development Planning: A Survey." *Journal of Development Economics* 1:1 (June 1974), 43-70.

Mathieson, Donald J., and Ronald I. McKinnon. "Instability in Underdeveloped Countries: The Impact of the International Economy," in Paul A. David and Melvin W. Reder, eds. *Nations and Households in Economic Growth: Essays in Honor of Moses Abramovitz.* New York: Academic Press, 1974, 315-332.

Michalopolous, Constantine. "Productivity Growth in Latin America: Comment." *American Economic Review* 59:3 (June 1969), 435-439.

Mikesell, Raymond F., and James E. Zinser. "The Nature of the Savings Function in Developing Countries: A Survey of the Theoretical and Empirical Literature." *Journal of Economic Literature* 11:1 (March 1973), 1-26.

Modigliani, Franco, and F. Tarantelli. "The Consumption Function in a Developing Economy and the Italian Experience." *American Economic Review* 65:5 (December 1975), 825-842.

Morawetz, David. "Employment Implications of Industrialization in Developing Countries: A Survey." *Economic Journal* 84:335 (September 1974), 491-542.

Mundell, R. *International Economics.* New York: Macmillan, 1968.

Musalem, Alberto. *Las Exportaciones Colombianas, 1959-1969.* Bogotá: 1970, unpublished.

——. *Demanda por Dinero y Balanza de Pagos en Colombia.* Bogotá: Banco de la República, 1971.

ODEPLAN. "Marco de referencia cuantitativo preliminar para la elaboración del programa 1970-80." Santiago: January 1970.

Okun, Arthur. *The Political Economy of Prosperity.* New York: W.W. Norton and Co., 1970.

Papanek, Gustav. "The Effect of Aid and Other Resource Transfers on Savings and Growth in Less Developed Countries." *Economic Journal* 327 (September 1972), 934-950.

——. "Aid, Foreign Private Investment, Savings and Growth in Less Developed Countries." *Journal of Political Economy* 81:1 (January/February 1973), 120-131.

Ranis, Gustav. "Short-Run Policy in Semi-Industrialized Economies: Comment." *Economic Development and Cultural Change* 22:3 (January 1974), 345-346.

Rao, V.K.R.V. "Investment, Income and the Multiplier in an Underdeveloped Economy." *The Indian Economic Review,* 1952. Reprinted in A. Agarwala and S. Singh, eds. *The Economics of Underdevelopment.* Oxford: Oxford University Press, 1958, 205-218.

Rosenstein-Rodan, Paul N. "Notes on the Theory of the 'Big Push'," in H. Ellis, ed. *Economic Development for Latin America.* New York: St. Martin's Press, 1961, 57-81.

Reynolds, Clark. "Development Problems of an Export Economy," in C. Reynolds and M. Mamalakis, eds. *Essays on the Chilean Economy.* Homewood, Ill.: Irwin Publishing Co., 1968, 203-398.

Schydlowsky, Daniel M. "Short-Run Policy in Semi-Industrialized Economies." *Economic Development and Cultural Change* 19:3 (April 1971), 391-413.

———. "Capital Utilization, Growth, Employment and Balance of Payments and Price Stabilization." This volume.

Sheahan, John, and Sara Clark. *Las Respuestas de las Exportaciones Colombianas a Variaciones en la Tasa Efectiva de Cambio.* Bogotá: FEDESARROLLO, 1972.

Taylor, Lance. "Short-Term Policy in Open Developing Economies: The Narrow Limits of the Possible." *Journal of Development Economics* 1:2 (September 1974), 85-104.

Tobin, James. "A General Equilibrium Approach to Monetary Theory." *Journal of Money, Credit and Banking* 1:1, (1969), 15-30.

United Nations Economic Commission for Asia and the Far East (UNECAFE). *Programming Techniques for Economic Development.* Bangkok: United Nations, 1960.

United Nations Conference on Trade and Development (UNCTAD). *Trade Prospects and Capital Needs of Developing Countries.* New York: United Nations, 1968.

Wachter, Susan. *Latin American Structuralist and Monetarist Inflation Theories: An Application to Chile.* Ph.D. Thesis, Boston College, September 1974.

Wachter, Susan "Structuralism vs. Monetarism: Inflation in Chile." This volume.

Zarnowitz, Victor. *An Appraisal of Short-Term Forecasts.* New York: NBER and Columbia University, 1967.

2

JERE BEHRMAN and JUAN RAFAEL VARGAS || A Quarterly Econometric Model of Panama*

1. INTRODUCTION

This paper reports on a new econometric model for a Latin American country—Panama. The purposes of this model are fourfold:

1. To provide a framework for the systematic analysis of the available short-run data about the Panamanian economy.
2. To make short-run predictions of developments in the Panamanian economy.
3. To provide a tool for simulating the effects of changes in policies and in other exogenous variables on the Panamanian economy.
4. To serve as a prototype for the development of similar models for other Latin American economies.

*Working Paper No. 4 (revised) ILPES—Ministerio de Planificacion y Política Económica Project, 16 June 1976. ILPES and the Ministerio de Planificación y Política Económica supported this project, but bear no responsibility for the analysis presented in this paper. The authors also would like to thank, but not implicate, James A. Hanson, Edelma M. Lopez, and Carlos A. Bhrugiati B. of the Departamento de Estudios Económicos y Sociales in the Controloria General de la República, and the following members of the Ministerio de Planificación y Política Económica: Nicolás Ardito Barletta, Jr., José Sokol, Reinaldo Deceraga, Juan Luis Moreno, Victoriano Moreno, Edgar Rojas, Ricaurte Vásquez, J. Stavrou, Mariana Reyes, Hermán Arboleda, and Hector Alexander.

Some previous econometric work on Panamá has been done by Stavrou and Arboleda. One of the features of the present model that distinguishes it from that model and most other econometric models of developing economies is that it is based on quarterly observations. To our knowledge this is the first time that a medium-scale, quarterly econometric model has been estimated for a developing economy. Other distinguishing features include the product and sectoral detail (especially for the critical agricultural sector), the effort to identify separate supply and demand considerations in a number of sectors, and the related distinction among sectors and products for which prices are set by the government, by the international market, or by internal balance between supply and demand.

The paper is organized as follows. Section 2 describes the structure of the model. Section 3 discusses its sample performance. Section 4 reports on some dynamic multiplier runs for changes in various policy instruments.

2. MODEL STRUCTURE

The model contains 97 endogenous and 71 exogenous variables. To determine the endogenous variables there are 55 estimated behavioral or technological relations and 42 identities. The sample period for relations estimated from quarterly data is generally 1965-1973, or 36 observations.[1] For some of the agricultural products the unit of observation is a year, in which case the sample period generally is 1962-1973, or 12 observations.

The estimation technique primarily used for estimated relations is ordinary least squares (although in some cases maximum likelihood procedures are utilized for autocorrelated error structures). The expected returns of adopting more sophisticated methods seemed less than the expected costs of doing so, given the nature of the data, some questions about the robustness of alternative estimators, and the opportunity costs of sophistication in estimation procedure in exploring various model structures. Polynomial distributed lags (including geometric and Almon lags as special cases) are used to represent adjustment processes and the creation of expectations. Dummy variables are included to explore the extent of seasonality due to annual patterns in agricultural production and demand, Christmas demand, and so on. (DM_i, where i indicates the quarter, with the fourth quarter as the reference point). For each estimated relation the coefficient of determination corrected for degrees of freedom ($\overline{R}^2$), the standard error of estimate (SE), the Durbin Watson statistic (D),[2] and the sample period are presented after the estimates. The t-statistics are given in parentheses under the point estimates.

The model is specified basically in real terms (i.e., stock and flow variables generally are deflated). Both demand and supply features enter into the determination of the macroeconomic aggregates of interest, given the history of past values of all variables, current government policies, current international prices and market conditions, and other variables exogenous to the Panamian economy. Capacity adjustments on the supply side tend to occur less rapidly than many adjustments on the demand side, however, so in an immediate sense the model is as much demand as supply determined.

The discussion of the model specification below is organized around seven blocks of variables: government policies, production of value added in real terms, final demand, prices, wages and the labor market, the monetary sector, and identities. With this specification the model can be used to explore the impact of changes in a number of government policies (subsection 2.1) or other exogenous variables on the following major areas of macroeconomic policy concern:

1. Nominal stability (i.e., the rate of change of prices).
2. Real stability (i.e., the rate of utilization of available physical and human resources).
3. Structural change (i.e., relative shifts in sectoral production and in demands).
4. Income distribution (i.e., real wages, employment, sectoral conditions—including particular emphasis on agriculture).
5. International economic position (i.e., level of reserves, balance of trade in goods and services).
6. Growth (i.e., level and composition of physical and human resource investment).

2.1 Government Policies

Within the framework in which the Panamian government has operated some of the major policy tools that most governments use are not available. This is particularly true in the international monetary area, where the Balboa has been maintained completely convertible at parity into the United States dollar, with the latter actually serving as the paper currency in circulation, and where there has been no central bank to engage in the usual type of monetary policy. Nevertheless, the government has a number of policy variables that can be assumed to be exogenous in this model. Of course, for some of these instruments the degree of exogeneity depends on the time period of reference and/or the availability of external resources. Government expenditures and revenues, for example, while somewhat independent in the short run, combine to determine the government deficit (surplus) and are constrained by the availability of means of covering that deficit. The maintenance of complete convertibility also obviously limits the range of many policy options, once other basic decisions have been taken.[3]

2.1.1 Government Expenditures: include current consumption $(\overline{C}_g)$, investment $(\overline{I}_g)$, and net transfers to families $(\overline{TR}_i)$ and to government enterprises $(\overline{TR}_{ge})$. Government investment basically includes the creation of new or replacement capital stock but also some purchases of private plant and equipment (most notably during the sample, the purchase of private utilities).

2.1.2 Government Revenues (including loans): Taxes include those on imports $(\overline{TX}_M)$, sales, production and other indirect $(\overline{TX}_{SP})$ and direct income $(\overline{TX}_D)$. As is the case for most developing countries, indirect taxes are relatively more important than in the developed countries. Nontax inflows include net income from government enterprises $(\overline{Y}_{ge})$, net income to the government from casinos, hippodromes, and lotteries $(\overline{Y}_{gche})$, and net loans to the government $(\overline{L}_g)$.

2.1.3 Canal Zone: The net income from the canal zone $(\overline{Y}_{cz})$ is presumed to be the result of negotiations with the United States Government and of canal usage. Although it is far from completely under the control of the Panamian Government and thus not a direct policy instrument in the sense of some of the other variables considered in this section, it is appropriate to treat it as exogenous to the model.

2.1.4 Free Zone: The net income from the free zone of Colon $(\overline{Y}_{fz})$ depends upon the level of intra- and inter-American trade and the capacity of the zone. In recent years the government has taken steps to expand that capacity, but, unfortunately, within the resource constraints for this study data could not be located that permit the endogenization of this variable. Therefore, net income from the free zone is considered to be an exogenous government policy instrument, even though it is the net result of a whole set of policies and of the level of international trade activity.

2.1.5 Government Set Prices and Minimum Wages: The government sets prices $(\overline{P}_i)$ for some major products (e.g., basic agricultural and food staples; see subsection 2.2.2.1 below). It then regulates international trade flows to assure that such price policies are effective. It also sets sectoral minimum wages $(\overline{W}_i)$ although adjustments in these minimums during the sample period were very infrequent.

2.1.6 Monetary Variables: As is suggested above, within the framework of complete convertibility maintained through the sample period, the options for monetary policy have been quite limited. Nevertheless an attempt has been made to fix interest rates $(\overline{R})$[4] and to control sectoral credit allocations $(\overline{CRDT_i/CRDT})$. While there is no direct representation of the factors associated with the substantial expansion of international banking activity in Panama following the 1970 banking law, Johnson (1976) concluded that the benefits to Panama have been limited. Nonetheless, the expansion of this activity certainly has had an impact on the real value added from banks and other financial institutions within the model framework.

2.2 Production of Value Added (V) and Exports (X) in Real Terms

It is convenient to distinguish among three major categories of goods and services: export oriented, other traded and tradable, and nontraded.[5]

2.2.1 Export-Oriented Goods and Services[6]

2.2.1.1 Agricultural and Fishing: Panama's major nonpetroleum goods exports come from this sector. Within the model two major products are emphasized.

The real export value of *bananas* $(\overline{X}_B)$ is assumed to be determined by the banana-producing companies, independently of the rest of the model. Attempts to estimate banana export functions on the basis of responses to variables such as deflated prices (both short- and long-run) and weather conditions were not fruitful.

The real export value of shrimps $(\overline{X}_{SH})$ is dominated by a negative shift in the first quarter, when fishing has been limited to maintain the stocks, and a positive response to relative prices with a lag of over a year:

$$SHRIMP = -0.0081 \quad\quad DM1 \quad\quad\quad (2.2.1.1-1)$$
$$(-6.64)$$

$$+0.0002 \quad\quad P_{SHR}/P_{WH}$$
$$(.08)$$

$$-0.0020 \qquad P_{SHR}/P_{WH-1}$$
$$(-1.81)$$

$$-0.0032 \qquad P_{SHR}/P_{WH-2}$$
$$(-3.74)$$

$$-0.0033 \qquad P_{SHR}/P_{WH-3}$$
$$(-2.37)$$

$$-0.0024 \qquad P_{SHR}/P_{WH-4}$$
$$(-1.52)$$

$$-0.0005 \qquad P_{SHR}/P_{WH-5}$$
$$(-.35)$$

$$+0.0025 \qquad P_{SHR}/P_{WH-6}$$
$$(2.07)$$

$$+0.0066 \qquad P_{SHR}/P_{WH-7}$$
$$(3.08)$$

$$+0.0116 \qquad P_{SHR}/P_{WH-8}$$
$$(2.88)$$

$$+0.0179 \qquad P_{SHR}/P_{WH-9}$$
$$(2.82)$$

$\bar{R}^2 = 0.733, SE = 0.0024, D = 2.36, 1968.2 - 1973.4$

Second-degree Almon polynomial distributed lag unconstrained,

$$\Sigma\alpha_i = 0.0095$$
$$(1.40)$$

The initial negative price response is somewhat puzzling, but explorations with alternative specifications have not led to a preferable formulation.

   These agriculture and fishing exports enter into the determination of total agricultural and fishing production (Q_A) and total real agricultural and fishing value added (V_A) together with the other primary products that are considered in subsection 2.2.2.1 below.

   2.2.1.2 Petroleum Products: Since the establishment of a refinery in Panama, this subsector has been a major subsection of gross output within the industrial production and export subsectors. Because of the need to import petroleum inputs and because the production mix of petroleum products does not coincide exactly with the domestic consumption mix, imports remain important for this subsector. Within the model, production (Q), value added (V), domestic demand (D), imports (M), and exports (X) for this subsector (FL) are determined by the following set of relations:[7]

$$Q_{FL} = 10.5145 * P_{FL}/P_{WH_{IND}} + 0.3730 * V_{IND} \qquad (2.2.1.2\text{-}1)$$
$$\quad\; (0.923) \qquad\qquad\qquad (3.11)$$
$$+\, 0.4148 * Q_{FL_{-1}} \qquad -\, 11.6128$$
$$\quad (2.30) \qquad\qquad (-1.05)$$

$\bar{R}^2 = 0.941, SE = 0.8885, D = 1.61, 1965.3 - 1972.4$

$$V_{FL} = 0.1147 * Q_{FL} + 1.1171 + 0.7764 * u_{-1} \qquad (2.2.1.2\text{-}2)$$
$$\quad (1.45) \qquad\qquad (0.767)$$

$\bar{R}^2 = 0.751, SE = 0.5206, D = 1.81, 1965.3 - 1972.4$

$$D_{FL} = 0.1755 * V - 9.3326 * P_{FUEL}/P_{WHOLESALE} \qquad (2.2.1.2\text{-}3)$$
$$\quad (9.35) \qquad\quad (-2.19)$$
$$+\, 2.8671 * DM2 + 1.2431 * DM3$$
$$\quad (2.52) \qquad\qquad (1.26)$$
$$-\, 2.66 * DM1 + 0.2658 * u_{-1}$$
$$\quad (-2.66)$$

$\bar{R}^2 = 0.854, SE = 2.16, D = 1.98, 1965.4 - 1972.4$

$$M_{FL} = 0.0098 * V + 0.6828 * M_{FL_{-1}} - 3.9775 * DM1 \qquad (2.2.1.2\text{-}4)$$
$$\quad (1.17) \qquad\quad (4.55) \qquad\quad (-6.92)$$
$$-\, 0.2928 * DM2 + 3.7647$$
$$\quad (-0.53) \qquad\qquad (2.17)$$

$\bar{R}^2 = 0.68, SE = 1.2384, D = 2.12, 1965.3 - 1973.4$

$$X_{FL} = Q_{FL} + M_{FL} - D_{FL} \qquad (2.2.1.2\text{-}5)$$

Real production responds to the price of petroleum products relative to the industrial wholesale price index (which represents the cost of inputs) and to the current level of domestic industrial real value added. This response occurs with a lag due to adjustment processes but still is fairly quick. The estimated relation is consistent with most of the variance in the dependent variable (and with a higher proportion of the variance than in the other three estimated relations in this set).

In the estimated relation between real value added and production the assumption is made that there is no substitution between primary factors and intermediate inputs in the production process. Real value added is estimated to be only 11 percent of real production at the margin with a substantial degree of positive autocorrelation. This low value reflects the great importance of material inputs—especially crude petroleum—in the production process. As a result, value added per unit of petroleum production is relatively limited (with no significant trend).

Real domestic demand is estimated to respond positively to total real value added (representing general economic activity) and negatively to the price of petroleum products deflated by the wholesale index with some positive serial correlation. The estimated marginal propensity to demand petroleum products out of total value added is about 18 percent. There also is evidence of a negative seasonal effect for the first quarter and a positive one for the second and possibly the third.

Imports might be interpreted as an adjustment toward general economic activity as represented by total real value added. The estimated marginal propensity to import petroleum products out of total value added is only about 1 percent—much smaller than that noted above for domestic demand. The levels of significance of the variables, however, suggest that this relation basically reflects an autocorrelated structure. In any case there is evidence of a significantly negative downturn in the first quarter, which is parallel to that observed in the domestic demand relation (although here there is less evidence of significant seasonal effects for the next quarter).

Exports, finally, are that part of supply that is not consumed domestically. This assumes that undesired inventories are not accumulated, but regulated through changing production or foreign trade. This also assumes that petroleum products can be considered to be relatively homogenous.

2.2.1.3 Services: Exports of services are much more important than exports of goods in the Panamanian case. As is indicated in subsections 2.1.3 and 2.1.4 above, two important components of these services are treated as exogenous—net income from the canal and from the free zone. Exports of other services are estimated to depend on the level of tourism[8] and on the degree of overall international trade activity as represented by exports:

$$X_{OS} = 1.0809 * \overline{TOUR} + 0.2972 * X - 19.5711 \qquad (2.2.1.3\text{-}1)$$
$$(9.30) \qquad\qquad (5.32) \qquad\quad (-4.56)$$

$$\overline{R}^2 = 0.895,\ SE = 3.595,\ D = 1.85,\ 1967.1 - 1973.4$$

Both of these variables probably are serving partially as proxies for nontourism activity in business and finance by foreigners in Panama. Multicolinearity makes it very difficult to identify the relative importance of tourists versus others.

2.2.2 Other Trade and Tradable Goods and Services: This category is subdivided into two groups, depending upon whether or not the government plays a major role in fixing prices.

2.2.2.1 Prices Set by Government with Imports to Fill the Gap: For nonexported, basic agricultural goods and staples the government effectively sets prices and allows imports to cover any shortfalls in production. The prices are set early enough each year so that farmers can know with certainty harvest prices before planting. The hope is that the elimination of price uncertainty induces higher production (see Behrman [1968] for evidence of such an effect in the case of another developing country). However, the prices are set, if anything, below the level required to clear the market using only domestic supplies in hopes of keeping the price of wage goods low for nonagricultural laborers. Of course, although the government may increase domestic supplies through the reduction of uncertainty, it cannot set domestic prices significantly below marginal international prices and still obtain the necessary imports unless it provides subsidies.

For each of the major agricultural products a supply function is included in the model. In cases in which two crops are harvested each year (i.e., corn, rice, and beans) separate functions are estimated for each crop. Whether there are one or two crops per year, the functions are based on annual data. Within the quarterly model these annual outputs are allocated to quarters under the assumption that the harvest occurs uniformly each year over the harvest months reported by the Controloría in the original data source. To obtain total real value added in agriculture and fishing (V_A), a price weighted average of these products plus those in subsection 2.2.1.1 is constructed (Q_A), and the following autocorrelated quarterly relation is used:[9]

$$V_A = 7.2811 * DM3 - 10.5548 * DM2 - 7.0837 * DM1 \quad (2.2.2.1\text{-}1)$$
$$ (6.58) \qquad\qquad (-9.61) \qquad\qquad (-4.32)$$

$$+ 0.1822 * Q_A + 31.9352 + 0.1604 * u_{-1}$$
$$ (8.03) \qquad\quad (22.85)$$

$$\bar{R}^2 = 0.903, SE = 2.2765, D = 2.24, 1965.2 - 1972.4$$

The coefficient of Q_A includes the effects both of including only the major products in the weighted index and of translating from total value to value added (although the positive autocorrelation and constant terms make interpretation somewhat difficult). The dummy variables are included to explore the possibility that the seasonality of the agricultural and fishing products not included in the Q_A index differs from those included. The point estimates suggest that, indeed, total real agricultural value added is relatively lower in the first half year and higher in the second than the Q_A index implies.

The supply functions for the individual major products underlying the aggregate index are as follows:

$CORN\ 1 = 435.6612 * [[P(NEW\ CORN) * 5.0$ (2.2.2.1-2)
              (3.56)
            $+ P(DRY\ CORN)]/2*I.\ DEF.\ AGRO]$

          $- 21.7018 * R + 25.8653 * AREA\ 1 - 1927.2855$
          (-3.27)   (8.80)   (-3.35)

$\bar{R}^2 = 0.943, SE = 62.93, D = 2.21, 1962 - 1973$

$CORN\ 2 = 73.4465 * [P(DRY\ CORN)/$ (2.2.2.1-3)
              (1.27)
            $AGRICULTURAL\ WAGE * 0.0015]_{-1}$

          $+ 5.9953 * WEATHER - 396.4975$
          (5.20)   (-1.22)

$\bar{R}^2 = 0.827, SE = 70.94, D = 1.57, 1966 - 1973$

$RICE\ 1 = 605.5264 * [(PRICE_1 RICE$ (2.2.2.1-4)
              (3.71)
            $+PRICE_2 RICE)/2.0(I.\ DEFL.\ AGR. * 0.01)]$

          $+ 5.2289 * WEATHER$
          (2.13)

          $- 1.0063 * AGRIC.\ WAGES/(IMPL.\ DEFL.\ AGR. * 0.01)$
          (-.81)

          $- 1279.5138 * DUMMY65$
              (-1.55)

$\bar{R}^2 = 0.407, SE = 300.44, D = 1.53, 1962 - 1973$

$RICE\ 2 = 276.1946 * [PRICE_1 RICE/$ (2.2.2.1-5)
              (1.78)
            $(IMP.\ DEFL.\ AGR. * 0.01)]$

+ 3.8095 $WEATHER$ + 2.2038 $WEATHER_{-1}$ - 1791.5229
 (3.32)   (1.93)   (-1.74)

$\bar{R}^2$ = 0.716, SE = 52.00, D = 2.38, 1963 - 1973

Second-degree Almon, polynomial, distributed lag constrained to be zero at $t - 1$,

$$\Sigma \alpha_i = 6.01$$
$$(2.94)$$

$BEAN\ 2$ = 12.3289 * [$PRICE_2 BEAN$/   (2.2.2.1-6)
  (1.65)
  ($IMPL.\ DEFL.\ AGR.$ * 0.01)]

  + 1.1258 * $WEATHER$ - 120.7988
  (6.37)   (-1.61)

$\bar{R}^2$ = 0.810, SE = 14.98, D = 2.47, 1961 - 1973

($BEAN\ 2$ + $BEAN\ 1$) = 4.9668 * [$PRICE_2 BEAN$/   (2.2.2.1-7)
  (1.05)
  ($IMPL.\ DEFL.\ AGR.$ * 0.01)]

  + 1.1222 * $WEATHER$ - 42.9709
  (9.95)   (-.92)

$\bar{R}^2$ = 0.917, SE = 10.29, D = 1.78, 1961 - 1973

$BEAN\ 1 \equiv (BEAN\ 2 + BEAN\ 1) - BEAN\ 2$ (2.2.2.1-8)

$TOBACCO$ = 0.2737 * [$P(TOBACCO)$/   (2.2.2.1-9)
  (3.32)
  ($AGRIC.\ WAGE$ * 0.0015)]

  + 7.3248 * $AREA$ + 3.5294
  (3.10)   (1.14)

$\bar{R}^2$ = 0.787, SE = 1.32, D = 1.64, 1965 - 1973

$COFFEE$ = 1.0993 * [$P(COFFEE)$/   (2.2.2.1-10)
  (1.44)
  ($IMPL.\ DEFL.\ AGRIC.$ * 0.01)]$_{-1}$

  + 0.3666 * $WEATHER$ + 33.8494
  (4.28)   (1.45)

$\bar{R}^2$ = 0.616, SE = 5.32, D = 2.51, 1962 - 1973

$SUGAR = 7.2779 * [AGRIC. CREDIT/$ (2.2.2.1-11)
    (2.33)
    $(IMPL. DEFL. AGRIC. * 0.01)]$

    $- 187.3050 * DUMMY\ 65 + 0.8600 * WEATHER$
    (-2.78) (1.15)

    $+ 299.6557 * P(SUGAR)/(IMPL. DEFL. AGRIC. * 0.01)_{-1}$
    (4.55)

    $- 958.6281$
    (-2.93)

$\bar{R}^2 = 0.943, SE = 63.99, D = 2.10, 1961 - 1973$

$CHICKEN = 18.9480 * LIVESTOCK\ CREDIT/$ (2.2.2.1-12)
    (2.76)
    $(IMPL. DEFL. AGRO. /100)$

    $+ 15550.3872 * P(CHICKEN)/$
        (3.72)
    $(IMPL. DEFL. AGRO./100)$

    $- 2953.6937$
      (-2.10)

$\bar{R}^2 = 0.944, SE = 130.86, D = 2.55, 1964 - 1973$

$EGG = 51.3208 * AGRICULTURAL\ CREDIT/$ (2.2.2.1-13)
  (10.29)
    $(IMPL. DEFL. AGRO./100)$

   $+ 3767.7559 * P(EGGS)/(IMPL. DEFL. AGRO. /100)$
    (19.12)

$\bar{R}^2 = 0.930, SE = 165.64, D = 3.17, 1964 - 1973$

On a general level, these individual supply functions seem to be reasonably satisfactory.[10] All but two of the relations are consistent with over 70 percent of the variance in the dependent variable over the sample period. With the exception of eggs, serial correlation is not an apparent problem. However, the number of observations is quite limited in some of these estimates (e.g., CORN 2) because of the lack of critical data for the earlier years.

On a more detailed level, these supply results may be summarized as follows:

1. The price (or weighted averages of prices for various qualities) of the product of concern, relative to the price of alternatives (as

represented by the agricultural deflator) or relative to the agricultural wage has a significantly positive coefficient in each of the estimated relations.[11] As has been found in many other studies of developing agriculture (see Behrman [1968, 1973a] and the references therein), significant price responses are pervasive in Panamanian agriculture. In one particular respect, however, these results differ from previous studies. The response in Panamanian agriculture generally is to the current actual price, not to some representation of expected prices based on past experience. This difference, of course, reflects the government policy of announcing fixed harvest prices before planting so that farmers expectations for the harvest prices are in fact the actual prices.[12]

2. Following the traditional Nerlovian agricultural supply model (e.g., Nerlove [1958] Behrman [1968]) the possibility of adjustment lags was explored in all of the relations. In no case, however, is evidence obtained of an adjustment process longer than a year.[13] The implied rapid adjustment well may reflect the same characteristic as described above. With certainty about product prices, farmers can be less cautious in switching from one product to another.[14]

3. Originally it was hoped that data from the survey of area planted would be available quickly enough so that data from this survey could be used in forecasts for one or two quarters into the future and the specification could distinguish between the allocation of area and the allocation of other inputs to the production process. Currently, however, the survey data are not processed sufficiently quickly to permit the possibility of using planting data from the survey in ex ante forecasts of harvests. For all of the agricultural crops except for the first corn crop and tobacco, moreover, combining the area allocation decision with the rest of the production process results in a formulation at least as consistent with the variation in production as when area is treated separately, and therefore area is not included as a separate variable.

4. The government has attempted to affect agricultural production by channeling credit to it. In each relation, therefore, the effects of the real quantity of credit[15] and the cost of credit were explored. Significantly positive coefficient estimates for the quantity of real credit are presented for sugar, chicken, and egg production. A significantly negative coefficient estimate for the cost of credit is indicated for the first crop of corn. Thus these credit variables do appear to have had some significant impact on the quantities of agricultural production, with the quantity of credit being more important than the cost, as has also been found in other

studies of developing economies. It is not clear from the estimates, of course, whether only these farm products are responsive to such credit variables or only the producers of these products have had access to credit.

5. In the agricultural sector much more than in most other sectors of the economy, the magnitude of output depends on weather conditions. As a partial index of these conditions, crop-specific rainfall indices (in which provincial rainfalls are weighted by the shares of the provinces in total national production of each specific crop) are included. For seven of the nine crops (all but the first corn crop and tobacco), such rainfall indices have significant positive coefficient estimates. Of course, more sophisticated indices (e.g., incorporating humidity, sunlight, the timing of rainfall, the deviations of rainfall from some ideal amount, etc., might lessen substantially more the unexplained residuals).

To this point in this subsection, emphasis has been on agricultural production. The rest of the subsection is devoted to the food-processing industries, which, of course, utilize agricultural production and imports as their major intermediate inputs.

The treatment of the food-processing industries within the model is somewhat similar to the treatment of petroleum products (see subsection 2.2.1.2 above). Production (Q), value added (V), exports (X), domestic demand (D), and imports (M) for this subsector are determined by the following set of relations based on quarterly data:[16]

$$Q_{FD} = 4.7919 * CRDT_{IND}/P_{FD} + 0.9523 * Q_{FD_{-1}} \qquad (2.2.2.1-14)$$
$$\phantom{Q_{FD} = }(1.13) \phantom{* CRDT_{IND}/P_{FD} + } (21.95)$$
$$+ 1.1667$$
$$(1.67)$$
$$\bar{R}^2 = 0.983,\ SE = 0.6224,\ D = 2.18,\ 1965.2 - 1972.4$$

$$V_{FD} = 0.2186 * Q_{FD} + 3.5761 + 0.7528 * u_{-1} \qquad (2.2.2.1-15)$$
$$\phantom{V_{FD} = }(4.03) \phantom{* Q_{FD} + }(2.59)$$
$$\bar{R}^2 = 0.916,\ SE = 0.3900,\ D = 2.28,\ 1965.2 - 1972.4$$

$$D_{FD+A} = 0.1476 * C_p - 9.3819 * DM2 - 15.63 * DM3 \qquad (2.2.2.1-16)$$
$$\phantom{D_{FD+A} = }(1.15) (-1.32) (-2.23)$$
$$+ 50.4920 * DM1 + 43.1742 + 0.4840 * u_{-1}$$
$$(7.82) (2.06)$$
$$\bar{R}^2 = 0.769,\ SE = 14.9650,\ D = 1.97,\ 1965.3 - 1972.4$$

$$M_{FD+A} = 0.4933 * M_{FD+A_{-1}} + 0.0064 * V \qquad (2.2.2.1\text{-}17)$$
$$\phantom{M_{FD+A} =} (3.4943) \phantom{* M_{FD+A_{-1}}} (1.1945)$$
$$+ 0.0161 * C_P$$
$$ (3.3820)$$
$$- 1.4044 * DM1 - 0.6331 * DM2$$
$$ (-5.3254) (-2.1227)$$

$\bar{R}^2 = 0.828$, $SE = 0.5899$, $D = 2.0793$, 1965.3 - 1973.4

$$X_{FD+A} = Q_{FD} + M_{FD+A} - D_{FD+A} \qquad (2.2.2.1\text{-}18)$$

These relations imply that real food processing basically is auto-correlated with a weak response to the availability of real industrial credit. Unfortunately (at least in regard to tying this production into the rest of the model), no statistical support could be found for a response to such variables as relative prices or the availability of domestic and/or imported agricultural inputs.

Real value added is an autocorrelated function of gross production (once again under the assumption of no substitution between intermediate and primary inputs). Note that real value added at the margin is about 22 percent of gross production in the food-processing subsectorial—about twice as high as in petroleum (relation 2.2.1.2-2 above).

Real domestic demand for processed food depends primarily on overall private consumption (C_P) with significant positive autocorrelation and with some upward shifts in the first and third quarters. The marginal propensity to purchase processed food out of private consumption expenditures is about 15 percent. The positive constant implies that this marginal propensity is lower than the average propensity.

Real import demand for processed food basically is a geometric adjustment toward total private consumption with negative seasonal effects for the first half of the year. The different seasonal pattern between this and the domestic demand relation and the slower adjustment in this case may reflect greater supply lags for imported commodities. From the point of view of integrating these relations with the rest of the model, unfortunately there is once again no evidence of significantly nonzero price responses in either the domestic demand or the import estimates. Real exports from this subsector, finally, are residually determined and thus reflect all of the considerations in the other relations.

2.2.2.2 Prices Set by World Markets and Tariff Adjustments: The rest of the industrial sector (i.e., total industry minus food processing

and petroleum products) is combined into a set of relations anal-
ogous to those for the other two industrial subsectors:

$$Q_{OT} = 0.1583 * Q_{OT_{-1}} + 3.4557 * P_{OT}/P_{WH} \qquad (2.2.2.2-1)$$
$$\phantom{Q_{OT} =} (1.03) \phantom{* Q_{OT_{-1}}} (4.60)$$
$$\phantom{Q_{OT} =} + 34.8404$$
$$\phantom{Q_{OT} =} (4.39)$$
$$\phantom{Q_{OT} =} - 0.5101 * DM1 - 0.2989 * DM2 + 0.9409 * u_{-1}$$
$$\phantom{Q_{OT} =} (-1.85) (-1.15)$$

$\bar{R}^2 = 0.987, SE = 0.8153, D = 2.01, 1965.4 - 1972.4$

$$V_{OT} = 0.0057 * Q_{OT} * TIME + 12.4302 \qquad (2.2.2.2-2)$$
$$\phantom{V_{OT} =} (8.76) \phantom{* Q_{OT} * TIME} (11.16)$$
$$\phantom{V_{OT} =} + 0.7704 * u_{-1}$$

$\bar{R}^2 = 0.981, SE = 0.5400, D = 2.03, 1965.3 - 1972.4$

$$D_{OT} = 0.7987 * D_{OT_{-1}} + 0.1646 * C_P \qquad (2.2.2.2-3)$$
$$\phantom{D_{OT} =} (14.67) \phantom{* D_{OT_{-1}}} (4.85)$$
$$\phantom{D_{OT} =} - 9.2818 * DM1$$
$$\phantom{D_{OT} =} (-5.29)$$
$$\phantom{D_{OT} =} - 2.4753 * DM3 - 6.0372$$
$$\phantom{D_{OT} =} (-1.23) (-1.52)$$

$\bar{R}^2 = 0.961, SE = 3.3099, D = 2.59, 1965.4 - 1972.4$

$$M_{OT} = 0.1264 * V + 0.4826 * M_{OT_{-1}} \qquad (2.2.2.2-4)$$
$$\phantom{M_{OT} =} (2.7440) (2.0806)$$
$$\phantom{M_{OT} =} - 11.4924 * DM1$$
$$\phantom{M_{OT} =} (-6.9608)$$
$$\phantom{M_{OT} =} - 2.2004 * DM2 - 2.9536 * DM3$$
$$\phantom{M_{OT} =} (-1.3768) (-1.9903)$$

$\bar{R}^2 = 0.8512, SE = 3.1806, D = 2.1664, 1965.3 - 1973.4$

$$X_{OT} = Q_{OT} + M_{OT} - D_{OT} \qquad (2.2.2.2-5)$$

In comparison to the other industrial subsectors, these relations
seem to be relatively successful as evidenced, for example, in the
degree of consistency with the variance in the dependent variables.
Production in this sector basically adjusts with substantial positive
serial correlation to the deflated product price with some possibility
of a downward shift during the first half year. Real value added is a
secularly increasing proportion of real gross product with substantial

positive serial correlation. Real domestic demand slowly adjusts positively to real private consumption expenditures with significant downward shifts in the first and third quarters. The marginal propensity to purchase other industrial products out of real private consumption expenditures is about 19 percent. Real imports adjust toward total economic activity (as represented by total real value added) with significant seasonal shifts downward for the first three quarters (probably reflecting the relative concentration of these imports prior to Christmas sales). Real exports, finally, are determined as a residual.

2.2.3 Noninternationally Traded Products: The rest of the economy (i.e., that not included in subsectors 2.2.1 and 2.2.2) is composed primarily of various service sectors: construction, utilities, commerce, banking, insurance, real estate and other finance, housing, transportation, public administration, and services not otherwise covered. These sectors constitute a substantial proportion of total value added. Unfortunately, however, comparatively little data are available for exploring the determinants of production in these sectors. In the specifications estimated, therefore, recourse had to be made to reduced-form adjustments to overall economic activity (or to some component thereof).[17] Although these formulations probably represent important links among sectors, the implicit lack of substitution that is assumed probably overstates real world rigidities.

The estimated relations follow (in the same order as indicated above):

$$V_{CNT} = 0.1372 * (I_{PL} + I_H) + 1.8825 * DM1 \qquad (2.2.3\text{-}1)$$
$$\phantom{V_{CNT} =} (2.79) (2.52)$$
$$\phantom{V_{CNT} =} + 0.6742 * V_{CNT_{-1}}$$
$$\phantom{V_{CNT} =} (6.17)$$
$$\bar{R}^2 = 0.742, SE = 1.77, D = 1.94, 1966.3 - 1973.4$$

$$V_{UTL} = 0.9789 * V_{UTL_{-1}} - 0.6152 * DM3 + 0.0028 * Y \qquad (2.2.3\text{-}2)$$
$$\phantom{V_{UTL} =} (23.98) (-2.74) (1.67)$$
$$\phantom{V_{UTL} =} - 0.3071 * u_{-1}$$
$$\bar{R}^2 = 0.942, SE = 0.5476, D = 1.92, 1966.2 - 1974.4$$

$$V_{CMM} = 0.0695 * Y - 0.4310 * DM2 + 6.3565 \qquad (2.2.3\text{-}3)$$
$$\phantom{V_{CMM} =} (10.06) (-2.87) (5.00)$$
$$\phantom{V_{CMM} =} + 0.6479 * u_{-1}$$
$$\bar{R}^2 = 0.949, SE = 0.4008, D = 2.37, 1966.3 - 1973.4$$

$$V_{BNK} = 0.9583 * V_{BNK_{-1}} + 0.0648 * (DD^T \qquad (2.2.3\text{--}4)$$
$$\quad (12.69) \qquad\qquad (1.08)$$
$$\quad + CRDT^T)/P_{WH}$$
$$\quad + 0.2266$$
$$\quad (.860)$$

$\bar{R}^2 = 0.989, SE = 0.3209, D = 2.21, 1965.3 - 1973.4$

$$V_H = 0.5933 * V_{H_{-1}} + 0.0109 * K_H - 0.3277 \qquad (2.2.3\text{--}5)$$
$$\quad (4.87) \qquad\qquad (3.65) \qquad\quad (-2.95)$$

$\bar{R}^2 = 0.998, SE = 0.1086, D = 1.60, 1965.3 - 1973.4$

$$V_{TRN} = 4.1809* (P_{WH}/W_{TRN}) + 0.0427 * V \qquad (2.2.3\text{--}6)$$
$$\quad (1.83) \qquad\qquad\qquad (1.31)$$
$$\quad + 0.1711 * X$$
$$\quad (1.72)$$
$$\quad - 5.5711 * DM3 - 9.0422$$
$$\quad (-7.16) \qquad\qquad (-3.79)$$

$\bar{R}^2 = 0.826, SE = 1.97, D = 2.33, 1965.1 - 1973.4$

$$V_{PA} = 0.1910 * \bar{C}_G + 0.9101 \qquad (2.2.3\text{--}7)$$
$$\quad (9.38) \qquad\quad (1.78)$$

$\bar{R}^2 = 0.7190, SE = 0.681, D = 2.02, 1965.2 - 1973.4$

$$V_{SRV} = 0.1656 * Y - 0.4424 * DM1 - 0.2996 * DM3 \qquad (2.2.3\text{--}8)$$
$$\quad (57.22) \qquad (-2.56) \qquad\qquad (-1.79)$$
$$\quad + 0.8024 * u_{-1}$$

$\bar{R}^2 = 0.981, SE = 0.6375, D = 1.96, 1966.2 - 1974.4$

With the exception of construction and possibly transportation, these relations are quite consistent with the variations in the dependent variables. Not too much should be made of this fact, however, given the preponderance of autocorrelated structures and that the data for most of these sectors are constructed from assuming rigid relations with similar activity variables.

Taken at face value, the relations suggest that the following activity indices are highly related with value added in each of the sectors: real investment in plant and housing for construction, real national income for utilities, commerce and other services, real demand deposits and credit for banks and other financial institutions, total real value added, and exports for transportation and real government consumption for public administration. Real value added in housing services is more of a production relation with output dependent on the stock of houses. Only for transportation is there any evidence of substitution possibilities in a response to relative prices. Seasonal dummies suggest a relative upward shift in the first quarter for construction (during which time rain is relatively limited) and downward shifts in the first quarter for other services, in the second quarter for commerce, and in the third quarter for utilities and transportation. Adjustments are estimated to be slowest (in order) for utilities, banks and other financial institutions, and construction and housing, which does not seem to be an obviously unreasonable ordering (although the autocorrelated terms for utilities, commerce, and other services make such a ranking tentative).

2.3 Final Demand:

In most macroeconometric models aggregate product is determined primarily or exclusively by aggregate demand. Such a feature is a common criticism of many of the models for developing economies since the critical bottlenecks are often thought to be on the supply side.

Within the present study demand continues to have an important role because for quarterly time units there may be more possibility for flexibility in demand than in supply (although such a statement really holds much more for supply capacity than for capacity utilization). However, an attempt is made to incorporate supply features and their interaction with demand factors (see subsection 2.2). For the three industrial subsectors (i.e., petroleum products, food processing, and other industry) the data permit a fairly satisfactory approximation to the representation of a supply and demand framework.[18] For the other sectors, subsectors, and products considered in section 2.2, the available data do not permit satisfactory representation of individual demand relations. Therefore, relations are included for the traditional major components of aggregate demand so that the model can be closed on an aggregate level.

2.3.1 **Private Consumption** (C_P):[19] A number of different hypotheses about private consumption behavior were considered—permanent and life cycle income, wealth and liquidity effects (as represented by the real value of capital stock and of demand deposits), the impact of sectoral and factoral distribution, and the role of the credit market (both in terms of cost and credit availability). The most satisfactory function is the following:

$$C_P = -0.8865 * RR + 0.9446 * YD - 1.8497 * DM1 \qquad (2.3.1\text{-}1)$$
$$(-1.21) \qquad\quad (58.59) \qquad\quad (-2.39)$$
$$- 1.3446 * DM3 + 9.8786 + 0.8268 * u_{-1}$$
$$(-1.58) \qquad\quad (1.35)$$
$$\bar{R}^2 = 0.994,\ SE = 2.559,\ D = 2.77,\ 1965.2 - 1973.4$$

This relatively simple function states that real private consumption is a positively autocorrelated function of disposable income (YD) with negative seasonal shifts in the first and third quarters and possibly a negative response to real interest rates (RR). The fast adjustment and the relatively high marginal propensity to consume of 0.94 imply a relatively large multiplier, *ceteris paribus*. However, because of supply constraints and monetary behavior, many of the traditional total multipliers are relatively small within this model. (See section 4 below.) The possible inverse response to real interest rates is explicable in light of the way in which the consumption series is calculated as well as any intertemporal substitution effect. Basically, consumption is a residual, given the assumption that inventory changes are proportional to output changes. The negative response to real interest rates thus may reflect the response to the cost of holding inventories on that part of inventories that is not proportional to output.

2.3.2 **Investment (I):** Investment is a much smaller component of total final demand than is consumption but generally is thought to be quite important because of its relatively great volatility. Careful empirical investment studies for developing countries are few in number. Conventional wisdom about investment functions for the developing economies emphasizes the importance of quantitative variables such as the availability of credit and foreign exchange instead of neoclassical considerations although Behrman (1972b, 1976b) presents some evidence of behavior consistent with the neoclassical model for a relatively high per capita income Latin American economy.

For the quarterly Panamanian model a number of alternatives have been explored. Within the model real investment is determined by an adding up identity and a set of five estimated relations, one each for investment in plant and other nonhousing construction (I_{PL}), private housing investment (I_{H_P}), investment in machinery and equipment (I_M), change in inventories ($D[INV]$), and depreciation(DEP):

$$I_{PL} = 0.0505 * (CRDT/P_{PL}) + 0.0339 * (CRDT/P_{PL})_{-3} \qquad (2.3.2\text{-}1)$$
$$\phantom{I_{PL} = }(4.05) \qquad\qquad\qquad (2.11)$$

$$+ 0.0414 * VP_{-4} - 1.1443$$
$$(1.22) \qquad (-.23)$$

$\bar{R}^2 = 0.784, SE = 3.341, D = 1.80, 1966.1 - 1973.4$

$$I_{H_P} = -9.7786 * (P_H/P_C) + 0.0582 * K_H \qquad (2.3.2-2)$$
$$(-2.62) \qquad\qquad (10.2)$$

$$+ 1.4856 * DM1 + 1.7189 * DM2 - 8.7722$$
$$(1.77) \qquad\quad (2.06) \qquad\qquad (-2.86)$$

$\bar{R}^2 = 0.837, SE = 1.922, D = 1.43, 1965.4 - 1973.4$

$$I_M = 2.1949 * DM3 + 0.3648\, CRDT_{IND}/P_M \qquad (2.3.2-3)$$
$$(1.12) \qquad\quad (1.66)$$

$$+ 0.4086 * I_{M_{-1}} + 0.5615 * \%UT + 0.8801 * \%UT_{-1}$$
$$(2.98) \qquad\quad (1.39) \qquad\qquad (2.32)$$

$$+ 0.9380 * \%UT_{-2} + 0.6674 * \%UT_{-3} - 285.1436$$
$$(2.83) \qquad\qquad (1.80) \qquad\qquad (-2.99)$$

$\bar{R}^2 = 0.660, SE = 4.721, D = 2.10, 1966.2 - 1973.4$

Almon polynomial distributed lag; third-degree constrained zero at $t - 4$,

$$\sum_i^3 a_i = 3.0470$$
$$(3.04)$$

$$D(INV) = 3.7326\, DM1 + 1.7406\, D(V) - 1.4326 \qquad (2.3.2-4)$$
$$(1.23) \qquad\quad (16.89) \qquad\quad (-.97)$$

$\bar{R}^2 = 0.899, SE = 7.420, D = 2.67, 1965.3 - 1973.4$

$$DEP = 0.0111 * K - 3.5784 + 0.3155 * u_{-1} \qquad (2.3.2-5)$$
$$(10.22) \qquad (-1.55)$$

$\bar{R}^2 = 0.870, SE = 1.436, D = 1.39, 1965.3 - 1973.4$

These estimates suggest that real investment in plant and other nonhousing construction responds primarily to the real value of credit (with some lag in the complete response) and perhaps some-what to replacement needs as represented by the lagged value of potential output (i.e., the secular trend through the peak of real value added). Real private investment in housing apparently is par-tially for replacement needs (and therefore, related to the stock of housing, K_H) with an upward seasonal shift for the first half year, but also there is some evidence of a price response on the demand side to the tradeoff between housing and other consumer items (P_H/P_C). Real investment in machinery and equipment is a distributed lag adjustment to the degree of capacity utilization ($\%UT$) and the availability of real industrial credit ($CRDT_{IND}/P_M$) with an upward shift in the third quarter. Inventory change depends on the change in real value added, possibly with an upward shift in the first quarter (but the part of inventories not proportional to real value added are included with private consumption, see subsection 2.3.1 above). Real depreciation depends on the stock of real physical capital with some positive autocorrelation.

2.3.3 Net Foreign Demand: The conventional wisdom is that fluctuations in net foreign demand are a major source of instability in developing economies.[20] For the Panamanian model total exports equal the sum of those from agriculture and fishing (subsection 2.2.1.1), petroleum (subsection 2.2.1.2), services (subsection 2.2.1.3), processed food and agricultural (subsection 2.2.2.1), and other industrial products (subsection 2.2.2.2). Total imports equal the sum of petroleum products (subsection 2.2.1.2), processed food and agriculture (subsection 2.2.2.1), other industrial products (subsection 2.2.2.2), imported machinery and equipment (subsection 2.3.2), and services. Therefore, the following function for the real imports of services is the last that is required to determine net foreign demand. However, see subsection 2.7 below for a further discussion of import response to exogenous changes within the complete model.

$$M_S = 0.0221 * YD + 0.3490 * (X + M) - 31.5263 \qquad (2.3.3-1)$$
$$\quad (2.79) \qquad\quad (15.20) \qquad\qquad (-7.09)$$
$$+ 0.8599 * u_{-1}$$
$$\bar{R}^2 = 0.9709, SE = 1.6279, D = 1.1033, 1965.3 - 1973.4$$

This function states that the real import of services depends on the level of international trade activity ($X + M$) and the level of real disposable income (YD) with a high degree of positive serial correlation.

2.4 Prices (P):
For price determination, goods and services are divided into three basic groups: (1) items for which the government sets prices, (2) internationally tradable items for which the international market (with

some adjustment for tariffs and other trade barriers) determines prices, and (3) nontradable items for which domestic market pressures determine prices.

For the first of these groups the only estimated relation necessary is one to translate the weighted average price of specific agricultural products included in the model (see subsection 2.2.2.1) into an overall deflator for agriculture:

$$P_A = 10.9430 * \Sigma Q_i/P_i/\Sigma Q_i + 111.9623 \qquad (2.4\text{-}1)$$
$$\quad\;\;(4.49) \qquad\qquad\qquad (30.29)$$
$$\bar{R}^2 = 0.732, SE = 3.4167, D = 1.50, 1965 - 1973$$

In the second of these groups two price indices are included, one for petroleum products and the other for other manufacturing:

$$P_{FL} = 1.8321 * DM2 + 0.7347 * P_{FL_{-1}} \qquad (2.4\text{-}2)$$
$$\quad\;\;(1.83) \qquad\quad (10.83)$$
$$\quad + 0.1430 * P_{VPETRO} + 11.3827$$
$$\quad\;\;(8.34) \qquad\qquad\;\; (2.09)$$
$$\bar{R}^2 = 0.962, SE = 2.4642, D = 2.40, 1965.3 - 1973.4$$

$$P_{OT} = 0.9880 * P_{USXFMN} + 20.0116 * DM1 \qquad (2.4\text{-}3)$$
$$\quad\;\;(2.03) \qquad\qquad\;\; (2.13)$$
$$\quad + 0.8083 * P_{OT_{-1}} - 102.9787$$
$$\quad\;\;(8.03) \qquad\quad\;\; (-1.93)$$
$$\bar{R}^2 = 0.889, SE = 23.12, D = 2.14, 1965.3 - 1973.4$$

Both of these prices are distributed lag adjustments to international prices—the Venezuelan petroleum price (P_{VPETRO}) for petroleum products and the U.S. price for finished manufactured goods (P_{USXFMN}) for other industrial goods. In both cases there is evidence of upward seasonal shifts—in the second quarter for petroleum products and in the first quarter for processed food. In both cases the simple formulation is consistent with a high proportion of the variance in the domestic price under examination.

For the third group, the estimation of price-determination relations is much more difficult because of the shortage of data. The general assumption maintained below is that substantial pressures carry over from the internationally traded commodities to these nontradables. For housing, in addition to this general influence as represented by the wholesale price level (P_{WH}), some evidence is found for markup behavior on construction wages (W_{CNS}) within an autocorrelated structure:

$$P_H = 0.0112 * P_{WH} + 0.0017 * W_{CNS} \qquad\qquad (2.4\text{-}4)$$
$$\quad\ (2.77) \qquad\qquad (1.56)$$
$$\quad - 0.5392 + 0.3704 * u_{-1}$$
$$\quad (-2.27)$$

$\bar{R}^2 = 0.840$, $SE = 0.1006$, $D = 1.46$, 1966.1 - 1973.4

In addition to these three groups of product prices, the model contains relations to determine the wholesale (P_{WH}) and consumer price indices (P_C):

$$P_{WH} = 6.02 * P_Q * (1 + TXR_{PS}) \qquad\qquad (2.4\text{-}5)$$
$$\qquad (1.85)$$
$$\quad + 0.89 * P_M * (1 + TXR_M) + 39.14 * P_{FD}/P_{FL}$$
$$\quad (20.62) \qquad\qquad\qquad (2.01)$$
$$\quad + 74.69 * P_{FL}/P_{OT} - 56.9146 * P_{FD}/POT - 60.5515$$
$$\quad (2.10) \qquad\qquad (-2.02) \qquad\qquad (-2.18)$$

$\bar{R}^2 = 0.987$, $SE = 1.4785$, $D = 1.32$, 1965.3 - 1974.3

$$P_C = 1.8120 * P_{FL}/P_{OT} + 0.2176 * P_{WH} * (1 + TXR_{PS}) \qquad (2.4\text{-}6)$$
$$\quad (2.40) \qquad\qquad (6.57)$$
$$\quad + 0.7638 * P_{C_{-1}}$$
$$\quad (19.16)$$

$\bar{R}^2 = 0.994$, $SE = 0.6366$, $D = 2.21$, 1965.3 - 1973.4

Both of these relations are consistent with most of the variance in the dependent variables. The wholesale price index depends on the weighted average of the prices for the first two groups discussed above with an adjustment for the production and sales tax rate ($P_Q * [1 + TXR_{PS}]$) and on the price of imports with an adjustment for the import tax rate ($P_M * [1 + TXR_M]$). In addition, three ratios of the components of P_Q are included to reflect the fact that the weights in creating PQ differ significantly from those used in the wholesale price index. The consumer price index is a lagged adjustment to the wholesale price index with a correction for the sales and production tax and with one additional included price ratio to reflect the compositional differences between the two indices.

2.5 Wages (W) and Labor (N) Market:

Eight wage rates are determined within the model. The following sectors or subsectors are included: agriculture (A), food processing (FD), other industry (OT), construction (CNT), utilities (UTL), transportation (TRN), commerce (CMM), and services (SRV). No evidence could be found for a significant impact of plausible variables on the wage of the petroleum-processing subsector so this wage is exogenous. The lack of association with the domestic labor market probably reflects the fact that this industry has a small, highly specialized, and relatively internationally mobile labor force.

The estimated wages relations are:

$$W_A = 0.4614\, W_{A_{-1}} + 2.1749\, P_C + 55331.3496\, V_A/N_A \qquad (2.5\text{-}1)$$
$$\ (2.86) \qquad\quad (3.22) \qquad\qquad (1.88)$$
$$\ - 17.1230\, DM1 + 43.1449\, DM2 - 213.1050$$
$$\ (-1.78) \qquad\quad (2.83) \qquad\quad (-2.66)$$
$$\bar{R}^2 = 0.690,\ SE = 20.74,\ D = 2.12,\ 1966.2 - 1973.4$$

$$W_{FD} = 6.9257\, P_C + 50598.4709\, Q_{FD}/N_{FD} \qquad (2.5\text{-}2)$$
$$\phantom{W_{FD} =}\ (4.19) \qquad\quad (1.59)$$
$$\phantom{W_{FD} =}\ - 59.2853\, DM1 - 491.5117$$
$$\phantom{W_{FD} =}\ (-3.59) \qquad\quad (-3.58)$$
$$\bar{R}^2 = 0.678,\ SE = 38.30,\ D = 2.94,\ 1965.2 - 1972.4$$

$$W_{OT} = 78732.7534 * (Q_{OT}/N_{OT}) + 7.9330 * P_C \qquad (2.5\text{-}3)$$
$$\phantom{W_{OT} =}\ (1.62) \qquad\qquad\quad (8.76)$$
$$\phantom{W_{OT} =}\ - 70.0145 * DM1 - 544.1401 - 0.5741 * u_{-1}$$
$$\phantom{W_{OT} =}\ (-4.49) \qquad\qquad (-5.05)$$
$$\bar{R}^2 = 0.763,\ SE = 35.13,\ D = 2.21,\ 1965.4 - 1972.4$$

$$W_{CNT} = 23.8715\, W_{MIN_{CNT}} - 9.0375\, DM1 \qquad (2.5\text{-}4)$$
$$\phantom{W_{CNT} =}\ (1.85) \qquad\qquad (-1.54)$$
$$\phantom{W_{CNT} =}\ + 1.0673\, P_C + 0.1910\, W_{CNT_{-1}} + 0.1483\, W_{CNT_{-2}}$$
$$\phantom{W_{CNT} =}\ (2.23) \qquad (1.15) \qquad\qquad (1.06)$$
$$\phantom{W_{CNT} =}\ + 0.1455\, W_{CNT_{-3}} + 0.1853\, W_{CNT_{-4}}$$
$$\phantom{W_{CNT} =}\ (1.17) \qquad\qquad (1.11)$$
$$\bar{R}^2 = 0.934,\ SE = 11.77,\ D = 1.92,\ 1966.3 - 1973.4$$

Almon polynomial distributed lag: fourth-degree constrained zero at $t - 4$,

$$\sum_i a_i = 0.6701$$
$$(4.06)$$

$$W_{UTL} = 1.3888 * W_{IND} - 259.6693 + 0.7337 * u_{-1} \qquad (2.5\text{-}5)$$
$$(22.72) \qquad\qquad (-6.84)$$
$$\bar{R}^2 = 0.958, SE = 24.67, D = 1.78, 1966.2 - 1974.4$$

$$W_{TRN} = -129.4224\, U_{TRN} + 58.1994\, DM1 + 210.3900 \qquad (2.5\text{-}6)$$
$$(-1.61) \qquad\qquad (3.64) \qquad\qquad (14.46)$$
$$\bar{R}^2 = 0.313, SE = 37.24, D = 2.10, 1966.2 - 1973.4$$

$$W_{CMM} = 14.3458 * W_{MIN_{CMM}} + 0.2945 * P_C \qquad (2.5\text{-}7)$$
$$(0.84) \qquad\qquad\qquad (0.85)$$
$$+ 0.7982 * W_{CMM_{-1}} - 4.5012 * DM2 + 36.6111$$
$$(6.52) \qquad\qquad (-1.08) \qquad\qquad (1.30)$$
$$\bar{R}^2 = 0.830, SE = 9.51, D = 2.09, 1966.3 - 1973.4$$

$$W_{SRV} = -841.2583 * U - 56.7755 * DM1 \qquad (2.5\text{-}8)$$
$$(-8.25) \qquad\qquad (-6.63)$$
$$+ 52.1794 * DM2$$
$$(5.81)$$
$$+ 1.3078 * P_C + 1.7437 * P_{C_{-1}} + 1.3078 * P_{C_{-2}}$$
$$(8.84) \qquad\qquad (8.84) \qquad\qquad (8.84)$$
$$- 129.9296 - 0.3549 * u_{-1}$$
$$(-1.29)$$
$$\bar{R}^2 = 0.940, SE = 19.52, D = 1.99, 1966.2 - 1974.4$$

Polynomial Almon distributed lag: third-degree constrained at $t - 3$,

$$\sum_i^3 \alpha_i = 4.3592$$
$$(8.84)$$

The underlying model of wage determination in each case basically assumes that the level of sectoral wages adjusts in a manner described by a polynomial to (some of) a set of six variables:

1. The unemployment rate (U) has significantly negative coefficients in only two sectors—transportation and services. Although these sectors employ a fairly considerable number of workers, it is hard

to argue that there is evidence of widespread Phillips curvelike phenomena.[21]

2. Minimum wages have been in effect for most of the sample period. However, there has been relatively little variance in the legal minimums. Only for construction and commerce is there evidence of any significant effect of the legal minimums on actual levels. Perhaps this pattern reflects the fact that in most other sectors average wages have been significantly above the minimum levels.

3. In discussions of sectoral wage determination one frequently encounters suggestions that particular sectors act as pacemakers for other sectors. Some evidence supporting such a phenomenon is present in estimated dependence of wages in utilities on the industrial wage (which is defined as the weighted average of the wages of the three industrial subsectors).

4. Expectations concerning the level of prices are widely thought to be an important determinant of wage levels. In a sectoral quarterly study of Chilean wage determination Behrman and Garcia (1973) report that such expectations are the most important single determinant of wages (although that study is for a country with a much more inflationary history). In the present study current and lagged values of the consumer price index are used to represent such expectations. Its impact is fairly pervasive in that it enters directly with a significantly positive coefficient at the 5 percent level in five cases and indirectly through the industrial wage in a sixth (utilities). The only exceptions are commerce (where it is significantly nonzero only at the 30 percent level) and transportation.

5. Neoclassical theory predicts that at the margin wages depend on productivity. The data do not really permit consideration of marginal changes in this study. However, for the three goods-producing sectors (i.e., agriculture, food processing, and other industry) positive coefficients are obtained for average productivity (Q/N or V/N), thus lending some support to the hypothesis that labor productivity influences wages.

6. Dummy variables are included to represent seasonal shifts. The dominant such shift is a negative one for the first quarter, which occurs in five cases: agriculture, food processing, other industry, construction, and services. A negative shift also occurs in commerce in the second quarter. Positive shifts are indicated for transportation in the first quarter and for agriculture and services in the second quarter.

In addition to sectoral wages, the number of workers (N) demanded by each sector is determined within the model. Because of

data inadequacies, no attempt is made to explore elaborate hypotheses about the determination of these variables. Instead a fixed
coefficient relation between laborers per unit of output (N/Q for the
goods-producing sector, N/V for the rest) is posited at any point of
time, but the possibility is explored of secular trends or seasonal
effects.

In the same order as the above sectoral wage equations (but with
the addition of petroleum products) the estimated relationships so
obtained are:

$$N_A/Q_A = 390.8770 * DM3 - 373.8969 * DM1 \qquad\qquad (2.5-9)$$
$$ (7.13) \qquad\qquad (-6.56)$$
$$ - 2.0573 * TIME$$
$$ (-0.99)$$
$$ + 783.9133 - 0.0487 * u_{-1}$$
$$ (9.08)$$
$$\bar{R}^2 = 0.811, SE = 129.7989, D = 1.96, 1965.2 - 1973.4$$

$$N_{FL}/Q_{FL} = -0.6932 * TIME + 78.1941 + 0.7182 * u_{-1} \qquad (2.5-10)$$
$$\phantom{N_{FL}/Q_{FL} =} (-1.92) \qquad\qquad (5.36)$$
$$\bar{R}^2 = 0.682, SE = 5.15, D = 1.91, 1965.2 - 1972.4$$

$$N_{FD}/Q_{FD} = -1.0684 * TIME + 268.9546 + 0.6483 * u_{-1} \qquad (2.5-11)$$
$$\phantom{N_{FD}/Q_{FD} =} (-2.61) \qquad\qquad (16.48)$$
$$\bar{R}^2 = 0.815, SE = 7.17, D = 2.19, 1965.2 - 1972.4$$

$$N_{OT}/Q_{OT} = -1.1640 * TIME + 462.7063 + 0.4350 * u_{-1} \qquad (2.5-12)$$
$$\phantom{N_{OT}/Q_{OT} =} (-2.29) \qquad\qquad (23.47)$$
$$\bar{R}^2 = 0.486, SE = 14.29, D = 1.98, 1965.2 - 1972.4$$

$$N_{CNT}/V_{CNT} = 5.6457 * TIME + 1055.9553 \qquad\qquad (2.5-13)$$
$$\phantom{N_{CNT}/V_{CNT} =} (1.18) \qquad\qquad (5.40)$$
$$\phantom{N_{CNT}/V_{CNT} =} + 0.3643 * u_{-1}$$
$$\bar{R}^2 = 0.160, SE = 181.7, D = 1.45, 1965.2 - 1973.4$$

$$N_{UTL}/V_{UTL} = -10.5935 * TIME + 1120.2303 \qquad\qquad (2.5-14)$$
$$\phantom{N_{UTL}/V_{UTL} =} (-1.88) \qquad\qquad (4.64)$$
$$\phantom{N_{UTL}/V_{UTL} =} + 0.7285 * u_{-1}$$
$$\bar{R}^2 = 0.706, SE = 91.39, D = 1.16, 1965.2 - 1973.4$$

$$N_{TRN}/V_{TRN} = -12.0572 * TIME + 1188.8130 \qquad (2.5\text{-}15)$$
$$(-3.12) \qquad\qquad (7.68)$$
$$\bar{R}^2 = 0.200, SE = 301.6, D = 2.92, 1965.2 - 1973.4$$

$$N_{CMM}/V_{CMM} = 24.8742 * TIME + 815.7081 \qquad (2.5\text{-}16)$$
$$(7.00) \qquad\qquad (5.63)$$
$$+ 0.3448 * u_{-1}$$
$$\bar{R}^2 = 0.771, SE = 139.1, D = 1.41, 1965.2 - 1973.4$$

$$N_{SRV}/V_{SRV} = 4.9557 * TIME + 2668.9864 \qquad (2.5\text{-}17)$$
$$(1.90) \qquad\qquad (25.34)$$
$$\bar{R}^2 = 0.071, SE = 156.2, D = 1.91, 1965.2 - 1973.4$$

The dominant pattern in these relations is a negative secular time trend in labor demanded per unit output, quite possibly with positive serial correlation. In seven of the nine cases the estimated coefficients of time are significantly nonzero at the 5 percent level. Five of these seven are negative, indicating secular increases in average labor productivity. Two of these seven are positive, indicating declines in average labor productivity in commerce and services (perhaps due to overcrowding because of the absorption of underemployed labor?). For agriculture and construction, the coefficients (negative and positive, respectively) are significantly nonzero only at the 25 percent level. For agriculture alone, there is evidence of seasonal patterns with a downward shift in the first quarter and an upward shift of approximately the same magnitude in the third quarter (during which many of the major crops are harvested).

The last relations in the labor market part of the model allow measurement of sectoral unemployment, defined as the difference between the exogenous secular trends through the peaks of sectoral labor usage and the sectoral demands for labor as estimated from the last set of relations. Total unemployment is obtained by summing these residuals across sectors. The unemployment rate (U) is defined by dividing unemployment by the secular trend. Notice this measure need not coincide with the usual sample survey measurement of unemployment, nor is it likely that full employment, so defined, is a desirable target.

2.6 Monetary Sector:
As noted in the discussion of government policy variables in subsection 2.1, the complete convertibility of the Balboa and the U.S.

dollar substantially limits the effectiveness of monetary policy. The use of the U.S. dollar for paper currency, in fact, makes it impossible even to measure accurately the complete Panamanian money supply. Panamanian prices reflect these institutional arrangements by being relatively dependent on international prices as compared to domestic monetary policy even in the short run (see subsection 2.4 above).[22]

Within the model, as also noted above, credit (both total and sectoral allocations) is exogenous. The only monetary variables that are endogenous in the model are domestic demand deposits in real terms (DD/P_C) and (sometimes) the interest rate (R):

$$DD/P_C = -6.6000 * R(P_C) + 0.9455 * [DD/P_C]_{-1} \qquad (2.6\text{-}1)$$
$$ (-1.84) \qquad\qquad (16.11)$$

$$- 0.0333 * R_{US} + 0.0014 * Y + 0.0024 * Y_{-1}$$
$$(-1.64) \qquad\quad (0.83) \qquad\quad (1.86)$$

$$+ 0.0027 * Y_{-2} + 0.0020 * Y_{-2} - 0.8232$$
$$(1.80) \qquad\quad (1.05) \qquad\quad (-1.92)$$

$$\bar{R}^2 = 0.994, SE = 0.130, D = 2.40, 1966.2 - 1973.4$$

Almon polynomial distributed lag: third-degree constrained zero at $t - 4$,

$$\sum_i^3 \alpha_i = 0.0085$$
$$(2.25)$$

$$R = 1.7901 * (CRDT^T/DD^T) + 0.4636 * R_{-1} \qquad (2.6\text{-}2)$$
$$(4.92) \qquad\qquad\qquad\quad (3.97)$$

$$+ 0.0924 * R_{-2} - 0.0711 * R_{-3} - 0.0267 * R_{-4}$$
$$(1.39) \qquad\quad (-0.79) \qquad\quad (-0.43)$$

$$+ 0.2254 * R_{-5} + 1.5112$$
$$(1.47) \qquad\quad (1.62)$$

$$\bar{R}^2 = 0.949, SE = 0.4291, D = 2.06, 1966.2 - 1974.4$$

Almon polynomial distributed lag: second-degree unconstrained,

$$\sum_i \alpha_i = 0.7295$$
$$(4.82)$$

Both of these relations are consistent with considerable portions of the dependent variables.

The holding of real demand deposits depends on a fairly slow lagged adjustment to factors that determine desired real demand deposits. The first of these is permanent income as represented by a distributed lag over four periods. The other two factors are related to opportunity costs. The rate of inflation $(R(P_C))$ represents the opportunity cost in terms of holding real goods. The U.S. interest rate (R_{US}) represents the opportunity cost in terms of holding foreign debt instruments. No evidence was found of a response to domestic interest rates.

The interest rate depends on a polynomial adjustment to demand versus supply pressures as represented by total credit relative to total demand deposits. No evidence was found of a direct tie to international interest rates (an indirect tie exists through demand deposits) despite the increasing integration of Panama into international markets in the 1970s. Possibly this reflects the dominance in the sample of the period before the structural shift caused by the banking law of 1970. In that earlier period local interest rates seem to have been relatively independent of international money markets.

2.7 Identities:

A number of identities are included in the model. For the most part, these merely define various aggregates as the sum of their components (i.e., total value added equals the sum of individual sectoral values added, total exports equal the sum of the individual exports, total imports equal the sum of the individual imports, total aggregate demand equals the sum of the components of final demand, etc.). There are also identities that define such residuals as the balance of trade (equal to exports minus imports) and the government deficit (equal to expenditures minus inflows).

The most important question related to the identities is how to close the model given that both aggregate demand and supply are independently estimated. Total product or income can be defined as the sum of sectoral value added[23] (with, perhaps, the change in inventories defined as a residual between total supply and the other estimated components of demand instead of using the estimated relation for the change in real inventories in subsection 2.3 above) or, as is more commonly done, the sum of the components of final demand[24] (with, perhaps, value added in services defined as a residual between total demand and the other components of supply). The function of the model clearly differs under these two assumptions. Because of the hypothesized importance of supply variables in developing economies, the Panamanian model was closed by the former alternative.

However, there are obviously physical and economic limits to which inventories may be drawn down when increased nominal expenditures encounter a given production level. At some point there will be an additional reaction; either prices or the deficit on the current account must increase. Given the size and openness of the Panamanian economy, it seems appropriate to assume that, after some initial reduction of inventories, the basic response to an increase in nominal expenditures that is not accompanied by an increase in production takes the form of higher net imports financed by capital inflows. Since international reserves do not really exist in the Panamanian case, in such a situation, therefore, there may be additional imports beyond those indicated in the above estimated relations. Allowing for such a variation in imports would lead basically to the same general results as are obtained from the monetary model of balance of payments.[25] It is important to keep this additional reaction in mind when predicting the effects of specified policy disturbances. It is interesting to note that some of the results of the model as it is in fact closed, such as small multipliers for government expenditures (see section 4), do suggest reactions of this type.

3. WITHIN SAMPLE SIMULATIONS

This section presents the results of within sample complete model simulations in order to give some idea of the degree of success of the model in tracking the quarterly behavior of major economic variables in the Panamanian economy. These simulations are of two types: single period and dynamic. Before presenting these simulations, four important characteristics of the simulation procedure are mentioned.

1. The structure of the model outlined in the previous section is assumed to be the true structure of the Panamanian economy in the period of interest for these simulations. If biases exist in the estimated coefficients, such biases have an impact on the simulation results. Sensitivity analysis, of course, can be used to explore the effect of any such biases in specific parameter values or in particular relations in the model. Nevertheless, some possibly very important phenomena—such as changes in psychological and political attitudes—are not well incorporated into the model.[26]
2. The simulations presented in this study are all nonstochastic.

3. Except for the set of within sample period single-period simulations presented below, all of the simulations used in this work are dynamic in that in the nth simulation period, simulated lagged endogenous values from the first $n - 1$ simulation periods are used instead of actual lagged endogenous values. This procedure permits the tracing out of the time paths of the responses to a given change.
4. Because the model is nonlinear, it cannot be solved by simple matrix inversion. Instead, a Gauss-Seidel iterative procedure is utilized.

Table 2-1 presents summary statistics for the mean of fourteen different single-period simulations and one fourteen-quarter (or three and a half years) dynamic simulation, which is a fairly long period for testing this model. Although the particular results depend on the particular starting points used, they are suggestive of the short-run and medium-run success of the model in tracing out the sample. Both cases include the mean predicted value as a percentage of the actual, the root mean squared percentage error, and the mean absolute percentage error for ten major endogenous variables: total real value added, the major components of real final demand (private consumption, private investment, exports, and imports), the unemployment rate, two representative wage rates (agriculture and other industry[27]), and demand deposits.

Examination of these statistics and graphs of the dynamic simulation (available on request) leads to the conclusion that, for the most part, the model seems to track aggregate behavior fairly well. The mean absolute percentage errors (for the average of the single-period simulations and for the dynamic simulation, respectively) are 1.2 and 1.6 percent for total real value added, 0.4 and 1.0 percent for the consumer price index, and 1.8 and 6.6 percent for demand deposits. For some of the more disaggregated variables (especially private investment, the consumer price index, and demand deposits) and for variables defined as a residual (e.g., the unemployment rate[28]), there appears to be some serial correlation in the errors. As would be expected, generally (but not exclusively, see the agricultural wage) the errors are smaller for the single-period simulation than for the dynamic simulation. All in all, however, the model appears to trace the sample period relatively well in regard to the size of percentage errors and the identification of turning points. This performance leads to some confidence in using the model as a tool to examine the short- and medium-run operations of the Panamanian economy.

Table 2-1. Summary Statistics for Single Period and Dynamic Simulations for Ten Major Variables Behrman Vargas Panama Model

Variables	14 Single-Period Simulations			One 14-Period Dynamic Simulation		
	Mean Predicted as Percentage of Actual	Root Mean Squared Percentage Error	Mean Absolute Percentage Error	Mean Predicted as Percentage of Actual	Root Mean Squared Percentage Error	Mean Absolute Percentage Error
Total real value added (V)	100.2	1.8	1.2	100.9	2.2	1.6
Real private consumption (C_p)	100.4	2.7	1.9	100.6	3.1	2.3
Real private investment (I_p)	104.7	17.4	10.9	122.3	33.1	25.6
Total real exports (X)	100.7	9.9	6.4	101.9	11.8	8.8
Total real imports (M)	100.0	9.3	5.2	101.0	11.5	8.1
Unemployment rate (U)	104.1	20.7	13.9	102.4	21.6	15.2
Consumer price index (P_c)	99.9	0.5	0.4	100.0	1.2	1.0
Agricultural wages (W_A)	100.3	8.7	6.2	100.6	8.5	5.6
Other industrial wages (W_{OT})	100.0	5.4	3.1	99.7	6.7	4.8
Demand deposits (DD)	100.6	2.7	1.8	103.7	9.1	6.6

4. MULTIPLIER RUNS FOR POLICY-RELATED VARIABLES

This section presents the results of multiplier runs for changes in four exogenous policy-related variables: government consumption, sales and production taxes, nonagricultural credit, and net income from the canal. Changes in these particular variables are examined to illustrate the workings of the model. Many other multiplier runs, of course, are possible (e.g., see the list of exogenous policy instruments in subsection 2.1 above).

For each of these four exogenous variables two simulations are presented. In the first, the variable of interest is changed by one unit (i.e., 10^6 Balboas) for one period and then it returns to its previous level. In the second, the change of one unit is sustained for all subsequent quarters. For each simulation only the explicitly indicated alteration in the exogenous variable of interest is made. All other exogenous variables and parameters are fixed at their base simulation values in order not to confuse the impact of the change under examination with other changes.[29]

The base simulation used as a point of reference is the dynamic simulation of the previous section. Table 2-2 presents the multiplier results for each of the simulations described above for the same ten major variables considered in section 3. For total value added, private consumption, private investment, exports and imports, the entries in this table are the changes from the base simulation included in the respective variables as measured in millions of real Balboas. For the unemployment rate, the entries are the changes in terms of a unitless ratio (i.e., percentages divided by 100). For the consumer price index, the entries are changes with reference to a base of 100. For other industrial and agricultural wages the entries are changes in Balboas per quarter. For demand deposits the entries are changes as measured in millions of current Balboas. For each variable in each simulation these changes from the base simulation values are given in Table 2-2 for the first three quarters and the eighth quarter after the initial exogenous change. This allows a reasonably concise presentation of the immediate and medium-term response paths. For the variables measured in millions of Balboas the time paths of the induced changes are really time paths of dynamic multipliers since the exogenous changes are all unit changes.

An examination of Table 2-2 and the data underlying it suggest eight major characteristics that merit emphasis.

1. Because of the simultaneous nature of the system, variables

Table 2-2. Multipliers for Major Economic Variables due to Exogenous Policy-Related Changes[a]
Behrman Vargas Panama Model

| | Current Government Expenditure | | | | | | | | Sales and Production Taxes | | | | | | | |
| | One-Period Shock | | | | Sustained Shock | | | | One-Period Shock | | | | Sustained Shock | | | |
Variables	1	2	3	8	1	2	3	8	1	2	3	8	1	2	3	8
Total value added (V)	0.23	-0.01	-0.01	-0.00	0.23	0.22	0.21	0.18	-0.11	-0.03	-0.01	0.03	-0.11	-0.10	-0.12	-0.27
Private consumption (C_P)	0.22	-0.01	-0.01	-0.01	0.22	0.20	0.19	0.14	-0.13	-0.02	-0.02	-0.02	-0.13	-0.10	-0.11	-0.24
Private investment (I_P)	0.08	0.16	0.19	-0.01	0.08	0.33	0.31	0.54	-0.04	-0.26	-0.11	0.08	-0.04	-0.29	-0.30	-0.46
Total Exports (X)	-0.16	-0.14	-0.04	0.01	-0.16	-0.20	-0.23	-0.35	-0.65	0.02	0.04	-0.06	-0.65	-0.42	-0.36	-0.74
Total imports (M)[b]	-0.03	-0.00	-0.01	-0.00	-0.03	-0.03	-0.03	-0.07	-0.38	-0.01	0.01	-0.01	-0.38	-0.26	-0.23	-0.46
Unemployment rate (U)	-0.01	0.00	0.00	0.00	-0.01	-0.00	-0.00	-0.00	-0.02	-0.02	-0.02	-0.01	-0.02	-0.03	-0.02	-0.00
Consumer price index (P_C)	0.00	0.00	0.00	0.00	0.00	0.00	0.00	0.00	0.44	0.33	0.25	0.06	0.44	0.64	0.80	1.36
Other industrial wages (W_{OT})	0.00	0.00	-0.00	-0.01	0.00	-0.00	0.00	0.03	3.46	2.64	2.01	0.47	3.46	5.08	6.31	10.82
Wages in agriculture (W_A)	0.00	0.00	-0.00	*	0.00	0.00	0.00	*	0.95	1.16	1.08	*	0.95	1.83	2.57	*
Demand deposits (DD)	0.03	0.09	0.14	0.07	0.03	0.22	0.27	0.96	-2.03	-1.33	-0.92	0.46	-2.03	-2.80	-3.26	-3.31

Table 2-2. continued

| | Nonagricultural Credit | | | | | | | | Net Income from Canal Zone | | | | | | | |
| | One-Period Shock | | | | Sustained Shock | | | | One-Period Shock | | | | Sustained Shock | | | |
Variables	1	2	3	8	1	2	3	8	1	2	3	8	1	2	3	8
Total value added	0.03	0.02	0.02	-0.01	0.03	0.05	0.07	0.10	1.88	-0.05	-0.06	-0.04	1.87	1.80	1.75	1.54
Private consumption (C_P)	0.01	0.02	0.02	-0.01	0.01	0.02	0.04	0.03	1.77	-0.06	-0.08	-0.07	1.77	1.68	1.60	1.17
Private investment (I_P)	0.41	0.17	0.11	0.15	0.41	0.56	0.66	0.98	0.67	1.34	1.61	0.04	0.67	1.93	3.35	4.57
Total exports (X)	0.01	0.01	0.02	-0.08	0.01	0.03	0.03	-0.02	2.38	-0.28	-0.30	-0.13	0.67	1.90	3.34	4.55
Total imports (M)b	0.01	0.02	0.02	-0.01	0.01	0.03	0.04	0.06	1.79	0.06	-0.05	-0.05	1.79	1.81	1.70	1.22
Unemployment rate (U)	-0.02	-0.03	-0.02	-0.01	-0.02	-0.03	-0.03	-0.00	-0.03	-0.03	-0.02	-0.01	-0.03	-0.03	-0.03	-0.01
Consumer price index (P_C)	-0.00	-0.00	-0.00	-0.00	-0.00	-0.00	-0.00	-0.01	-0.08	-0.06	-0.05	-0.01	-0.08	-0.11	-0.13	-0.17
Other industrial wages (W_{OT})	-0.00	-0.00	-0.01	-0.05	-0.00	-0.00	-0.01	-0.07	-0.62	-0.50	-0.38	-0.10	-0.63	-0.85	-1.03	-1.32
Wages in agriculture (W_A)	-0.00	-0.00	-0.00	*	-0.00	-0.00	-0.00	*	-0.17	-0.22	-0.20	*	-0.17	-0.31	-0.43	*
Demand deposits (DD)	0.01	0.02	0.03	0.40	0.01	0.02	0.04	0.59	0.64	0.99	1.37	1.12	0.64	1.47	2.71	8.40

aThe top column headings give the exogenous policy-related variables that are changed for each respective simulation. The next column heading distinguishes between a one-period shock and a sustained shock. The next column heading refers to the quarter, starting with the one in which the exogenous change is first experienced. The individual entries give the deviations from the base run in that quarter for that variable due to the exogenous change indicated in the column heading. The mean values of the endogenous variables (with the units in parentheses if they are not 10^6 real Balboas) are: V (176.9), C_P (137.1), I_g (31.2), X (72.4), M (80.9), U (0.15, unitless), P_C (106.2, unitless), W_{OT} (472.3 Balboas per quarter), W_A (169.9 Balboas per quarter), and DD (241.3 10^6 Balboas).

bFor these simulations it is assumed that inventories are sufficiently large so that they can absorb the residual shock of increased expenditures that are unaccompanied by equal incrementation in production. If this is not the case, then in such a situation imports will rise more than is indicated here, thereby increasing the deficit on the current account, but without any immediate feedback on the rest of the model. See subsection 2.7.

*Not calculated.

throughout the economy are affected by exogenous changes—the direct impact of which may be limited to a narrow part of the economy. This simultaneity is one factor that makes it difficult to analyze the impact of macroeconomic policy changes without an explicit model with empirically based parameters.

2. Although the more detailed results are not presented here, on a more disaggregated level some of the induced changes are greater than for these aggregates. Such compositional changes may imply results different from those predicted by traditional textbook models (see point 4).

3. The induced changes generally are in the direction that the textbook macroeconomic models suggest. For example, reduced sales and production taxes and increased government expenditures as well as nonagricultural credit or net income from the canal zone all result in immediate increased total value added, private consumption, private investment, and demand deposits.

4. However, there are exceptions. For example, imports decline due to compositional changes when government consumption increases.[30] Also prices (and therefore, wages) increase when sales and production taxes increase because the cost-push aspect of increased taxes outweighs the reduced demand. Furthermore, the compositional changes and increased supplies cause prices (and therefore, wages) to decline when nonagricultural credit or net income from the canal rises—even though the unemployment rate also declines. Finally, increased sales and production taxes cause compositional changes that reduce unemployment even though total production declines.

5. The effects of many of the policy-related variables are immediate. However, some of the major variables (e.g., private investment in the first and third one-period shock simulation or demand deposits in all but the second one-period shock simulation) have their maximum impact only after a lag of several quarters. In other cases there is a sign reversal after an immediate impact in the direction suggested by textbook models (e.g., total value added and private consumption in the first and fourth one-period stock simulations). Such lag patterns complicate the analysis substantially, and therefore, point again to the need for an explicit empirically based model for the analysis of macroeconomic policy changes and contribute to outcomes different (transitorily, at least) from those predicted by traditional textbook models.

6. The sustained shocks generally result in sustained and sometimes somewhat larger changes in the same direction as the initial effects of the one-period shocks. Because of the nonlinearities and overall

constraints of the system, however, once again an explicit model is needed to analyze changes. The impact of a sustained change often cannot be deduced merely by adding up the effects of a number of one-period shocks.

7. Some of the multipliers are of considerable size (e.g., the value-added multiplier of changes in net income from the canal). However, in many cases the multipliers are much smaller than suggested by traditional textbook models (e.g., in response to changes in government expenditures or sales and production taxes) because of the importance of supply constraints. Thus government policy must be selected on the basis of the potential effects (given policy goals) within the Panamanian economy, not on the basis of what is thought to be effective elsewhere and is uncritically transferred to this economy.

8. Although some government policies have substantial effects, that others do not implies that the government has a difficult time trying to attain macroeconomic goals simultaneously. Thus, as economists with as differing points of view as Friedman (1974) and Taylor (1974) recently have emphasized, the lot of a policymaker in an economy such as Panama is indeed difficult.

NOTES

1. The sample period is constrained by the availability of data. For some relations it is shorter or longer. The basic data were constructed from a large number of quarterly series and the parallel annual series. The quarterly national accounts so constructed are consistent with the annual national accounts. For details of the data construction see Vargas (1976).

2. As is well known, in cases in which lagged values of the dependent variables are included on the right-hand side, the Durbin-Watson statistic is biased toward two.

3. If this model were to be developed further, some of the government variables now considered exogenous could be endogenized by imposing government budgetary constraints and by adding behavioral functions (e.g., tax collections as functions of the tax base, tax rates, and expectational variables). For an example of another Latin American situation in which such endogeneity is very important, see Behrman (1976a, 1976b).

4. Before 1968 this effort reportedly was successful.

5. Of course, it is difficult to be precise about the division among such categories since relative prices in principle could change so as to move a particular good or service into any of these categories. When one examines the details of actual transactions, moreover, the distinctions become quite fuzzy in a number of cases. On a broad level for plausible relative prices, however, the distinctions have some empirical content and usefully characterize the general picture.

6. Included in this subsection are the export-oriented products, not all exports. Some minor exports are discussed below in regard to relations 2.2.2.1 to 18 and 2.2.2.2 to 5.

7. The production and value-added data for petroleum are not "clean" in that they are not separated from "other miscellaneous industries." However, it is clear that the refineries dominate this category.

8. In a subsequent stage tourism could be linked to activities in other countries.

9. Actually V_A also includes some mineral products, but during the sample they were a very small percentage of the total.

10. For the first bean crop ($BEAN$ 1), however, it was not possible to find a relation that is reasonably consistent with a priori expectations and with variations in production. Therefore, $BEAN$ 1 is calculated by subtracting from total bean production, the estimate of $BEAN$ 2 (see relations 2.2.2.1-6 through 8).

11. For the second crops of the three major staples (i.e., corn, rice, and beans) and for coffee the levels at which the price coefficients are significantly nonzero are somewhat less satisfactory (i.e., 10 to 20 percent) than in the other cases. For $RICE$ 1 the coefficient of the second price term (actually defined as the inverse of the ratio of the two terms mentioned in the text) is significantly nonzero only at the 25 percent level. In this same relation incidentally, a dummy variable is included for 1965 and the earlier years ($DUMMY$ 65) to represent the mean effect of the second price for these years for which wage data are not available.

12. In three of the eleven cases, a one-year lag in the price ratio is more consistent with variations in the dependent variable than is the current price ratio. For two of these three exceptions, however, the gestation period is sufficiently long that annual government announcements do not preclude the need for forming expectations on some other basis.

13. The gestation period of several years for coffee, of course, precludes such rapid complete long-run adjustment. For this tree crop, however, we have not been able to find evidence of a significant long-run price response—perhaps because of the shortness of our sample.

14. That there is no evidence of an adjustment process when there is no reason to have expected prices depend on the past price history brings to mind that in the original Nerlovian formulation, it was not possible to distinguish, that is, identify statistically, the price expectations coefficient from the adjustment coefficient. By including additional variables related to expected yields on farm demand and uncertainty in the desired production relation, however, Behrman (1968) was able to identify the expectations and adjustment parameters.

15. Because of problems of data consistency over the whole sample period, when credit was included in a relation the possibility of a significant coefficient for a dummy variable for 1965 and before ($DUMMY$ 65) was investigated (e.g., $SUGAR$).

16. It should be noted that the international trade data and the subsectoral production data are not defined for exactly the same aggregates so the distinction between processed food and agricultural goods is not as clear as would be desired. Therefore, the imports and domestic demand relations include some

important agricultural commodities in addition to processed food. The major agricultural exports, however, are separated out as is indicated in subsection 2.2.1.1 above.

17. Such treatment for these sectors is common in macroeconometric models. For an example in which more extended treatment is undertaken, see Behrman (1972a, 1972b, 1972c, 1973b, 1973c, and 1976b).

18. For petroleum products "supply" is a misnomer given the market structure. Perhaps a "production reaction function" would be better terminology in this case.

19. Government consumption is an exogenous policy variable (subsection 2.1.1).

20. Recent studies have raised questions about the validity of this hypothesis (e.g., MacBean [1966], Mathieson and McKinnon [1974], and the references therein).

21. These estimates are not Phillips curves in the normal sense because the dependent variable is not in rate of change form. Attempts to specify the relations in such a form were not successful. For more successful efforts see Behrman (1971a, 1976b) and Behrman and Garcia (1973) for a discussion of the Chilean case.

22. For a slightly different view, see Borts and Hanson (Chapter 9, this volume).

23. The Chilean model in Behrman (1976b), for example, generally is closed in this way.

24. See Beltrán del Rio (1974) for a summary of Latin American models.

25. See Borts and Hanson (Chapter 9, this volume) for a simplified application to Panama.

26. For example, the psychological and political impact of the advent of the Torrijos government in 1968 or of the discussions regarding the future of the canal are very difficult to incorporate. However, the model can be used to give some insight about such effects. If such a change results in different priorities among macroeconomic goals, then the model can be used to explore the trade-offs among these objectives. If such a change has an impact on particular parameters (e.g., the productivity of labor, the marginal propensity to consume or export), sensitivity analysis can be used to explore the results.

27. Agriculture is included because of interest in the rural sector. Other industry is included as a representative of a relatively modern sector. (Total industry is not used because the wage in petroleum products is exogenous.)

28. It should be emphasized that the summary statistics in Table 2-1 refer to the error in predicting the unemployment rate in percentage terms for that rate. That is, the unemployment rate averaged about 13 percent over the period examined. A mean absolute percentage error of 15.2 in the dynamic simulation implies an average absolute error in the unemployment rate of less than 2 percentage points (i.e., 15.2 percent times 13 percentage points).

29. Of course, it also may be desirable to explore what happens when a whole package of policy changes are adopted by changing several different policy instruments at the same time.

30. This statement presumes that inventories are sufficiently large to absorb

the increased government expenditures. If inventories are not large enough, imports increase in response to the increased expenditures unaccompanied by equal increments in production. See subsection 2.7 above.

REFERENCES

Behrman, Jere R. *Supply Response in Underdeveloped Agriculture: A Case Study of Four Major Annual Crops in Thailand, 1937-1963.* Amsterdam: North-Holland Publishing Co., 1968.

——. "The Determinants of the Annual Rates of Change of Sectoral Money Wages in a Developing Economy." *International Economic Review* 12:3 (October, 1971a), 431-447.

——. "Sectoral Elasticities of Substitution between Capital and Labor in a Developing Economy: Time Series Analysis in the Case of Postwar Chile." *Econometrica* 40:2 (March 1972a), 311-327.

——. "Sectoral Investment Determination in a Developing Economy." *American Economic Review* 62:5 (December 1972b), 825-841.

——. "Short-Run Flexibility in a Developing Economy: The Postwar Chilean Experience." *Journal of Political Economy* 80:2 (March-April 1972c), 292-313.

——. "Aggregate Market Response in Developing Agriculture: The Postwar Chilean Experience," in R. Eckaus and P.N. Rosenstein-Rodan, eds. *Analysis of Development Problems: Studies of the Chilean Economy.* Amsterdam: North-Holland Publishing Co., 1973a, 229-250.

——. "Cyclical Sectoral Capacity Utilization in a Developing Economy," in R. Eckaus and P.N. Rosenstein-Rodan, eds. *Analysis of Development Problems: Studies of the Chilean Economy.* Amsterdam: North-Holland Publishing Co., 1973b, 251-268.

——. "Price Determination in an Inflationary Economy: The Dynamics of Chilean Inflation Revisited," in R. Eckaus and P.N. Rosenstein-Rodan, eds. *Analysis of Development Problems: Studies of the Chilean Economy.* Amsterdam: North-Holland Publishing Co., 1973c, 369-398.

——. "Variable Definitions and Data Sources for Panamanian Quarterly Econometric Model." Philadelphia: University of Pennsylvania, Working Paper No. 2, ILPES-Ministerio de Planificación y Política Económica Project, 1975a.

——. "Proposed Specification of Quarterly Panamanian Econometric Model." Philadelphia: University of Pennsylvania, Working Paper No. 3, ILPES-Ministerio de Planificación y Económica Project, 1975c.

——. *Foreign Trade Regimes and Economic Development: Chile.* New York: NBER and Columbia University Press, 1976a.

——. *Macroeconomic Policy in a Developing Country: An Econometric Investigation of the Postwar Chilean Experience.* Amsterdam: North-Holland Publishing Co., 1976b.

Behrman, Jere, and M. Jorge García, "A Study of Quarterly Nominal Wage Change Determinants in an Inflationary Developing Economy," in R. Eckaus and R.N. Rosenstein-Rodan, eds. *Analysis of Development Problems: Studies of the Chilean Economy.* Amsterdam: North-Holland Publishing Co., 1973, 399-416.

Behrman, Jere, and James A. Hanson. "Tentative Data Sources and Specifications for a Quarterly Panamanian Model." Panama, Working Paper No. 1, ILPES-Ministerio de Planificación y Política Económica Project, 1975a.

Borts, G.H., and J.A. Hanson. "The Monetary Approach to the Balance of Payments with Empirical Application to the Case of Panama." This volume.

Friedman, Milton. "Monetary Policy in Developing Countries," in Paul A. David and Melvin W. Reder, eds. *Nations and Households in Economic Growth: Essays in Honor of Moses Abramovitz.* New York: Academic Press, 1974, 265-278.

Johnson, Harry G. "Panama as a Regional Financial Center: A Preliminary Analysis of Development Contribution." *Economic Development and Cultural Change*, 24:2 (January 1976), 261-286.

MacBean, Alasdair I. *Export Instability and Economic Development.* Cambridge, Mass.: Harvard University Press, 1966.

Mathieson, Donald J., and Ronald I. McKinnon. "Instability in Underdeveloped Countries: The Impact of the International Economy," in Paul A. David and Melvin W. Reder, eds. *Nations and Households in Economic Growth: Essays in Honor of Moses Abramovitz.* New York: Academic Press, 1974, 315-332.

Morawetz, D. "Employment Implications of Industrialization in Developing Countries: A Survey." *Economic Journal* 84:335 (September 1974), 491-542.

Nerlove, Marc. *The Dynamics of Supply: Estimation of Farmers' Response to Price.* Baltimore: Johns Hopkins Press, 1958.

Stavrou, J., and H. Arboleda. "An Econometric Model of the Panamanian Economy." WEFA, University of Pennsylvania, 1975 (mimeo.).

Taylor, Lance. "Short-Term Policy in Open Developing Economies: The Narrow Limits of the Possible." *Journal of Development Economics* 1:2 (September 1974), 85-104.

Vargas, Juan Rafael. "Data Definitions and Sources for the Panamanian Quarterly Econometric Model." Philadelphia: University of Pennsylvania, Working Paper No. 5, ILPES-Ministerio de Planificación y Política Económica Project, 1976.

3

LUIS DURÁN DOWNING and JOSÉ FÉLIX SOLÍS

An Econometric Model for Nicaragua-Dusol*

1. INTRODUCTION

The purpose of this work is to present the progress made in a project undertaken by the Central Bank of Nicaragua aimed at developing a macroeconometric model of the Nicaraguan economy.

The growing need to quantify the effects of different policies on the economic welfare of our countries renders it increasingly necessary to have instruments of analysis and simulation, such as macroeconometric models, that incorporate the vast complexity and interrelations of the economic system. This need contrasts with the limitations in the availability of data and in our knowledge of economic behavior, particularly in the short term, with which our

*We wish to express our gratitude for valuable guidance and assistance in carrying out this study to Doctor Roberto Incer Barquero, President of the Central Bank of Nicaragua, Francisco Suárez, Executive Director of the International Monetary Fund; Robert Heller, Ichiro Otani, Moshin Khan, members of the Staff of the International Monetary Fund, and particularly Délano Villanueva and Niranjan S. Arya, IMF Staff members who worked long and hard with us in Washington on the specification of the equations and the simulation of the model. Also to Ligia Elizondo, Juan Carlos Morales, Ligia Pérez and other members of the Department of Economic Studies of the Central Bank of Nicaragua who helped us in the statistical work and members of the staff of ILPES for their helpful comments.

countries are particularly concerned, making it necessary to reach a compromise between needs and limitations.

The model presented here adopts this compromise approach and represents no more than a stage in the achievement of more ambitious objectives. Basically it stresses a series of interrelationships that we assume to be distinctive features of the Nicaraguan economy. In the development of the model a number of requirements for statistics have arisen that ultimately will improve our understanding of the behavior of the Nicaraguan economy.

This study contains five sections. Section 2 sketches some previous econometric research on the Nicaraguan economy. Section 3 contains the description of the model, its distinctive features and basic assumptions, and the specification of the equations in the different sectors of economic analysis. Section 4 is devoted to testing its predictive accuracy in the sample period of the model and includes a test of the stability of its coefficients. Finally, Section 5 summarizes the conclusions and prospects for future research in this field.

2. BACKGROUND

The construction of econometric models for Nicaragua was begun only recently. The isolated efforts of this kind were based on very different motivations, and this is reflected in the features of the studies in question. Three previous models—by INCAE, SIECA, and the World Bank—will be discussed; recently some others have also been estimated.[1]

The INCAE[2] model is a variant of the one used by M.B. Chenery and M. Bruno in Israel, a model that has three constraints, namely, the rate of capital formation, the balance of payments, and the supply of labor. These three constraints are basic features of the Israeli economy, and the INCAE authors assume that they are also features of the Nicaraguan economy.

The model consists of twelve equations; seven of them are structural, three specify constraints, and two are definitions. The estimates of the equations are given, but the significance tests are omitted, and therefore the reader does not know the probability level that determines whether the results of the model are accepted or rejected. In addition, the model is not tested to verify its convergence and the stability of the coefficients.

The production function is given in the following form:

$$Vn = Vo + b(Kn - Ko)$$

where b represents the marginal output to capital ratio, which is assumed to be constant and equal to that observed in the period 1965/1971. V is the gross domestic product, and K is total installed capital. This specification follows Leontief; that is it assumes that during the period under consideration there is no substitution between labor and capital and that the proportions in which both factors are used remain constant. This assumption might be valid for some sectors but probably is incorrect at the aggregate level because there has been a strong absorption of capital and technology in the agricultural sector, which is basically the dynamic motor of the economy. It is precisely in the 1970s that the country made intensive use of land by replacing subsistence crops with highly commercial products, implying a consequent introduction of labor-saving technology.

By the production function

$$Vn - Vo = b(Kn - Ko) \text{ or } \Delta \ V = bI$$

investment becomes a fixed proportion, b, of the change in gross domestic product. The second equation for net capital formation

$$In = c(Vn - Vc)$$

is therefore redundant unless interpreted as a saving-equal-investment equilibrium, because it repeats what the production function has already described.

Apart from this redundancy, the rigidities and limitations involved in this naive conception of the accelerator are well known, especially bearing in mind the unutilized productive capacity at the aggregate level in the Nicaraguan economy and the lagged way in which the accelerator principle usually works.

The model also specifies labor supply and demand functions which in structural terms do not play a strategic role in the Nicaraguan economy. In this model the condition of equilibrium between the supply of and demand for labor would be expressed in the relationship $W/P = \delta X/\delta L$. In economies like that of Nicaragua, an expression $W/P = \delta X/\delta L \gtrless 0$ would reflect more reliably certain structural relationships observed in the conditions of production as well as the underlying model. Nevertheless, the virtues of specifying functions which are ex ante in disequilibrium are obscure and in general not recommended in econometric literature.

In sum, a production function from which a capital formation process cannot usefully be derived and a neoclassical labor market constitute an excessively restricted description of the economic processes, though one that often has been forced upon econometric investigators.

In addition, the model lacks an explicit consumption function, thereby giving a somewhat partial view of the overall economic structure. On the other hand, this model does include a savings function. Although correctly defined as a function of changes in production, it probably does not possess the explanatory potential that would come from the inclusion of financial variables or foreign saving. Moreover, since the levels of significance of the functions are not given, there is no criterion to judge explanatory and predictive properties of the saving function.

An effort wholly separate from the INCAE study was made by the Permanent Secretariat of the Treaty for Central American Economic Integration (SIECA),[3] which developed econometric models for each country belonging to the Central American Common Market (MCCA) in order to estimate the impact of economic integration in the Central American area.

The model, which consists of seven behavioral equations, is aimed more at forecasting than explanation and has a Keynesian connotation for the purposes of comparative analysis. The specifications of the gross domestic product and aggregate demand equations were made following the principle of principal components. This is an effective way of retaining sufficient degrees of freedom in statistical analysis and of reducing the problem of multicollinearity.

The model disaggregates and formulates behavioral equations for the various components of effective demand both inside and outside the Central American area. A parallel line of analysis using sectoral production functions was abandoned because of statistical limitations.

The model has two other distinctive features—the lag structure and the introduction of an export function. The inclusion of lagged variables for consumption, investment, and imports in the system of equations is a step forward, giving it a dynamic character and permitting the corresponding short- and long-term marginal propensities to be calculated. Nevertheless, the use of mainly aggregate annual data and the difficulty of breaking down the statistics by quarters means that the functions with lagged variables probably do not reflect the structure of reactions to the changes in signals from the economy (data on prices, profits, resources, etc.). The formulation of one-year lags is the result more of a statistical limitation than a different formulation of behavioral reactions with regard to, for example, consumption and investment.[4]

If the introduction of lagged variables represents a step forward, the form in which the equations are finally specified, through the acceptance or rejection of included variables on the basis of their Student's *t* statistic, weakens the theoretical structure of the model. Thus in certain periods and for certain countries consumption is explained by the gross domestic product (and not disposable income), and in other periods for the same country it appears to be explained by consumption with a lag. The same type of criticism holds for the investment function. Obviously, these specifications are somewhat inconsistent, perhaps because the selection of independent variables may have been influenced by multicollinearity.

In addition to this problem, when the consumption function is estimated in two successive periods it often shows different marginal propensities to consume (MPC). In economic theory short-term marginal propensities to consume may differ not only from long-term propensities, but also among themselves when estimated over different periods. This has been attributed to the influence of the economic cycle through its redistributive effect on income. In the SIECA model the explanation of different short-term MPCs is attributed to both this Keynesian effect and a growth effect. When a MPC is lower than another similar short-term MPC, it means that the marginal propensity to save is higher, which translates itself into a higher demand for investment. This consumption behavior also should be reflected in the structure of the lags, which is not the case when consumption is formulated as a function of the gross domestic product (GDP) of the same period. In addition, the study lacks a statistical test of the proposition that the different short-term MPCs stem from a single long-term function.

A second novel feature of the SIECA model is its specification of an export function both to the Central American area and outside the area. Exports outside the area are treated as exogenous. Exports to the Central American region are a function of three explanatory variables: aggregate GDP of the other countries of the region; relative prices, that is, the ratio between the general price level of the other countries and that of the exporting country; and imports of the exporting country from the other countries of the area with a lag. The specification of the equation is linear in the logarithms of the explanatory variables. In all the countries the demand factor—aggregate GDP of the other countries of the area—was statistically significant for the period following integration. However, except for Nicaragua, the relative price variable before integration was insignificant. The significance of the export function for the Central American area is an indicator of the growth of intrazonal trade, and its formulation was of considerable interest.

A third econometric modeling effort was made by the World Bank through the Minimum Standard Model, which is aimed at projecting external aid needs, although the same model also can be used from an availabilities standpoint. In general terms, the requirements model represents an ordinary two-gap model, which estimates the external assistance necessary to achieve a predetermined growth rate, given a minimum import elasticity, the marginal capital-product ratio, and a maximum marginal savings rate. The availabilities version estimates the GDP that can be achieved with specific foreign aid inputs, given a minimum import elasticity, a minimum marginal capital-product ratio, and a maximum marginal savings rate.

The limitations of this model stem from the fact that the three main structural parameters are given (although their value may change from year to year). These parameters are the marginal capital-product ratio, the minimum elasticity of imports, and the maximum marginal savings rate. Thus, rather than being a purely econometric model, the results of the Minimum Standard Model are a test of the consistency of the initial assumptions and a useful tool for the purposes of external assistance.

Pursuing this trend of econometric investigation, a new model is being developed by the Central Bank of Nicaragua and INCAE. The model attempts to cover both the supply and the demand side and to include the financial flows of the Nicaraguan economy. Nevertheless, the statistical requirements of the model are sophisticated, relative to the type of information available in Nicaragua. In addition, the model is still in the process of estimation, and therefore its results cannot be evaluated as yet.

The less ambitious model developed here, starting from certain basic assumptions about the experience and features of the Nicaraguan economy, attempts to quantify its behavior following the identification of functional relationships. As befits such an initial effort, the model basically explores the simplest relations—in most cases between GDP and/or credit variables and the dependent variables. Thus the model presented here should be viewed as the starting point for a more general effort to systematize, using an econometric approach, the structural properties and the process of economic growth of Nicaragua. Later efforts could use more complicated specification to eliminate the autocorrelation that occasionally appears and to investigate alternatives to some of the dummy variables. However, the model does have some interesting features that correct some of the questions raised in the above resumé of previous work.

In sum many of these features respond to the following questions and needs:

1. Integration of real and financial variables. The preceding summary indicates that earlier models concentrated primarily on real factors, and therefore in this type of research the explanatory or forecasting role of financial variables has not been included.
2. As a result of the above interrelationship, the model should permit simulations with monetary and fiscal policy variables and to establish short-term projections. This would constitute an additional empirical test of the basic assumptions that are set out below.
3. To test the consistency of the statistical series and determine further information needs. Hitherto the type of research done by the Central Bank of Nicaragua has been of a partial nature and thus the interdependence of the economic sectors has not been verified statistically. The DUSOL model enables us to observe the margins of measurement errors in our stock of information as well as to establish further needs.

The model contains 24 structural equations of which 10 are behavioral and 14 are identities. It presents 24 endogenous variables, 5 lagged variables, and 25 exogenous variables, including 6 economic policy variables and 3 dummy variables. The sample period runs from 1960 to 1974; structural changes and other qualitative variations within the sample period were corrected with dummy variables, and the dynamic simulation or test of convergence and stability of the coefficients covers the sample period.

3. DESCRIPTION OF THE MODEL

3.1 Distinctive Features and Basic Assumptions

The econometric model of Nicaragua presented here is a short-term model. Thus it does not include a series of features typical of growth models, such as technical restrictions on production, the dynamics of capital formation and population, and growth of the labor force. It is instead a demand-oriented model, in which the effective determination of the gross domestic product results from the basic identity of national accounts, and consists of the sum of domestic expenditure and the balance of payments surplus on current account.[5]

This formulation implicitly assumes that potential domestic production in a specific year is determined by the availability of factors of production and their respective marginal productivities plus a residual factor that accounts for the effects of the environment and technological change. For Nicaragua the effective use of such productive factors is thought to be influenced by the behavior of demand, with external demand or demand for exports and the internal and external flow of credit occupying preponderant positions. The effect of external demand on the domestic product is unquestioned, but the impact of the financial flow is not, because it could chiefly affect total money expenditure, but not necessarily production. That is, to the extent that the supplies of the other factors of production do not respond with sufficient elasticity in the short term and production does not increase *pari passu*, the excess demand for goods and services resulting from flow of credit would be resolved either through the external sector or the price level.

In the model described here, while domestic credit and external resources may be viewed to a certain extent as inputs of the production process, beyond this limit they become transformed directly into a country's imports, given the level and structure of national production. This last point is a distinctive feature of the economic system described in this model. On the other hand, the rate of inflation, measured in Nicaragua as the percentage change in the wholesale price index, is an autonomous element of the model. The explanation for this assumption lies in the relative openness of the Nicaraguan economy, its relative insignificance in world markets, and the free movement of goods and capital that exists in the country. Thus the variation in the price level is closely linked to the behavior of the prices of the products and services that actually or potentially enter into the flow of external trade. As a result, the resolution referred to in the previous paragraph is assumed to lie in Nicaraguan case primarily in the external sector and only temporarily, if at all, in the price level.

These features of the Nicaraguan economy are reflected in the treatment of the domestic money and financial markets in the model by the omission of the explicit function explaining supply of money or liquid assets, which is used by many of the traditional models. In the specifications of the financial sector, only the demand for money or liquid assets is included. The implicit assumption in this formulation is that the duration of the process of adjustment of the disequilibria between domestic expenditure and production is less than a year and therefore the quantity of money or liquid assets existing in the country is the quantity demanded from period to period.

On the other hand, in the model domestic credit to the private sector is not considered to be established by demand because it reflects to a large extent the explicit intentions of the monetary authorities or the financial system—the former to provide resources for economic activities, and the latter to place productively the resources tapped from other sources. Thus changes in domestic credit to the private sector may be interpreted as the main source of the variation that would occur in the nominal supply of money or liquid assets if there were no external sector; or, in the case of Nicaragua, the potential variation in the supply of money before the adjustment process through the external sector occurs. Consequently, the net international reserves of the banking system, or more precisely the changes in them, which are equivalent to the overall annual balance-of-payments, are determined in this model by the interaction between the demand for liquid assets and credit.

One of the objectives of the model is to detect the form and amount in which the financial variables affect the real aggregates of the economy. From the above it may be seen that the model uses the credit variable and not the money variable in the formulation of the equations determining private investment, consumption, and imports. That is, assuming that the process of adjustment is carried out in a one-year period and that the quantity of money is determined by demand, any effect on real aggregates occurs through the changes in credit and not through changes in the quantity of money.

Another feature of the model is the explicit assumption that external capital flows to the public sector occur in response to needs. To be specific, gross use of external resources results from the disequilibrium in the flow of its internal resources once the financing received by the domestic financial system and its capital expenditure have been fixed exogenously. This would seem to overlook the importance of the elasticity of supply of external credit for the country. However, it is felt that the impact of changes in the interest rate or in the schedule of debt payments, at least within reasonable limits, is small in the short run and therefore would not be captured by the model. In any case, for small changes the division between expenditure and financing is more exogenous than structural. However, this feature does suggest a limitation of the model that must be kept in mind if it is used for simulation of large changes in policy.

3.2 Specification of the Equations in the Different Sectors

The model contains three clearly differentiated markets (domestic goods, external goods, and financial). These are broken down and made compatible so as to show the gross domestic product expenditure account and the flow of funds into and out of four basic sectors of the economy, namely, balance of payments, or foreign sector, public sector, financial system, and private sector. All these variables are expressed in constant (1958) prices.

The behavioral equations and identities of the model of the different economic sectors are described below. The figures that appear in brackets beneath the regression coefficients are the corresponding values of the Student's t. The coefficient of determination, adjusted by degrees of freedom, which measures the goodness of fit of the equation, the Durbin-Watson statistic, which measures the level of autocorrelation, the standard error for each equation, and the estimated value of RHO—the first-order autocorrelation—are also given.

The equations were run using ordinary least squares. Since the variables are expressed in levels, much of the goodness of fit reflects the trend and not explanatory power per se. In particular, it would seem that the model is not suitable to grasp abrupt changes in the dependent variables. Nonetheless, as will be shown below, the results of the dynamic simulation reveal acceptable predictive properties for the model.

3.2.1 Financial System: In the model the financial system is broken down into two subsectors—the banking system and the rest of the financial system. The latter differs from the former not only in the nature of its operations but also in its recent dynamic development and in the lower degree of control that the monetary authorities exercise over it.

A number of earlier studies[6] have accepted the hypothesis that in Nicaragua the nominal quantity of money or liquid assets existing in the economy is determined by the public's demand for them and therefore the Central Bank cannot permanently influence their level or rate of growth.

In accord with this theory, the resources obtained from the public, both by the banking system ($L2$) and by the rest of the financial system ($L3 - L2$), are expressed in the model as structural demand relationships. The explanatory variables are the gross domestic product (PIB) and a dummy variable ($DUMY$) for the years 1972, 1973, and 1974.

The estimated equation for $L2$ was as follows:

$$L2 = -147.26 + 0.179\, PIB + 237.81\, DUMY \qquad (3\text{--}1)$$
$$(-2.37) \quad (11.24) \qquad (5.62)$$
$$\bar{R}^2 = 0.97;\ DW = 1.93;\ SE = 0.07;\ RHO = 0.0239$$

The coefficients both of *PIB* and *DUMY* are acceptable at a level of significance of 1 percent; the Durbin-Watson shows no problem of autocorrelation, and the $\bar{R}^2$ indicates that 97 percent of the variance in *L2* is explained by *PIB* and *DUMY*.

Another alternative describing the demand for *L2* would involve discrete and incomplete adjustment instead of an instantaneous process of adjustment as established in the basic assumptions; the proportion of adjustment would depend on the value of an adjustment coefficient. However, this alternative would introduce as an argument the lagged value of *L2*, a variable that is strongly correlated with the gross domestic product (*PIB*). Another alternative would be to include the rate of inflation as an indicator of the alternative cost of keeping liquid assets; this variable was not statistically significant. This is not surprising for the Nicaraguan economy shows great price stability for the sample period with the exception of 1973 and 1974. Perhaps the effect of this change in the behavior of prices or the lagged adjustment in this period is captured by the dummy variable. The dummy may also pick up some of the non-homogeneity of the linear form.

Credit to the private sector from the banking system (*FIB*) is an exogenous variable in the model. Such variables will be denoted by a bar. Although part of FIB could be considered fixed by demand, there is a high degree of implicit regulation by the Central Bank in determining its size. Likewise the net credit of the banking system to the government (*FIG*), basically related to Central Bank operations, was introduced as an exogenous variable. As a consequence, net international reserves (*RIN*) of the banking system are determined from the identity existing in the monetary accounts. The specifications are, therefore, as follows:

$$FIB = FIB_{-1} + \overline{\Delta\ FIB} \qquad (3\text{-}2)$$

$$FIG = FIG_{-1} + \overline{\Delta\ FIG} \qquad (3\text{-}3)$$

$$RIN = L_2 + \overline{OPNB} + \overline{FEB} - \overline{FIB} - \overline{FIG} \qquad (3\text{-}4)$$

As may be seen in the identity of the net international reserves, the only source of error is the demand for liquid assets (*L2*), which is the variable that exhibits the lowest prediction error in the model within the sample period.[7]

The demand for liquid assets issued by the rest of the financial system is represented by the variable *L3* - *L2*. The estimated equation was as follows:

$$L3 - L2 = -197.20 + 0.070 \, PIB + 168.75 \, DUMY \qquad (3-5)$$
$$(-4.83) \, (6.67) \qquad\qquad (6.05)$$
$$\bar{R}^2 = 0.95; DW = 0.88; SE = 0.23; RHO = 0.4896$$

The equation has a very low Durbin-Watson, indicating autocorrelation in the residuals. In order to obtain a better specification of the residuals the equation was corrected by means of a reestimation using the *RHO* coefficient.[8]

The equation thus corrected naturally has a much higher Durbin-Watson, and the variance is smaller. However, although this new equation was more acceptable, the predictive error (*MSE*) of $L3 - L2$ using it in the dynamic simulation of the model was higher than the predictive error with the uncorrected equation, and therefore the latter was retained in the model.

A number of alternative specifications were run for the variable $L3 - L2$. The formulation in logarithmic terms showed acceptable results at a reliability level of 1 percent. However, in the simultaneous results of the model the predictive error (*MSE*) of the logarithmic equation also was greater than that of the equation in absolute terms, and therefore the latter was retained.

The level of credit that the rest of the financial system grants to the private sector (*FIF*) is obtained through the identity:

$$FIF = (L3 - L2) + \overline{FEF} + \overline{OPNF} \qquad (3-6)$$

In this formulation the only one source of error is the result of the variable $L3 - L2$. The other two variables, defined as exogenous, are the medium- and long-term financing received from the external sector (*FEF*) and other net liabilities of the rest of the financial system (*OPNF*).

The remaining definitions for the financial sector are as follows:

$$\Delta FIF = FIF - FIF_{-1} \qquad (3-7)$$

$$\Delta FI = FIF + \Delta FIB \qquad (3-8)$$

3.2.2 Public Sector: The accounts of the public sector are broken down into two subsectors, the general government and the rest of the public sector. This difference is fundamental both for the purposes of making the figures compatible with the national accounts as well as for economic analysis and programming. Another reason for the breakdown is the different nature of both the income and the expenditure of the autonomous entities and financial intermediaries relative to those of the general government.

Current income of the general government is broken down into three categories: direct taxes (*ID*), indirect taxes (*II*), and other net income (*OINCG*), which constitutes an exogenous variable.

Direct taxes (*ID*) are expressed as a function of national income (*Y*), that is, of payments to the factors of production, and of a dummy variable (*DNEW*) for the period 1969-1974, which reflects two fundamental changes:

1. A change in the system of payments of the mining sector from a progressive to a proportional system that considerably weakened revenue levels
2. The impact of the earthquake and of inflation. The estimated equation is as follows:

$$ID = -75.04 + 0.048\ Y + 29.11\ DNEW \qquad (3\text{-}9)$$
$$(-7.85)\quad (18.32)\quad\ \ (7.97)$$
$$\bar{R}^2 = 0.96; DW = 1.65; SE = 0.09; RHO = 0.055$$

The results are accepted at a confidence level of 1 percent, there is no problem of autocorrelation, and $\bar{R}^2$ is high.

Indirect taxes (*II*) are expressed as a function of total domestic expenditure (*GI*) and of a dummy variable (*DUMY*), which covers short-term economic pressures on the taxation system in the years 1972, 1973, and 1974. The estimated equation is the following:

$$II = 39.52 + 0.075\ GI + 71.80\ DUMY \qquad (3\text{-}10)$$
$$(1.43)\quad (10.66)\quad\ \ \ (4.00)$$
$$\bar{R}^2 = 0.96; DW = 1.72; SE = 0.06; RHO = 0.0878$$

The equation is highly acceptable with no problem of autocorrelation and a high goodness of fit.

General government consumption (*CG*), a concept equivalent to that of the national accounts, depends on the gross domestic product (*PIB*):

$$CG = 94.42 + 0.039\ PIB \qquad (3\text{-}11)$$
$$(5.47)\ (9.78)$$
$$\bar{R}^2 = 0.87; DW = 1.83; SE = 0.06; RHO = 0.0755$$

The equation is highly acceptable, the Durbin-Watson is high, and the $\bar{R}^2$ indicates that 87 percent of the variance in CG is explained by PIB.

Interest on the external debt ($IDECG$) is defined as exogenous; current account savings are defined as the difference between current expenditure and income. As may be seen there are three sources of errors in the identity, direct and indirect taxes and current expenditure.

$$AG = ID + II + \overline{OINCG} - CG - \overline{IDECG} \qquad (3\text{-}12)$$

General government capital expenditure consists of real investment (ICG) and capital transfers (TK), which are specified in the model as exogenous variables (the latter includes the movement of capital resources under the heading of Grants of Loans and Transfers proper, which flow from the central government to the rest of the public sector). Another exogenous concept in the capital account is amortization of the external debt ($ADECG$).

The financing of operations of the general government subsector is carried out by recourse to external borrowing ($RDECG$); savings on current account; financing received from the financial system (FIG); and the variation in the other net assets concerned. Since the latter two variables are determined exogenously in the model, the external borrowing amounts to defining a need for gross external financing to achieve the real and financing investment plans and the servicing of the external debt.

$$RDECG = \overline{ICG} + \overline{ADECG} + \overline{TK} - AG - \overline{\Delta\ FIG}$$
$$- \overline{\Delta\ OANCG} \qquad (3\text{-}13)$$

The rest of the public sector, made up of the public companies producing goods and services and the financial intermediaries, have as a source of income the revenue from tariffs and interest on placements ($INTRG$); the equation for $INTRG$ is the following:

$$INTRG = -101.30 + 0.075\ PIB \qquad (3\text{-}14)$$
$$(-3.79)\ (11.80)$$
$$\bar{R}^2 = 0.91; DW = 1.34; SE = 0.12; RHO = 0.3198$$

The result is highly acceptable with autocorrelation in the indeterminate range and an explanatory power of 91 percent of the variance of $INTRG$.

Current expenditure for the rest of the public sector (CRG) is specified as a function of current income (*INTRG*). When *INTRG* was replaced by the gross domestic product (*PIB*) a rather low $\bar{R}^2$ was obtained. The result of the equation is the following:

$$CRG = 50.03 + 0.211\ INTRG \hspace{3cm} (3\text{-}15)$$
$$(5.46)\ (5.17)$$

$$\bar{R}^2 = 0.65; DW = 0.68; SE = 0.14; RHO = 0.6925$$

This variable presents a similar problem to that of the variable (*L3 - L2*). The equation for *CRG* reveals problems of autocorrelation, and therefore one could respecify the residuals through a re-estimation of the *RHO* coefficient. The corrected equation improves the goodness of fit by three percentage points. However, since the fundamental purpose of the model is its forecasting power as a simultaneous system of equations, the corrected equation was not used because of the high margins of error (MSE) that it generated for this variable in the dynamic simulation.

To complete the current account of the rest of the public sector, interest on the external public debt is defined as exogenous as is the residual heading, Other Current Expenditure.

The capital account for this subsector includes real investment (*IRG*), which is formulated in exogenous terms, and the amortization of the external public debt (*ADERG*), which is also considered as exogenous. The financing headings are made up of the change in other net assets ($\Delta\ OANRG$), savings on current account (*INTRG - CRG - $\overline{IDERG}$ - $\overline{OCRG}$*), capital transfers from the general government (*TK*), and external borrowing (*RDERG*), which is formulated as a requirement:

$$RDERG = \overline{IRG} + \overline{ADERG} - INTRG + CRG \hspace{2cm} (3\text{-}16)$$
$$+ \overline{IDERG} + \overline{OCRG} - \overline{TK} - \overline{\Delta\ OANRG}$$

The sources of errors for *RDERG* stem from *INTRG* and *CRG*.

3.2.3 Balance of Payments: In the balance-of-payments accounts, the model treats exports of goods and services, excluding payments to factors abroad, as an exogenous variable.

Imports of goods and services (*M*), again excluding payments to factors abroad, are made to depend functionally on the gross domestic product (*PIB*) and the change in total credit to the private sector ($\Delta\ FI$).

It should be noted that this specification implies that imports are

one of the mechanisms through which the country adjusts to any disequilibrium in the financial market. The estimated equation was as
follows:

$$M = 31.80 + 0.24\ PIB + 1.78\ \Delta\ FI \qquad\qquad (3\text{-}17)$$
$$\qquad (0.20)\ (5.17) \qquad (4.84)$$

$$\bar{R}^2 = 0.93;\ DW = 2.62;\ SE = 0.10;\ RHO = 0.3412$$

The equation yields a high $\bar{R}^2$, there is no problem of autocorrelation and the coefficients are acceptable at a level of significance of 1
percent.

Some of the remaining components of the balance of payments
are determined in other sectors included in the model. Thus external
borrowing (*RDECG* and *RDERG*) constitutes an additional need for
resources in the public sector. Similarly, the behavior of net international reserves is determined in the accounts of the financial sector.

Other net income from external factors (*OINFE*), net gifts from the
external sector (*DN*), and other net external borrowing (*ORNDE*),
which round off the official capital account of the balance of payments, are also introduced as exogenous variables.

3.2.4 Private Sector (Enterprises and family units):   In the private
sector it is considered that private consumption (*CP*) is explained by
disposable income (*YD*) and by the change in total credit to the
private sector with a lag ($\Delta\ FI_{-1}$). The estimated equation is the
following:

$$CP = 537.60 + 0.739\ YD + 1.30\ \Delta\ FI_{-1} \qquad\qquad (3\text{-}18)$$
$$\qquad (4.33)\ (4.99) \qquad (2.75)$$

$$\bar{R}^2 = 0.98;\ DW = 1.94;\ SE = 0.03;\ RHO = 0.0126$$

The results are highly acceptable, the Durbin-Watson is quite close
to 2, the $\bar{R}^2$ is high, and the Student *t*s are statistically significant.

Private investment (*IP*) is specified as a function of the gross domestic product (*PIB*), the change in total credit ($\Delta\ FI$), and a dummy
variable *DU* for the years 1970 and 1972. The dummy variable cor-
rects the very high residuals registered in 1970 because the war
between Honduras and El Salvador in 1969 caused trade to be
diverted toward Nicaragua with a consequent effect on expectations
and investment levels. In 1972 a fiscal reform of indirect taxes dis-
couraged investment, and thus the estimated *IP* function overestimates the real value. The resulting equation was as follows:

$$IP = 68.56 + 0.072\,PIB + 1.75\,\Delta\,FI + 193.14\,DU \qquad (3\text{-}19)$$
$$ (1.66)\ (5.90) \qquad (17.85) \qquad\quad (7.88)$$

$\bar{R}^2 = 0.99; DW = 1.78; SE = 0.05; RHO = 0.099$

The equation is highly acceptable with no problem of autocorrelation.

Private sector savings (*AP*) are the difference between total domestic savings and general government savings.

$$AP = PIB - CP - CG - \overline{IDECG} - \overline{IDERG} + \overline{OINFE} \qquad (3\text{-}20)$$
$$ + \overline{DN} - AG$$

As may be seen, in the *AP* identity there are four sources of error, namely, *PIB*, *CP*, *CG*, and *AG*. Finally, the net external financing needed by the private sector (*FEP*) is specified as exogenous.

3.2.5 National Accounts: Domestic expenditure (*GI*) is defined as the sum of total consumption (*CP* + *CG*) and total investment (*IF* + *ICG* + *IRG*). The gross domestic product (*PIB*) is the result of domestic expenditure (*GI*) plus the surplus of imports over exports (*M* - *X*). National income (*Y*) is defined as the net domestic product (0.96 *GDP*) minus indirect taxes (*II*) minus interest on the external public debt (*IDECG* and *IDERG*) plus other net income from factors abroad (*$\overline{OINFE}$*). For disposable income (*YD*) the method of calculation used is explained in the appendix.

$$GI = CP + CG + IP + \overline{ICG} + \overline{IRG} \qquad (3\text{-}21)$$

$$PIB = GI + \overline{X} - M \qquad (3\text{-}22)$$

$$Y = 0.96\,PIB - II - \overline{IDECG} - \overline{IDERG} + \overline{OINFE} \qquad (3\text{-}23)$$

$$YD = 0.931105Y - ID \qquad (3\text{-}24)$$

3.3 SUMMARY OF THE MODEL AND DEFINITION OF VARIABLES

Banking System

$$L_2 = -147.26 + 0.179\,PIB + 237.81\,DUMY \qquad (3\text{-}1)$$
$$ (-2.37)\ (11.24) \qquad (5.62)$$

$\bar{R}^2 = 0.97; DW = 1.93; SE = 0.07; RHO = 0.0239$

$$FIB = FIB_{-1} + \overline{\Delta\ FIB} \qquad (3\text{--}2)$$

$$FIG = FIG_{-1} + \overline{\Delta\ FIG} \qquad (3\text{--}3)$$

$$RIN = L2 + \overline{OPNG} + \overline{FEB} - \overline{FIB} - \overline{FIG} \qquad (3\text{--}4)$$

Rest of the Financial System

$$L3 - L2 = -197.20 + 0.070\ PIB + 168.75\ DUMY \qquad (3\text{--}5)$$
$$(-4.83)\ (6.67) \qquad\quad (6.05)$$
$$\bar{R}^2 = 0.95;\ DW = 0.88;\ SE = 0.23;\ RHO = 0.4896$$

$$FIF = (L3 - L2) + \overline{FEF} + \overline{OPNF} \qquad (3\text{--}6)$$

$$\Delta\ FIF = FIF - FIF_{-1} \qquad (3\text{--}7)$$

$$\Delta\ FI = \Delta\ FIF + \Delta\ FIB \qquad (3\text{--}8)$$

Central Government

$$ID = -75.08 + 0.048\ Y + 29.11\ DNEW \qquad (3\text{--}9)$$
$$(-7.85)\ (18.32) \qquad (7.97)$$
$$\bar{R}^2 = 0.96;\ DW = 1.65;\ SE = 0.09;\ RHO = 0.55$$

$$II = 39.52 + 0.075\ GI + 71.80\ DUMY \qquad (3\text{--}10)$$
$$(1.43)\ (10.66) \qquad (4.00)$$
$$\bar{R}^2 = 0.96;\ DW = 1.72;\ SE = 0.06;\ RHO = 0.0878$$

$$CG = 94.42 + 0.039\ PIB \qquad (3\text{--}11)$$
$$(5.47)\ (9.78)$$
$$\bar{R}^2 = 0.87;\ DW = 1.83;\ SE = 0.06;\ RHO = 0.0755$$

$$AG = ID + II + \overline{OINCG} - CG - \overline{IDECG} \qquad (3\text{--}12)$$

$$RDECG = \overline{ICG} + \overline{ADECG} + \overline{TK} - AG - \overline{\Delta\ FIG} - \overline{\Delta\ OANCG} \qquad (3\text{--}13)$$

Rest of the Public Sector

$$INTRG = -101.30 + 0.075\ PIB \qquad (3\text{--}14)$$
$$(-3.74)\ (11.80)$$
$$\bar{R}^2 = 0.91;\ DW = 1.34;\ SE = 0.12;\ RHO = 0.3198$$

$$CRG = 50.03 + 0.211 \, INTRG \quad\quad\quad (3\text{--}15)$$
$$(5.46)\,(5.17)$$
$$\bar{R}^2 = 0.65; DW = 0.68; SE = 0.14; RHO = 0.6925$$

$$RDERG = IRG + ADERG - INTRG + CRG + \overline{IDERG} \quad (3\text{--}16)$$
$$+ \, \overline{OCRG} - \overline{TK} - \Delta \, \overline{OANRG}$$

Balance of Payments

$$M = 31.80 + 0.24 \, PIB + 1.78 \, \Delta \, FI \quad\quad\quad (3\text{--}17)$$
$$(0.20)\,(5.17) \quad\quad (4.84)$$
$$\bar{R}^2 = 0.93; DW = 2.62; SE = 0.10; RHO = 0.3412$$

Private Sector

$$CP = 537.60 + 0.74 \, YD + 1.30 \, \Delta \, FI_{-1} \quad\quad (3\text{--}18)$$
$$(4.33)\,(14.99) \quad\quad (2.75)$$
$$\bar{R}^2 = 0.98; DW = 1.94; SE = 0.03; RHO = 0.0126$$

$$IP = 68.56 + 0.072 \, PIB + 1.75 \, \Delta \, FI + 193.14 \, DU \quad (3\text{--}19)$$
$$(1.66)\,(5.90) \quad\quad (17.84) \quad\quad\quad (7.88)$$
$$\bar{R}^2 = 0.99; DW = 1.78; SE = 0.05; RHO = 0.099$$

$$AP = PIB - CP - CG - \overline{IDECG} - \overline{IDERG} + \overline{OINFE} \quad (3\text{--}20)$$
$$+ \, \overline{DN} - AG$$

National Accounts

$$GI = CP + CG + IP + \overline{ICG} + \overline{IRG} \quad\quad\quad (3\text{--}21)$$

$$PIB = GI + \overline{X} - M \quad\quad\quad (3\text{--}22)$$

$$Y = 0.96 \, PIB - II - \overline{IDECG} - \overline{IDERG} + \overline{OINFE} \quad (3\text{--}23)$$

$$YD = 0.931105 \, Y - ID \quad\quad\quad (3\text{--}24)$$

DEFINITION OF VARIABLES

ENDOGENOUS VARIABLES RESULTING FROM THE STRUCTURAL EQUATIONS

1. $L2$ Real Demand for Money of the Private Sect_r. Includes: cash and demand, savings and time deposits in the banking system. Deflator: Implicit GDP index. Source: Monetary data.

2. $L3 - L2$ Real demand for liquid assets of the rest of the financial system by the private sector. Includes: savings and time deposits and outstanding securities. Deflator: Implicit GDP index.

3. ID Real direct taxes of the general government on households and companies. Deflator: Implicit GDP index. Sources: National accounts, compatibilized with public sector data.

4. II Real indirect taxes of the general government. Deflator: Implicit GDP index. Source: National accounts compatibilized with public sector data.

5. $INTRG$ Real nontax income of the rest of the public sector: Includes: Income from assets, sale of goods and services, other income and current transfers. Deflator: Implicit GDP index. Source: public sector data.

6. CG Real consumption of the general government. Deflator: Implicit CG index. Source: National accounts compatibilized with public sector data.

7. CRG Real consumption of the rest of the public sector. Includes: Payments and purchase of goods and services. Deflator: Implicit CG index. Source: Public sector data.

8. M Real imports of goods and services, exluding payments to factors abroad. Deflator: Implicit M index. Source: National accounts compatibilized with balance-of-payments data.

9. CP Real consumption of the private sector. Deflator: Implicit CP index. Source: National accounts.

10. IP Real investment of the private sector. Deflator: Implicit IP index. Source: National accounts.

ENDOGENOUS VARIABLES FROM IDENTITIES AND EQUILIBRIUM CONDITIONS

11. *FIB*   Real credit of the banking system to the private sector. Deflator: Implicit GDP index. Source: Monetary data.

12. *FIG*   Real credit of the financial system to the public sector. Deflator: Implicit GDP index. Source: Monetary data.

13. *RIN*   Real net international reserves of the banking system. Deflator: Implicit M index. Source: Monetary data, compatibilized with balance-of-payments data.

14. *FIF*   Real credit of the rest of the financial system to the private sector. Deflator: Implicit GDP index. Source: Monetary data.

15. Δ *FI*   Change in total real credit of the financial system in the private sector.

16. *AG*   Real savings of the general government on current account. Deflator: Implicit GDP index. Source: National accounts compatibilized with public sector data.

17. *RDECG*   Real external debt drawings of the general government. Deflator: Implicit M index. Source: Public sector accounts, compatibilized with balance-of-payments data.

18. *RDERG*   Real external debt assets of the rest of the public sector. Deflator: Implicit M index. Source: Public sector data, compatibilized with balance-of-payments data.

19. *AP*   Real savings of the private sector (companies and family units).

20. *GI*   Real domestic expenditure. Source: National accounts.

21. *PIB*   Real gross domestic product. Deflator: Implicit GDP index. Source: National accounts.

22. *Y*   Real national income. Deflator: Implicit GDP index. Source: National accounts.

23. *YD*   Real disposable income.* Deflator: Implicit GDP index. Source: National accounts.
24. Δ *FIF*   Variation in real credit of the rest of the financial system to the private sector.

EXOGENOUS AND LAGGED VARIABLES

25. Δ *FIB*   Change in real credit of the banking system to the private sector. Deflator: Implicit GDP index. Source: Monetary data.
26. Δ *FIG*   Change in real credit of the financial system to the public sector. Deflator: Implicit GDP index. Source: Monetary data.
27. Δ *OPNB*   Change in other real net liabilities of the banking system. Deflator: Implicit GDP index. Source: Monetary data.
28. Δ *OPNF*   Change in other real net liabilities of the rest of the financial system. Deflator: Implicit GDP index. Source: Monetary data.
29. $\overline{OINCG}$ Other real net income of the general government. Source: Public sector data.
30. $\overline{OCRG}$ Other real consumption of the rest of the public sector. Source: Public sector data.
31. $\overline{ICG}$ Real investment of the general government. Deflator: Implicit *ICG* index. Source: National accounts.
32. $\overline{TK}$ Transfer of capital resources from the central government to the rest of the public sector. Includes: Loans and capital transfers.
33. $\overline{\Delta\ OANCG}$ Change in other real net assets of the central government. Source: Public sector data.
34. $\overline{\Delta\ OANRG}$ Change in other real assets of the rest of the public sector. Source: Public sector data.
35. $\overline{X}$ Real exports of goods and services excluding payment of factors abroad. Deflator: Implicit X index. Source: National accounts with balance of payments.

*YD = Disposable Income equals National income less Companies' savings ($-0.075Y$) less Government income from property and companies ($-0.004Y$) less Direct taxes *ID* plus Interest on the public debt ($0.01Y$) plus Net current transfers of the general government ($0.000055Y$) plus Net current transfers from the rest of the world ($0.00005Y$) equals $0.931105Y - ID$.

36. $\overline{OINFE}$ Other real net income from factors abroad. Source: Balance of payments.

37. $\overline{DM}$ Real net gifts of the rest of the world. Deflator: Implicit M index. Source: Balance of payments.

38. $\overline{ORNDE}$ Other real net borrowings. Source: Balance of payments.

39. $\overline{IDECG}$ Real interest on the external debt of the general government. Deflator: Implicit M index. Source: Balance of payments compatibilized with public sector data.

40. $\overline{IDERG}$ Real interest on the external debt of the rest of the public sector. Deflator: Implicit M index. Source: Balance of payments compatibilized with public sector data.

41. $\overline{IDECG}$ Real amortization of the external debt of the general government. Deflator: Implicit M index. Source: Balance of payments compatibilized with public sector data.

42. $\overline{ADERG}$ Real amortization of the external debt of the rest of the public sector. Deflator: Implicit M index. Source: Balance of payments compatibilized with public sector data.

43. $\overline{IRG}$ Real investment of the rest of the public sector. Deflator: Implicit IG index. Source: National accounts compatibilized with public sector data.

44. $\overline{FEB}$ Medium- and long-term real external resources of the banking system. Deflator: Implicit GDP index. Source: Monetary data.

45. $\overline{FEF}$ Medium- and long-term real external resources of the rest of the financial system. Deflator: Implicit GDP index. Source: Monetary data.

46. $\overline{FEP}$ Net movement of external capital, including errors and omissions. Deflator: Implicit M index. Source: Balance of payments.

47. $DUMY$ Binary variable for $L2$, $L3 - L2$, and M. 1972, 1973, and 1974 = 1; rest of the period = 0.

48. $DNEW$ Binary variable for ID. 1969, 1970, 1971, and 1972 = -1; 1973, 1974 = 1; rest of the period = 0.

49. DU Binary variable for IP. 1970 = 1; 1971 = -1; rest of the period = 0.

50. FIB_{-1} Real credit of the banking system to the private sector with a lag.

51. FIG_{-1}　　　Real credit of the banking system to the public sector with a lag.

52. FIF_{-1}　　　Real credit of the rest of the financial system to the private sector with a lag.

53. ΔFI_{-1}　　　Change in real total credit of the financial system in the private sector with a lag.

54. RIN_{-1}　　　Real net international reserves of the banking system with a lag.

4. SIMULATION AND VALIDATION OF THE MODEL[9]

Dynamic simulation of the model involves grouping all the individual equations and identities into a simultaneous system whose interactions indicate whether or not the model is acceptable. Dynamic simulation is useful to determine the validity of the model as well as to identify the problem areas that could be improved to give better results. The validity of the model is tested through the following criteria: (1) a high degree of goodness of fit for the system of simultaneous equations, which ultimately is represented by the convergence of the model; (2) the conditions of stability of the model, which are tested by introducing an exogenous disturbance, for example, an increment of 20 percent in an economic policy variable, and observing whether the system returns to the initial value at the outset; (3) in order to quantify the goodness of fit of the system an analysis of errors is made through suitable indicators.

    4.1 Goodness of fit of the Entire System: The percentage of the variance of the dependent variable that is explained by an individual equation may be measured by the coefficient of determination, R^2. However, this explained percentage of the variance may change when we insert the equation into a simultaneous system. In order to test what we have called, following convention, the goodness of fit, a dynamic simulation was carried out and then a graph was drawn of the estimated value of the simulation and the actual value for each endogenous variable. Some sample graphs are shown in Figure 3-1. Obviously the scale affects the degree of deviation in visual inspection, but the latter is combined with an analysis of the errors (Table 3-1) in which the deviation is quantified.

    There are some functions, such as those of the demand for liquid assets of the banking system ($L2$) (shown), net international reserves (RIN) (shown), and credit from the rest of the financial system

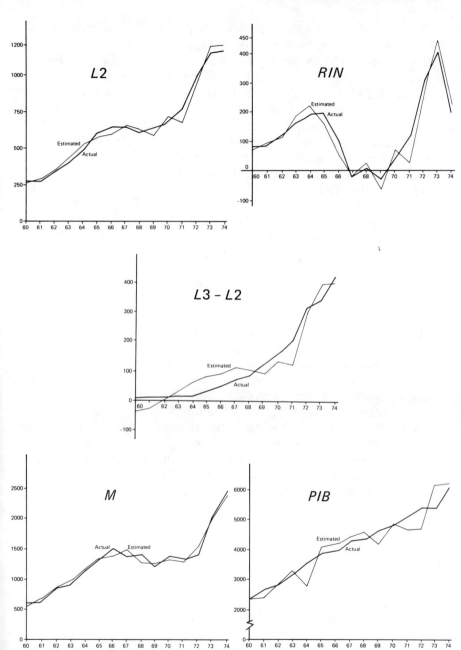

FIGURE 3-1. Comparison of Actual and Estimated Values, Selected Variables, Dusol—Nicaragua Model

(*FIF*), in which the estimated values identify the inflection points of the actual values, and both series show the same trend.

The model also simulates, although to a less satisfactory degree, indirect taxes (*II*), consumption of the general government (*CG*) and imports (*M*) (shown). Although the estimated values show a similar trend to that of actual values, certain inflection points are not well predicted by the model. Indirect taxes and imports are highly correlated; they both follow the same cyclical processes and reflect strong structural changes. It is therefore possible that the same variable is missing, which prevents us from capturing this behavior in full. For the consumption of the general government, the simulation accurately reflects the actual values until 1970, and from then on the trends diverge. The years 1971 and 1972 show a change in the composition of consumption between the public and private sectors, the former becoming more important; this break in the trend is not caught by the equation; likewise, the years 1973 and 1974 reflect the impact of the earthquake that affected public consumption; however, after being corrected by a binary variable this was not significant.

There are other variables such as private consumption (*CP*), total domestic expenditure (*GI*) and the gross domestic product (*PIB*) (shown) that in quantitative terms present errors below 10 percent; however, inspection of the graph shows that the estimated values simulate quite well until 1967 or 1968, after which the inflection points are not well captured by the model. As a consequence of the methodology used to calculate national income (*Y*) and disposable income (*YD*), both variables have the same behavior as the gross domestic product (*PIB*) with respect to the estimated values. The demand for liquid assets of the rest of the financial system (*L3 - L2*) (shown) and the consumption of the rest of the public sector (*CRG*) do not present acceptable results, graphically speaking, but this is partially due to the problem of specification of the errors in the two equations.

The direct taxes of the general government (*ID*) and the current income of the rest of the public sector (*INTRG*) are, of course, influenced by the behavior of the gross domestic product (*PIB*) and disposable income (*YD*). The simulations of the identities are less acceptable, perhaps due to the sources of errors in their definitions.

4.2 Stability: Once the model converges showing an acceptable goodness of fit as a whole, it is tested to verify its stability. Exogenous variables were chosen that greatly affect the economic system or are of great importance from the point of view of monetary and fiscal policy. These variables were exports (X), real investment both of the general government and of the rest of the public sector (IRG and ICG), and the change in the real credit of the banking system to the private sector. Each of these variables was raised autonomously by 20 percent.

The reaction of certain macroeconomic and financial variables to this impact was then observed. The stability of the model is shown in Figure 3-2 by the fact that the exogenous disturbance creates a short-term (two or three years) divergence relative to the base run; however, asymptotically the variables thus disturbed converge on what could be viewed as an equilibrium point. If the system were unstable the trend would be divergent. Given that the information used in this simulation is annual, the reaction of the variables to an exogenous disturbance appears to be much slower and more insensitive than if the data were quarterly, for example. However, it may be seen that the changes stemming from exports have a greater effect on the gross domestic product (PIB) than those from the fiscal and monetary variables, and in turn the effect of fiscal variables is more noticeable than that of the monetary variables.

4.3 Analysis of Errors: This section describes quantitatively the predictive accuracy of the model. In particular the graphic analysis of the deviations is supplemented by three criteria concerning the calculation of these deviations shown in Table 3-1. Even excluding the variables expressed in first differences such as Δ *FIF* and Δ *FI*, the error in percentage terms $(RMSE)$ is large. The variable $L3 - L2$ shows the greatest error. As mentioned above, the rapid changes in stocks in this subsector and its process of dynamic growth have not been accurately captured by the structural equation. While net international reserves captured the inflection points in the series, the relative predictive error is high. The other main macroeconomic variables show a somewhat lower relative predictive error as may be seen in the case of private consumption (CP), internal expenditure (GI), the gross domestic product (PIB), national income (Y), and disposable income (YD). The demand for liquid assets of the banking system shows the lowest predictive error. The deviation as well as the percentage difference between the arithmetic mean of the estimated values and the actual values are also shown. In general terms the deviation is rather low except in the case of the saving of the general government (AG).

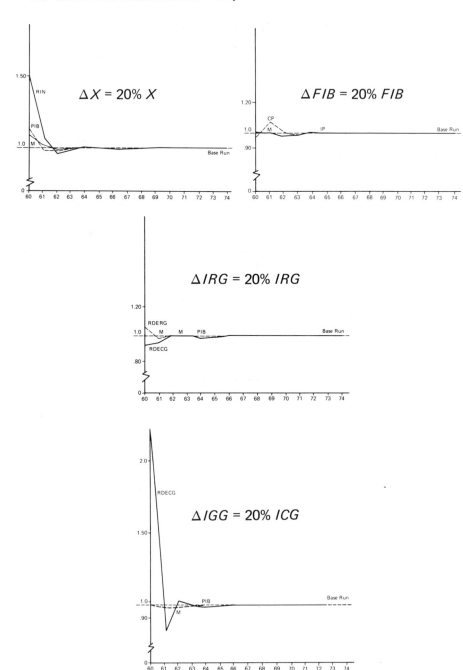

FIGURE 3-2.   Simulations of Stability Properties, Dusol—Nicaragua Model

Table 3-1. Forecasting Errors in the Sample Period
DUSOL Nicaragua Model

	MSE^1	$RMSE^2$ %	$Deviation^3$
L2	34.6822	5.74	-0.0050
RIN	34.6822	28.72	0.0072
L3—L2	39.3311	32.91	0.0531
FIF	39.3311	8.02	-0.0024
ΔFIF	40.9364	51.24	-0.0468
ΔFI	40.9364	26.80	-0.0068
ID	15.7096	18.36	-0.0124
II	23.0996	6.75	-0.0052
CG	23.2780	9.62	-0.0027
AG	19.4091	15.74	-0.1555
RDECG	19.4091	23.80	0.0279
INTRG	27.2936	13.96	-0.0064
CRG	12.1008	13.72	-0.0030
RDERG	26.4989	19.14	0.0071
M	61.2476	5.02	-0.0055
CP	247.3117	8.64	-0.0066
IP	84.5449	13.85	-0.0065
AP	69.5052	11.50	0.0082
GI	305.7616	7.86	-0.0060
PIB	300.1831	7.72	-0.0058
Y	270.2719	8.20	-0.0066
YD	207.4770	6.93	-0.0105

$$^1 MSE = \frac{\sqrt{\sum_{i=1}^{} (Y - Y)^2}}{n}$$

$$^2 RMSE = MSE/\overline{Y} \times 100$$

$$^3 Deviation = \overset{\Delta}{Y} - \overline{Y}/\overline{Y}$$

Where: $\overset{\Delta}{Y}$ = Arithmetic mean of estimated values.

$\overline{Y}$ = Arithmetic mean of real values.

5. CONCLUSIONS AND PROSPECTS

As a result of the experience described above, we wish to state once again that the model given here is part of a larger scale program that the Central Bank of Nicaragua intends to develop further. The results obtained, viewed in the light of their forecasting errors, should be accepted as a first attempt at simulation and in no way as a definitive test of the validity of the model. The testing of the convergence and stability of the model has illustrated problem areas that require further improvement and, obviously, raise fresh needs for statistical information. Until now the predictive effort has been limited to the sample period; a further test of validity is short-term projection for the purposes of economic policy, by no means an easy task in an economic system subject to great dynamic changes that it is difficult to summarize in a mathematical formulation. This effort will be followed up by further econometric research in the country, an effort that we hope will result in a more thorough understanding of our economy and its problems and of the best solutions to them.

NOTES

1. J. Nugent, *Economic Integration in Central America: Empirical Applications* (Baltimore: Johns Hopkins, 1975).

2. Instituto Centroamericano de Administración de Empresas—Centro de Asesoramiento, "Modelo Macroeconómico de Nicaragua," Doc. N° NI/PL–002 (Marzo: 1973).

3. Secretaría Permanente del Tratado General de Integración Económica Centroamericana, "El Desarrollo Integrado de Centroamérica en la Presente Década," IDB-INTAL. Volume 2, Evolution 1960-1970 and Outlook 1970-1980.

4. Nonetheless an attempt has been made to rationalize the difference in length of the lags between the developed and the developing countries. Thus it has been said that there is greater impulsiveness or less planning on the consumption side in the developing countries, while on the investment side although the lag in decisionmaking may be shorter, the implementation lag is greater than in the developed countries.

5. Excluding net payments to factor abroad and net transfers.

6. *Capacidad y Posibilidad del Banco Central para manejar la Oferta de Dinero: El caso de Nicaragua*, document presented by Dr. Roberto Incer Barquero, at the XVIII Meeting of Governors of Latin American Central Banks, Caracas, Venezuela, April 24, 1974. *Dificultades Inherentes a la Programación Monetaria*, XII Meeting of Governors of Central Banks of the American continent and XX Meeting of Governors of Latin American Central Banks, May 1975, Panama, Republic of Panama.

7. By error we are referring to the following expression:

$$MSE = \sqrt{\frac{\sum_{i=1}^{n} (\hat{Y} - Y)^2}{n}}$$

This expression is an indicator of the goodness of fit of the variable not as an individual unit but including the interdependence of the system.

8. A process of first-order autoregression was assumed so that if the error term of an equation is U_t, it is assumed that:

$$U_t = RHO\ (U_{t-1}) + e_t$$

9. The organization of this section largely follows I. Otani, and Y.C. Park, "A Monetary Model of the Korean Economy," International Monetary Fund, 1975. (Unpublished.) Moshin S. Khan and Délano P. Villaneuva, "A Simultaneous Model of the Interest Rate and Money Supply in the United States," International Monetary Fund, 1975. (Unpublished).

REFERENCES

Evans, Michael K. *Macroeconomic Activity Theory, Forecasting, and Control.* New York: Harper and Row, 1969.

Goldberger, Arthur S. *Econometric Theory*, New York: John Wiley and Sons, 1964.

Instituto Centroamericano de Administración de Empresas Centro de Asesoramiento, "Modelo Macroeconómico de Nicaragua." Managua, 1973.

Khatkhate, Deena R., Vicente G. Galbis, and Délano P. Villanueva. "A Money Multiplier Model for a Developing Economy: The Venezuelan Case." *Staff Papers.* XII: 3 (November 1974), IMF.

Kogiku, K.C. *An Introduction to Macroeconomic Models.* New York: McGraw-Hill Book Co.

Otani, Ichiro, and Yung Chul Park. "A Monetary Model of the Korean Economy." IMF 1975 (unpublished).

Ruggles, Nancy D. *The Role of the Computer in Economic and Social Research in Latin America.* A Conference of the National Bureau of Economic Research. New York: Columbia University Press, 1974.

Secretaría Permanente del Tratado de Integración Económica Centroamericana. "El Desarrollo Integrado de Centroamérica en la Presente Década." BID-INTAL Tomo 2.

Theil, Henri. *Principles of Econometrics.* New York: John Wiley and Sons, 1971.

Villanueva, Délano P., and Mohsin S. Khan. "A Simultaneous Model of the Interest Rate and Money Supply in the United States." IMF, 1975 (unpublished).

4

ABEL BELTRÁN DEL RIO

Econometric Forecasting for Mexico: An Analysis of Errors in Prediction

The central question about the utility of econometric models relates to their predictive accuracy. While evaluations have been made of predictions generated by developed country models,[1] no such attempt has been made for econometric forecasts of developing countries.

Evaluations may be made either through an analysis of the usual statistics of fit of the estimated equations of the model—the correlation coefficients, t-statistics, and Durbin-Watson statistics—or through a consideration of the (ex post) predictive accuracy of the forecasts over the sample period, which is the usual method.[2] It is evident, however, that an evaluation made a posteriori, based on ex ante prediction, is more satisfactory. This approach does require a relatively long period of predictions for computing the errors through a comparison of the actual figures with predictions made at different times. Such a procedure not only permits an appreciation of the relative magnitude of errors in the predictions made with different time horizons, but also illustrates whether the errors are reduced as the time horizon shortens.

The accumulated experience of the Wharton EFA econometric

project for Mexico (DIEMEX) provides a vehicle for this type of evaluation. More than seven years of regular forecasts have been made using successive versions of the annual econometric model. From this experience we choose to present, for purposes of this study, an evaluation corresponding to Version V of the model, which is presently in use. Before performing that evaluation it is necessary to describe the model briefly.

DIEMEX-WHARTON EFA MODEL V

Version V of the Mexican econometric model was finished in 1971 and has been used uninterruptedly since that time in making ex ante projections.

The model consists of 143 equations, of which 40 are estimated. The rest are identities. There are 46 exogenous variables. The model generates forecasts of the components of aggregate demand, the external balance on current account, aggregate output, labor force, certain demographic variables, accumulation of capital and creation of productive capacity, public finances, prices, and wages.[3] Basically it is concerned with real variables and contains a minimum of monetary detail. The equations were estimated using ordinary least squares.

The flow chart—Figure 4-1—provides a condensed description of the model and its six endogenous blocks. The economic process delineated there contains the following lines of causation among the blocks, which are numbered in parentheses in what follows: the magnitude of internal demand and its decomposition into consumption and investment in (1) determine the accumulation of capital and generation of productive capacity (3), with effects upon the demand for labor (4) and the division of income (5). Internal demand and its composition also determine the magnitude and composition of imports (especially the division of imports into consumption and investment goods, which is not shown in the diagram) within (1). The imports are (partially) paid for with exports, also within block (1), all of which is detailed in nine of the model's equations. Exports depend fundamentally on the U.S. economy, which is the most important exogenous factor in the model.

The rest of the diagram shows that production (2) is the result of demand (1). The demographic process of (4)—population and urbanization—depends on the regional distribution of capital and the creation of productive capacity (3). The distribution of income (5) is the result of the general level of economic activity determined in (1), of demand for labor, and of wages and prices. These last two

Figure 4-1. Mexico Macro Model—Condensed Flow Chart

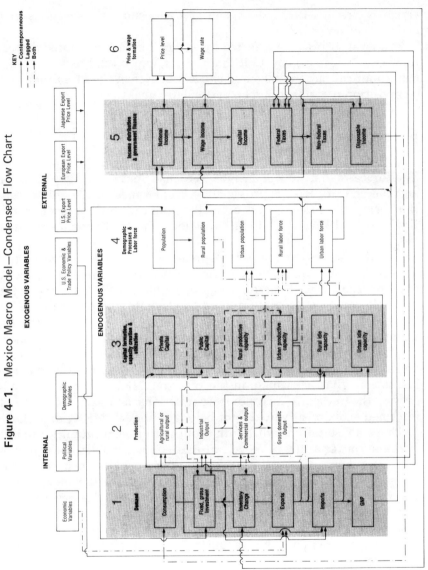

variables are interdependent and also depend on exogenous and endogenous processes.

The level of prices is affected by external inflation (United States, Europe, and Japan), by unit labor costs, and by indirect taxes. Finally political factors, taken as exogenous, affect the magnitude and composition of demand in (1), particularly investment.

PREDICTIVE METHOD

The forecasts that we will analyze were made between mid-year 1971 and the end of 1974, approximately every semester; the only exception being the forecast that normally would have been made in the first part of 1973, which in fact was postponed to September of that year.

Usually more than one set of predictions is made in a semester. This is done for two reasons. At times when uncertainty exists about the direction that domestic economic policy will take, the most probable policy outcomes are used to generate two or more predictions. In addition, our procedure, following the method used by Wharton EFA with its U.S. models,[4] consists of a preliminary projection and a revision (or revisions in the above case). These revisions are done in the semestral meetings of the economists representing the institutions that participate in the Wharton-DIEMEX project. In addition, the revisions incorporate corrections and suggestions from informed economists who do not belong to the DIEMEX group.

These consultations with both groups are an important source of information regarding the levels of exogenous variables in the model and the behavioral equations through adjustment of their errors for the period of projection. This is especially true for the short run as we indicate below. It should be emphasized that frequently these adjustments to the estimated equations are considerable. In general we are correcting the equation in question with more recent knowledge of the expert in the area and/or incorporating official revisions in the data.

Such a predictive procedure is neither simplistic nor mechanistic—in comparison to a simple extrapolation (by using, for example, the growth rate in the exogenous variables and "freezing" the last regression error of the behavioral variables for the period of projection). The comparison of the predictive errors generated by both methods, the simplistic versus the one we follow, favors the approach used here, as shown in Table 4–7 which will be discussed below.

THE ERRORS OF PREDICTION: PERCENTAGES AND DIFFERENCES

A simple way of illustrating the magnitude of the errors obtained in the predictions made since mid-1971 is to compare in tabular form the published official figures with the projections and compute the percentage errors, taking the official figure as 100 percent.

where

$$E_t = (P_t - A_t)/A_t$$
$$P_t = \text{projection of level or flow;}$$
$$A_t = \text{actual figure}$$

In the case of rates of growth, the absolute difference between actual and projected growth rates is perhaps a more convenient way to calculate errors in this type of variable.

where

$$D_t = (P_t - A_t)$$
$$P_t = \text{projected rate of growth}$$
$$A_t = \text{actual rate}$$

These two forms of calculation have been used in the tables that follow.

Since at the time this paper was written the published figures for 1972, 1973, and 1974 were available, we have taken the corresponding projections that were made for these three years. Here it should be mentioned that the Mexican authorities (fundamentally, the Banco de Mexico) publish preliminary figures for the previous year in March and revised figures in September. Thus the figures for 1972 and 1973 are revised while those for 1974 were still preliminary at the time of writing.

Tables 4-1, 4-2, and 4-3 contain in the top ten rows, the percentage errors (E_t) made in the projections (P_t) of the levels based on the actual figures (A_t) (taken as 100 percent), which are shown in the last column. Aside from the price deflator of GDP, expressed with base 1950 = 1.00, and federal government income and income taxes, which are expressed in billions of current pesos, all variables are expressed in billions of real 1950 pesos. (Rows 11 to 20 present the errors in predicted growth rates (D_t) with the final column reproducing the actual growth rates. The last two rows of these tables, 21

Table 4-1. Errors of 11 Ex Ante DIEMEX-Wharton Forecasts: Forecasted Year 1974

Row Symbol	Concept	1 Jun. 71	2 Jun. 71	3 Apr. 72	4 Nov. 72	5 Nov. 72	6 Sep. 73	7 Nov. 73	8 Dec. 73	9 Apr. 74	10 Jun. 74	11 Nov. 74	Actual Value 1974
Forecasts of Levels						*Percent Error*							
GDPR	Gross domestic product	2.70	0.13	-1.75	-0.45	-1.03	1.17	-0.05	0.44	-0.95	-0.25	0.08	180.17
XIR	Primary product	18.38	15.62	10.98	5.28	4.93	0.41	0.41	0.23	4.46	3.35	-0.06	17.03
X2R	Secondary product	4.67	5.24	5.73	2.29	-1.36	1.97	-1.34	-2.18	-3.08	-0.97	0.10	61.03
X3R	Tertiary product	-1.10	-2.69	-5.26	-1.54	-1.83	0.81	0.64	0.48	-0.58	-0.43	0.08	102.11
PGNP	Prices	-22.57	-25.88	-22.79	-21.23	-21.23	-12.17	-6.85	-5.31	-9.51	-4.42	-0.88	4.52
BGSFR*	External balance	-55.46	-68.19	-64.04	-45.92	-50.62	-36.38	-38.31	-43.57	-30.15	-26.83	-9.13	-7.23
EGSFR*	Exports	-2.61	0.0	-1.10	5.98	6.04	5.17	4.94	3.72	-0.29	2.32	3.54	17.21
MGSFR*	Imports	-23.49	-20.17	-19.68	-9.37	-10.72	-7.16	-7.05	-10.31	-9.12	-6.30	-0.20	24.49
TFC	Federal revenues	-24.71	-29.40	-29.12	-25.67	-26.22	-24.96	-21.17	-20.38	-11.64	-4.23	-1.20	70.71
TFIC	Income tax revenues	-26.96	-31.27	-35.21	-32.34	-32.64	-25.27	-23.32	-22.33	-14.31	-10.06	-1.10	35.50
Forecasts of Rates of Growth (%)						*Error*							
GDRP%	Gross domestic product	1.21	0.13	-0.05	1.18	0.55	0.82	-0.83	-1.25	-1.26	-0.53	0.08	6.30
X1R%	Primary product	3.36	2.22	-0.85	2.21	1.82	1.83	3.09	2.90	2.80	1.69	-0.06	2.63
X2R%	Secondary product	0.44	-1.21	-0.57	1.15	-0.10	0.73	-2.27	-3.17	-3.13	-0.04	0.11	8.02
X3R%	Tertiary product	1.33	-2.59	0.12	1.04	-0.73	0.68	-0.66	-0.83	-0.87	-0.71	0.09	5.72
PGNP%	Prices	-19.77	-20.41	-19.09	-18.07	-18.20	-12.82	-12.41	-10.58	-11.66	-5.37	-1.00	23.63
BGSFR%	External balance	-73.66	-90.41	-74.84	-57.63	-68.03	-62.20	-72.51	-81.43	-66.46	-61.19	-19.65	77.20
EGSFR%	Exports	2.16	4.42	1.87	1.14	1.20	2.72	0.03	-1.21	0.50	3.32	4.07	5.34
MGSFR%	Imports	-14.05	-13.26	-13.82	-11.16	-12.74	-10.32	-14.47	-17.27	-12.78	-9.45	-0.47	10.70
TFC%	Federal revenues	-24.26	-27.23	-24.87	-22.58	-23.41	-22.98	-26.04	-24.93	-19.48	-9.72	-1.77	35.80
TFIC%	Income tax revenues	-26.27	-29.25	-27.83	-25.64	-26.15	-25.59	-27.21	-25.70	-20.54	-14.57	-1.53	38.67
	Average error: levels	18.27	19.86	19.57	15.01	15.66	11.55	10.49	10.90	8.41	5.89	1.65	
	Average error: rate	16.64	18.18	16.32	14.18	15.29	14.07	16.05	16.94	13.95	10.75	2.88	

Columns 1 to 11 contain the errors made in the forecasts of the last column at the date shown. Actual data for 1974, tabulated in the last column, is taken as 100% for errors (E_t) in levels and as a subtraction in errors made or rates of growth. The date of publication of the official data was March 1975. The repetition of dates indicate two alternative forecasts were made at the same date. Positive signs indicate overestimations; negative signs, underestimations. * Dollar values.

Table 4-2. Errors of 7 Ex Ante DIEMEX-Wharton Forecasts: Forecasted Year 1973

Forecasts		1	2	3	4	5	6	7	Actual Value 1973
Row Symbol	Concept	Jun. 71	Jun. 71	Apr. 72	Apr. 72	Nov. 72	Sept. 73	Nov. 73	
Forecasts of Levels					*Percent Error*				
1 GDPR	Gross domestic product	1.55	0.00	-1.70	-0.51	-1.54	0.40	0.74	169.49
2 X1R	Primary product	14.65	13.20	10.07	10.79	3.13	-1.32	-2.47	16.59
3 X2R	Secondary product	4.25	1.66	1.10	3.66	-1.27	1.27	0.76	56.50
4 X3R	Tertiary product	-2.29	-3.23	-5.37	4.90	-2.50	0.18	1.28	96.40
5 PGNP	Prices	-7.67	-9.59	-8.49	-7.40	-2.50	-1.64	3.56	3.65
6 BGSFR*	External balance	-23.77	-35.05	-37.75	-25.74	-19.85	-1.96	4.41	-4.08
7 EGSFR*	Exports	-4.59	-4.04	-2.82	-3.85	4.83	2.51	4.90	16.34
8 MGSFR*	Imports	-8.42	-10.24	9.84	-8.23	-0.10	1.62	4.80	20.42
9 TFC	Federal revenues	-8.33	-11.70	-13.23	-10.85	-10.85	-9.68	-2.48	52.07
10 TFIC	Income tax revenues	-9.88	-12.89	-18.95	-16.99	-16.99	-8.36	-4.61	25.60
Forecasts of Rates of Growth (%)					*Error*				
11 GDPR%	Gross domestic product	-0.65	-1.62	-2.06	-0.65	-0.49	0.17	0.54	7.56
12 X1R%	Primary product	4.83	4.02	3.32	4.08	4.08	4.83	3.60	0.60
13 X2R%	Secondary product	-1.52	-3.00	-3.43	-0.54	-0.54	0.32	0.23	8.88
14 X3R%	Tertiary product	-1.20	-1.84	-2.23	-1.63	-1.31	-0.82	0.36	8.09
15 PGNP%	Prices	-7.38	-8.59	-8.30	-7.50	-7.50	-2.41	3.63	12.36
16 BGSFR%	External balance	-33.82	-46.26	-55.96	-40.22	-29.88	-16.92	-8.96	39.24
17 EGSFR%	Exports	-5.97	-4.68	-3.20	-3.97	-2.35	-1.93	0.65	11.93
18 MGSFR%	Imports	-10.85	-11.58	-12.20	-10.05	-6.94	-4.31	-0.76	16.50
19 TFC%	Federal revenues	-10.99	-13.37	-14.27	-11.47	-11.50	-11.85	-2.99	22.98
20 TFIC%	Income tax revenues	-9.64	-11.95	-13.86	-11.46	-11.46	-11.45	-6.89	22.95
21	Average error: levels	-8.54	10.16	10.93	9.29	6.85	2.89	3.00	
22	Average error: rate	8.69	10.69	11.88	9.16	7.61	5.50	2.86	

Columns 1 to 11 contain the errors made in the forecasts of the last column, tabulated in the last column. Actual data for 1974, tabulated in the last column, is taken as 100% for errors (E_t) in levels and as a subtraction in errors made or rates of growth. The date of publication of the official data was March 1975. The repetition of dates indicate two alternative forecasts were made at the same date. Positive signs indicate overestimations; negative signs, underestimations. * Dollar values.

Table 4-3. Errors of 5 Ex Ante DIEMEX-Wharton Forecasts: Forecasted Year 1972

Forecasts		1	2	3	4	5	Actual Value 1972
Row	Symbol Concept	Jun. 71	Jun. 71	Apr. 72	Apr. 72	Nov. 72	
Forecasts of Levels				*Percent Error*			
1	GDPR Gross domestic product	2.17	1.54	0.22	0.10	-1.09	157.57
2	X1R Primary product	9.40	8.85	6.61	6.49	-0.90	16.49
3	X2R Secondary product	5.67	4.55	4.39	4.18	-0.77	51.89
4	X3R Tertiary product	-1.20	-1.56	-3.37	-3.46	-1.30	89.19
5	PGNP Prices	-1.23	-2.15	-1.23	-0.92	-0.92	3.25
6	BGSFR* External balance	0.68	-2.73	4.10	4.44	2.05	-2.93
7	EGSFR* Exports	1.03	0.14	0.00	-0.34	7.05	14.60
8	MGSFR* Imports	0.97	-0.34	0.74	0.46	6.22	17.53
9	TFC Federal revenues	0.66	-0.92	-1.84	-1.68	-1.65	42.34
10	TFIC Income tax revenues	-2.21	-3.51	-8.65	-8.45	-8.45	20.82
Forecasts of Rates of Growth (%)				*Error*			
11	GDPR% Gross domestic product	-0.51	-1.17	-1.32	-1.45	-1.41	7.27
12	X1R% Primary product	5.64	5.11	3.43	3.35	3.72	0.48
13	X2R% Secondary product	-2.03	-3.16	-2.76	-2.97	-2.98	9.39
14	X3R% Tertiary product	-0.87	-1.26	-1.45	-1.54	-1.54	7.40
15	PGNP% Prices	-0.67	-1.65	-1.56	-1.16	-1.46	5.57
16	BGSFR% External balance	-5.77	-9.06	0.12	0.22	2.47	2.81
17	EGSFR% Exports	-3.98	-4.94	-4.81	-5.21	1.91	12.76
18	MGSFR% Imports	-4.30	-5.69	-3.94	-4.25	2.11	10.93
19	TFC% Federal revenues	-3.98	-5.74	-6.68	-6.49	-6.47	15.90
20	TFIC% Income tax revenues	-10.58	-12.08	-14.82	-14.59	-14.59	23.63
21	Average error: levels	2.52	2.63	3.12	3.05	3.04	
22	Average error: rate	3.83	4.98	4.09	4.12	3.85	

Columns 1 to 11 contain the errors made in the forecasts of the last column at the date shown. Actual data for 1974, tabulated in the last column, is taken as 100% for errors (E_t) in levels and as a subtraction in errors made or rates of growth. The date of publication of the official data was March 1975. The repetition of dates indicate two alternative forecasts were made at the same date. Positive signs indicate overestimations; negative signs, underestimations. * Dollar values

122

and 22, contain simple averages of the absolute errors in levels and growth rates of all predictions made at a given date:

$$(^{10}_{i}\Sigma|E_t|/10) \quad \text{and} \quad (^{10}_{i}\Sigma|D_t|/10)$$

The selection of the variables basically was determined by the availability of official statistics. For example, the lack of some figures, such as private consumption and investment, which were last published in 1968, prevents evaluations of the accuracy of the demand projections. Another basic criterion is that the official series has not been revised conceptually, which would impede comparisons.

ANALYSIS OF THE ERRORS

The most general observation that can be made is the tendency for the absolute size of the error to decline as the time horizon of prediction shortens. The predictions for 1974, made in June 1971, have an absolute error of 18.3 percent (or 19.9 percent) in the levels, depending on which prediction is chosen, and 16.6 percentage points (18.2) in the growth rates, as can be seen in rows 21 and 22 at the bottom of Table 4–1. (Most of this average error is due to the poor prediction of the external balance; for example, without that figure the average error of 18.3 would fall to 14.2 percentage points.) By comparison in November 1974, a half year from the publication of preliminary figures, the average errors were reduced to 1.7 percent and 2.9 percentage points, respectively (the 1.7 percent figure falls to 0.8 percent if we exclude again the balance-of-payments error). This tendency to improve the precision of the estimates as their date of announcement approaches is confirmed in the predictions for 1973. The tendency also exists for the predictions for 1972, although it is less obvious given the shortness of the sample of predictions.

The same tendency appears in the case of the majority of the specific variables. For example, in Table 4–2, which contains the most observations, the errors in predicting the price level, imports, federal government income, and income taxes all follow this tendency. The absolute errors in the levels of secondary and tertiary product also follow this tendency although the result is less clear for the growth rates.

There are also some interesting apparent deviations from this pattern; we say apparent because of the small sample size even for the predictions of 1974. For the prediction of the level and rate of change of gross domestic product (GDP) for 1974, the errors do not clearly decline. Although the maximum error, 2.7 percent, is found in column 1, the earliest prediction, the minimum, 0.5 percent, is not found in the most up-to-date prediction, but in column 7, corresponding to September 1973. It is, therefore, not apparent that the accuracy improved as we approached the date of publication.

A similar conclusion can be drawn from the errors in predicting GDP for 1973 and 1972. The amplitude of the "cycles" of prediction does not diminish. Nevertheless, given that in none of the three cases do the errors exceed the 2.7 percent obtained at the greatest "distance," one could say that the precision in predicting GDP was "good" at almost all points in time.

Another apparent exception is the prediction of exports. For all years the final errors are greater than those obtained at intermediate and even initial dates. Nearness to the date of announcement apparently led to a deterioration in predictive accuracy—with the exception of errors in the growth rates for 1972 and 1973.

What explains these two deviations, GDP and exports, from the general rule? Apart from the reduced sample size, there are particular explanations in both cases. For GDP, the so-called good prediction at almost all points is due apparently to a cancellation of the predictive errors of the components. Primary production was generally overestimated while secondary and tertiary production were underestimated. However, this is only part of the explanation. The predictions of tertiary output, the most important component of GDP, have been in general the most accurate over all time spans, never exceeding 5.3 percent in absolute error. The predictions of secondary output, although less accurate, never exceeded 5.7 percent in absolute error. In brief, the precision of the projections of secondary and tertiary production by canceling the elevated errors in predicting primary production yielded an accurate prediction of GDP.

In the case of exports there is a more obvious explanation. When the balance of payments deficit began to grow rapidly after 1972, we started a conscious predictive policy of optimism regarding exports in order to reduce the risk of being alarmist about the external disequilibrium. Consequently, we generally used the largest, reasonable values for those exogenous variables that enter the export equations such as domestic production of primary export products. The general result was an overestimate of exports after November 1972 as shown in Tables 4-1, 4-2, amd 4-3. The reverse was true for imports. Both types of errors translated into the large underestimates of the deficit in the balance of payments.

This brings us to a consideration of the signs of the errors. In addition to exports we have tended to overestimate (positive sign) primary production because of a similar policy of optimistic projections, again through positive adjustments in the econometric equation. This is especially clear in Table 4-2. On the other hand, we have regularly underestimated prices, imports, federal government revenues, and income taxes. For the last two, the underestimate is due to the imposition of the unforeseen Fiscal Reform of 1974, which increased federal revenues by about 20 billion pesos annually. As soon as the magnitude of the reform became apparent, the underestimate was reduced to less than half, as can be appreciated through a comparison of columns 8 and 9 of row 9, Table 4-1. The same is true for the income tax.

The underestimate of imports, aside from the effect of the already mentioned optimistic treatments of the external deficit and primary production, is due to an apparent increment in the import coefficient during the Echeverria administration, at least partially the result of a liberalized policy of imports.

Finally, the underestimate of prices can be explained by the unforeseen magnitude of world inflation in 1973, combined with an internal inflation generated by the excess demand of the public sector and the rapid increase in liquidity beginning in 1972. Again these errors were reduced substantially, to less than a third, as soon as these trends became clear, as can be appreciated through a comparison of columns 5 to 7, line 5 of Table 4-1.

Another convenient way of analyzing the errors is to average them according to "forecast time horizon." In this way one can appreciate the error incurred in forecasts of one, two, three, or more years of inflation. This method has been used to evaluate forecasts obtained from the U.S. quarterly econometric models in view of the great number of forecasts that they generate yearly.[5] In our own case, given the annual nature of the model and the few forecasts included in sample size of predictions, we have not rigorously followed this approach. Nevertheless, Tables 4-4, 4-5, and 4-6 give an idea of the forecasting errors obtained from predictions made from one half to three years in advance. The basic data for the averages are obtained from the indicated lines of Tables 4-1, 4-2, and 4-3. The figures in parentheses again correspond to an alternative forecast when two forecasts were made on the same date.

Comparing rows of the three tables, one can observe the improvement in the precision of the forecasts at shorter prediction "distances." The average error in predicting the ten levels at the bottom of Table 4-4 almost diminishes by half as the forecasting time horizon shortens from three years to one-half year, that is, 18.3 percent, 11.8 percent, 6.5 percent, and 2.6 percent. The same tendency appears clearly in the price predictions in Table 4-6. The exception

Table 4-4. Average Predictive Errors (%) of Forecasts Made with Different Anticipation Periods (Averages obtain from Tables 4-1, 4-2, and 4-3, Rows 21-22)

Forecasted Year	1/2 Year	1 1/2 Years	2 1/2 Years	3 Years
1974				
Average error: levels	1.65	10.49	15.01	18.27 (19.86)
Average error: rate	2.88	16.05	15.66	16.64 (18.18)
1973				
Average error: levels	3.00	6.85	8.54 (10.16)	
Average error: rate	2.86	7.61	8.69 (10.69)	
1972				
Average error: levels	3.04	2.52 (2.63)		
Average error: rate	3.85	3.83 (4.98)		
General average: levels	2.56	6.52	11.78	18.27
General average: rates	3.20	9.16	12.18	16.64

Note: The headings 1/2 year, 1 1/2 years, etc., are approximations using mid-March of the next year to that of the forecast as date when official data is known.

The general averages are the simple averages of the figures of each column.

The figures under each column were taken from the November forecasts, previous to the forecasted year. The exceptions are the figures in parenthesis, which come from the June 1971 forecasts.

Table 4-5. Average Predictive Errors (%) of Forecasts of the Real Gross Domestic Product Made with Different Anticipation Periods

(Averages obtain from Tables 4-1, 4-2, and 4-3, Rows 1-11)

Forecasted Year	1/2 Year	1 1/2 Years	2 1/2 Years	3 Years
1974				
Average error: levels	0.08	-0.05	-0.45	0.13 (2.70)
Average error: rate	0.08	-0.83	1.18	0.13 (1.21)
1973				
Average error: levels	0.74	-1.54	0.0 (1.55)	
Average error: rate	0.54	-9.49	-1.62 (-0.65)	
1972				
Average error: levels	-1.09	1.54 (2.17)		
Average error: rate	-1.41	-1.17 (-0.51)		
General average: levels	0.64	1.04	0.45	0.13
General average: rates	0.66	0.83	1.40	0.13

Note: The headings 1/2 year, 1 1/2 years, etc., are approximations using mid-March of the next year to that of the forecast as date when official data is known.

The general averages are the simple averages of the figures of each column.

The figures under each column were taken from the November forecasts, previous to the forecasted year. The exceptions are the figures in parenthesis, which come from the June 1971 forecasts.

Table 4-6. Average Predictive Errors (%) of Forecasts of the Price Level Made with Different Anticipation Periods (Averages obtain from Tables 4-1, 4-2, and 4-3, Rows 5-15)

Forecasted Year	1/2 Year	1 1/2 Years	2 1/2 Years	3 Years
1974				
Average error: levels	-0.88	-6.85	-21.23	-22.57 (-25.88)
Average error: rate	-1.00	-12.41	-18.20	-19.77 (-22.11)
1973				
Average error: levels	3.56	-7.40	-7.67 (-9.59)	
Average error: rate	3.63	-7.50	-7.38 (-8.59)	
1972				
Average error: levels	-0.92	-1.23 (-2.15)		
Average error: rate	-1.46	-0.67 (-1.65)		
General average: levels	1.79	5.15	14.45	22.57
General average: rates	2.03	6.86	12.79	19.77

Note: The headings 1/2 year, 1 1/2 years, etc., are approximations using mid-March of the next year to that of the forecast as date when official data is known.

The general averages are the simple averages of the figures of each column.

The figures under each column were taken from the November forecasts, previous to the forecasted year. The exceptions are the figures in parenthesis, which come from the June 1971 forecasts.

appears in the GDP predictions on Table 4-5. The early forecasts of June 1971, made with three years of anticipation, have the smallest errors. We feel, however, that a larger sample of forecasts of GDP will eventually fall into the same pattern.

A COMPARISON WITH
MECHANICAL FORECASTS

As mentioned above, an alternative method of forecasting would be to use a simplistic or mechanistic approach. Even without any knowledge of the economy and its recent evolution, it is easy to generate a mechanistic "forecast" with an econometric model. All that is required is a simple extrapolation of the exogenous variables, using its recent growth rates and the residuals (or errors of estimate)[6] of the stochastic variables, using for example, the most recent historical value. The rest is simply computer work.

Since it is useful to ask which of these methods is more accurate, we have included a comparison of their errors.[7] The only mechanical projection that is available, using the Mexican Model V, was made in April 1972, the same date as the nonmechanical forecast already presented in Tables 4-1, 4-2 and 4-3. Table 4-7 contains the comparison of both types of forecasts.

Although at first glance a comparison of lines 21 and 22 does not appear to decisively favor the nonmechanical method, in reality the latter results are superior. The substantial error reduction achieved in 1972, where the average errors in levels are halved by the nonmechanical forecasts (3.1 percent versus 6.3 percent of the mechanical forecast), is the result of the incorporation of the economic information available to the experts in the first quarter of that year.

On the other hand, the similarity of errors of the two types of forecasts for 1973 and for 1974 is due to the absence of such up-to-date information for those years in the nonmechanical forecasts. In other words, for these two years the "nonmechanical" forecasts were actually mechanically done.

CONCLUSION

The forecasting experience of the Wharton-DIEMEX Econometric Model of Mexico is encouraging about the use of this type of models for purposes of "economic meteorology" in developing countries. The accuracy of the ex ante forecasts, especially of the year in course and the following year, is acceptable. The average error of the sample of predictions made one-half year in advance is 3 percent; for those

Table 4-7. Error Comparison of a Mechanical Forecast Made on April, 1972 with the Nonmechanical of the Same Date

		1972			1973			1974	
		Mechanical	Non-mechanical 1	Non-mechanical 2	Mechanical	Non-mechanical 1	Non-mechanical 2	Mechanical	Non-mechanical
Errors in the Forecasts of Levels: Percents									
1	GDPR	Gross domestic product	-0.45	0.10	0.22	-3.23	-0.51	-1.70	-4.21	-1.75
2	X1R	Primary product	8.19	6.49	6.61	15.07	10.79	10.07	13.56	10.98
3	X2R	Secondary product	4.16	4.18	4.39	0.48	3.66	1.10	0.31	5.73
4	X3R	Tertiary product	-4.73	-3.46	-3.37	8.56	4.90	-5.37	9.88	-5.26
5	PGNP	Prices	-0.92	-0.92	-1.23	7.40	-7.40	-8.49	-61.08	-22.79
6	BGSFR*	External balance	26.96	4.44	4.10	-3.92	-25.74	-37.75	-37.20	-64.04
7	EGSFR*	Exports	-4.45	-0.34	0.00	11.32	-3.85	-2.82	-12.89	-1.10
8	MGSFR*	Imports	0.74	0.46	0.74	-9.84	-8.23	9.84	-20.09	-19.68
9	TFC	Federal revenues	-2.79	-1.68	-1.84	-13.85	-10.85	-13.23	-30.16	-29.12
10	TFIC	Income tax revenues	-9.51	-8.45	-8.65	-20.08	-16.99	-18.95	-36.79	-35.21
Errors in the Forecasts of Rates of Growth: Differences									
11	GDPR%	Gross domestic product	-2.03	-1.45	-1.32	3.00	-0.65	-2.06	1.08	-0.05
12	X1R%	Primary product	4.96	3.35	3.43	6.44	4.80	3.32	1.36	0.85
13	X2R%	Secondary product	-2.99	-2.97	-2.76	3.85	-0.54	-3.43	0.18	-0.57
14	X3R%	Tertiary product	-2.92	-1.54	-1.45	4.35	-1.63	-2.23	1.53	0.12
15	PGNP%	Prices	-1.18	-1.16	-1.56	7.32	-7.50	-8.30	19.41	-19.09
16	BGSFR%	External balance	22.44	0.22	0.12	33.86	-40.22	-55.96	-61.38	-74.81
17	EGSFR%	Exports	9.69	-5.21	-4.81	8.04	-3.97	-3.20	1.88	1.87
18	MGSFR%	Imports	-3.92	-4.25	-3.94	12.28	-10.05	-12.20	13.59	-13.12
19	TFC%	Federal revenues	7.73	-6.49	-6.68	13.99	-11.47	-14.27	25.73	-24.87
20	TFIC%	Income tax revenues	15.85	14.59	14.82	14.36	-11.46	-13.86	28.99	-27.83
21		Average error: levels	6.29	3.05	3.12	9.38	9.29	10.93	22.62	19.57
22		Average error: rate	7.37	4.12	4.09	10.75	9.16	11.88	15.51	16.32

made one and one-half years in advance it is less than 7 percent (see Table 4-4—Average Absolute Error).

Nevertheless, the tendency for the error to increase with the length of the prediction period decreases the confidence in forecasts of more than two years. The average error of forecasts made two and one-half years in advance is close to 12 percent; of those made more than three years in advance, over 18 percent.

The predictive accuracy of the variables differs substantially. In the case of GDP the error never exceeded 3 percent even for predictions over a three-year horizon. (Table 4-1, line 1) On the other hand, prices were underestimated by 23 percent (Table 4-1, line 5) and the external balance by over 55 percent in these medium-term forecasts.

The good short-run predictive accuracy that is generally obtained is apparently due to the method of incorporating the latest information available from experts and other data sources external to the model. That is, the combined method—experts and model—permits a substantial reduction in the predictive error of the current year's forecast to less than half of that made with a mechanical projection technique (Table 4-7, lines 21 and 22, for the year 1972).

If on top of the short-term precision attainable, when considerations of the scope of economic aspects that can be forecasted, the consistency obtained among them, and the excellent work discipline imposed upon the user are taken into account, then econometric models emerge as a superior tool for forecasting.

NOTES

1. For an example of an analysis of the predictive accuracy of a quarterly model of the United States see G.R. Green and L.R. Klein, "10th Anniversary, the Wharton Forecast Record: A Self Examination, *The Wharton Quarterly* 7: 2 (Winter 1972-1973).

2. See Y. Haitovsky, G. Treyz, and V. Su, *Forecasts with Quarterly Macro-Econometric Models*, Studies in Business Cycles, No. 23 (New York: NBER, 1974), p. 7.

3. A more complete description of Model V can be found in A. Beltrán del Rio and L.R. Klein, "Macroeconometric Model Building in Latin America: The Mexican Case," *The Role of the Computer in Economic and Social Research in Latin America* (New York: NBER, 1974), pp. 161-90.

4. For greater detail regarding this procedure, see G.R. Green and L.R. Klein, op. cit.

5. See Y. Haitovsky, G. Treyz, and V. Su, op. cit. The models analyzed are the OBE (Office of Business Economics) and Wharton quarterly models. See also G. Green and L.R. Klein, op cit.

6. If the last year of the sample used to estimate the regression is not the year

previous to the forecast (e.g., if the last year is 1970 and the forecast is for 1975-1980) the necessary intermediate errors can be obtained through a calculation of residuals or "residual check." This same check is indispensable when there have been revisions of the data over the sample period used for the regressions.

7. The superiority of the nonmechanical method is well documented for studies based on the broad sample of quarterly forecasts. See Y. Haitovsky, G. Treyz, and V. Su, op. cit., ch. 7.

5

ROQUE B.
FERNANDEZ

The Short-Run Output-Inflation Tradeoff in Argentina and Brazil

1. INTRODUCTION

The purpose of this chapter is to study the short-run relationship between output and inflation in the context of a macroeconomic model. Although a considerable number of economists have studied this subject, mainly from the point of view of the Phillips curve theory, most of them have used ad hoc hypotheses regarding the process through which expectations are formed. Other economists (e.g., Lucas, and Sargent and Wallace) have studied the same subject and have postulated a rational expectations hypothesis for analyzing the short-run tradeoff between inflation and output and for testing the "natural rate" hypothesis.

The analysis performed in this chapter is similar to that of Lucas and Sargent and Wallace. In fact, the analysis in Section 2 starts with the assumption that the model previously postulated by Sargent and Wallace (1975) is an appropriate theoretical framework for analyzing the short-run relationship between prices and output. In that section the model to be used is presented, as well as some of its main limitations and implications.

In Section 3 a summary of the results of the structural analysis of the model is presented as well as the estimation procedure followed in order to obtain the estimates for the structural equations of the system. These estimates, based on available information for Argentina and Brazil, are presented in Section 4.

In Section 5 of this chapter an attempt is made in order to analyze the short-run dynamics of price and output based on the empirical findings of Section 4. This obviously implies that the parameters of the model have to be assumed constant over the period of analysis. As argued below, the duration of this period is of particular importance given the assumption of rational expectations that is incorporated in the model.

2. THE MACROECONOMETRIC MODEL

As mentioned above, the model analyzed in this section is a standard macroeconomic model in which expectations will be assumed to be "rational" in the sense of Muth (1961). This assumption was incorporated in similar models by Sargent (1973) and Sargent and Wallace (1975). In this chapter some modifications are introduced in order to arrive at a direct, estimable relationship for a short-run output-inflation tradeoff.

The model consists of the following three equations:

(a) Aggregate supply

$$y_t = y_{n,t} + a(P_t - {}_tP^*_{t-1}) + k(y_{t-1} - y_{n,t-1}) + u_{1t}, a > 0 \qquad (5\text{-}1)$$

(b) Aggregate demand

$$y_t = y_{n,t} + g + c(r_t - ({}_{t+1}P^*_{t-1} - {}_tP^*_{t-1})) + u_{2t}, c < 0, g > 0 \qquad (5\text{-}2)$$

(c) Portfolio balance

$$\phi m_t = p_t + y_t + br_t + u_{3t} - \infty < b < 0 \qquad (5\text{-}3)$$

In these equations y_t, p_t and m_t are the natural logarithms of real income, the price level, and the nominal stock of money, g is a constant, and the $u_{i,t}$s, $i = 1, 2, 3$, are disturbance terms. The variable $y_{n,t}$ is a measure of normal productive capacity that will be represented by the trend in real output in the empirical application of the model. Therefore, $y_t - y_{n,t} = y_{c,t}$ represents cyclical or "detrended" output. The variable ${}_{t+1}P^*_t$ represents the public's expectation at time t of the logarithm of the price level expected to prevail at $t + 1$. The variable r_t is the nominal rate of interest.

The $u_{it}s$, $i = 1, 2, 3$, are random disturbances with zero means that may be serially and contemporaneously correlated.

Equation (5-1) is an aggregate supply equation relating detrended output to the gap between current price level and the public's prior expectation of the current price level. In this equation lagged detrended output indicates that deviations of aggregate supply from normal capacity may display some persistence. A formal derivation of Equation (5-1) can be found in the work of Lucas (1973), and the next few paragraphs will outline some major aspects of his work. However, similar reduced forms could be generated by other models, for example, those Phillips curve models based on an aggregation of multiple markets of the economy such as Lipsey and Hansen, among others, have proposed.

Lucas derives his equation under the assumptions that suppliers are located in a large number of scattered competitive markets and that demand for goods in each period is distributed unevenly over markets, leading to relative as well as general price movements. This means that the situation as perceived by individual suppliers may be different from the aggregate situation. Following Lucas and letting z index markets, supply in market z is:

$$y_t(z) = y_{n,t} + y_{c,t}(z) \qquad (5\text{-}1a)$$

The secular component $y_{n,t}$ is assumed to be common to all markets. The cyclical component varies with perceived relative prices and with its own lagged value:

$$y_{c,t}(z) = S \left[p_t(z) - E(p_t | I(z)) \right] + k y_{c,t-1} \qquad (5\text{-}1b)$$

where $p_t(z)$ is the log of the actual price in z at t and $E(p_t | I[z])$ is the mean current general price level, conditioned on information available in z at the end of $t - 1$, $I(z)$. While this information does not permit exact inference of p_t, it does determine a "prior" distribution on p_t, common to traders in all markets. We assume that this distribution is known to be normal with mean $\bar{p}_t$.

Now let z be the percentage deviation of the price in market z from the average p_t (so that markets are indexed by their price deviation from average). z is assumed normally distributed, independent of p_t with zero mean. Then

$$p_t(z) = p_t + z \qquad (5\text{-}1c)$$

This last expression is used by suppliers to calculate the distribution of p_t conditional on $p_t(z)$ and $\bar{p}_t$. By straightforward calculation it can be proved that the distribution of p_t is normal with mean

$$E(p_t|I(z)) = E(p_t|p_t(z), \bar{p}_t) = (1 - \theta)\, p_t(z) + \theta \bar{p}_t \qquad (5\text{-}1\text{d})$$

where θ is a ratio between the "relative" price variance and total price variance, that is, $V(z)/(V(\bar{p}_t) + V(z))$, where $V(\bar{p}_t)$ is the variance of the "prior" distribution.

Combining (5-1a), (5-1b), and (5-1c) and averaging over markets (integrating with respect to the distribution of z) gives Equation (5-1) where $a = \theta S$. This is a very important point because the *slope* of the aggregate supply function (1) varies with the fraction, θ, of *total* individual price variance that is due to *relative* price variation.

Equation (5-2) is an aggregate demand equation that relates the deviation of aggregate demand to the real rate of interest, which in turn is represented by the nominal rate of interest minus the expected rate of inflation. This equation resembles the Hicksian "IS" schedule utilized to represent the income expenditure sector in the model of Keynes. Of course, some major arguments of the Keynesian aggregate demand function have been neglected for analytical simplicity. A possible extension of the model could include some variables representing the fiscal action of the government (e.g., see, Sargent and Wallace [1975]).

Some limitations of Equation (5-2) are stated in Sargent (1973) as follows:

> An important thing about equation (2) is that it excludes as arguments both the money supply and the price level. . . . This amounts to ruling out direct real balance effects on aggregate demand. It also amounts to ignoring the expected rate of real capital gains on cash holdings as a component of the disposable income terms that belong in the expenditure schedules that underlie equation (2). Ignoring these things is usual in macroeconometric work.

Another aspect of this model is the lack of symmetry between Equation (5-1) and (5-2), that is, only suppliers have explicit misperceptions of prices and only demanders have an explicit responses to changes in the real rate of interest. Implicitly, the effect of the neglected variables in each equation could be captured if they induced some stable stochastic process in the error terms.

Equation (5-3) is a demand for money relationship with unit real income elasticity (this assumption is not crucial and will be relaxed later on) that summarizes the condition for portfolio equilibrium. In other words, when Equation (5-3) is satisfied owners of bonds and equities are satisfied with the division of their portfolio between money (assumed to be exogenous), on the one hand, and bonds and equities, on the other hand. ϕ is a polynomial in the lag operator (i.e., $\phi = \phi_0 + \phi_1 L^2 + \ldots$, where $\phi_0 + \phi_1 + \ldots = 1$) introduced in an effort to capture the effects of lagged changes of m_t on nominal income. The degree of this polynomial will be determined empirically.[1]

The u_{it}s, $i = 1, 2, 3$, are random disturbances with zero means that may be serially and contemporaneously correlated.

On pure theoretical ground there is not a strong justification for the existence of a lagged response of nominal income to changes in the quantity of money. However, the existence of lags is confirmed in many empirical works that relate money and prices.

The working of the model can easily be illustrated leaving aside the problem of how expectations are formed. This rules out some implications of the dynamics of the model as is usual in comparative statics. It will help understand the problem if we use a geometrical interpretation of the model along the familiar framework of the *IS-LM* analysis. Then Equation (5-2) has the form of a *IS* schedule in the (r, y) plane, Equation (5-3) has the form of a *LM* schedule in the (r, y) plane, and Equation (5-1) is a vertical line in the (r, y) plane at the full employment or natural rate level of real income. Equations (5-2) and (5-3) are drawn in the (r, y) plane under the assumption that the expected rate of inflation is zero (so the nominal and real rate of interest are the same). Then in Figure 5-1, y_0^s, y^d, and m_0 will denote Equations (5-1), (5-2), and (5-3), respectively.

Our starting point will be a nongrowth economy in full equilibrium with real output at its natural level (y_n), zero rate of inflation, and consequently nominal and real rate of interest equal. This situation is represented in Figure 5-1 by point A.

Now let us assume an unanticipated increase in the stock of money. From Equation (5-3) we see that with prices and income as yet unchanged, portfolio balance can be attained through a reduction in the rate of interest. There, the m_0 curve shifts rightwards to m_1. In the goods market a reduction in the rate of interest means an excess demand for goods, exerting an upward pressure on the price level as well as on real output. As has been argued in the derivation of Equation (5-1), individual suppliers have to assess whether a given price change is a "relative" price change or a "general" price change. In this last case suppliers are assumed not to respond because their supply functions are homogeneous of degree zero in absolute prices.

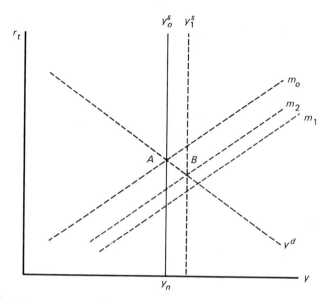

FIGURE 5-1.   A Geometrical Interpretation of the Model

Therefore, output changes are associated only with price misperceptions. Then in our case a new, temporary equilibrium with a higher
level of output and a lower interest rate is attained through a mis-
perception effect that shifts y_o^s to y_1^s. A point of temporary equilibrium like B can be reached with m_1 shifting leftward to m_2 due to
the price increase. The movement from B to A, that is, the long-run
equilibrium position, will depend upon the process of adjustment of
expectations. The same apparatus can be used to analyze other types
of shocks.

To complete the model we should specify how expectations are
formed. This is a delicate matter. It has been customary to postulate
different ad hoc hypotheses about the formation of expectations.
The most popular is Cagan's hypothesis of adaptive expectations although the explanations for its use were confined to the fact that
adaptive expectations seemed reasonable and proved useful in explaining data. The hypothesis of rational expectations used in this
chapter follows Muth's proposal that expectations are informed
predictions of future events based on the available information and
the relevant economic theory. This has a strong implication. With
this assumption the economist who is modeling an economy does not
have a superior knowledge of the "reality." This in turn is confirmed
by the fact that actual expectations "are more accurate than naive
models and as accurate as elaborate equations systems" (see Muth

[1961], p. 316). Thus, our model is completed with the following equations.

$$_t p^*_{t-1} = E p_t \tag{5-4}$$

$$_{t+1} p^*_{t-1} = E p_{t+1} \tag{5-5}$$

where $E p_t$ is the conditional mathematical expectation of p_t formed using the model and all the information assumed to be available as of the end of period $t - 1$ (hereafter the E operator will always be conditional on the information available as of the end of period $t - 1$).[2]

The algebra of rational expectations is tedious and is confined to Appendix A. The following two equations correspond to Equations (A5-12) and (A5-13) of Appendix A and they show expected prices as a function of the past and expected future behavior of the money supply. Indeed, this property is an essential feature of rational expectations. The equations are.

$$EP_t = [1/(1 - b)] \sum_{j=0}^{\infty} [1/(1 - b^{-1})]^j [E\phi m_{t+j} - y_{n,t+j}] \tag{5-6}$$

$$+ [J_3/(1 - J_0)] \sum_{j=0}^{\infty} [\alpha/(1 - b^{-1})]^j y_{c,t-1} + c_0$$

and

$$Ep_{t+1} = [1/(1 - b)] \sum_{j=0}^{\infty} [1/(1 - b^{-1})]^{j+1} [E\phi m_{t+j+1} \tag{5-7}$$

$$- y_{n,t+j+1}] + [J_3/(1 - J_0)] \sum_{j=0}^{\infty} [\alpha/(1 - b^{-1})]^{j+1} y_{c,t-1} + c_0$$

In these equations J_0, J_3, and c_0 are constants that are complicated functions of the structural parameters of the model.

From these equations, it is easy to illustrate the process of formation of expectations; let us assume for a moment that $b = 0$ (i.e., that the interest elasticity of the demand for money is zero). Then, after taking first differences (D operator), Equation (5-6) can be reduced to:

$$EDp_t = \phi_0 \, EDm_t - (\beta + kDy_{c,t-1}) + \phi_1 Dm_{t-1} + \phi_2 Dm_{t-2} + \ldots \quad (5\text{-}8)$$

where β is the trend in real output and $J_3/(1 - J_0) = -k$ when $b = 0$. Equation (5-8) clearly shows that the expected rate of change of prices depends upon the expected rate of change in the money supply in period t, the trend rate of growth in output (β), a term in the cyclical component of output in $t - 1$, and past rates of change of the money supply. If $b \neq 0$, then the results are not far from the quantity theory in expectation form although the algebraic expression representing the expectation formation process is more complicated.

The money supply on the basis of which the public makes its forecasts of the future path of m_{t+j} is of particular relevance. The empirical analysis of Section 4 considers two processes as determining the money supply; an ARIMA process that in its "inverted form" is

$$Dm_t = \pi_1 Dm_{t-1} + \pi_2 Dm_{t-2} + \pi_3 Dm_{t-3} + \ldots + v_{3t} \quad (5\text{-}9)$$

where the πs are parameters. The second process will be a model of the form

$$Dm_t = \pi_1' \, Dm_{t-1} + \pi_2' z_t + u_t \quad (5\text{-}10)$$

where π_1' can be a parameter or a polynomial in the lag operator and π_2' can be a row vector of parameters or a row vector of polynomials in the lag operator while z_t is a column vector of predetermined variables.[3]

The empirical tests will not be carried out directly in the form of Equations (5-9) and (5-10) but indirectly through the transfer functions of the next section.

3. TOWARD AN EMPIRICAL TEST OF THE MODEL

In this section we outline the method followed in order to get the estimates for the structural equations of the model. Thus two points are jointly developed, one is the computation of expected prices and the other is the endogeneity of p_t that precludes the straightforward estimation of Equation (5-1) using ordinary least squares.

At the estimation stage we shall concentrate on Equations (5-1) and (5-3). The main problem with equation (5-2) is the variable r_t for which data do not exist in Argentina and Brazil. This problem is eliminated in Equation (5-3) because it is assumed that variation in r_t is dominated by variation of the expected rate of inflation and the public's forecast of the rate of inflation (based on information available at $t-1$) is used as a proxy for r_t. It is obvious that this substitution cannot be made in Equation (5-2) because the term $(r_t - (_{t+1}p^*_{t-1} - _tp^*_{t-1}))$ would vanish if r_t were replaced by $_{t+1}p^*_{t-1} - _tp^*_{t-1}$. Nevertheless, the system formed by Equations (5-1) and (5-3) is perfectly determined when a proxy is used for r_t, let us say, $r'_t = Dp^*_t = _{t+1}p^*_{t-1} - _tp^*_{t-1}$.

For convenience, we write Equations (5-1) and (5-3) again:

$$y_{c,t} = a(p_t - _tp^*_{t-1}) + ky_{c,t-1} + u_{1t}, a > 0 \qquad (5\text{-}1)$$

$$p_t + y_t = \phi m_t - br'_t - u_{3t}, \qquad -\infty\ b < 0 \qquad (5\text{-}3)$$

where $y_{c,t} = y_t - y_{n,t}$ (detrended output).

Let us start with Equation (5-1). We know that a direct estimation of this equation is not possible because p_t and y_t are jointly determined and $_tp^*_{t-1}$ is not observable. Thus, in this section our objective is to obtain an estimable relationship to replace (5-1), making use of the relationships previously developed.

Let us consider first the case of $_tp^*_{t-1}$ that, as we said, is unobservable. Rational expectations imply that the actual log of the price level differs from the expected value by a random component, let us say, u_{4t}, so we can write

$$p_t = Ep_t + u_{4t} \qquad (5\text{-}14)$$

Now what we need is a process for forming expectations that, using the available information, the model's structure, and suitable coefficients, yields an unbiased forecast of p_t. This is obtained through some algebraic manipulations that are shown in Appendix B. The relevant equation for our ends is one in which the actual change in prices is a function of lagged variables as follows:

$$Dp_t = v(L) LDm_t + h_0 Dy_{c,t-1} + c + u_{5t} \qquad (5\text{-}14a)$$

where $v(L)$ is polynomial in the lag operator and c and h_0 are parameters.

To estimate Equation (5-14a), we have to consider the problem of collinearity, especially in the case of quarterly data, where a reasonable lag of two years would imply that m_t should be lagged eight times. A way of dealing with Equation (5-14a) is to consider it to be a multiple input transfer function. The transfer function form of Equation (5-14a) can be parsimoniously (in terms of the number of parameters) represented by

$$Dp_t = \frac{v_1(L)}{\alpha_1(L)} LDm_t + \frac{v_2(L)}{\alpha_2(L)} LDy_{c,t} + \frac{0(L)}{\theta(L)} u_t + c \quad {}_4 \tag{5-15}$$

The estimation of Equation (5-15) can be done using the Marquardt algorithm, and the forecast made using the estimated version of Equation (5-15) is a minimum mean square error forecast. Thus the problem of $_t p^*_{t-1}$ being unobservable is solved using the forecast yielded by the estimated version of Equation (5-15) over the sample period. In other words, from Equation (5-15) we can construct a series of "expected prices." The reader should realize that our Equation (5-15) substitutes for the popular hypothesis of adaptive expectations that constructs forecasts from an exponentially weighted, distributed lag polynomial.

Although, Equation (5-15) can be used to obtain an estimate of the unobservable $_t p^*_{t-1}$, Equation (5-1) still cannot be estimated directly because of the simultaneity between p_t and $y_{c,t}$. To solve this problem we follow a "two-stage" method, computing estimates for p_t from a "reduced-form equation" for p_t. A reduced form for p_t is given by Equation (A5-3) of Appendix A. Combining this equation with Equations (5-6), (5-7), and (5-9) and following the same algebraic manipulations to obtain (5-15) we get

$$Dp_t = \frac{\omega_1'(L)}{\alpha_1'(L)} Dm_t + \frac{\omega_2'(L)}{\alpha_2'(L)} LDy_{c,t} + \frac{\theta'(L)}{\phi'(L)} u_t' + c' \tag{5-16}$$

where the meaning of the notation is the same as in Equation (5-15). Notice that the main difference between (5-15) and (5-16) is that in (5-15) Dm_t appears lagged one period.

Now let me recall that Equation (5-9) represents the hypothesis that the money supply follows an ARIMA process. If we use the assumption (5-10) for the money supply, then Equations (5-15) and (5-16) should be extended to include terms in the components of z_t.

Although the algebraic analysis is rather long, its intuitive interpretation is quite simple and straightforward. The rational expectation feature of the model implies that the public forms their expectations using the information available as of the end of period $t - 1$. In forming these expectations the money supply expected to prevail in future periods is important, and it is assumed that the public forecasts future values of m_t by considering the history of m_t available at $t - 1$ (as well as other variables if (5-10) is used). But the history of m_t is not only relevant for forecasting future values; the recent past values of m_t also directly affect the price level because of the lagged response of prices to changes in the money supply. This is also considered in the expectations formation process. Equation (5-15) is oriented to capture this process.

Equation (5-16), although very similar to (5-15), is quite different. It is a reduced form for p_t implied by the system (5-1)-(5-5) and the assumption in (5-9) or (5-10) for the money supply. In (5-16), m_t directly affects the price level. The economy as a whole need not forecast m_t; it is an exogenous variable determined by monetary authorities in period t that will have an immediate effect on p_t.

The fitted values for p_t from (5-16) will be introduced in (5-1) in place of p_t and the fitted values of (5-15) will be introduced in (5-1) in place of $_tp^*_{t-1}$ in order to estimate Equation (5-1).

Consider now Equation (5-3). This equation assumes that the real income elasticity of demand for money is one. This assumption need not be maintained since all the previous algebraic expressions can be rearranged to include an additional parameter (the real income elasticity of the demand for money). Hereafter we will relax this assumption writing (5-3) as

$$y_t = \phi m_t - br'_t - u_{3t}$$

where $y_t = p_t + iy_t$, i representing the real income elasticity of demand for money. It should be noticed that if $i = 1$, then y_t is the log of nominal income. Then the system (5-1) - (5-3) can be interpreted as follows. Equation (5-3) determines nominal income and Equation (5-1) determines the division of nominal income between changes in prices and changes in output.

For analyzing the cases in which $i \neq 1$, we will evaluate the results for three possibilities: $i = 0.5$, 1.5, and 2. An attempt was made to estimate i using an instrumental variable for Dy_t and an ARIMA process; however, the results were not reliable because y_t behaves almost like a random walk. At the estimation stage, Equation (5-3) will be expressed in the form of a transfer function with all variables in first differences. The transfer function form will allow us to estimate the lag operator ϕ.

4. EMPIRICAL RESULTS

In this section we proceed to test and estimate the model presented in Sections 2 and 3 with the available data for Argentina and Brazil. First, we construct a series of expected prices on the basis of the results obtained in fitting Equation (5-15). Secondly, we construct a series of actual prices from the reduced form for prices, that is, Equation (5-16) (recall that this step is necessary in order to avoid the problem of simultaneity in estimating Equation (5-1). "Actual prices" minus expected prices give us the misperceptions of prices that are needed to estimate Equation (5-1). Finally, we estimate Equation (5-3) under different assumptions with respect to the real income elasticity of the demand for money and using a proxy for the interest rate.

4.1 The Data

All the data for Argentina were obtained from International Financial Statistics (International Monetary Fund). They include quarterly data for the index of industrial production, wholesale prices, currency and demand deposits, wages set in collective bargaining, and the balance of trade (all seasonally adjusted by the method of moving averages). The observations relate to the period 1956-I to 1973-II (this period was chosen in order to base the analysis on the maximum number of observations available for the index of industrial production).[5]

The log of the index of industrial production for Argentina was detrended splitting the data into two parts: from 1956-I to 1962-IV and from 1963-I to 1973-II. This was done because in the first period there is no apparent trend in real output and if a single trend line were fitted to the whole period we would lose most of the cyclical fluctuations.[6]

The data for Brazil were obtained from two sources: International Financial Statistics (IMF) and Goncalves (1974). From International Financial Statistics we obtained the series of wholesale prices (excluding coffee) and currency and demand deposits. From Goncalves we obtained a series of real output. All the observations relate to the period 1955-I to 1971-IV (this period was chosen in order to base the analysis on the maximum number of observations available for real output). The data were seasonally adjusted by the method of moving averages.

All the variables were expressed in first differences of logs prior to estimation except in the case of balance of trade. This variable was computed as the log of exports minus the log of imports (this because of the impossibility of taking the log of a negative number in the case of trade deficits).

The estimation of transfer functions was carried out using Marquardt's (1963) algorithm.

4.2 Estimates of the Transfer Function for Expected Prices

In Table 5-1 we present the estimates obtained for Equation (5-15), which is the expression that determines expected prices.[7] These models have been selected from a larger number of models with different lag structures and different error terms. The selection has been carried out using the likelihood ratio test proposed by Zellner and Palm (1974) (see Fernandez [1975] for a description and application of this test).

Models (1) and (2) for Argentina assume that the money supply follows a process as represented by Equation (5-9) and model (3) considers the assumption implied by Equation (5-10). In model (3) we have computed the transfer function with wages and balance of trade as input variables. We notice from Table 5-1 that in the case of Argentina there is a slight reduction in the RSS/DF and a small increase in the adjusted R^2 when passing from model (1) or (2) to model (3).[8]

At the bottom of the table we present the results obtained for Brazil, where an insignificant reduction in the RSS/DF occurs when we go from the simple lag structure of model (1) to the more complex lag structure of model (2).

4.3 Estimates of the Reduced Form for Prices

Table 5-2 shows the estimates of the transfer functions for prices (i.e., Equation (5-16). Here again, for the case of Argentina models (1) and (2) incorporate assumption (5-9) for the money supply while model (3) incorporates assumption (5-10). The models (1) and (2) are the best results obtained for each hypothesis regarding the money supply. In both Table 5-1 and Table 5-2, the coefficient of the balance of trade variable is significantly different from zero at the 5 percent level. Only in Table 5-2 does the balance of trade variable have a coefficient estimate with an algebraic sign that the theory predicts (i.e., positive sign).

For Brazil we observe again that no appreciable reduction in the RSS/DF is obtained in going from the simple lag structure of model (1) to the more complex lag structure of model (2).

In both Table 5-1 and Table 5-2, the estimates for the variables $DY_{c,\,t-1}$ and dummy or constant are small numbers not significantly

Table 5-1. Estimated Transfer Functions for Expected Prices

Model	Residual Sum of Squares (RSS)	Degree of Freedom (DF)	RSS/DF	Estimates of the AR and MA Parts of Dm_{t-1}	Estimates of $D^y_{c,t-1}$	Dummy or constant	Wages	Bal. of Trade	Estimates of the AR and MA Parts of u_t	Adjusted R^2
				Argentina 1956-I–1973-II						
(1)	0.122293	59	0.00207	$\dfrac{0.492}{1 - 1.041L + 0.785L^2}$ num (0.129); denom (0.082) (0.087)	−0.006 (0.094)	0.011 (0.012)			$\dfrac{1}{1 - 0.402L - 0.252L^2}$ (0.133) (0.130)	0.47
(2)	0.117639	57	0.00206	$\dfrac{0.693 - 0.317L}{1 - 1.112L + 0.719L^2}$ num (0.166) (0.221); denom (0.135) (0.102)	−0.060 (0.104)	0.011 (0.013)			$\dfrac{1}{1 - 0.376L - 0.271L^2}$ (0.135) (0.131)	0.48
(3)	0.116154	59	0.00197	$\dfrac{0.613}{1 - 1.009L + 0.741L^2}$ num (0.146); denom (0.099) (0.098)	−0.022 (0.091)	0.006 (0.009)	0.044 (0.081)	−0.004 (0.001)	$\dfrac{1}{1 - 0.436L}$ (0.124)	0.49
				Brazil 1955-I–1971-IV						
(1)	0.066609	60	0.00111	$\dfrac{0.188}{1 - 0.723L}$ num (0.122); denom (0.174)	−0.009 (0.077)	0.016 (0.024)			$\dfrac{1}{1 - 0.520L}$ (0.116)	0.46
(2)	0.065183	59	0.00110	$\dfrac{0.119}{1 - 1.388L + 0.556L^2}$ num (0.099); denom (0.662) (0.578)	−0.012 (0.078)	0.013 (0.023)			$\dfrac{1}{1 - 0.508L}$ (0.116)	0.46

Note: This table presents the estimates of Equation (5-15). The terms AR and MA represent the autoregressive and moving average parts, respectively, of the rational polynomials. Figures in parentheses are large sample standard errors.

Table 5-2. Estimated Transfer Functions for Prices

Model	Residual Sum of Squares (RSS)	Degree of Freedom (DF)	RSS/DF	Estimates of the AR and MA Parts of Dm_t	Estimates of $Dy_{c, t-1}$	Dummy or constant	Wages	Bal. of Trade	Estimates of the AR and MA Parts of u_t	Adjusted R^2
				Argentina 1956-I-1973-II						
(1)	0.125758	59	0.00213	$\dfrac{0.422\ (0.112)}{1 - 1.216L + 0.773L^2\ (0.102)\ (0.103)}$	0.049 (0.095)	0.004 (0.012)			$\dfrac{1}{1 - 0.400L - 0.216L^2\ (0.133)\ (0.132)}$	0.45
(2)	0.116639	57	0.00205	$\dfrac{0.224 + 0.346L\ (0.160)\ (0.202)}{1 - 1.073L + 0.763L^2\ (0.104)\ (0.091)}$	0.030 (0.105)	0.004 (0.012)			$\dfrac{1}{1 - 0.365L - 0.280L^2\ (0.135)\ (0.132)}$	0.48
(3)	0.113562	57	0.00199	$\dfrac{0.207 + 0.435L\ (0.180)\ (0.229)}{1 - 1.054L + 0.749L^2\ (0.116)\ (0.098)}$	0.010 (0.095)	-0.003 (0.010)	0.018 (0.084)	0.003 (0.001)	$\dfrac{1}{1 - 0.438L\ (0.124)}$	0.49
				Brazil 1955-I-1971-IV						
(1)	0.064908	61	0.00106	$\dfrac{0.212\ (0.117)}{1 - 0.716L\ (0.155)}$	-0.004	0.010 (0.023)			$\dfrac{1}{1 - 0.511L\ (0.113)}$	0.47
(2)	0.064130	60	0.00107	$\dfrac{(0.119)\ (0.190)}{1 - 1.389L + 0.546L^2\ (0.630)\ (0.611)}$	-0.005	0.008 (0.022)			$\dfrac{1}{1 - 0.498L\ (0.115)}$	0.47

Note: This table presents the estimates of Equation (5-16). The terms *AR* and *MA* represent the autoregressive and moving average parts, respectively, of the rational polynomials.

different from zero. This is not in contrast with the theoretical model because it is shown in Appendix A that these parameters can indeed be close to zero (See Equations (A5-12) and (A5-13) in Appendix A.)

4.4 Estimates of the Aggregate Supply

Recall that Table 5-1 provides the estimates of Equation (5-15), which in turn allow us to obtain a series of "expected prices" needed to estimate Equation (5-1) of our original model. By the same token Equation (5-16), whose estimates are given in Table 5-2, provides us with a series of "actual prices" to estimate Equation (5-1). Then the next step is to compute a one step ahead forecast from (5-15) that would give us a proxy variable for $_tp^*_{t-1}$. Similarly a one step ahead forecast from (5-16) would give us a proxy for p_t. The difference between the proxy of p_t and the proxy for $_tp^*_{t-1}$ is introduced in Equation (5-1) in place of $(p_t - {_tp^*_{t-1}})$, and the estimation of this equation provides us with an estimate of the slope coefficient of our short-run Phillips equation. Table 5-3 shows the results obtained by this procedure and indicates the different models used for forecasting prices and reduced forms used for prices.

On testing the significance of the Phillips parameter for Argentina using a two-tailed test we notice that at the 5 percent level only the last regression shows an estimate significantly different from zero. Using a one-tailed test (i.e., the alternative hypothesis is that the parameter is greater than zero), estimates of the last three regressions provide evidence for rejecting the null hypothesis at the 5 percent level of significance. In all five cases the Box and Pierce Q statistic favors rejecting the hypothesis of autocorrelated residuals.[9]

Perhaps it is convenient at this stage to take a closer look at the estimates of Table 5-3. Recall that the estimate of parameter "a" is an estimate of the slope of the Phillips curve. Our results for Argentina indicate that there is some evidence in favor of a short-run tradeoff between inflation and output given by the 95 percent confidence intervals for the estimates of the third through fifth regressions. These are (-0.089, 0.991), (0.0, 1.384), and (0.001, 2.268), respectively. This short-run tradeoff is not in contrast to the natural rate hypothesis of Friedman because, as Equation (5-1) indicates, if prices are anticipated correctly output will remain in its long-run trend (or "natural" level).

These results cannot provide evidence either in favor of the naive Phillips curve approach or in favor of the Solow-Tobin analysis. The naive Phillips curve approach says that there is only one Phillips curve indicating a positive tradeoff between inflation and output regardless

Table 5-3.   Estimates of the Aggregate Supply Equation

Model for Reduced Form	Model for Expected Prices	a	k	Adjusted R^2	Q-Statistics
		Argentina 1956-I – 1973-II			
(1) M_2	M_2	0.877 (0.594)	0.564 (0.102)	0.35	15.3
(2) M_2	M_1	0.647 (0.578)	0.574 (0.102)	0.34	16.5
(3) M_1	M_1	0.401 (0.295)	0.575 (0.102)	0.35	15.7
(4) M_1	M_2	0.692 (0.346)	0.569 (0.101)	0.36	14.2
(5) M_3	M_3	1.140 (0.564)	0.778 (0.102)	0.35	15.1
		Brazil 1955-I – 1971-IV			
(1) M_1	M_1	-0.272 (0.919)	0.664 (0.095)	0.430	15.1
(2) M_1	M_2	-0.492 (0.750)	0.660 (0.095)	0.433	16.0
(3) M_2	M_1	0.842 (1.328)	0.657 (0.095)	0.433	14.5
(4) M_2	M_2	-0.140 (1.390)	0.665 (0.095)	0.429	14.9
(5) Actual prices	M_1	0.168 (0.178)	0.634 (0.099)	0.437	15.8
(6) Actual prices	M_2	0.153 (0.172)	0.638 (0.099)	0.436	15.5

Note: Chi-square values from table:

$$\chi^2(24) = 33.2 \quad \text{0.10 level of significance}$$
$$\chi^2(24) = 36.4 \quad \text{0.05 level of significance}$$

The models used to represent prices and expected prices are symbolized in this table with the letter M and a subindex. Thus, M_2 in the column headed "Model for Reduced Form" means that model (2) of Table 5-2 is being used to represent actual prices in the aggregate supply equation.

of expectations. The Solow-Tobin analysis says that people adjust to changes in prices, but they are subject to some money illusion that allows for a permanent tradeoff between inflation and output. Both of these hypotheses are ruled out by the specification that when actual prices are equal to expected prices output will remain at its long-run natural level.

For Brazil we notice that in the first, second, and fourth equations the estimate of "a" is negative although not significantly different from zero at the 0.05 level in a two-tailed test. The third regression presents the right sign but its a estimate has a large standard error that makes it not significantly different from zero. In all cases the value of the Q statistics favor rejection of the hypothesis of autocorrelation in the residuals.

In order to compare our results with other results obtained for Brazil by Goncalves (1974) we estimated the last two models of Table 5-3 using actual prices instead of the forecast of the reduced form for prices. Goncalves performed a similar estimation under the assumption that the price level was exogenously determined (mainly due to strongly enforced price controls in most of his period of analysis). He worked with the period 1959-1969 and used another hypothesis for expectations formation. His results provide an estimate of a equal to 0.41 (standard errors are not reported in his work). Another of his results shows a equal to 0.27 when a dummy variable is included with a value of unity from 1961-I to 1963-II and zero elsewhere (this dummy variable is supposed to capture the effect of price controls). It should be noted that this last result, obtained by Goncalves, is close to the last two models of Table 5-3. From our results for Brazil we must conclude that the empirical evidence does not favor a stable short-run tradeoff between output and inflation even in the short run.[10]

4.5 Estimates of the Transfer Function
for Nominal Income

Now we proceed to the estimation of Equation (5-3) of our original model. Recall that in this equation we are using nominal income as the dependent variable when the real income elasticity of the demand for money is assumed equal to one, and we are using as dependent variable the term $p + iy$ where i is the real income elasticity for all the cases in which it is assumed that $i \neq 1$.

In addition, we are using the first difference in the one step ahead forecast for prices from model (1) of Table 5-1 as a proxy for the nominal rate of interest. The estimates for these transfer functions are presented in Table 5-4. In this table it is shown that for Argentina when i is greater than one both the degrees of polynomials estimated and the RSS/DF, are higher than when i is equal to or lower than one. I have no explanation for this except, as mentioned above, Dy_t is a very noisy series and as i becomes large it magnifies the noise of the series of "nominal income." The last transfer function reported for Argentina in Table 5-4 includes a second-order autoregres-

Table 5-4. Estimated Transfer Functions for Nominal Income

Model	Residual Sum of Squares (RSS)	Degree of Freedom (DF)	RSS/DF	Estimates of the AR and AM Parts of Dm_{t-1}	Estimates of the AR and MA Parts of Dr^1_t	Estimates of the AR and MA Parts of u_t	Adjusted R^2
				Argentina 1956 I – 1973 II			
(1) ($i = 1.5$)	0.249863	56	0.00446	$\dfrac{1.021 - 0.264L + 1.283L^2}{1 + 1.739L + 0.596L^2}$ $(0.269)\,(0.311)\,(0.247)$ $(0.208)\quad(0.234)$	0.565 (0.311)		0.27
(2) ($i = 1$)	0.140220	58	0.00242	$\dfrac{0.406 - 0.147L}{1 - 1.496L + 0.737L^2}$ $(0.149)\;(0.182)$ $(0.120)\;(0.106)$	0.504 (0.213)		0.38
(3) ($i = 0.5$)	0.139771	58	0.00241	$\dfrac{0.424 - 0.130L}{1 - 1.436L + 0.737L^2}$ $(0.165)\;(0.212)$ $(0.120)\;(0.106)$	0.475 (0.215)		0.38
(4) ($i = 0.5$)	0.121832	54	0.00225	$\dfrac{0.442 - 0.141L}{1 - 1.407L + 0.722L^2}$ $(0.194)\;(0.260)$ $(0.176)\;(0.141)$	0.266 (0.216)	$\dfrac{1}{1 - 0.276L - 0.171L^2}$ $(0.141)\;(0.150)$	0.41

151

Table 5–4 continued

Model	Residual Sum of Squares (RSS)	Degree of Freedom (DF)	RRS/DF	Estimates of the AR and AM Parts of Dm_{t-1}	Estimates of the AR and MA Parts of Dr^1_t	Estimates of the AR and MA Parts of u_t	Adjusted R^2
				Brazil 1955 I – 1971 IV			
(1) ($i = 1.5$)	0.377770	57	0.00593	$\dfrac{0.212 + 0.103L + 0.348L^2}{1 - 0.383L}$ $(0.348)\,(0.526)\,(0.521)$ (0.422)	-0.093 (0.516)		0.093
(2) ($i = 1$)	0.182688	57	0.00320	$\dfrac{0.253 - 0.272L + 0.356L^2}{1 - 0.419L}$ $(0.255)\,(0.389)\,(0.359)$ (0.306)	0.115 (0.380)		0.171
(3) ($i = 0.5$)	0.095822	57	0.00168	$\dfrac{0.292 - 0.161L + 0.366L^2}{1 - 0.466L}$ $(0.184)\,(0.285)\,(0.243)$ (0.213)	0.723 (0.375)		0.293
(4) ($i = 0.5$)	0.086180	53	0.00162	$\dfrac{0.197 - 0.061L + 0.221L^2}{1 - 0.613L}$ $(0.182)\,(0.272)\,(0.251)$ (0.226)	0.085	$\dfrac{1}{1 - 0.223L - 0.169L^2}$ $(0.167)\ \ (0.169)$	0.342

sive process for the error term that yields an appreciable reduction in the *RSS*.

For Brazil when the real income elasticity is relatively large (1 or 1.5) the adjusted R^2s are low. The best explanation is obtained with $i = 0.5$ and with a second-order polynomial in the disturbance term.

It should be noticed that if the estimate for the parameter "*a*" is assumed to be zero and if the real income elasticity of the demand for money is assumed to be one, our system is reduced to a special formulation of Friedman's theory of nominal income.

This can be explained as follows: If "*a*" is assumed equal to zero Equation (5-1) can no longer be used to break down the changes in nominal income obtained from Equation (5-3) into changes in prices and output. Thus the system explains only nominal income.

In this case, Equation (5-15) determines the price expectations (still under the hypothesis of rational expectations) that would dominate the changes in the nominal rate of interest in Equation (5-3). Let me recall that from Equation (5-15) we obtain the proxy Dr'_t for the nominal rate of interest.

Section 5, which analyzes the short-run dynamics of prices and output, makes use of the estimates of this section. In choosing the estimates that will represent our model we make use of models (1) of Table 5-1 and Table 5-2 for Argentina and models (1) of Table 5-1 and models (2) of Table 5-2 for Brazil—the models that most appropriately represent the process for expected prices and prices, respectively, under the hypothesis of Equation (5-9) for the money supply. This implies that the third equation of Table 5-3 (for both Argentina and Brazil) was used to represent the Phillips equation. Finally the second model for Argentina ($i = 0.5$, second order regressive error) and the first model for Brazil ($i = 0.5$) of Table 5-4 were used as transfer functions for nominal income.

5. The Short-Run Dynamics of Output and Prices

In this final section we analyze the short-run behavior of a system like that developed in Section 2. In doing so we will perform a deterministic simulation of a change in the rate of growth of the money supply in order to observe the short-run adjustment of the endogenous variables of the system.

By the adjustment process we mean the path followed for the variables from one long-run equilibrium position to another long-run equilibrium position when an exogenous force shocks the system. In our simulations the shock will be a shift in the rule governing the money supply. These long-run equilibrium positions have been already stated in the literature for models of this kind. So, for example, if the real income elasticity of the demand for money is unity and if we change the rate of growth of the money supply from 3 percent to 10 percent, then the long-run equilibrium position of nominal income will shift from 3 percent to 10 percent (this is no more than the quantity theory; for a discussion of this proposition see Friedman [1971], pp. 56-58). The question to be answered by the analysis of the short-run dynamics of the system is how the endogenous variables, for example, nominal income, moves from the 3 percent position to the 10 percent position.

In order to illustrate the short-run dynamics of prices and output implied by this model we use three different simulations concerning the behavior of the money supply. However, before proceeding, it is necessary to emphasize the circumstances under which these simulations can cast some light on the short-run dynamics of prices and output. Our model, under the hypothesis implied by equation (5-9) about the money supply, states that all the parameters of equation (5-15) are stable as long as the process followed by the money supply is the same. That is, if the money supply has followed an ARIMA (3, 1, 2) process, then the forecasts will be accurate as long as this process stays the same, mainly because the people compute their expectations as if they knew the process ARIMA (3, 1, 2) governing the money supply. If we change this process then the parameters of equation (5-9) will eventually change and consequently the parameters of equation (5-15). This can be proved mathematically. However, there also is a clear intuitive explanation. We cannot expect that people will continue indefinitely to form their expectations on the basis of one process ARIMA (3, 1, 2) for the money supply, when the monetary authorities have changed the rule governing the money supply to, let us say, a rate of growth of m_t at 10 percent per period. If this second rule has been in operation for a long enough time period, then in computing their expectations people will use the process $Dm_t = 0.10$ instead of the previous ARIMA process. From this discussion it should be clear that the implicit assumption that all the parameters of the model are constant while we change the rule governing the money supply, is a strong assumption, particularly if we want to analyze long periods of time.[11] Nevertheless, we assume that there will be a transition period during which people will utilize something approximating the old process. That is, perhaps the past is full of promises and attempts from the government or monetary authorities that prices will remain stable or that the rate of inflation will be lower or that monetary emission will slow down. Moreover, there are probably costs in changing the rule. Therefore, people take some time in assuming that any change in the rule governing the money supply is permanent. It is precisely during this period that our simulations will be relevant.

Figures 5-2 to 5-4 refer to Argentina. The first simulation, illustrated in Figure 5-2, shows the paths followed by the rate of change in nominal income, the rate of inflation, and the rate of change in detrended output when the money supply is shifted from a rate of growth of 0 percent to a rate of growth of 10 percent per period. The convergence to the new steady state is oscillatory for the three variables. Inflation accelerates during the first year, reaching a peak at the end of the fourth quarter; during the second year inflation slows down and then accelerates again reaching a second peak at the thirteenth quarter. The rate of change in detrended output also accelerates during the first year, but it peaks one period later than inflation; therefore during the first quarter of the second year output increases while the rate of inflation decreases. Similarly, the first trough of output is two periods later than the trough in the rate of

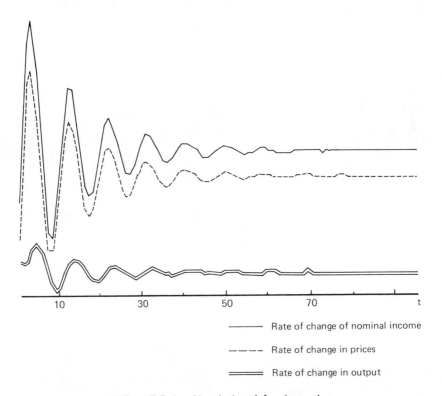

Rate of change of nominal income

Rate of change in prices

Rate of change in output

FIGURE 5-2. Simulation 1 for Argentina

inflation, and thus we observe inflation accelerating and output probably decreasing, a phenomenon known as stagflation. It should be noticed that from quarter 8 to 12 the rate of change in detrended output is negative so output will tend to be below the trend and consequently the unemployment rate above its natural level, while the rate of inflation is accelerating; this would be an illustration of a lower part of a counterclockwise loop in the conventional Phillips curve analysis. The other parts of the loop are readily observed in the following quarters as well as in the previous quarters.[12]

The second simulation, that is illustrated in Figure 5-3, assumes the rate of growth of the money supply shifts from 0 to 10 percent from period 1 to 30, and then it is shifted back to zero in period 31 and kept at that level thereafter. In this case we observe that the paths toward the final equilibrium levels of the variables oscillate and that a deep trough in the rate of inflation is reached four quarters after the reduction in the money supply while the trough in output is reached five periods after. One interesting aspect is illustrated in the four quarters between period 34 to period 37; during these quar-

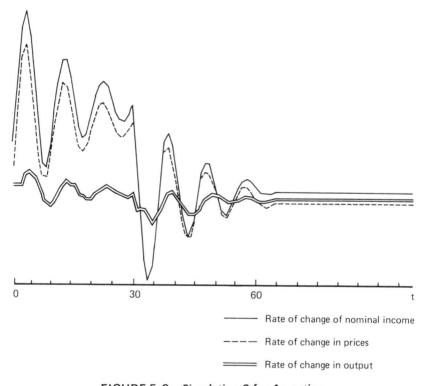

0   30   60   t

———— Rate of change of nominal income

— — — Rate of change in prices

===== Rate of change in output

FIGURE 5-3.   Simulation 2 for Argentina

ters output is certainly below the trend and consequently we should expect a relatively high unemployment rate. At the same time inflation is accelerating; this is a time when many people could think that the "old remedy to cure inflation does not work" because the reduction in the money supply not only has increased unemployment but also the rate of inflation is accelerating.

The third simulation is similar to the second but in place of an abrupt reduction in the money supply in period 31 we reduce the money supply to 8 percent in the first year, to 6 percent in the second year, and so on.

We observe that the fall in output is not as abrupt as it was in the previous case. In Figure 5-3 the trough in period 34 reached the value −3.4 percent while in Figure 5-4 the trough in period 47 reached the value 1.8 percent. In addition, it should be noticed that the convergence to the new steady state does not exhibit the large

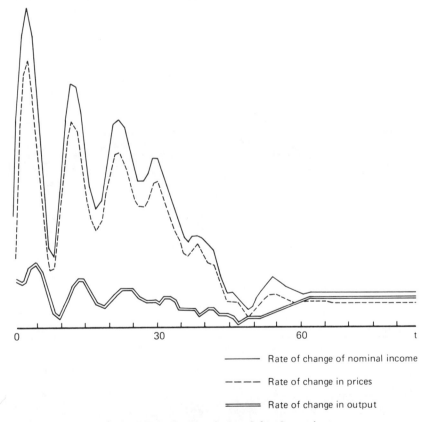

——— Rate of change of nominal income

− − − − Rate of change in prices

===== Rate of change in output

FIGURE 5-4. Simulation 3 for Argentina

oscillations of the previous case; that is, in this case convergence is smoother.

Figures 5-5, 5-6, and 5-7 illustrate the same types of simulations for the case of Brazil. In the first simulation (see Figure 5-5) we observe that the shift of the rate of growth of the money supply from 0 percent to 10 percent produces an initial overshoot of nominal income, prices, and output but after a few oscillations they converge to their long-run equilibrium values. We observe that nominal income and output reach a peak a quarter before prices; then during the fifth quarter we observe prices accelerating and output slowing down.[13]

The second simulation for Brazil (see Figure 5-6) shows a large fall in output produced by an abrupt shift of monetary policy from a rate of growth of the money supply of 10 percent to a rate of growth of 0 percent.

Finally, the third simulation for Brazil illustrates the advantages of gradualism in stabilizing the economy (this same conclusion is reached

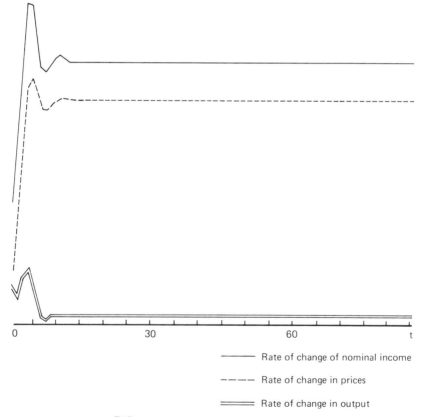

FIGURE 5-5.   Simulation 1 for Brazil

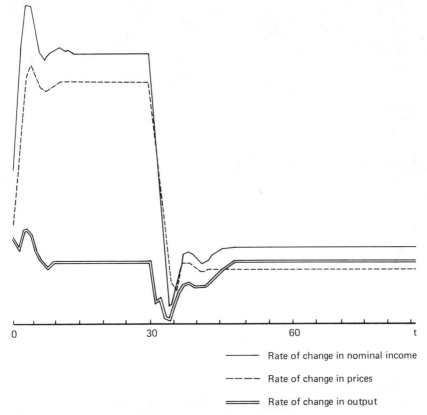

Rate of change in nominal income

Rate of change in prices

Rate of change in output

FIGURE 5-6. Simulation 2 for Brazil

by Goncalves [1974] for Brazil although in the context of a different model). We observe from Figure 5-7 that during the stabilization
period the fall in output is smaller than in the previous simulation
that assumed an abrupt change of monetary policy.

6. CONCLUSIONS

As indicated in the title of this paper we have tried to explain the
short-run dynamics of prices and output. An indicator of the degree
to which this objective has been achieved could be the part of the
variance in prices and output that has been explained by the model.
In other words, we could look at the R^2s obtained in our transfer
functions or regressions. For the case of Argentina, the R^2s for prices
and nominal income have been close to 0.50 while for detrended
output the R^2s have been on the order of 0.35.

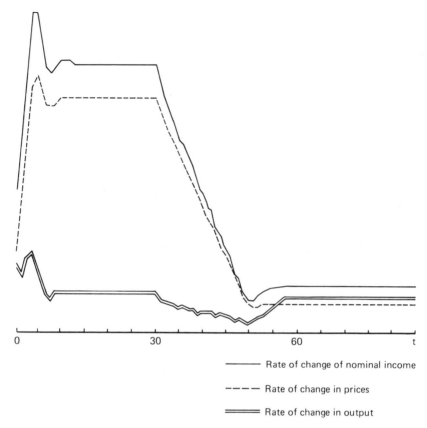

FIGURE 5-7. Simulation 3 for Brazil

For Brazil we obtained R^2s around 0.45 for prices, 0.30 for nominal income, and 0.43 for detrended real income.

Other indicators are the standard error of the estimates and the t values. Standard errors have been reported in the tables of Section 4. Not all the estimates of the parameters are significantly different from zero at the 0.05 level but many of them are indeed significantly different from zero at the 0.05 level in a two-tailed test. Other estimates are small in absolute value and not significantly different from zero—for example, in the case of the estimates of $Dy_{c,t-1}$ and c in the transfer functions for prices and expected prices—however, this does not contradict the theoretical model. As mentioned above, these parameters can be close to zero. Finally, there are other parameters that have large standard errors, in particular, the slope coefficient of our short-run Phillips curve, indicating that this relationship is empirically unstable.

In general, the estimates for Argentina are more precise than the estimates obtained for Brazil. In both countries better fits were obtained for the rate of change in prices than for detrended income. The good performance of the model in explaining the rate of inflation can be illustrated by plotting the actual and fitted values from the reduced form for prices. This is shown in Figure 5-8 for Argentina. Here we observe that the model behaves well in explaining inflation, and for only two observations—one near the beginning and one near the end of the period—do the observed rates of inflation differ substantially from the fitted values.

Figure 5-9 illustrates the case of Brazil. Here we also observe the good performance of the model in explaining the large oscillations of the rate of inflation. Only for a few observations near the middle of the period do actual values differ substantially from the fitted values.

Although our results seem to be good relative to many other empirical studies working with highly noisy quarterly series, we still are not sure that we have really separated the true signal from the

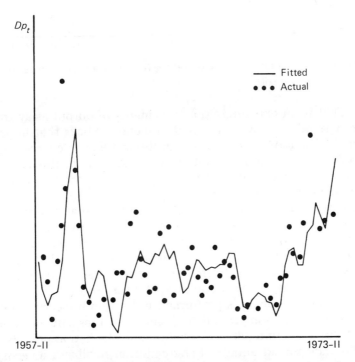

FIGURE 5-8. Actual and Fitted Values for the Rate of Change in Prices (Argentina)

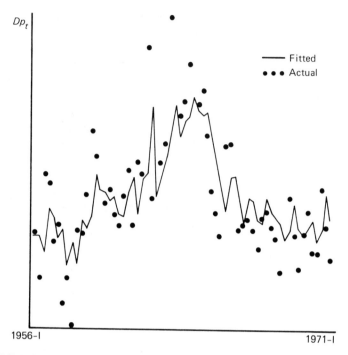

FIGURE 5-9.   Actual and Fitted Values for the Rate of Change in Prices (Brazil)

noise. That is, in explaining the movements of output away from its long-run trend we have only used monetary shocks that impeded a correct anticipation of prices, and in this sense people were surprised (or fooled) during short periods of time. As long as this is the only cause that produces cyclical fluctuations around the trend, then our model seems to behave well.

From a theoretical point of view we can say that our model uses two relatively new aspects of macroeconomic theory. One is the hypothesis of rational expectations and the other is a sort of Phillips equation to play the role of the "missing equation" that, according to Friedman, explains the difference between the quantity theory of money and the Keynesian income-expenditure theory.

The simulation analysis performed in Section 6 clearly illustrates many of the situations found in practice such as shifting short-run Phillips curves, counterclockwise loops, and stagflation periods. They also illustrate the advantage of gradualism in stabilizing an economy. It was shown that an abrupt fall in the rate of growth of the money supply introduces a big oscillation in the system in the case of Argentina and a deep fall in output in both Argentina and Brazil. On the other hand, a gradual reduction in the rate of growth of the money supply produces a different effect. First, no large oscillations are observed in the endogenous variables of the system. Secondly, the fall in output is not as large as it was in the previous case although the system reaches its new steady state in a longer period of time. It must be emphasized again that this simulation depends upon the hypothesis that the same structure (parameters of the model), including the structure of the expectations formulation, continues to prevail even when policy changes. This assumption is less credible with abrupt policy changes than with gradual ones, and therefore this simulation might overstate the true difference between "gradualism and shock treatment."

NOTES

1. Equation (5-3) can be derived from the simple quantity theory. That is, let

$$Y_t \cdot \frac{1}{V_t} = M_t \tag{5-3'}$$

Now in order to capture the lagged effect of M_t on the left-hand side we have to specify something like

$$Y_t \cdot \frac{1}{V_t} = f(M_t, M_{t-1}, M_{t-2}, \cdots)$$

and a specific construction is

$$Y_t \cdot \frac{1}{V_t} = \exp(\phi \ln M_t) \tag{5-3''}$$

where ϕ is a polynomial in the lag operator (notice that if $\phi = 1$ we get (5-3')).

Assuming $(1/V_t) = \exp(br_t)$ and taking logs on both sides of (5-3'') we get Equation (5-3) of the text.

2. Some testable implications of the model can be derived from a structural analysis of the system. This analysis, following the method suggested in Zellner and Palm (1974), is presented in Fernandez (1975) where the final equations of the system 1 (5-1 to 5) were derived and checked with the data. Also in that work a variant of the system is analyzed in which an adaptive expectation hypothesis was used for prices. This version was *incompatible* with the available information for both Argentina and Brazil while the rational expectations

version of the model (system (5-1 to 5) was compatible under certain conditions. The method of analysis can be described briefly. Given a system of structural equations we can work out the "final equations" for the variables of the system. These are in the form of ARIMA (Autoregressive integrated moving average) processes. On the other hand, we can identify the actual ARIMA processes for the variables using the available information on each variable. If the structural equations of the model are correct, the final equations derived for each endogenous variable should have the same structure as the ARIMA processes identified for those variables from the available information. If this is the case, we say that the model is *compatible* with the available information.

3. In searching for a process determining the money supply we can choose either to postulate a model for the money supply by relating it to a set of "predetermined variables" relative to the model (5-1 to 3) (so m_t still remains as if it were exogenous or determined outside of the system (5-1 to 3) or we can identify a Box-Jenkins ARIMA process. It has been customary in the economics profession to call these models "naive models" because of their rather simple structure by which only past values of a variable are used to predict future values of the same variable. However, it has recently been shown (see Zellner and Palm [1974]) that these models might not be naive at all. Indeed these models (the ARIMA models) represent the "final form" for a variable implied by a highly sophisticated model. I will briefly illustrate this point with a model for the nominal money supply. Let us assume that in a given country the money supply is generated by the following relationship:

$$Dm_t = c_1 + a_1 Dm_{t-1} + b_1 Dg_t + e_1 Dx_t + v_t \qquad (5\text{-}11)$$

where g_t could be the federal budget relative to lagged GNP, x_t could be the lagged balance of payment surplus relative to GNP, and v_t an error term stochastically independent of the errors in the structural equations. In our case a_1, b_1, and e_1 are assumed to be constants for simplicity, but in a more general analysis we could assume a_1, b_1, and e_1 to be polynomials in the lag operator.

Now we shall show that Equation (5-11) implies a final equation for m_t that is in the form of an ARIMA process. Equation (5-11) can be written as

$$(1 - a_1 L) Dm_t = c_1 + b_1 Dg_t + e_1 Dx_t + v_t \qquad (5\text{-}12)$$

Now the predetermined variables g_t and x_t can follow any process over time, that is, both could follow a random walk or one could follow a random walk and the other a given ARIMA process, and so on. To illustrate the problem at hand we will assume that:

$$Dg_t : \text{ARIMA } (2, 1) \text{ or } \phi (2) Dg_t = \theta (1) v_{1t}$$

$$Dx_t : \text{Random walk or } \phi (0) Dx_t = \theta (0) v_{2t}$$

where the vs are stochastically independent of the disturbances in the structural equations. Multiplying both sides of (5-12) by ϕ (2) ϕ (0), we have:

$$(1 - a_1 L)\, \phi\, (2)\, \phi\, (0)\, Dm_t = \phi\, (2)\, \phi\, (0)\, c + b\phi\, (0)\, \theta\, (1)v_{1t} \tag{5-13}$$
$$+ e\phi\, (2)\, \theta\, (0)v_{2t} + \phi\, (2)\, \phi\, (0)v_t$$

In this last expression we notice that we have obtained an ARIMA (3, 2) process (if no cancellation occurs) for m_t, using Equation (5-11) and the assumption for the predetermined variables g_t and x_t. This clearly illustrates that if we obtain the process ARIMA (3, 2) for m_t this may not be a naive model at all, but on the contrary it could be reflecting the "true" model governing the behavior of the money supply.

Now we go back to our original problem of finding a process for m_t on the basis of which the public makes its forecasts of the future path of the money supply. The above discussion demonstrates that we cannot talk about "alternative models" when we evaluate a model of the sort of Equation (5-11) with respect to a model like (5-13) because (5-13) could be the final form of (5-11). Nevertheless, we have considered it appropriate to check empirically the ARIMA hypothesis for m_t, as well as a model of the sort implied by Equation (5-11). However, no further attention is dedicated to the "theory of the money supply" that underlies our hypothesis of the money supply process, a subject that goes beyond the scope of this chapter.

4. The analysis of transfer functions can be found in Chapters 10 and 11 of Box and Jenkins (1970). The derivation of a transfer function, different from the one presented in this chapter for a simultaneous equation model can be found in Zellner and Palm (1974).

5. The index of industrial production is used for Argentina as a proxy for real income because it is more reliable and complete than existing series of real output. For Brazil the only available information corresponds to real output.

6. As a matter of fact this was exactly the procedure originally followed. The procedure was abandoned because the detrended output obtained in this manner showed an initial period in which output was mostly above the trend, a second period of almost "seven years" in which output was below the trend, and a third period where output was above the trend. A detailed explanation about some institutional aspects that could explain the difference in the trend of real output mentioned above can be found in Fernandez, pp. 36–39.

7. The column headed "dummy" corresponds to the constant c in Equation (5-15). The dummy appears in the empirical results for Argentina because the constant c is a term in the slope coefficient of the trend line for output. As we split the data into two periods and in each period there is a different slope coefficient a dummy with the value of one from 1956-I to 1962-IV and two from 1963-I to 1973-II was incorporated in the transfer function to capture the effect of the change in trend.

8. The adjusted R^2 reported in the tables for transfer functions takes account of the correction for degree of freedom. That is, $1 - R^2$ adj $= n - 1/n - k\, (1 - R^2)$.

9. The Q statistic is calculated from the first K autocorrelations $\hat{r}_k$ ($k = 1, 2, \ldots, K$). If the fitted model is appropriate,

$$Q(K) = n \sum_{k=1}^{K} \hat{r}_k^2$$

is approximately distributed as X^2 ($k - p - q$). If the model is wrong the value of Q will be inflated. For Table 5-3, $p = q = 0$ because there are no autoregressive or moving average parameters in the noise model.

10. It is important to mention here an interesting result obtained by Lucas (1973). He found, in a sample of eighteen countries and working with annual observations, that "in a stable price country like the United States, policies which increase nominal income tend to have a large initial effect on real output, together with a small positive initial effect on the rate of inflation. Thus the apparent short-term trade-off is favorable, as long as it remains unused. In contrast, in a volatile price country like Argentina, nominal income changes are associated with equal, contemporaneous price movements with no discernible effect on real output" (see Lucas [1973] pp. 332-333). Our results for Argentina and Brazil tend to confirm this finding and the underlying theory that specifies that a favorable tradeoff between output and inflation depends upon "fooling" suppliers, which becomes difficult when the variance of the demand shifts becomes large.

11. Of course this might be a problem too for the stability of our estimates. If the ARIMA process is not stable neither can be the parameters of the transfer functions.

12. There are two factors playing an important role in the determination of the loops. One is the lag structure in the transfer functions and the other is the autoregressive term in detrended income.

13. The difference in the oscillatory pattern of nominal income between Brazil and Argentina should be noticed. This is due to the different lag structure in the transfer functions for nominal income.

REFERENCES

Box, G. and G. Jenkins. *Time Series Analysis.* San Francisco: Holden-Day, 1970.

Fernandez, Roque B. "Short-Run Dynamics of Output and Prices." Ph.D. Thesis, Department of Economics, University of Chicago, 1975.

Friedman, Milton. "A Theoretical Framework for Monetary Analysis." National Bureau of Economic Research, Occasional Paper 112, 1971.

Goncalves, A.C. "The Problem of Stopping Inflation." Ph.D. Thesis, Department of Economics, University of Chicago, 1974 (mimeo).

Hansen, Bent. "Excess Demand, Unemployment, Vacancies, and Wages." *Quarterly Journal of Economics* LXXXIV:1 (February 1970), 1-23.

Lipsey Robert. "The Relationship between Unemployment and the Rate of Change of Money Wages in the United Kingdom 1862-1957: a Further Analysis." *Economica* 37: (February 1960) 1-31.

Lucas, Robert E. "Some International Evidence on Output-Inflation Trade-offs." *American Economic Review* LXV (June 1973), 326–334.

Marquardt, D.W. "An Algorithm for Least-Squares Estimation of Nonlinear Parameters." *Journal of the Society for Industrial and Applied Mathematics* 2 (1963), 431–441.

Muth, John F. "Rational Expectations and the Theory of Price Movements." *Econometrica* 29:2 (July 1961), 315–335.

Sargent, Thomas. "Rational Expectations, the Real Rate of Interest, and the Natural Rate of Unemployment." *Brookings Papers on Economic Activity*, 1973:2.

Sargent, Thomas J., and Neil Wallace. "Rational Expectations, the Optimal Monetary Instrument and the Optimal Money Supply Rule." *Journal of Political Economy* 83 (April 1975), 241–254.

Zellner, A., and F. Palm. "Time Series Analysis and Simultaneous Equation Models." *Journal of Econometrics* 2 (May 1974).

Appendix 5-A | The Algebra of Rational Expections

The methodology of this appendix is similar to the methodology developed by Sargent and Wallace (1975).

We start from the system (5-1 to 3) and first solve Equation (5-3) for r_t

$$r_t = b^{-1}\phi m_t - b^{-1}p_t - b^{-1}y_t - b^{-1}u_{3t}$$

Substituting this last expression and (5-4) and (5-5) in (5-2) gives

$$\begin{aligned} y_t - y_{n,t} &= g + cb^{-1}\phi m_t - cb^{-1}p_t - cb^{-1}y_t - cb^{-1}u_{3t} \\ &\quad - cEp_{t+1} + cEp_t + u_{2t} \end{aligned}$$

Adding $(cb^{-1}y_{n,t} - cb^{-1}y_{n,t})$ in the above expression gives

$$\begin{aligned} y_t - y_{n,t} + cb^{-1}(y_t - y_{n,t}) &= g + cb^{-1}\phi m_t - cb^{-1}p_t \\ &\quad - cEp_{t+1} + cEp_t - cb^{-1}y_{n,t} + u_{2t} - cb^{-1}u_{3t} \end{aligned}$$

Then

$$\begin{aligned} y_t - y_{n,t} &= g/(1 + cb^{-1}) + (cb^{-1}/[1 + cb^{-1}])\phi m_t \qquad\qquad \text{(A5-1)} \\ &\quad - (cb^{-1}/[1 + cb^{-1}])p_t \\ &\quad - (c/[1 + cb^{-1}])Ep_{t+1} + (c/[1 + cb^{-1}])Ep_t \end{aligned}$$

$$-(cb^{-1}/[1 + cb^{-1}])\, y_{n,t} + (1/[1 + cb^{-1}])u_{2,t}$$
$$-(cb^{-1}/[1 + cb^{-1}])u_{3t}$$

Equating this last expression to (5-1) we have

$$ap_t - aEp_t + ky_{c,t-1} + u_{1t} = g/(1 + cb^{-1}) + (cb^{-1}/[1 + cb^{-1}])\,\phi m_t$$
$$-(cb^{-1}/[1 + cb^{-1}])p_t - (c/[1 + cb^{-1}])Ep_{t+1} + (c/[1 + cb^{-1}]\,Ep_t$$
$$-(cb^{-1}/[1 + cb^{-1}])\, y_{n,t} + (1/[1 + cb^{-1}])u_{2t}$$
$$-(cb^{-1}/[1 + cb^{-1}])u_{3t}$$

Solving the last expression for p_t the following expression is obtained

$$p_t = J_0 Ep_t + J_1 Ep_{t+1} + J_2\,(\phi m_t - y_{n,t}) + J_3 y_{c,t-1} \qquad (A5\text{-}2)$$
$$+ J_4 u_{1t} + J_5 u_{2t} + J_6 u_{3t} + J_7$$

where

$$J_0 = (a + c/[1 + cb^{-1}])/\theta$$
$$J_1 = (-c/[1 + cb^{-1}])/\theta$$
$$J_2 = (cb^{-1}/[1 + cb^{-1}])/\theta$$
$$J_3 = -k/\theta$$
$$J_4 = -1/\theta$$
$$J_5 = (1/[1 + cb^{-1}])/\theta$$
$$J_6 = -J_2$$
$$J_7 = (g/[1 + cb^{-1}])/\theta$$
$$\theta = a + cb^{-1}/(1 + cb^{-1})$$

Equation (A5-2) can be written more compactly as

$$p_t = J_0 Ep_t + J_1 Ep_{t+1} + N_t \qquad (A5\text{-}3)$$

where

$$N_t = J_2(\phi m_t - y_{n,t}) + J_3 y_{c,t-1} + J_7 + w_t$$

and

$$w_t = J_4 u_{1t} + J_5 u_{2t} + J_6 u_{3t}$$

is a random variable normally distributed with zero mean.

Taking expectations in (A5-3) conditional on the information available as of the end of period $t - 1$ the following expressions are obtained:

$$Ep_t = J_0 Ep_t + J Ep_{t+1} + EN_t \qquad (A5\text{-}4)$$

and

$$Ep_t = (J_1/[1 - J_0]) Ep_{t+1} + (1/[1 - J_0])EN_t \qquad (A5\text{-}5)$$

this last expression can be generalized to

$$Ep_{t+j} = (J_1/[1 - J_0]) Ep_{t+j+1} + (1/[1 - J_0]) EN_{t+j} \qquad (A5\text{-}6)$$

Repeatedly substituting (A5-6) in (A5-5), we obtain,

$$Ep_t = (1/[1 - J_0]) \sum_{j=0}^{\infty} (J/[1 - J_0])^j EN_{t+j} \qquad (A5\text{-}7)$$
$$+ (J_1/[1 - J_0])^{n+1} Ep_{t+n+1}$$

Now notice that $0 < J_1/(1 - J_0) = 1/1 - b^{-1}) < 1$, then it is assumed that $\lim_{n \approx \infty} (J_1/[1 - J_0])^{n+1} \approx 0$. Then the limit of (A5-7) for n approaching infinity gives the following equation

$$Ep_t = (1/[1 - J_0]) \sum_{j=0}^{\infty} (J_1/[1 - J_0])^j /EN_{t+j} \qquad (A5\text{-}8)$$

or, for period $t + 1$

$$Ep_{t+1} = (1/[1 - J_0]) \sum_{j=0}^{\infty} (J_1/[1 - J_0])^j EN_{t+j+1} \qquad (A5\text{-}9)$$

From Equations (A5-8) and (A5-9) we notice that we should obtain some workable relationship for EN_{t+j} in order to get an expression representing the formation of expected prices. We know from (A5-3) that

$$N_{t+j} = J_2 (\phi m_{t+j} - y_{n,t+j}) + J_3 y_{c,t+j-1} + J_7 + w_{t+j} \qquad (A5\text{-}10)$$

In order to apply the expectation operator above we need an assumption about the stochastic process followed by $y_{c,t}$. For simplicity I will assume that $y_{c,t}$ follows an autoregressive process

$$y_{c,t} = \alpha y_{c,t-1} + e_t$$

where e_t is an independently distributed random term with zero mean. This assumption is not restrictive; any other process in the class of ARIMA processes can be assumed without loss of generality. It can be proved that the nature of the process for $y_{c,t}$ will be reflected in the autoregressive-moving average terms for $y_{c,t}$ in the transfer function for p_t (see Appendix B for the derivation of the transfer function).

Applying the expectation operator in (A5–10) we obtain

$$EN_{t+j} = J_2 (E\phi m_{t+j} - y_{n,t+j}) + J_3 \alpha^j y_{c,t-1} + J_7 \tag{A5-11}$$

Substituting (A5–11) in (A5–8)–(A5–9), and considering that $J_2/(1 - J_0) = 1/(1 - b)$ and that $J_1/(1 - J_0) = 1/1 - b^{-1})$ we have

$$Ep_t = (1/[1 - b]) \sum_{j=0}^{\infty} (1/[1 - b^{-1}])^j (E\phi m_{t+j} - y_{n,t+j}) \tag{A5-12}$$

$$+ J_3/(1 - J_0) \sum_{j=0}^{\infty} (\alpha/[1 - b^{-1}])^j y_{c,t-1} + c_0$$

or

$$Ep_{t+1} = (1/[1 - b]) \sum_{j=0}^{\infty} (1/[1 - b^{-1}])^{j+1} (E\phi m_{t+j+1} \tag{A5-13}$$

$$- y_{n,t+j+1}) + (J_3/[1 - J_0]) \sum_{j=0}^{\infty} (\alpha/[1 - b^{-1}])^{j+1} y_{c,t-1} + c_0$$

where

$$c_0 = (g/c[b^{-1} - 1]) \sum_{j=0}^{\infty} (1/[1 - b^{-1}])^j$$

It should be noticed that in Equations (A5-12) and (A5-13) the term $(\alpha/[1 - b^{-1}])$ is less than one so the coefficient of $y_{c,t-1}$ converges to a finite number.

Equations (A5-12) and (A5-13) correspond to Equations (5-6) and (5-7) of Section 2.

Appendix 5-B | Derivation of Transfer Functions for Prices

The hypothesis of rational expectations in our model implies that the expected p_t is computed as if the public attempted to obtain an optimal unbiased forecast of p_t using Equation (5-6). Combining (5--14) and (5-6) we can write:

$$p_t = (1/[1-b]) \sum_{j=0}^{\infty} (1/[1-b^{-1}])^j (E\phi m_{t+j} - y_{n,t+j}) \qquad \text{(B5-1)}$$

$$+ [J_3/(1-J_0)] \sum_{j=0}^{\infty} (\alpha/[1-b^{-1}])^j y_{c,t-1} + c_0 + u_{4t}$$

In (B5-1) we have a term in $E\phi m_{t+j}$. Developing this term for $j = 0,1,\ldots$ taking expectations and recalling that

$$\phi = \phi_0 + \phi_1 L + \phi_2 L^2 + \ldots,$$

we have

$$E\phi m_{t+j} = E\phi_0 m_t + \phi_1 m_{t-1} + \phi_2 m_{t-2} + \ldots \qquad j = 0$$

$$E\phi m_{t+j} = E\phi_0 m_{t+1} + E\phi_1 m_t + \phi_2 m_{t-1} + \ldots \qquad j = 1$$

$$E\phi m_{t+j} = E\phi_0 m_{t+2} + E\phi_1 m_{t+1} + E\phi_2 m_{t-1} + \ldots \qquad\qquad j = 2$$

Recall that the E operator is conditional on the information in period $t - 1$, so $Em_{t-1} = m_{t-1}$, and so on, for periods before period $t - 1$. Now provided that we use the process (5-12) to obtain Em_{t+j}, $j = 1$, 2, . . . , we notice that the forecasts of m_t are obtained through linear combinations of m_{t-1}, m_{t-2}, m_{t-3}, ... These linear combinations should be combined with the other terms in m_{t-1}, m_{t-2}, m_{t-3}, · · · that appear because of the lagged response of prices to changes in m_t, and with $y_{n,t+j}$, $j = 1,2,$ . . . and $y_{c,t-1}$ to forecast p_t. Then we can rearrange the terms in m_{t-1}, m_{t-2}, m_{t-3}, . . . , and rewrite (B5-1) as

$$p_t = v(L)Lm_t - (1/[1 - b])\sum_{j=0}^{\infty} (1/[1 - b^{-1}])^j y_{n,t+j}$$

$$+ (J_3/[1 - J_0]) \sum_{j=0}^{\infty} (\alpha/[1 - b^{-1}])^j y_{c,t-1} + c_0 + u_{4t}$$

The first difference form of this equation is:

$$Dp_t = v(L)LDm_t + h_0 Dy_{c,t-1} + c + u_{5t} \qquad\qquad (\text{B5-3})$$

where c accounts for the term in $y_{n,t+j}$ after differencing (recall that $y_{n,t}$ is a trend and differencing it yields the trend) and h_0 represents the coefficient of $y_{c,t-1}$.

Equation (B5-3) is reproduced in the text as equation (5-14-a), which in turn is parsimoniously (in terms of the number of parameters) represented by the transfer function (5-15).

6

ROBERT J.
BARRO

Money and Output in Mexico, Colombia, and Brazil*

This chapter investigates the effects of changes in the quantity of money on economic activity in Mexico, Colombia, and Brazil. On a theoretical level, the impact of monetary shocks on economic activity has been analyzed in modern theories of the Phillips curve by Friedman (1968), Phelps (1970), Lucas (1973), and Barro (1976). In these models cyclical movements in output are generated by shifts in prices relative to expected values of prices, where these expectations refer either to future periods or to alternative markets. Increases in wages or prices above their expected or normal values lead to increases in factor supplies and to corresponding increases in employment and output.

Monetary shocks can increase output in this type of framework because these shocks may not immediately and fully be recognized as nominal in origin. A fully perceived nominal disturbance to aggregate demand—that is, "anticipated money growth"—will raise actual and expected prices by equal amounts. Since this type of disturbance does not produce a gap between actual and expected prices, it does not stimulate factor supplies, and it therefore has no impact on output. On the other hand, the aggregate demand shift implied by

*This paper was prepared under a contract from the United Nations Development Programme and ILPES. I am grateful for research assistance from Nasser Saidi. Jim Hanson provided some useful comments.

177

"unanticipated money growth" will appear to market participants as partly a change in relative prices—that is, as partly a real shock to excess demand for particular products or services. Expected prices—either over time or across markets—will lag behind actual prices when this underlying demand shift is not fully perceived as an aggregate, purely nominal disturbance. In this circumstance factor supplies will respond positively to the (incorrectly) perceived improvement in relative prices, and there will be a cyclical boom in output. Negative values of unanticipated money growth imply a corresponding contractionary effect on economic activity.

A key element in the theory is the extent to which money movements are anticipated or unanticipated. Hence, the completion of the theoretical model requires an approach to expectation formation. Individual expectations will depend in part on the information available at the current date. Notably, the confusion between nominal and real shocks that is central to modern theories of the Phillips curve requires some lag in the transmission of information about the values of nominal shocks. Given incomplete knowledge of the absolute price level, money stock, and so on, it is natural (because of the lack of a serious alternative) to assume rational formation of expectations. That is, individuals are assumed to forecast prices, and so on, in an optimal manner subject to their limited information. Accordingly, the present study identifies anticipated money growth as the value that is predictable for the future (one year ahead) based on experiences with money and other variables that influence the money supply process. The implicit one-year lag in information transmittal is an empirical construct that worked well in my previous investigations of the U.S. economy (Barro, 1977). As in that study, an important test of the underlying theory is whether money growth influences economic activity only when it differs from the anticipated value of money growth.

For the United States I was able to isolate three types of predictable influences on money—first, a positive response of money to a rise in government spending above its "normal" level (as measured by a distributed lag of past values of government spending); second, a countercyclical response of money to the level of economic activity; and third, a positive correlation with previous growth rates of money. For the three Latin American cases that I consider in this chapter I have been unable to find a systematic relation between money growth and the first two types of variables. However, in the Mexican and Colombian cases there are some effects on money growth of a measure of the departure of prices from purchasing power parity and of the behavior of money growth in the United States. In addition, these two cases show a time pattern of negative serial correlation in money growth rates. For the Brazilian case the only money predictor that I have isolated is based on a positive correlation with the previous year's money growth rate.

The estimated money growth relations for the three cases are used to form time series for anticipated money growth. The differences between actual and anticipated growth are then measures of unanticipated money growth—the monetary variable that is supposed to influence real variables like output and employment.

In the Mexican case I have found some important effects of money on output as well as effects that involve the level of output in the United States, the value of Mexican prices relative to purchasing power parity, and an index of the terms of trade. Since the model performed well in its (ex ante) prediction for 1974, there should be some interest in its predictions for 1975 and beyond. These (ex ante) forecasts indicated a period of substantial output contraction for 1975-1976. One notable implication of the results is that a devaluation of about 25 percent, which would restore approximate purchasing power parity (and which turned out, ex post, to be the actual order of magnitude for the first devaluation made in late 1976), would be a substantial stimulant to Mexican output for 1976.

A less cheerful aspect of the Mexican results is that they do not provide supporting evidence for the underlying hypothesis that only the unanticipated portion of money growth affects output—that is, the actual and unexpected money growth variables had about the same explanatory power for output. In this respect the results for Mexico contrast sharply with those found elsewhere for the United States.

For Colombia I have been unable to find any link from money (unanticipated or otherwise) to output, whereas in the Brazilian case there is only a weak indication of a contemporaneous link from unanticipated money growth to output. Hence, these two experiences look very different from both Mexico and the United States.

1. MEXICO

1.1 Behavior of Money Growth
The money growth equation for Mexico involves three types of variables: first, the past history of money growth (up to three annual lags); second, the behavior of money growth in the United States; and third, a lagged index of the departure of prices from purchasing power parity. This index is measured by the Mexican exchange rate times the ratio of U.S. prices (the implicit price deflator for gross

national product) to Mexican prices (the implicit price deflator for gross domestic product).

Because the Mexico/U.S. exchange rate was fixed from 1955 to the end of the sample period at 12.5 pesos per U.S. dollar, the expectation over this period is that a change in U.S. money growth would lead—through actual or anticipated movements in the balance of payments—to a corresponding change in Mexican money growth. Since the money growth equation is used to generate a forecast, $\hat{DM}_t$, for date t based on information available in the previous year, it is desirable to measure U.S. monetary behavior from the standpoint of date $t - 1$ information. From my previous study (Barro, 1977, Table 3), I have available the forecasted values of U.S. money growth for date t, $\hat{DM}_{US_t}$, based on date $t - 1$ information.[1] These values are reproduced in Table 6-1, column 7. The expectation is that in the "long run," under a fixed exchange rate regime and with the appropriate other variables held fixed, a one percentage point increase in $\hat{DM}_{US}$ would lead to a one percentage point increase in the Mexican money growth rate.

During the 1948 to 1955 period in Mexico there were devaluations in 1948, 1949, 1950, 1954, and 1955. The impact of $\hat{DM}_{US}$ on Mexican DM over this period is less apparent, although the effect would still be positive to the extent that Mexico was attempting to maintain a fixed exchange rate during this period.

The index of departure from purchasing power parity (PP) is measured by the exchange rate (constant since 1955) times the ratio of U.S. to Mexican prices (Table 6-1, column 9). (The variable has been normalized so that its average value over 1948 to 1974 is equal to zero.) The price measures used in this calculation were GNP and GDP deflators, respectively, although "traded goods" price indices (perhaps proxied by wholesale prices) are typically used to construct this type of index. Particularly because of the prominence of "invisible" trade between the United States and Mexico, it seemed that the concept of traded goods should be broadened to encompass the entire spectrum of economic transactions. It is also implicit in the calculation that the underlying price ratio that corresponds to purchasing power parity remained constant over the sample period.

A high (lagged) value of the PP index signifies that the Mexican currency is undervalued, which implies upward pressure on the Mexican money stock. In the present context there is assumed to be symmetric downward pressure on Mexican money when the PP index is low. Again, the impact of the PP variable on Mexican DM is clearer during the fixed rate period since 1955 than in the earlier period.

Table 6-1. Mexico Independent Variables and Predictions of Monetary and Real Growth

	(1) DM	(2) D̂M	(3) DMR	(4) ỹ	(5) ŷ̂	(6) ỹ − ŷ̂	(7) D̂M_US	(8) ỹ_US	(9) PP	(10) TT	(11) X̃
1948	0.056	0.033	0.023	0.047			0.014	-0.003	-0.17	100.7	-0.18
9	0.108	0.119	-0.011	0.038			0.005	-0.039	0.13	85.5	0.08
1950	0.202	0.165	0.037	0.061			0.005	0.015	0.12	100.0	0.16
1	0.258	0.158	0.100	0.066			0.038	0.053	0.00	98.5	0.13
2	0.040	0.075	-0.035	0.040			0.046	0.046	-0.05	103.4	0.06
3	0.073	0.017	0.056	-0.023			0.047	0.052	-0.03	86.3	-0.08
4	0.101	0.081	0.020	0.011	0.026	-0.015	0.023	0.001	0.17	93.7	0.16
1955	0.192	0.180	0.012	0.028	0.020	0.007	0.026	0.036	0.15	92.0	0.29
6	0.116	0.154	-0.038	0.026	0.030	-0.004	0.029	0.017	0.12	91.4	0.25
7	0.088	0.082	0.006	0.031	0.018	0.013	0.020	-0.006	0.09	82.6	0.03
8	0.065	0.091	-0.026	0.018	0.004	0.014	0.021	-0.055	0.06	83.9	-0.06
9	0.117	0.131	-0.014	-0.019	-0.008	-0.011	0.032	-0.031	0.04	82.5	-0.10
1960	0.113	0.151	-0.039	-0.013	-0.028	0.015	0.039	-0.044	0.04	68.2	-0.13
1	0.062	0.107	-0.045	-0.037	-0.027	-0.010	0.022	-0.062	-0.01	68.3	-0.15
2	0.077	0.109	-0.032	-0.056	-0.055	-0.001	0.039	-0.036	-0.03	64.4	-0.09
3	0.134	0.122	0.012	-0.042	-0.024	-0.018	0.034	-0.035	-0.01	65.1	-0.08
4	0.181	0.134	0.047	0.005	-0.010	0.016	0.037	-0.019	-0.02	62.0	-0.06
1965	0.087	0.104	-0.017	-0.002	0.000	-0.002	0.040	0.005	-0.02	62.4	-0.04
6	0.080	0.073	0.007	-0.001	0.009	-0.010	0.044	0.030	-0.04	61.3	-0.04
7	0.085	0.105	-0.020	-0.007	-0.004	-0.003	0.045	0.018	-0.06	60.8	-0.18
8	0.103	0.122	-0.019	0.005	-0.004	0.005	0.042	0.026	-0.06	65.6	-0.15
9	0.095	0.135	-0.040	-0.001	-0.006	0.005	0.052	0.015	-0.05	64.3	-0.08
1970	0.100	0.120	-0.021	0.000	0.002	-0.003	0.047	-0.027	-0.04	70.1	-0.19
1	0.073	0.119	-0.046	-0.033	-0.033	0.000	0.044	-0.032	-0.03	66.9	-0.19
2	0.144	0.144	-0.001	-0.030	-0.032	0.002	0.061	-0.009	-0.06	69.4	-0.06
3	0.223	0.141	0.082	-0.023	-0.023	0.000	0.057	0.010	-0.12	69.4	0.14
4	0.189	0.092	0.097	[-0.032]	-0.028	[-0.004]	0.058	-0.049	-0.24		0.19
1975		-0.006		[-0.057]	-0.059	[0.002]	0.052	-0.086			
6		0.000			-0.093		0.053				

181

Table 6-1 continued

Notes to Table 6-1

$DM_t \equiv \log(M_t) - \log(M_{t-1})$, where M is an annual average of the money stock in billions of pesos (obtained from Manuel Cavazos of the Mexican Central Bank). $\hat{DM}_t$ is an estimated value from Equation (6-1). $DMR_t \equiv DM_t - \hat{DM}_t$.

$\tilde{y}_t \equiv \log(y_t) - 3.161 - 0.0666 \cdot t$ is output relative to trend, where y is real gross domestic product (billions of pesos at 1960 prices) from *International Financial Statistics* (henceforth, *IFS*). $\hat{y}$ is an estimated value from Equation (6-4).

$\hat{DM}_{USt}$ is the predicted value of DM in the United States for year t from Barro, 1977. $\tilde{y}_{US}$ is U.S. output (real gross national product in 1958 prices) relative to trend from Barro, 1977.

PP, the index of departure from purchasing power parity, is the peso–U.S. dollar exchange rate (*IFS*) times a ratio of the GNP deflator in the United States (1958 base) to the GDP deflator in Mexico (*IFS*, 1960 base). This variable is measured relative to its mean value over the 1948 to 1974 period.

TT is an index of the terms of trade (ratio of U.S. dollar export prices to U.S. dollar import prices with a base of 1950 = 100) from Griffiths, 1972, Appendix Table 4, p. 141, up to 1967, and from *Economic Survey of Latin America*, 1975, Table 17, p. 42, since 1967.

$\tilde{X}_t \equiv \log(X_t) - 1.510 - 0.0314 \cdot t$ is real exports relative to trend, where X is the peso value of exports (*IFS*) divided by the Mexican GDP deflator.

Finally, the money growth equation also includes some lagged values of the dependent variable. Since lagged values of four or more years were unimportant to the fit, the equation incorporates the first three annual lags: DM_{t-1}, DM_{t-2}, and DM_{t-3}.

For the United States I found some important money supply influences from the level of government spending relative to "normal" and from a lagged value of the level of economic activity (a countercyclical response of money). I have been unable to detect any influences of this sort for Mexico. However, the failure of the government expenditure variable may reflect a data problem—the available series involve ambiguities over which types of expenditure to classify as governmental and they also contain changes in coverage over time.

The principal money growth equation that I have used for the Mexican case, estimated from annual observations over 1948 to 1973, is (with standard errors of the coefficients in parentheses)[2]

$$DM_t = 0.14 - 0.03\ DM_{t-1} - 0.49\ DM_{t-2} - 0.24\ DM_{t-3} \qquad (6\text{-}1)$$
$$\ (0.03)\ (0.21)\qquad\quad (0.19)\qquad\quad (0.17)$$
$$+ 1.41\ \hat{DM}_{US_t} + 0.29\ PP_{t-1},$$
$$\ (0.73)\qquad\quad (0.11)$$
$$R^2 = 0.49,\ DW = 1.59,\ \hat{\sigma} = 0.044$$

where DM_t ($\equiv \log\ [M_t] - \log\ [M_{t-1}]$) is an annual average of the money growth rate with M_t measured as an annual average of the money stock in year t. (The mean value of Mexican money growth over 1948 to 1973 is 0.114 per year with a standard deviation of 0.055.) The fit of the equation is indicated by the $\hat{\sigma}$ value of 0.044, which signifies an estimation error of about ± four and one-half percentage points per year in the money growth rate. By contrast, the value of $\hat{\sigma}$ for the United States over the 1946 to 1973 period is about 0.015, but the mean value of U.S. money growth for that period is only about 3.4 percent per year.

The estimated form of Equation (6-1) implies a tendency for Mexican money growth to return to a normal or long-run rate, $\overline{DM}$, that is determined by the values of the constant term and $\hat{DM}_{US}$ (assuming a long-run average value of PP equal to zero). The relation for this long-run money growth rate can be determined by setting $DM_t = DM_{t-1} = DM_{t-2} = DM_{t-3} = \overline{DM}$ and $PP = 0$ in Equation (6-1) to obtain

$$\overline{DM} = 0.080 + 0.80\ \hat{DM}_{US} \qquad (6\text{-}2)$$

For example, at $\hat{DM}_{US} = 0.03$ per year (a typical value for the 1948 to 1963 period), the value of $\overline{DM}$ is 10 percent per year. At $\hat{DM}_{US} = 0.058$ per year—the value applicable to 1974—the result is $\overline{DM} = 13$ percent per year. Since the estimated coefficient on $\hat{DM}_{US}$ in Equation (6-2) does not differ significantly from one, there is support for the theoretical idea that the long-run effect of $\hat{DM}_{US}$ on Mexican DM is one to one.

The negative coefficients on DM_{t-2} and DM_{t-3} in Equation (6-1) (only the DM_{t-2} coefficient is individually significantly different from zero) indicate that years in which DM is above $\overline{DM}$ tend to be followed by years in which DM is below $\overline{DM}$. This type of behavior would be expected from the pressure generated by a fixed exchange rate system to restore a particular relationship between the *levels* of Mexican and U.S. money stocks.

The estimated coefficient of 0.29 on PP_{t-1} (*t*-value relative to zero of 2.6) reflects the hypothesized positive response of DM to an undervaluation of the currency. An undervaluation by 10 percent produces an increase of about three percentage points in next year's money growth rate.

It is of interest to compare the results from the overall 1948 to 1973 sample with those obtained solely from the fixed-rate period from 1955 to 1973. Over the latter period the estimated equation is

$$DM_t = 0.091 + 0.10\ DM_{t-1} - 0.52\ DM_{t-2} - 0.26\ DM_{t-3} \qquad (6-3)$$
$$(0.075)\ (0.28) \qquad\quad (0.27) \qquad\quad (0.27)$$
$$+ 2.23\ DM_{US_t} + 0.32\ PP_{t-1}$$
$$(1.26) \qquad\quad (0.21)$$
$$R^2 = 0.50,\ DW = 1.64,\ \hat{\sigma} = 0.037$$

Statistically, one cannot reject the hypothesis that the observations from 1948 to 1954 are generated by the same model (with the same coefficients) that generated the data over the fixed rate period from 1955 to 1973 (though there is little power in this test). Comparison of Equation (6-3) with Equation (6-1) indicates that the main difference is a higher coefficient for $\hat{DM}_{US}$ over the fixed rate period. Although this behavior is consistent with the view that Mexican money was more closely related to U.S. money during the fixed-rate period than during the devaluation period from 1948 to 1954, the high standard errors make it impossible to obtain any firm statistical evidence on this point. In any event there is no empirical evidence that would invalidate the use of Equation (6-1) over the entire period from 1948 to 1973.

The estimated values from Equation (6-1), denoted by $\hat{DM}_t$, are contained in Table 6-1, column 2. The residuals from this equation, $DMR_t \equiv DM_t - \hat{DM}_t$ (Table 6-1, column 3), are used in the subsequent analysis of Mexican output.

1.2 Behavior of Output

The equation for output (real gross domestic product in 1960 prices) includes the following variables:

1. Current and lagged values of money growth rates. One type of equation involves only the unanticipated part of money growth, $DMR \equiv DM - \hat{DM}$, as calculated from Equation (6-1). Another type includes the actual money growth rate, DM. In both cases values of money growth up to two annual lags turn out to be important.
2. A direct effect from the level of economic activity in the United States. This influence is measured by the (lagged) value of U.S. output (real gross national product in 1958 prices) relative to a time trend, $\tilde{y}_{US}$, as tabulated in Table 6-1, column 8. This variable captures effects of U.S. demand for Mexican output—particularly for invisible exports[3]—and would also proxy for influences that work through international capital markets. Empirically, only a one-year lag of $\tilde{y}_{US}$ was significant in the Mexican output equation. The inclusion of U.S. (unanticipated) money growth rates (with $\tilde{y}_{US}$ excluded) has effects that are similar though somewhat inferior in terms of fit, to those produced by $\tilde{y}_{US}$. This result suggests that the $\tilde{y}_{US}$ variable proxies partly for the effects of U.S. money on Mexican output and partly for the effects of other U.S. output influences on Mexican output.
3. The magnitude of departure from purchasing power parity, $|PP_t|$. The idea here is that these departures in either direction constitute relative price distortions[4] that would tend to depress output. The algebraic value of the departure, PP_t, turns out to be insignificant in the output equation.
4. A measure of Mexican terms of trade, (TT_t), (Table 6-1, column 10), which should have a positive effect on output.
5. A time trend variable, intended to hold constant the growth of "normal" output.

The estimated equation that includes DMR values from Equation (6-1) is, when estimated from annual observations for 1954 to 1973,

$$\log(y_t) = 2.70 + 0.23\ DMR_t + 0.18\ DMR_{t-1} \tag{6-4}$$
$$\ (0.22)\ (0.12)\qquad\quad (0.13)$$
$$+\ 0.28\ DMR_{t-2} + 0.57\ \tilde{y}_{US_{t-1}} - 0.39\ |PP_t|$$
$$\ (0.11)\qquad\quad\ (0.14)\qquad\ (0.16)$$
$$+\ 0.11\ \log(TT_t) + 0.0666 \cdot t,$$
$$\ (0.05)\qquad\quad\ (0.0009)$$
$$R^2 = 0.9993,\ DW = 2.68,\ \hat{o} = 0.0125,\ SSE^5 = 0.00188$$

A test for joint influence of the three *DMR* variables in Equation (6-4) yields the statistic, $F^3_{12} = 4.1$, which is significant at the 5 percent level (critical value = 3.5). Hence, there is evidence of a positive effect of Mexican money growth on Mexican output. The magnitude of the effect of an increase in unexpected money growth (*DMR*) by one percentage point per year that is sustained over a three-year period is determined by the sum of the three lag coefficients to be an increase in output by 0.7 percent.

There is also a strong positive effect on Mexican output from the lagged value of U.S. output relative to trend, $\tilde{y}_{US}$ (coefficient of 0.57, standard error = 0.14). Since my previous results for the United States (Barro, 1977, section III) indicated an effect of U.S. *DMR* values on $\tilde{y}_{US}$ with a sum of coefficients equal to 3.0, the implication is that U.S. unanticipated money growth affects Mexican output with a total coefficient of 1.7 (3.0 × 0.57). Hence, the effect of all unanticipated money growth (both U.S. and Mexican) on Mexican output involves a total coefficient of 2.4—that is, a sustained increase by one percentage point per year in all *DMR* values would raise output by 2.4 percent. This total value is similar to the magnitude found for the United States, although in the Mexican case only about 30 percent of the total effect of money on output is attributable to Mexican money.

Equation (6-4) indicates an important effect of the purchasing power parity variable in the hypothesized negative direction. The coefficient implies that a 10 percent deviation of Mexican prices from par value (or, equivalently, a 10 percent "error" in the exchange rate) reduces output by 4 percent. The symmetry of the |*PP*| variable should be stressed—that is, the undervaluation of the peso by 12 percent in 1956 is estimated to have the same depressing effect on output as the overvauation by 12 percent in 1973. The effect of this variable is especially important for predictions (see below), since the 1974 value of the *PP* variable (Table 6-1, column 9) shows an overvaluation by 24 percent.

If the algebraic value of *PP* is added to Equation (6-4), it enters insignificantly although the |*PP*| variable remains significant. Hence, there is support for the view that the relative price distortions associated with exchange rate "errors" reduce output, but no support for the Keynesian notion that the aggregate demand influence of these errors—which would distinguish under- from overvaluation—is the important consideration.

Finally, Equation (6-4) also indicates a positive, though relatively minor, effect of the terms-of-trade variable on output. A 10 percent improvement in the terms of trade is estimated to produce a 1 percent increase in output.[6]

The fit of Equation (6-4) can be indicated by the value of $\hat{\sigma}$, which shows an estimation error for output of about ± 1-1/4 percent.[7] Values of output relative to the time trend are shown in Table 6-1, column 4, together with estimated values (column 5) and residuals (column 6) from Equation (6-4).

Equation (6-4), which was estimated through 1973, can be used to generate predictions for 1974 and beyond. For 1974 the predicted value of output relative to the time trend[8] is -0.028 (about three percentage points below trend)—as compared with an actual value of -0.032 relative to trend. Hence, the estimated equation performs well for 1974. The role of the |*PP*| variable in this prediction should be stressed: the value *PP* = -0.24 for 1974 implies a negative contribution of -9 percent to output (which more than offsets the direct positive contribution of the *DMR* variables[9] from 1973 and 1974). In other words the model implies on this count that a 25 percent devaluation—which would restore approximate purchasing power parity—would raise Mexican output by about 9 percent over what would have otherwise occurred.

For 1975 and 1976—assuming no change in the purchasing power parity and terms-of-trade variables and using *DMR* values of zero for 1975 and 1976—the predicted output values relative to trend are -0.059 and -0.093, respectively. Hence, the model predicts a period of strong contraction in the absence of a devaluation or major changes in money or the terms of trade. (The actual value of output relative to trend in 1975 turned out to be -0.057, which is remarkably close to the [ex ante] prediction. The results for 1976 probably were affected by the sharp devaluation of the peso and perhaps also by a shift in underlying purchasing power parity associated with an increased risk of political confiscation.)

An output equation based on actual money growth rates, *DM*, rather than on the unanticipated portion, *DMR*, is the following:

$$\log (y_t) = 2.84 + 0.29 \, DM_t + 0.5 \, DM_{t-1} + 0.20 \, DM_{t-2} \tag{6-5}$$
$$\quad\;\;(0.19)\ (0.10)\qquad\;(0.09)\qquad\quad(0.09)$$
$$+ 0.74 \, \tilde{y}_{US_{t-1}} - 0.35 \, |PP_t| + 0.08 \log (TT_t)$$
$$(0.15)\qquad\quad (0.16)\qquad\;\;(0.04)$$
$$+ 0.653 \cdot t,$$
$$(0.0008)$$
$$R^2 = 0.9994, \, DW = 2.26, \, \hat{o} = 0.0120, \, SSE = 0.00173$$

The fit of this output equation, based on the *DMs*, is slightly better than that based on the *DMRs*—although the main observation is that Equations (6-4) and (6-5) appear similar.[10] Hence, unlike the situation in the United States (Barro, 1977, section II.E), the calculation and use of the *DMR* variables is not important for the analysis of the link between money and output. However, it can be noted that Equation (6-5), which is based on *DM* values, does not perform as well for predicting 1974 output relative to trend—this predicted value is -0.019, as compared with the actual value of -0.032 and the predicted value from Equation (6-4) of -0.028.[11] It can also be observed that Equation (6-5) is similar to Equation (6-4) in respect to the effects of the $|PP|$ and *TT* variables although Equation (6-5) does suggest a somewhat larger impact of the $\tilde{y}_{US}$ variable.

The slightly poorer performance of the *DMR* output equation can be attributed to the presence of the PP_{t-1} variable in the *DM* relation, Equation (6-1).[12] If this variable is omitted, the *DM* equation over 1948 to 1973 becomes

$$DM_t = 0.129 + 0.20 \, DM_{t-1} - 0.30 \, DM_{t-2} - 0.32 \, DM_{t-3} \tag{6-6}$$
$$\quad\;\;(0.034)\ (0.21)\qquad\;\;(0.20)\qquad\quad(0.19)$$
$$+ 0.76 \, \hat{DM}_{US_t},$$
$$(0.78)$$
$$R^2 = 0.32, \, DW = 1.92, \, \hat{o} = 0.049$$

With the *DMR* values based on the residuals from Equation (6-6), the output equation over 1954 to 1973 becomes

$$\log (y_t) = 2.85 + 0.27 \, DMR_t + 0.23 \, DMR_{t-1} \tag{6-7}$$
$$\quad\;\;(0.16)\ (0.09)\qquad\quad(0.09)$$
$$+ 0.28 \, DMR_{t-2} + 0.67 \, \tilde{y}_{US_{t-1}} - 0.37 \, |PP_t|$$
$$(0.07)\qquad\quad (0.11)\qquad\;\;\;(0.13)$$
$$+ 0.08 \log (TT_t) + 0.0670 \cdot t,$$
$$(0.04)\qquad\qquad (0.0007)$$
$$R^2 = 0.9996, \, DW = 2.83, \, \hat{o} = 0.0098, \, SSE = 0.00115$$

Although this equation fits better than Equation (6-5), which was based on *DM* values, this result does not provide much support to the idea that only the unanticipated part of money expansion, *DMR*, is relevant for output. If a readily available and apparently important money predictor such as a measure of departure from purchasing power parity is not incorporated into anticipated money growth, then there is not much content in the distinction between anticipated and unanticipated money movements. My conjecture is that a better procedure would be to look for some additional money growth predictors that were omitted from Equation (6-1), rather than deleting the PP_{t-1} variable. One candidate for an omitted variable is domestic holdings of international reserves relative to a target level of these reserves, which could reflect a policy response of the monetary authority. I have not yet explored this possibility.

2. COLOMBIA

2.1 Behavior of Money Growth

For the Colombian case the period since 1957 has been characterized by a flexible exchange rate at least in the sense that the rate has depreciated more or less continuously with the increases in the domestic price level relative to that in the United States. For the entire 1951 to 1972 period, an estimated money growth equation is[13]

$$DM_t = 0.307 - 0.65\,DM_{t-1} - 0.38\,DM_{t-2} + 0.62\,\hat{DM}_{US_t} \qquad (6\text{-}8)$$
$$(0.078)\ (0.22) \qquad\quad (0.22) \qquad\quad (1.00)$$
$$+ 0.64\,PP_{t-1},$$
$$(0.037)$$
$$R^2 = 0.39,\ DW = 2.18,\ \hat{\sigma} = 0.043$$

This equation is similar to that estimated for Mexico in Equation (6-1) although in the Colombian case the negative lag pattern appears sooner and the $\hat{DM}_{US}$ and PP_{t-1} (Table 6-2, column 7) variables are quantitatively less important. The value of $\hat{\sigma}$ for Colombia is almost identical to that for Mexico.

Equation (6-8) implies that money growth in Colombia tends to return to a normal rate of about 16 percent per year ($\hat{DM}_{US}$ does not significantly affect this normal rate). The mean value of *DM* over 1949 to 1973 was, in fact, 0.160 per year with a standard deviation of 0.057. Values of *DM*, together with estimated values and residuals from Equation (6-8), are indicated in Table 6-2, columns 1 to 3.

A money growth equation for Colombia that is limited to the flexible exchange rate period from 1957 to 1972 is

Table 6-2. Colombia: Independent Variables and Predictions of Monetary and Real Growth

	(1) DM	(2) $\hat{DM}$	(3) DMR	(4) $\tilde{y}$	(5) $\hat{y}$	(6) $\tilde{y}-\hat{y}$	(7) PP	(8) P_x	(9) $\tilde{X}$
1949	0.202						-0.75	121	0.13
1950	0.042			0.020			-0.86	158	0.30
1	0.153	0.172	-0.019	0.023			-0.62	162	0.36
2	0.155	0.181	-0.026	0.061			-0.58	153	0.34
3	0.161	0.140	0.020	0.074	0.076	-0.002	-0.61	160	0.53
4	0.172	0.119	0.053	0.089	0.084	0.005	-0.70	205	0.59
1955	0.037	0.106	-0.068	0.073	0.068	0.005	-0.68	164	0.42
6	0.220	0.192	0.028	0.056	0.057	-0.001	-0.73	182	0.40
7	0.126	0.115	0.011	0.028	0.026	0.002	-0.31	156	0.18
8	0.118	0.135	0.054	-0.001	0.007	-0.008	0.01	129	0.02
9	0.108	0.157	-0.050	0.015	0.014	0.001	-0.02	110	0.01
1960	0.095	0.189	-0.094	-0.002	0.000	0.002	-0.09	108	-0.05
1	0.218	0.213	0.005	-0.001	-0.014	0.013	-0.15	103	-0.16
2	0.192	0.144	0.048	-0.002	-0.006	0.004	-0.12	97	-0.13
3	0.109	0.113	-0.004	-0.021	-0.023	0.003	-0.10	93	-0.21
4	0.186	0.180	0.006	-0.015	0.002	-0.017	-0.24	108	-0.05
1965	0.146	0.154	-0.008	-0.034	-0.010	-0.023	-0.15	105	-0.10
6	0.131	0.159	-0.028	-0.033	-0.033	-0.001	-0.01	98	-0.22
7	0.208	0.193	0.014	-0.048	-0.046	-0.003	0.02	85	-0.27
8	0.135	0.149	-0.014	-0.041	-0.040	-0.001	0.08	84	-0.24
9	0.199	0.178	0.021	-0.031	-0.039	0.008	0.11	83	-0.23
1970	0.202	0.163	0.039	-0.020	-0.021	0.001	0.13	96	-0.13
1	0.112	0.136	-0.023	-0.020	-0.032	0.012	0.14	82	-0.26
2	0.240	0.205	0.035	-0.005	-0.005	0.000	0.15	89	-0.09
3	0.268	0.149	0.119	0.011	0.026	-0.015	0.08	110	0.14
4		0.084							
1975		0.188							

190

$DM_t \equiv \log(M_t) - \log(M_{t-1})$, where M is annual money stock end of year—see the text-billions of pesos, from *IFS*. $\dot{DM}$ is an estimated value from Equation (6-8). $DMR \equiv DM - \dot{DM}$.

$\tilde{\hat{y}}_t \equiv \log(y_t) - 2.445 - 0.0533 \cdot t$, where y is real gross domestic product in 1958 prices (*IFS*). $\tilde{\hat{y}}$ is an estimated value from Equation (6-12).

PP is the official exchange rate (*IFS*) times a ratio of the U.S. GNP deflator (1958 base) to the Colombian GDP deflator (*IFS*, 1958 base). The variable is measured relative to its mean value from 1958 to 1973.

P_x is a U.S. dollar index of export prices (*IFS*, 1963 base) divided by the United States GNP deflator.
$\tilde{\hat{X}}_t \equiv \log(X_t) - 5.829 - 0.0256 \cdot t$, where X is exports in millions of U.S. dollars (*IFS*) divided by the United States GNP deflator.

191

$$DM_t = 0.264 - 0.64\ DM_{t-1} - 0.38\ DM_{t-2} + 1.56\ \hat{DM}_{US_t} \qquad (6\text{-}9)$$
$$(0.092)\ (0.29) \qquad\quad (0.27) \qquad\qquad (1.47)$$
$$+ 0.006\ PP_{t-1},$$
$$(0.081)$$
$$R^2 = 0.37,\ DW = 2.07,\ \hat{\sigma} = 0.043$$

Not surprisingly, the effect of PP_{t-1}—which appeared weakly in Equation (6-8)—vanishes when the fixed exchange rate years are removed from the sample. (Although the $\hat{DM}_{US}$ coefficient is actually higher in Equation (6-9) than in equation (6-8), the large standard errors suggest that nothing can be inferred from this result.) The negative coefficients on DM_{t-1} and DM_{t-2} remain even when the sample is limited to the flexible exchange rate period.

2.2 Behavior of Output

For the purpose of explaining output in Colombia, it turns out to make little difference whether Equation (6-8) or Equation (6-9) is used to generate unanticipated money growth, *DMR*. In fact, I have been unable to isolate any monetary effects on output for Colombia. A typical result for output, using Equation (6-8) to calculate *DMR*s and including $\tilde{y}_{US}$ and a measure of real exports relative to a time trend, $\tilde{X}$, (Table 6-2, column 9) as explanatory variables, is (for the 1953 to 1972 period)[14]

$$\log(y_t) = 2.44 - 0.06\ DMR_t - 0.03\ DMR_{t-1} \qquad (6\text{-}10)$$
$$(0.01)\ (0.07) \qquad\quad (0.06)$$
$$- 0.09\ DMR_{t-2} - 0.20\ \tilde{y}_{US_{t-1}} + 0.17\ \tilde{X}_t$$
$$(0.07) \qquad\qquad (0.08) \qquad\quad (0.02)$$
$$+ 0.0538 \cdot t,$$
$$(0.0008)$$
$$R^2 = 0.9992,\ DW = 1.51,\ \hat{\sigma} = 0.0095,\ SSE = 0.00118$$

The *DMR* variables are insignificant with the wrong sign and the $\tilde{y}_{US}$ variable also appears with the "wrong" sign. My expectation in regard to the U.S. output variable was that its effect on Colombian output would be smaller than in the case of Mexico because of the weaker direct connection between the Colombian and U.S. economies. However, the negative sign on $\tilde{y}_{US}$ is difficult to understand. Otherwise, the only variable other than the time trend that shows up strongly is the export variable—the exogeneity of which can be questioned.[15]

The output results are similar when *DM* is substituted for *DMR*:

$$\log (y_t) = 2.45 - 0.01\, DM_t + 0.01\, DM_{t-1} + 0.01\, DM_{t-2} \qquad (6\text{-}11)$$
$$ (0.02)\ (0.06) \qquad (0.07) \qquad\quad (0.06)$$

$$ - 0.20\, \tilde{y}_{US_{t-1}} + 0.16\, \tilde{X}_t + 0.533 \cdot t,$$
$$ (0.08) \qquad\ (0.02) \qquad (0.0009)$$

$$R^2 = 0.9991,\ DW = 1.26,\ \hat{\sigma} = 0.0102,\ SSE = 0.00135$$

When the monetary variables are excluded entirely the output equation becomes

$$\log (y_t) = 2.45 - 0.20\, \tilde{y}_{US_{t-1}} + 0.16\, \tilde{X}_t + 0.0533 \cdot t, \qquad (6\text{-}12)$$
$$ (0.01)\ (0.08) \qquad\ (0.02) \qquad (0.0007)$$

$$R^2 = 0.9991,\ DW = 1.32,\ \hat{\sigma} = 0.0092,\ SSE = 0.00136$$

Actual and estimated values of output relative to the time trend from Equation (6-12) are shown in Table 6-2, columns 4 to 6. Although this equation has a low value of $\hat{\sigma}$—indicating an estimation error for output of only about ± 1 percent—the sign of $\tilde{y}_{US}$ is peculiar and most of the "explanatory" power comes from the export variable.

I have very little useful to say about the Colombian output results. One possibility is that there really is no Phillips curve type of relation between money and output in Colombia. Another, and more probable, explanation is that such a relation exists, but I have not been able to isolate it. One excuse is the quality of the data. Anecdotal evidence supports the view that measured real output in Colombia has little to do with actual output.[16] Of course, it is always convenient to blame the data when empirical results are unsuccessful. Another possibility is that the monetary data refer to the end of each year rather than, as perhaps would be more appropriate, annual averages. Hanson (1976) reports somewhat better results when annual average figures are used.

3. BRAZIL

The Brazilian case is much more extreme than the previous two in terms of the mean and variability of money growth (the average value of DM over 1949 to 1973 is 0.295 per year with a standard deviation of 0.129). Furthermore, except for 1949 to 1951, the period is characterized by continuous and rapid devaluation of the exchange rate. Not surprisingly, the U.S. money behavior and an index of departure from purchasing power parity have no impact on Brazilian money growth. There is also no indication of the negative serial correlation in the DM series that characterized the money processes for Mexico and Colombia.[17] In fact, the only useful predictor for Brazilian money growth that I have been able to isolate is the previous year's money growth rate. The equation for the 1950 to 1972 period is

$$DM_t = 0.08 + 0.76 \, DM_{t-1}, \qquad \qquad (6\text{-}13)$$
$$(0.14) \; (0.13)$$
$$R^2 = 0.62, DW = 1.79, \hat{\sigma} = 0.081$$

Equation (6-13) implies a normal money growth rate of about 32 percent per year. The positive coefficient of DM_{t-1} implies that values of DM above the norm tend to be followed by additional above-normal years—that is, there is no tendency for the money stock to return to a normal level relative to trend. The value of $\hat{\sigma}$ for Brazil is about twice as high as those estimated for Mexico and Colombia. Values of DM for Brazil, together with estimated values and residuals from Equation (6-13), are indicated in Table 6-3, columns 1 to 3. Since the money growth equation contains only a lagged value of DM, there is little distinction that can be made between using DMR and DM values to explain fluctuations in output.[18]

An output equation for Brazil is the following:[19]

$$\log (y_t) = 5.22 + 0.11 \, DMR_t - 1.16 \, \tilde{y}_{US_{t-1}} + 0.18 \, \tilde{X}_t \qquad (6\text{-}14)$$
$$(0.03) \; (0.09) \qquad \quad (0.23) \qquad \quad (0.04)$$
$$+ \, 0.0569 \cdot t,$$
$$(0.0013)$$
$$R^2 = 0.996, DW = 1.44, \hat{\sigma} = 0.027, SSE = 0.0119$$

where $\tilde{X}$ is a measure of real exports relative to a time trend (Table 6-3, column 9). Additional lagged values of DMR are insignificant. The results are similar to those found for Colombia in Equation (6-10) in terms of the unexpected negative sign on the $\tilde{y}_{US}$ coefficient (though the Brazilian coefficient is much higher in magnitude) and the highly significant positive effect of $\tilde{X}$. However, DMR_t does appear weakly with a positive sign for Brazil,[20] and the value of $\hat{\sigma}$ is almost three times as high as that for Colombia. In a sense the higher value of $\hat{\sigma}$ for Brazil makes it more plausible that the measured real output series is reflecting some real phenomena unlike the situation in the Colombian case.

The appearance of a weak reduction between money and output in Brazil is not surprising, given the large prediction variance for DM

Table 6-3. Brazil: Independent Variables and Predictions of Monetary and Real Growth

	(1) DM	(2) $\hat{DM}$	(3) DMR	(4) $\tilde{y}$	(5) $\hat{y}$	(6) $\tilde{y}-\hat{y}$	(7) PP	(8) P_x	(9) X
1949	0.120			0.044			−0.14	122	0.74
1950	0.216	0.170	0.047	0.038			−0.13	172	0.88
1	0.143	0.242	−0.099	0.027			−0.27	193	1.01
2	0.210	0.187	0.023	0.043	0.027	0.016	−0.19	186	0.71
3	0.169	0.237	−0.068	−0.001	0.027	−0.028	−0.11	178	0.72
4	0.195	0.206	−0.012	0.027	0.015	0.012	0.06	205	0.65
1955	0.175	0.226	−0.051	0.025	0.039	−0.015	0.08	161	0.48
6	0.187	0.211	−0.024	−0.012	−0.008	−0.004	−0.10	149	0.42
7	0.211	0.220	−0.009	−0.003	−0.014	0.011	−0.14	147	0.26
8	0.289	0.238	0.050	0.003	−0.016	0.019	0.26	132	0.05
9	0.240	0.297	−0.057	−0.011	0.020	−0.031	−0.09	110	0.00
1960	0.327	0.260	0.067	0.013	−0.011	0.023	−0.12	106	−0.09
1	0.367	0.326	0.041	0.042	0.006	0.037	0.00	110	−0.07
2	0.433	0.356	0.077	0.025	−0.009	0.034	0.12	95	−0.29
3	0.458	0.406	0.052	−0.028	−0.029	0.001	−0.02	93	−0.22
4	0.622	0.426	0.196	−0.068	−0.026	−0.041	−0.03	110	−0.28
1965	0.606	0.550	0.057	−0.109	−0.055	−0.054	0.15	109	−0.26
6	0.337	0.538	−0.201	−0.128	−0.112	−0.016	0.07	102	−0.26
7	0.278	0.334	−0.056	−0.149	−0.152	0.002	0.02	98	−0.41
8	0.353	0.289	0.064	−0.137	−0.120	−0.017	0.03	96	−0.39
9	0.280	0.346	−0.066	−0.106	−0.127	0.021	0.12	94	−0.29
1970	0.249	0.290	−0.041	−0.085	−0.103	0.018	0.10	91	−0.24
1	0.266	0.267	−0.011	−0.046	−0.059	0.013	0.13	93	−0.30
2	0.292	0.280	0.012	−0.015	−0.013	−0.002	0.12	99	−0.07
3	0.358	0.299	0.059					131	0.25
4		0.349							
1975									

Table 6-3 continued

$DM_t \equiv \log(M_t) - \log(M_{t-1})$, where M is an annual average of the money stock in millions of Cruzeiros (*IFS*). DM is an estimated value from Equation (6-13). $DMR \equiv DM - DM$.

$\tilde{y}_t \equiv \log(y_t) - 5.257 - 0.0684 \cdot t$, where y is real gross domestic product in billions of 1949 Cruzeiros (*IFS*). $\hat{\tilde{y}}$ is an estimated value from Equation (6-14).

PP is the exchange rate (*IFS* trade conversion factor since 1959; earlier figures correspond to estimates of free market rates, as reported in *IFS*) times a ratio of the U.S. GNP deflator (1958 base) to the Brazilian GDP deflator (*IFS*, 1949 base).

P_x is an index of export prices in U.S. dollars (1963 base) divided by the U.S. GNP deflator.

$\tilde{X}_t \equiv \log(X_t) - 6.352 - 0.0654 \cdot t$, where X is exports in billions of U.S. dollars divided by the U.S. GNP deflator.

in Equation (6-13). The analysis of Lucas (1973) and Barro (1976) predicts that the magnitude of a given DMR stimulus on output would diminish as the predictability of DM increases. In this respect, and aside from the unexplained negative coefficient on $\tilde{y}_{US}$ in Equation (6-14), the Brazilian results are less difficult to understand than those for Colombia.

4. CONCLUSIONS

Although the model has some explanatory power for the money supply processes in Mexico and Colombia, and some predictive value for output in Mexico, the main results of this study are disappointing. The output results for Colombia and Brazil are not very useful and those for Mexico do not support the U.S. finding that the switch from actual to unanticipated money growth is an important empirical concept. In the Mexican case the results may improve by an extension of the money growth equation to include variables like the reserve stock and the behavior of government spending (if useful data on the latter can be constructed). It may also be useful to extend the sample period for output back to 1948. For Colombia and Brazil I am less hopeful that the output results can be improved.

It may be more useful to extend the empirical analysis by considering some additional cases instead of refining the results for the present three. Venezuela would be an interesting case because of the relative stability in its money and price behavior. At the other extreme it would be of interest to see whether the Argentine and Chilean cases appear similar to the Brazilian experience. If a money/output relation were satisfactorily isolated for a number of countries, it would be possible to carry out a test of the Lucas proposition that the magnitude of the Phillips curve slope diminishes when money and prices become less predictable. There was some indication of this effect from a comparison of Mexico and Brazil, but the present results are surely inconclusive in this respect.

NOTES

1. Alternatively, the underlying determinants of $\hat{DM}_{US_t}$—which were lagged money growth in the United States, a measure of the government budget in the United States, and a lagged value of the United States unemployment rate—could have been entered into the Mexican money growth equation. This alternative entails an unnecessary loss of degrees of freedom.

2. DW is the Durbin-Watson statistic for serial correlation of the residuals (which is not very useful for an equation that contains a lagged dependent variable) and $\hat{\sigma}$ is the estimated standard error of the disturbance term.

3. The $\tilde{y}_{US}$ variable does not have a significant effect on real Mexican exports as measured—see note 6 below. Furthermore, real exports do not have a significant effect on Mexican output, given the other variables that are included in Equation (6–4) below.

4. Some of these distortions could be the result of government policies associated with maintaining the "wrong" exchange rate.

5. *SSE* is the error sums of squares for the equation.

6. As indicated in note 3 above, a real export variable does not enter significantly when added to Equation (6–4). An equation to "explain" real exports is the following:

$$\log (X_t) = -0.82 + 1.6\,DMR_t + 1.1\,DMR_{t-1} + 1.2\,DMR_{t-2}$$
$$\quad\;\;(2.31)\;(0.7)\qquad\;\;(0.9)\qquad\qquad(0.7)$$
$$+ 0.06\,\tilde{y}_{US_{t-1}} - 0.04\,PP_t + 0.54\log (TT_t)$$
$$\;\;(0.79)\qquad\quad\;(1.05)\qquad(0.30)$$
$$+ 0.031\,t,$$
$$\;\;(0.010)$$
$$R^2 = 0.83,\, DW = 1.69,\, \hat{\sigma} = 0.086$$

The three *DMR* variables together appear significantly in this equation (F_{12}^3 = 4.2, 5 percent critical value = 3.5) although the mechanism by which *DMR* affects exports positively is not apparent.

7. The Durbin-Watson statistic indicates absence of positive serial correlation in the residuals. A lagged value of y is not significant when added to Equation (6–4).

8. Assuming that the terms-of-trade index remains at its 1973 value, but using the 1974 value of *DMR* = 0.097.

9. In a complete model that included price determination, there would also be an effect of cumulated monetary experience on the *PP* variable (assuming the maintenance of a fixed exchange rate).

10. An output equation with the *DMR*s and *DM*s included simultaneously yields an *SSE* of 0.00085. Based on this value, a test that (all three of) the *DMR*s are irrelevant to the determination of output, given the inclusion of the *DM*s, yields the statistic, $F_9^3 = 3.1$, which is less than the 5 percent critical value of 3.9. Similarly, a test that the *DM*s are irrelevant, given the inclusion of the *DMR*s, yields $F_9^3 = 3.6$. The implication is that either the *DMR*s or the *DM*s (but not both sets of variables) can be deleted without significantly affecting the fit.

11. Equation (6–5) also predicts a substantially larger contraction of output relative to trend for 1975 and 1976 if the very low values of $\hat{DM}$ (Table 6–1, column 2) for 1975 and 1976 are used in these calculations. The predicted value for output relative to trend in 1975 is –0.107 and that for 1976 is –0.150. (Recall that the actual value for 1975 is –0.057.)

12. In my earlier study of Mexico (Barro, 1975), the PP_{t-1} variable was not included in the *DM* equation.

13. A measure of government expenditures relative to "normal," the type of

variable that was important in my study for the United States, did not enter significantly when added to Equation (6-8).

14. The $|PP_t|$ variable is insignificant when added to Equation (6-10), as is an export price index, P_x (Table 6-2, column 8). A lagged value of y added to Equation (6-10) has a coefficient of 0.25, standard error = 0.15.

15. When the $\widetilde{X}$ variable is omitted the output equation becomes

$$\log (y_t) = \underset{(0.12)}{2.54} + \underset{(0.16)}{0.11 \, DMR_t} + \underset{(0.14)}{0.09 \, DMR_{t-1}} + \underset{(0.15)}{0.12 \, DMR_{t-2}}$$

$$+ \underset{(0.18)}{0.15 \, \widetilde{y}_{US_{t-1}}} + \underset{(0.0010)}{0.0476 \cdot t}$$

$$R^2 = 0.9947, DW = 0.72, \hat{\sigma} = 0.024, SSE = 0.00809$$

Although the DMR and $\widetilde{y}_{US}$ variables have the "right" signs here, they are all insignificantly different from zero ($F_{14}^3 = 0.3$ for the three DMR variables simultaneously). Furthermore, the deletion of the $\widetilde{X}$ variable has a dramatically negative effect on the fit. An equation to "explain" exports is

$$\log (X_t) = \underset{(1.39)}{2.68} + \underset{(0.67)}{0.25 \, DMR_t} + \underset{(0.56)}{0.43 \, DMR_{t-1}} + \underset{(0.62)}{0.41 \, DMR_{t-2}}$$

$$+ \underset{(0.76)}{0.44 \, \widetilde{y}_{US_{t-1}}} - \underset{(0.18)}{0.25 \, PP_t} + \underset{(0.27)}{0.66 \, P_{x_t}} + \underset{(0.0096)}{0.0256 \cdot t,}$$

$$R^2 = 0.82, DW = 0.93, \hat{\sigma} = 0.089$$

where P_x is an export price index (Table 6-2, column 8). The three DMR variables are jointly insignificant in this equation ($F_{12}^3 = 0.3$).

16. One such anecdote is that output predictions and ex post measurements of output are made by the same persons. It turns out that only small modifications are ever required in the measurement stage. This story may also explain the low value of $\hat{\sigma}$ in Equation (6-12).

17. In this respect the monetary behavior in Brazil is similar to that found earlier for the United States. See Barro (1977, section II.B).

18. A form with DMR values would be equivalent to a (restricted) form with DM values that contained one additional lag term. However, the pattern of money growth rate coefficients in the output equation would be affected by the switch from DMR to DM.

19. An export price index, P_x (Table 6-3, column 8), and an index of departure from purchasing power parity, $|PP_t|$ (Table 6-3, column 7), are insignificant, given the inclusion of the export variable, $\widetilde{X}$. An estimated equation for exports is

$$\log (X_t) = \underset{(1.5)}{0.2} - \underset{(0.35)}{0.61 \, DMR_t} + \underset{(0.36)}{0.01 \, DMR_{t-1}} - \underset{(1.26)}{1.52 \, \widetilde{y}_{US_{t-1}}}$$

$$- \underset{(0.27)}{0.37 \, PP_t} + \underset{(0.29)}{1.52 \, P_{x_t}} + \underset{(0.011)}{0.070 \cdot t,}$$

$$R^2 = 0.80, DW = 1.34, \hat{\sigma} = 0.110$$

20. With DM_t substituted for DMR_t the output results are

$$\log(y_t) = 5.26 - 0.08\,DM_t - 1.32\,\tilde{y}_{US_{t-1}} + 0.14\,\tilde{X}_t$$
$$(0.04)\ (0.07)\quad\ (0.22)\qquad\quad (0.04)$$
$$+\,0.0577\cdot t,$$
$$(0.0013)$$
$$R^2 = 0.996,\ DW = 1.91,\ \hat{\sigma} = 0.027,\ SSE = 0.0120$$

REFERENCES

Barro, R.J. "Money and Output in Mexico." Paper presented at the ILPES/ National Bureau of Economic Research Conference on Short-Term Macroeconomic Policy in Latin America, October 1975.

——. "Rational Expectations and the Role of Monetary Policy." *Journal of Monetary Economics* 2:1 (January 1976), 1-32.

——. "Unanticipated Money Growth and Unemployment in the United States." *American Economic Review* 67:1 (March 1977), 101-15.

E.C.L.A *Economic Survey of Latin America.* New York: United Nations, 1975.

Friedman, M. "The Role of Monetary Policy." *American Economic Review* 58:1 (March 1968), 1-17.

Griffiths, B. *Mexican Monetary Policy and Economic Development.* New York: Praeger, 1972.

Hanson, J.A. "The Short-Run Relation Between Growth and Inflation in Latin America: A Quasi-rational Expectations Approach." Brown University Working Paper No. 76-3, October 1976.

Lucas, R.E. "Some International Evidence on Output-Inflation Tradeoffs." *American Economic Review* 63:3 (June 1973), 326-34.

Phelps, E.S. "The New Microeconomic in Employment and Inflation Theory," in Phelps, ed. *Microeconomic Foundations of Employment and Inflation Theory.* New York: W.W. Norton Publishing Co., 1970.

7

MARIO S. BRODERSOHN*

The Phillips Curve and the Conflict Between Full Employment and Price Stability in the Argentine Economy, 1964-1974

The publication in 1958 of Phillips's work (1958), which brought out empirically an inverse and nonlinear functional relation between the percentage changes in money wages and the rate of unemployment, made a considerable impact on the academic world. Contradicting as it did the widespread, simple version of the Keynesian model, Phillips's empirical relation suggested that the rate of inflation might increase considerably before the goal of completely full employment was reached. That is, if we accept the hypothesis that the Phillips curve is stable through time, this means that in order to achieve a lower level of unemployment (or a lower rate of inflation) we must pay the price of increasing the rate of inflation (or raising the level of unemployment) before we have reached the point of completely full employment.

Phillips's original version was limited to the development of an empirical model without probing deeply into its theoretical basis. It can therefore be considered that the theoretical advances in Phillips' empirical relation began with the work of Lipsey (1960) and, subsequently acquired a new dimension with Phelps's (1967) and Friedman's (1968) inclusion of the concept of the expected rate of

*The views expressed in this document are entirely the responsibility of the author and do not necessarily reflect those of the Instituto Torcuato Di Tella.

inflation. A different line of reasoning which also gave rise to important contributions in the analysis of the Phillips curve is connected with Hines's work (1964) on the role of the trade unions as an explanatory factor in wage demands.

The purpose of the present work is to evaluate empirically, for the period 1964–1974, whether these various formulations of the Phillips curve are applicable to the Argentine economy.

Quite apart from the numerous theoretical concepts underlying the Phillips curve, however, the very question of the measurement of each variable may be decided in various ways, yielding results that are incompatible with each other. For example, in some studies the price of labor is expressed in terms of the basic wage established by labor contracts while in others use is made of the wages effectively paid, which may yield different results.[1] Similarly, we must state whether we are limiting ourselves to the manufacturing sector or are speaking in terms of the whole economy.

A further example is the price variable. What should we use: the cost-of-living index, wholesale prices, or the implicit price index? It is usually assumed that the first mentioned has a more direct impact on wage demands. Still a further difficulty concerns the employment variable. It is highly possible that in order to provide a better explanation of the state of the labor market one would have to include concealed unemployment and the rates of participation of certain groups that make up the reserve labor force, for example, women and youths of working age. Alternatively, in some versions of the Phillips curve attempts have been made to measure the degree of tension in the labor market by breaking down the demand for and the supply of labor as follows:

$$\frac{D-S}{S} = \frac{(E+PV)-(E+M)}{E+M} = \frac{PV}{E+M} - \frac{M}{E+M}$$

where

$$E = \text{the number of persons employed}$$
$$PV = \text{the number of vacancies}$$
$$M = \text{the number of unemployed}$$

One limitation of this approach is that very few countries have statistical data on vacancies.

These difficulties also extend to other variables used in the Phillips model. In these circumstances, it can be seen that the conflicting results of different empirical studies may stem from the different concepts used for defining the same variables as well as from the different variables that are included in the Phillips functional relation.[2]

While it is certainly interesting to investigate the implications of different variable definitions, in our analysis of the Argentine case the definition and selection of variables, as well as the period of time selected, were dictated purely by the availability of statistical data. Lack of more than one possible series generally prevented us from observing in what way the conclusions might vary as a function of other variable definitions.

The statistical series for unemployment, wages, and prices are those published by the National Institute of Statistics and Censuses (INDEC). Although the series for unemployment begins in July 1963, the period actually considered extends from the first half of 1964 to the first half of 1974 because of the statistical constructions employed. For unemployment, these data cover the percentage of unemployed in the Greater Buenos Aires area compared with the economically active population. Unemployment surveys are carried out three times a year: in April, July, and October.[3] In our case, we took the April figure as an indicator for the first half of the year and that of October for the second half; the month of July was not considered. For wages, we took the contractually negotiated basic wage for unskilled industrial workers in the Federal Capital as a reflection of hourly money wages. The simple average of the six months in each semester was used. For prices, the cost-of-living index for the Federal Capital (corrected to remove seasonal variations) was used, again taking the average over each semester.

Finally, in all our estimates we used simple least squares. For the models including the price variable this procedure may be vulnerable to simultaneous equations bias since, if we take a complete system of price equations, prices should be included as an independent variable in the wage equation while the money wage should be included as an independent variable in a price equation.

1 Simple Version of the Phillips Curve

The basic equations of the model are:

$$\Delta W_t = a + b\ U_t^{-1} + c\ U_t^{-2}$$

where

$$\Delta W_t = \frac{W_t - W_{t-2}}{W_{t-2}}$$

W_t being the average of the basic wages fixed by agreement for un-skilled industrial workers.[4]

and

$$U_t = \frac{1}{2} [\hat{U}_t + \hat{U}_{t-1}]$$

$\hat{U}_t$ being the percentage of unemployed industrial workers in Greater Buenos Aires relative to the economically active population in the months of April or October of each year.

The results obtained are as follows (the t-statistic is in brackets):

$$\Delta W_t = 76.90 - 243.18 \, U_t^{-1} \qquad\qquad R^2 = 0.16 \quad (7\text{-}1)$$
$$ (3.25) \quad\; (1.92) \qquad\qquad\qquad R_A^2 = 0.12$$
$$\qquad\qquad\qquad\qquad\qquad\qquad\qquad F(19) = 3.67$$

$$\Delta W_t = 55.62 - 674.46 \, U_t^{-2} \qquad\qquad R^2 = 0.18 \quad (7\text{-}2)$$
$$ (4.57) \quad\; (2.03) \qquad\qquad\qquad R_A^2 = 0.13$$
$$\qquad\qquad\qquad\qquad\qquad\qquad\qquad F(19) = 4.11$$

$$\Delta W_t = -32.88 + 957.59 \, U_t^{-1} - 3194.48 \, U_t^{-2} \qquad R^2 = 0.21 \quad (7\text{-}3)$$
$$ (0.29) \quad\;\; (0.78) \qquad\qquad (0.99) \qquad\qquad R_A^2 = 0.12$$
$$\qquad\qquad\qquad\qquad\qquad\qquad\qquad\qquad F(18) = 2.32$$
$$\qquad\qquad\qquad\qquad\qquad\qquad\qquad\qquad FG(1) = 83.76$$
$$\qquad\qquad\qquad\qquad\qquad\qquad\qquad\qquad DW = 0.56$$

These results completely rule out the applicability of a simple ver-sion of the Phillips curve. In expression (7-3) the rate of unemploy-ment only explains 21 percent of the rate of change in money wages, and the coefficients are not significantly different from zero. More-over, the Equations (7-1) and (7-2) show a sign opposite to the one expected for the coefficient of unemployment: the rate of growth of money wages *increases* as the level of unemployment rises.

For Equation (7-3)—$\Delta W_t = f \, (U_t^{-1}, \, U_t^{-2})$—the function attains a maximum value when the level of unemployment is 6.7 percent. It is only above that level that the percentage variation of wages begins to fall as the rate of unemployment increases. This result would sug-gest that the usual Phillips functional relation only occurs beyond an unemployment rate of 6.7 percent. However, apart from the weak statistical basis of this conclusion, levels of unemployment above 6.7

percent were only observed in two cases—April 1964 (7.5 percent) and April 1972 (7.4 percent)—so the relation shown lies outside the usual performance of the economy and therefore is not really relevant.

In brief, and always bearing in mind the fact that these econometric estimates are far from satisfactory, the results achieved thus far suggest that the state of the labor market, insofar as this is adequately reflected by the rate of unemployment, fails to explain the variation in money wages during the period 1964–1974.

In fact, the last functional relation (7–3) suggests that only a substantial increase in the level of unemployment to more than 6.7 percent, that is, much greater than that normally experienced in the Argentine economy, could slow the rate of increase of money wages (to rates below 40 percent per year). Of course, in such a case we would have to make a joint evaluation of the social cost of such high levels of unemployment and the possible social benefits of curbing the rate of inflation. If it is assumed that a sharp increase in unemployment is the "only" way of controlling inflation, it is obvious that the price of freeing ourselves of the latter may be socially unacceptable. If the Phillips option were put this way, there is little doubt that society would rather live with inflation than maintain an unacceptable level of unemployment.

But if the state of the labor market as measured by unemployment rates alone does not explain the behavior of money wages, then what are the variables that influence wage changes? Let us begin by making an empirical analysis of the role of the expectation of inflation in order to evaluate to what extent the rate of increase in wages is influenced by anticipated future rates of inflation. The latter will in turn call for a study of the manner in which expectations of future inflation are formed. Since expectations are not directly observable a generally accepted indirect approach is to assume that the formation of such expectations is influenced by the past history of the real rate of inflation. In other words, two models must be prepared simultaneously—one on the manner in which expectations of inflation are formed and the other on the way in which the behavior of wages is affected by changes in such expectations.

2 The Phillips Curve, Taking Account of Expected Inflation

The basic equation of the model for determining money wages on the basis of expectations of inflation is as follows:

$$\Delta W_t = a_0 + a_1\, U_t^{-1} + a_2\, \Delta P_t^e \tag{7-4}$$

where

ΔW_t = the average percentage change in W over the period t (negotiated basic wages of unskilled industrial workers);

U_t^{-1} = average level of unemployment over the period t (Greater Buenos Aires);

ΔP_t^e = the expected future rate of inflation projected over the period t

   In view of the lack of direct observations of price expectations, the variable ΔP_t^e must be replaced, using a model of expectations that employs observable statistical data. Some expectation models are as follows.

2.1 STATIC EXPECTATIONS

In this model the expectations for the period t are (approximately) the same as the actual rate of inflation in that period:

$$\Delta P_t^e = \Delta P_t \qquad (7-5)$$

Substituting (7-5) in (7-4), we have:

$$\Delta W_t = a_0 + a_1 U_t^{-1} + a_2 \Delta P_t$$

   In our calculations, P_t, the cost-of-living index in the Federal Capital was estimated on the basis of two assumed trends. The first defines $\Delta P_t = \Delta P_t^{(1)}$ as follows:

$$\Delta P_t^{(1)} = \frac{1}{2}\left[\frac{P_t - P_{t-2}}{P_{t-2}} + \frac{P_{t-1} - P_{t-3}}{P_{t-3}}\right]$$

   In this case it is assumed that what is important is the moving average of the percentage changes in prices that occur up to the time of the increases in money wages (or wage negotiations); in other words, during the year preceding the wage increase. The limitation of this model is that it may reflect either the formation of future expectations or the process of adjusting wages to past inflation.
   The second assumption on the percentage variation in prices is the following:

$$\Delta P_t^{(2)} = \frac{1}{2}\left[\frac{P_t - P_{t-1}}{P_{t-1}} + \frac{P_{t-1} - P_{t-2}}{P_{t-2}}\right]$$

In this case, $\Delta P_t^{(2)}$ is defined on the basis of the percentage variation in the prices prevailing at the same time as the increases in wages.[5] Again this model does not clearly show a causal relationship between prices and wages. The introduction of a one-semester time lag would be necessary to show that the percentage variation in the cost of living precedes that in money wages.[6]

For the period under study, we developed three equations (with $\Delta P_t^{(1)}$, $\Delta P_t^{(2)}$, and $\Delta P_{t-1}^{(2)}$). The best results were provided by the following expressions with the t-statistic given in brackets:

$$W_t = 0.26 + 10.39\ U_t^{-1} + 1.00\ \Delta P_t^{(1)}$$
$$\quad (0.02)\quad (0.13)\qquad\ (6.87)$$

$$R^2 = 0.77 \quad (7\text{--}6)$$
$$R_A^2 = 0.74$$
$$FG(1) = 4.72^7$$
$$F(18) = 29.9$$
$$DW = 1.126$$

$$\Delta W_t = -12.67 + 73.34\ U_t^{-1} + 1.14\ \Delta P_t^{(2)}$$
$$\qquad (0.66)\quad (0.85)\qquad\ (6.52)$$

$$R^2 = 0.75 \quad (7\text{--}7)$$
$$R_A^2 = 0.72$$
$$F(18) = 27.13$$
$$FG(1) = 7.08$$
$$DW = 1.04$$

From the results provided by the three estimations (including $\Delta P_{t-1}^{(2)}$ which is not shown), the following conclusions can be drawn: (a) the variable U_t is of no significance and in one case its coefficient is perverse, as in our simple Phillips model;[8] (b) the expectations variable is significant in all the examples, showing that the percentage change in the cost-of-living index does play a role in determining money wages; (c) in all the examples the autocorrelation in the residual is significant at the 5 percent level, which suggests that we can improve the specification of the model by introducing additional variables; (d) in Equations (7-6) and (7-7) the coefficient of expectations of inflation is not significantly different from unity, which would permit acceptance of the Friedman-Phelps hypothesis, in the sense that it is not valid to assume that money illusion exists in the short term. At the same time the hypothesis that demand pressures, working through the proxy U_t, determine money wages is rejected since the coefficient of this variable is not significantly different from zero.

In sum, in accordance with this simple version of expectations of inflation we may draw the conclusion that the percentage change in *real* wages affects the behavior of the labor market (since the coefficient of ΔP_t^e is not different from unity), although we cannot accept the hypothesis that the change in wages is a stable function of the rate of unemployment since it appears that the behavior of money wages is independent of the level of unemployment disequilibrium in the labor market.

So far, we have developed an oversimplified version of the formation of expectations because we assume that the knowledge of the recent or actual rate of inflation is sufficient for their formulation. However, it seems more reasonable to assume that the past history of inflation rates plays a role in the formation of expectations. Moreover, as discussed earlier, the use of $\Delta P_t^e = \Delta P_t^{(1)}$ does not enable us to determine whether this reflects a static model of expectations or a mechanism for adjusting money wages to past inflation. Therefore, other models of expectations are needed for a more detailed analysis. In general, the following models of the formation of expectations[9] have been used.

2.2 EXTRAPOLATIVE MODEL

$$\Delta P_t^e = \Delta P_t + \theta (\Delta P_t - \Delta P_{t-1})$$

where θ is the rate of extrapolation.

This equation shows that the expected rate of inflation that exists at the moment t is equal to the rate of change in prices in the period t plus a correction factor through which account is taken of the recent trend in the rate of inflation. If $\theta > 0$ it is expected that the growth differential between the present rate of inflation and the past rate will continue in the future, while if $\theta < 0$ it is expected that the reverse will follow (regressive expectations). The special case $\theta = 0$ corresponds to the model developed earlier for $\Delta P_t^e = \Delta P_t$.

Substituting the equation for the formation of expectations in (7-4), we have

$$\Delta W_t = a_0 + a_1 U_t^{-1} + a_2 \Delta P_t + a_2 \theta (\Delta P_t - \Delta P_{t-1})$$

However, this model of the formation of expectations is unsatisfactory and suffers from the same defect as the model of static expectations because of the fact that it only takes account of current inflation and that of the preceding period; in other words, it does not take account of the information that extensive past experience may offer.

2.3 ADAPTIVE MODEL

$$\Delta P_t^e = \Delta P_{t-1}^e + \gamma(\Delta P_t - \Delta P_{t-1}^e) \quad 0 \leqslant \gamma \leqslant 1 \qquad (7\text{-}8)$$

where γ is the rate of adaptation.

As is well known Equation (7-8) can be shown to be a weighted geometric average of all past rates of inflation. The equation shows that the change in expectations $(\Delta P_t^e - \Delta P_{t-1}^e)$ is equal to a fraction γ of the error of prediction between what was expected in the preceding period and what actually occurred in that period. If γ is equal to 1, only the current rate of inflation is important—again $(\Delta P_t^e = \Delta P_t)$. If γ is close to zero the weightings $\gamma(1 - \gamma)^i$ decrease slowly, thus taking into account a long history of prices. With γ close to 1 the weightings fall rapidly and memory is short.

Equation (7-8) gives the following result:

$$\Delta P_t^e - (1 - \gamma) \, \Delta P_{t-1}^e = \gamma \, \Delta P_t \qquad (7\text{-}9)$$

Using a program prepared by the Central Bank we obtained the values of ΔP_t^e for γ from 0.1 to 1.0.[10]

For each value of γ and its corresponding ΔP_t^e we estimated the values of ΔW_t using least squares. Taking the equation in which R^2 is at its maximum $(\gamma = 0.7)$:[11]

$$\Delta W_t = -10.45 + 46.98 \, U_t^{-1} + 1.243 \, \Delta P_t^e \qquad R^2 = 0.78 \quad (7\text{-}10)$$
$$ (0.60) \quad (0.61) \qquad (7.20) \qquad\qquad R_A^2 = 0.76$$
$$F(18) = 32.65$$
$$FG(1) = 5.83$$
$$DW = 1.14$$

Thus in this adaptive expectations model the present semester and the previous one represent 91 percent of the total weightings of the past history of price changes.[12]

From the results of Equation (7-10) the following conclusions can be drawn:

(i) The coefficient of U_t is not significantly different from zero, thereby corroborating the previous results.

(ii) The test of the hypothesis that the coefficient of $\Delta P_t^e = 1$ yields a t-statistic $= 1.41$ for 18 degrees of freedom, showing that we cannot reject the hypothesis that it is equal to 1 at a significance level of 5 percent.

(iii)   As compared to Equations (7-6) and (7-7), although the R_A^2 improves slightly, we still cannot reject the hypothesis of autocorrelation, although in this case we are also unable to accept it at a significance level of 1 percent. This result again invalidates the hypothesis test for the estimated coefficients and once more suggests the need for improving the specification of the model by introducing other variables.

The unemployment variable in the Phillips curve attempts to illustrate the role of excess demand in determining money wages and can therefore be visualized as one means of showing—of course, in a very primitive and crude manner—the effects that a policy based on the control of demand has on the rate of wage inflation. Insofar as that variable reflects excess aggregate demand, the fact that the coefficient U_t is not significant points to the limitations for the Argentine economy of using this variable as a means of curbing inflation.

Furthermore, the results of Equation (7-10), although limited by the autocorrelation suggested by the Durbin-Watson statistic, do suggest that for the period 1964–1974 workers were not affected by the money illusion even though the coefficient of adaptation is greater than unity.[13]

Of course, the foregoing conclusion about the role of the expected rate of inflation in determining the rate of change in money wages must be examined with the greatest care in view of the existing theoretical limitations about the true model adopted by economic units in forming their future expectations. There is no doubt that the past history of prices is one important factor to be taken into consideration. But even if we accept this simple general rule, many unknown quantities remain. First, what is the right weighting structure that ought to accompany each of the past prices? In our case the results suggest that only the current semester and the past semester really count. It is highly possible that for the hectic period 1964–1974 with six presidents, three of whom acquired office through revolutions or coups d'etat and three through constitutional elections, so short a memory may provide an accurate picture of real economic behavior. But it is also highly probably that by taking prices alone we may be overlooking much more important sociopolitical variables. In this connection Solow (1969), in his analysis of the United States and England, suggests that these institutional factors should be considered as irregular deviations from the systematic relation based on the past history of prices. Obviously, political trends in Argentina seem to suggest that such deviations are the rule rather than the exception, which in all probability caused the economic agents to accept certain hypotheses of behavior based on past experience regarding the inter-relationship between political change and the economic model. Second, we may accept intuitively the idea that percentage variations in past prices fit the Argentine case, with its almost permanent history of fluctuating inflation, much more readily than the absolute level of prices. But it can also be argued that what really counts are the variations in the historical trend of the rate of inflation (approximately 27 percent per year in (1950–1972) in view of the fluctuations around this rate during that period. For example, in 1964–1974 the average rate of inflation was 28 percent per year, falling in 1969 to 7.6 percent, rising again in 1970–1971, racheting upward between the first half of 1972 and the first half of 1973 to 71.5 percent and then dropping sharply to 17.9 percent between the first half of 1973 and the first half of 1974.

All these observations serve to place the role of the expected rate of inflation, and in particular the model of the formation of expectations, in its proper perspective.

3 The Phillips Curve and Incomes Policy

The results based on the model of adaptive expectations, which roughly coincide with those of the less sophisticated model of static expectations, lead to the conclusion that in the short term there is no traditional tradeoff; the Argentine economy is not faced with the well-known inverse relation between variations in money wages and the level of unemployment. However, expectations regarding the future rate of inflation have a significant effect on the behavior of wages, an effect that is nearly independent of the level of unemployment in the labor market. Hence, a policy that operates on inflationary expectations such as an incomes policy, could be successful.[14] In other words, incomes policy may serve as a way of preventing the past history of prices from being a suitable means of predicting the future inflation.

This hypothesis leads us to an analysis of the role played by the different incomes policies followed in the period 1964–1974. The first problem that arises in such an analysis is to define those periods in which an incomes policy was actually in force. This is not an easy task, because, although nearly all the governments formally announced price and wage controls, in several cases they went no further than a formal declaration, particularly as regards price fixing. Throughout the period a common practice of the governments was to fix maximum prices for products making up the family consumption basket as well as to decide wage increases unilaterally.

However, the behavior of prices and wages clearly shows a lack of effective obedience to these regulations. For this reason, we must distinguish between periods of effective controls and those with mere formal declarations of controls.

In view of the confused socioeconomic situation during the years under study, we are obliged to use two criteria simultaneously for defining periods when an incomes policy was effectively applied. The first is the existence of a series of formal regulations on prices and wages. The second is the respect shown by the different social groups for these regulations, recognizing in this manner the political power of the government as an arbitrator in the income distribution struggle. The second criterion introduces a high degree of subjectivity into the analysis.

In view of the above criteria, we have selected two subperiods during which incomes policy generally is considered to have had some effect. The first subperiod is associated with Ongania-Krieger Vasena and runs from the second half of 1967 to the second half of 1969. Although the fact that the government was changed as a result of the incidents in Cordoba in May 1969 sheds some doubt on the inclusion of the second half of 1969, we feel that the regulations governing prices and wages continued to be effective. The second, and much more recent experience in the field of incomes policies, is connected with the Cámpora-Perón-Gelbard period and runs from the second half of 1973 to the first half of 1974. For the first period we used the dummy variable I_1 (1 for the Krieger Vasena period and zero for the remainder of the period) and for the second the dummy variable I_2 (1 for the Gelbard period and zero for the remainder of the period). The purpose of introducing a different dummy variable for each of these periods, instead of a single dummy variable for the whole period covered by incomes policy, was to reflect the different institutional contexts in which these incomes policies were applied.[15]

Table 7-1 shows the results using $\Delta P_t^{(2)}$ and ΔP^e (corresponding to $r = 0.7$), both including and excluding U_t^{-1}. The table shows that the inclusion of the dummy variable improves the results of Equation (7-10) by eliminating the autocorrelation (at the 5 percent level). The coefficient of determination adjusted for degrees of freedom (R_A^2) increases from 0.76 to 0.86. The price expectations variable continues to be significant and does not differ from unity. The elimination of the variable U_t generally improves the estimates.

An interesting point is raised by the different signs of the incomes policy. For the Krieger Vasena period (II: 1967 to II: 1969), as a result of the application of an incomes policy, the annual rate of growth of money wages was 11 percent lower than would have been the case without such a policy. For the Gelbard period, however,

Table 7-1. Argentine Phillips Curves

Using $\Delta P_t^{(2)}$	Coefficient of: Constant	U_t^{-1}	Expectations	I_1	I_2	R^2	R_A^2	F	FG	DW
(7-11)	7.08 (0.50)	8.66 (0.13)	0.89 (6.64)	-11.01 (2.69)	17.86 (3.11)	0.89	0.87	33.26	14.86	1.91
(7-12)	8.88 (2.30)	-	0.88 (8.02)	-10.92 (2.79)	18.16 (3.56)	0.89	0.87	47.05	4.82	1.92
(7-13)	2.71 (0.17)	25.05 (0.35)	0.99 (6.11)	-13.04 (3.06)	8.71 (1.32)	0.88	0.85	29.09	16.33	2.00
(7-14)	8.03 (1.88)	-	0.96 (7.40)	-12.76 (3.13)	9.88 (1.77)	0.88	0.86	40.85	5.29	1.99

the dummy variable is positive, thus indicating that the incomes policy was directed toward increasing money wages at an annual rate 17.86 percent higher than that achieved without that policy. Since prices were also controlled, the overall real effect of the two income policies cannot fully be estimated if only these coefficients are taken into account. Nevertheless, since there was a sharp drop in the annual rate of inflation in both periods the figures would tend to suggest that the incomes policies in question took different approaches to distribution. Whereas Krieger Vasena attempted to hold down both prices and wages by his income policy, Gelbard tried to make a lower rate of increase in prices compatible with a higher annual growth rate in wages through his anti-inflationary program. We must point out that these results are insufficient for us to express an opinion on the ultimate redistributive impact of the prices and wages policy because that would call for the formulation of a simultaneous equation model with prices and wages playing in turn the role of dependent and independent variables. Furthermore, the Krieger Vasena period, which covers five semesters, was characterized by a sharp increase in wages in the first semester and a slower increase subsequently. Therefore, its coefficient, which reflects both phases, can only show that the last stage, with a lower annual growth rate of wages, canceled out the sharp initial positive effect. In contrast, the shortness of the Gelbard period, which covers only two semesters, may be insufficient for making an accurate evaluation of the direction and long-run effects of the incomes policy.[16]

In any event, and even in the light of the foregoing observations, it is obvious that an incomes policy need not necessarily be associated with a distributive scheme involving the containment of wages. On the contrary, the central theme of any anti-inflationary scheme based on incomes policy continues to be the guidelines on income distribution proposed to the community by the government.

This distributive variable is of special relevance for a country that has functioned in an inflationary setting for a long period of time. In such a long-standing context of inflation, the different social groups have produced sufficient antibodies to prevent any anti-inflationary policy from causing real deterioration in their relative position in terms of income distribution. Thus, after a long experience of stop-go efforts to stabilize prices, the system of relative prices ceases to be regarded mainly as an instrument for assigning productive resources and becomes the central mechanism in income distribution. This stop-go approach to anti-inflationary policies tends to convince the economic groups that the short term is of prime importance in the distributive struggle and that their natural means of self-defense are based mainly on relative prices, since possible compensatory schemes based on fiscal policy, requiring a longer period in which to operate, do not usually have a lasting effect.

The high significance of the price expectations and incomes policy coefficients and the insignificant contribution of the unemployment variable suggest that wage inflation in Argentina develops in a context of continuous redistributive friction between social groups with different capacities for domination of the market. This implies that if an economic policy program is to be successful, it is not enough to explain its distributive targets. The government must also have sufficient political backing to impose new rules of the game for income distribution. For those countries with a long tradition of respect for the electoral aspect of politics, the questioning of the government's power of arbitration does not imply any breaking of the institutional norms that govern the running of a country. However, in Argentina an important means of questioning government decisions has been the weakening of the very bases of the representative institutions, thereby creating conditions that lead to the subsequent overthrow of governments. For this reason, governments anxious for their survival shirk their role of distributive arbitration and become mere instruments for rubber-stamping the demands of those groups with the political capacity to impose their own distributive guidelines. This sets in motion a circular process of attempted redistribution that feeds inflation and culminates in the questioning of the very role of the government. This mechanism, which was clearly described by Guillermo O'Donnell, lies outside the immediate scope of this work, and for this reason we shall not dwell on it. The point to which we do wish to draw attention is that, other things being equal, the traditional assumption of *ceteris paribus* as regards the social, political, and institutional variable eliminates from the analysis, for a period as hectic as that of 1964–1974, factors that are of major importance in the dynamics of inflation. We do not believe that a satisfactory explanation of those dynamics is possible unless the entire range of factors affecting them is covered by an interdisciplinary approach.

4 The Phillips Curve and Trade Union Pressure

The foregoing remarks are linked with the sociological explanation of the dynamics of inflation and were set out in Argentina by Javier Villanueva among others. In this view inflation is the result of the distributive struggle among social sectors with some degree of domination of the market.

In the specific matter of the Phillips curve, the analysis made so

far would be incomplete without considering the role of union aggressiveness in determining money wages. For this analysis a definition of aggressiveness in terms of variations in the percentage level of
union membership (Hines's approach) is not suitable since, as a result
of the nature of Argentine labor legislation, that percentage, which is
not only high but also stable over time, does not reflect any increase
or fall in union pressure.[17] For this reason we shall define this variable
in terms of working days lost as a result of strikes and stoppages (the
Godfrey approach). The Ministry of Labor publishes statistics on the
labor conflicts recorded in the Federal Capital, indicating the number
of cases, the workers affected, and the number of days lost. This statistical series covers both strikes (temporary interruptions in work
that last for more than one working day) and stoppages (interruptions that do not exceed a working day).[18] While the annual figures
are broken down on the basis of economic sectors and the causes of
the labor conflicts (economic improvements, wage claims, dismissal
and suspension of workers, disciplinary measures, organization and
conditions at working places), such a breakdown unfortunately is
not available on a monthly basis. Therefore, this variable is not limited to the industrial sector, as would be required to bring it in line
with the money wages concept, but covers all the productive sectors
and the whole range of economic and noneconomic causes of strikes
and stoppages.[19] The working days lost variable, which is assumed to
express the degree of union pressure, was estimated as:

$$\Delta S_t = \frac{S_t - S_{t-2}}{S_{t-2}}$$

where S_t is the total number of days lost in the semester t. The series
covers 1964–1971 since these particular statistics were not prepared
after the latter year.

   We have used ΔS_t instead of the absolute level S_t for two reasons.
The first is the likely seasonal nature of the series since the first half
of the year includes the holiday period during which there is less likelihood of labor conflicts. The variable S_t is, therefore, found by linking S_t with S_{t-2} and not with the previous semester (S_{t-1}). The
second reason is a more delicate one since it is assumed that union
aggressiveness is a function of the changes in intensity of the conflict
and not the total number of disputes that occur in the semester. A
possible justification for this assumption is that wages are usually
fixed unilaterally by the government or, if this is not the case, there
is at least stronger government pressure to keep wage increases within
its guidelines, which may not necessarily have been fixed publicly

and explicitly. In this context, a likely model of behavior would be that the unions, in order to obtain higher wages, would try to create an escalating climate of conflict so as to win a more favorable attitude from the government. This suggests that the rate of increase in money wages should move in the same direction as the increase in the rate of union aggressiveness, measured by ΔS_t.

The equation estimated for the period 1964-1971 is as follows:[20]

$$\Delta W_t = 6.920 + 1.002 \; \Delta P_t^e + 0.024 \; \Delta S_t \qquad R^2 = 0.87 \qquad (7\text{-}15)$$
$$\quad\;\; (1.38) \quad (5.12) \qquad\quad (2.05) \qquad\qquad R_A^2 = 0.83$$
$$\quad -13.329 \, I_1 \qquad\qquad\qquad\qquad\qquad F(12) = 25.86$$
$$\qquad (4.36) \qquad\qquad\qquad\qquad\qquad\qquad FG(3) = 4.90$$
$$\qquad\qquad\qquad\qquad\qquad\qquad\qquad\qquad DW = 1.85$$

We originally estimated an equation similar to (7-15) including U_t. The results show that the latter's coefficient has a sign different from that expected, that it is not significant, and that it introduces some multicollinearity. For this reason, we excluded that variable from expression (7-15). The results thus achieved are clear and compatible with our previous estimates:

(i)   the coefficient of adaptation to price expectations does not differ from unity;

(ii) the dummy variable I_1, which expresses the income policy during the Krieger Vasena period, has the expected sign and is significantly different from zero;

(iii) the proxy variable of union pressure ΔS_t has the expected sign and is significant at 5 percent.[21] It is noted that an annual increase of 10 percent in such pressure through strikes and stoppages gives an annual increase in money wages of 2.4 percent;

(iv) the variable ΔS_t is not closely linked with the employment situation in the labor market, which suggests that union pressure is exercised somewhat independently of the level of excess demand for labor.[22]

5 Conclusions on the Applicability of the Phillips Curve to the Argentine Economy

In our empirical analysis of the Phillips curve for the Argentine economy for the period 1964-1974 we started with the simplest version:

$$\Delta W_t = a_1 + a_2 \; U_t^{-1} + a_3 \; U_t^{-2}$$

and observed not only that the state of the labor market is not a significant variable in the determination of the rate of growth of money wages but also that its behavior is the opposite of that expected—the level of unemployment increases with the rate of increase of wages.

Since the econometric estimates based on the previous equation were far from satisfactory, the second step was to show the effect of the expected rate of inflation on the behavior of money wages. For this purpose, we first had to formulate a model of the expectations of the rate of inflation and then substitute the expected rate of inflation in the wages equation. To this end, we began by defining a very simple model of static expectations. The results obtained confirm the low level of significance of the variable U_t while at the same time showing the important role of the rate of inflation in explaining the rate of change in wages.

Since this model only took account of present inflation, ignoring the impact of earlier history of rates of inflation, a model of adaptive expectations was used in which

$$\Delta P_t^e = \gamma\, \Delta P_t + \gamma(1 - \gamma)\, \Delta P_{t-1} + \gamma(1 - \gamma)^2\, \Delta P_{t-2} + \ldots, \; 0 \leqslant \gamma \leqslant 1$$

In this model, the closer that γ is to unity, the shorter is the memory of the economic units and the greater is the influence of the more recent periods in the formation of the expected rates of inflation.

The estimates made, while again discarding the contribution of U_t, serve, on one hand, to bring out the significance of the expected rate of inflation and, on the other hand, to show the importance of the present and previous semesters in the formation of expectations—the value of R_A^2 is maximized in the wage equation when $\gamma = 0.7$.

An important limitation of the previous estimates is the presence of autocorrelation in the residuals, which makes it difficult to carry out meaningful tests of the significance of the estimated coefficients. This also suggests that the estimated model could be improved by introducing new variables. To this end, we introduced two dummies representing experiences with incomes policy in the period 1964–1974—that of Krieger Vasena and that of Gelbard.

The results obtained again rule out the importance of U_t and highlight the significance of expectations of inflation and of incomes policies, which together account for 86 percent of the change in money wages. The elimination of the autocorrelation in the residuals made it possible to accept confidently the hypothesis that the coefficient of adaptation does not differ from unity and that while the incomes policy of Krieger Vasena was used to slow down the growth rate of money wages, that of Gelbard helped during its short period of application to accelerate that growth.

The verification that the level of unemployment (U_t) is not a significant variable in the explanation of the rate of change in money wages led finally to the formulation of another model in which wages were influenced by union aggressiveness (ΔS_t):

$$\Delta W_t = a_1 + a_2 \, \Delta P_t^e + a_3 \, \Delta S_t + a_4 \, I_1$$

The results of this model, which were applied only to the period 1964-1971 owing to limitations in statistical sources, show that the coefficient of ΔP_t^e does not differ from unity, that the incomes policy of Krieger Vasena was significant, and that union aggressiveness helped to increase the rate of growth of wages. In particular, it is observed that union pressure is largely independent of the employment situation in the labor market.

In sum, the estimates carried out for the Argentine economy for the period 1964-1974 reject the well-known tradeoff between a lower level of unemployment and a higher rate of growth of money wages. In contrast, the expected rate of inflation and the degree of pressure exercised by unions do influence the rate of growth of money wages.

The long-standing inflation that is characteristic of the Argentine economy apparently has served to create in certain social groups the necessary antibodies that help prevent the germs of inflation from affecting them adversely. In the labor sector this process took place without the need for any inoculation with an explicit dose of indexation (adjustment for inflation) of money wages. The unitary coefficient of adaptation to expected rates of inflation shows the impossibility of continually fooling wage earners through a rising rate of inflation. Not only are they not subject to monetary illusion, but in a stop-go context of contradictory economic policy programs, wage earners form their expectations of inflation on the basis of a model in which a 90 percent weight is given to what occurs in the current and previous semesters.

This capacity of wage earners to transfer the expected increase in prices to wages, together with the upward pressure exercised by union militancy, suggests that the explanation of Argentine wage inflation cannot be found in the traditional Phillips curve interpretation of excess demand for labor as a catalytic factor. If we accept that the latter variable is adequately represented by the level of unemployment, the acceleration of inflation takes place independently of the state of the labor market. On the contrary, Argentine inflation is more readily explained by expectations and the influence exercised on the level of prices by aspirations about the distribution of national income that go beyond the global capacity of the country to satisfy them. These aspirations were forced into compatibility in a context of stable prices on the occasions on which the government rose above conflicting aspirations and directed and controlled the distributive struggle. In the period 1964–1974 this occurred on two occasions: in 1967–1969 (Ongania-Krieger Vasena), where as mentioned earlier de Pablo has argued that fiscal restraint was used as an instrument to affect expectations, and in 1973–1974 (Perón-Gelbard), where wages were raised and prices fixed. But it is also possible to see that the socioeconomic strain, which such stabilizing shocks implied, in a country that is accustomed to thinking and operating in terms of permanent and fluctuating inflation led, once this controlling capacity had been exhausted and had disappeared, to a subsequent period of galloping inflation of the type experienced in 1971–1972 and from the second half of 1974 to 1977. In other words, although the incomes policy may shift the Phillips curve toward the left, it tends to go back toward the right.

This suggests that, for a country that is accustomed to average rates of inflation of 25 to 30 percent per year, it is not advisable to apply a sharp brake to inflation because the strains that accumulate during that brief interregnum of price stability later lead to a corresponding price explosion. Thus, just as it is not easy for a country with price stability to adjust to the situation prevailing under inflation, it is no less difficult if the process of adaptation is reversed.

Although the incomes policies of Krieger Vasena and Gelbard seem to have been successful during their short period of application, when they are examined in a wider context it seems that they were only transitory examples of repressed inflation. These results suggest that if the capacity of the government to act as arbitrator in the distributive struggle is exercised gradually for a certain period of time, it may be possible not only "to educate" the economic units as to how to operate with a certain degree of price stability but also to reduce the strain on distribution and to cushion the natural erosion of the arbitrating power of the government, provided that this can be done in a context of steadily expanding the income available for distribution. It does not seem advisable to us, nor politically viable for a country that for twenty-five years has known no other way of dealing with income distribution than through changes in relative prices, to change these patterns of behavior suddenly, since it is highly possible that with suddenly stable prices the majority of the social groups will all feel cheated simultaneously. In such a context of collective dissatisfaction the incomes policy becomes a brief period of transition that may terminate with the expulsion of the arbitrator when his capacity for enforcing the rules of the distributive game is exhausted politically.

This view of the dynamics of inflation has been taken in a context of moderate and fluctuating growth resulting from the external sector's limited capacity to satisfy a level of production compatible with full employment. Full employment implies that the determinants of money wages cannot be analyzed in the context of a closed economy, such as that depicted by the Phillips curve, but that their analysis must take account of the relation between the exchange policy followed (fixed versus flexible rates of exchange) and the internal and external inflation differential.

To the extent that the rate of growth of domestic prices in a context of fixed exchange rates exceeds world inflation, the international competitive capacity of the country will be affected as a result of the overvaluation of its currency. The progressive tendency toward external imbalance arising from such a state of affairs will lead to subsequent devaluation in order to find equilibrium once more. The Argentine experience shows that the last-mentioned measure, if accompanied by a policy for containing money wages, gives rise to a redistribution of income that is unfavorable to wage earners. Since they have a bigger marginal propensity to spend than nonwage earners, devaluation depresses the level of domestic demand and with it the level of production and employment in view of the low elasticity of supply of export products in the short term. This mechanism indicates that external equilibrium is achieved in the short term more often through the contractionary effect of devaluation on the domestic demand for imports and exports than through the effect of a change in relative prices. In the short term, the final result of devaluation will be an upswing in inflation and a slowing down in the rate of growth of the product and employment.

The process described above is obviously most applicable to the policy of fixed exchange rates followed up to 1964. From then on this type of policy was cast aside and the government began to apply more flexible exchange rates, including as part of them concealed devaluations in the form of reductions in taxes on exports. To some extent, however, the devaluations of March 1967 and the end of 1971, suggest that the rate of exchange was not adjusted fully in relation to the disparity between domestic and world inflation. This lag in the real rate of exchange and its subsequent adjustment helps to explain the slowing down in the rate of growth of economic activity and employment in the period following the 1971 devaluation.

The most important contribution of the new scheme based on a certain degree of exchange flexibility, compared with that applied in the period preceding 1964, is that, while in the latter period the adjustment to external equilibrium was associated with contractions in the absolute level of the gross domestic product (e.g., 1952, 1959, and 1962–1963), in the period beginning in 1964 the increases and decreases in the rate of growth of the GDP did not involve a drop in its absolute level.

The whole range of queries raised in the analysis by the introduction of the external sector would extend this chapter far beyond its immediate scope and for this reason the interested reader is referred to the numerous existing works on the subject, for example those by Díaz Alejandro (1965), Mallon and Sourrouille (1975) and the author (1974).

NOTES

1. Mackay and Hart (1974) show that the Phillips curve, expressed in terms of contractual wage rates, may yield different results from those obtained if wages effectively paid are used. In England the first would yield a higher Phillips curve in the postwar period. Contractual wages may be more suitable for measuring the influence of the labor market on collective agreements; whereas the wages effectively paid more suitable for measuring demand pressures.

2. Rothschild (1971:274) presents an interesting table that shows the different results obtained in terms of unemployment levels for a constant rate of change in money wages by varying the period of time chosen, the structure of the model, and introducing additional variables.

3. For a description of their methodology see the regular INDEC publications on unemployment.

4. This form of measurement, although it has the advantage of eliminating seasonal changes, has a disadvantage in that it includes superimpositions on the percentage variations in each semester, and therefore, may introduce autocorrelation into the residuals.

5. The series for the half year was adjusted to reflect annual percentage variations in order to make it compatible with the other statistical series.

6. Perry's (1964) analysis for the United States concludes that $\Delta P_t^{(2)}$, with a time lag of three months, provides the best estimate of ΔW_t.

7. Farrar-Glauber's multicollinearity test.

8. The failure of U_t to make any contribution can be seen from the following result:

$$\Delta W_t = 3.12 + 1.06 \ \Delta P_t^{(2)} \qquad R^2 = 0.74$$
$$\quad (0.69) \ (7.37) \qquad\qquad R_A^2 = 0.73$$

9. See Turnovsky and Wachter (1972).

10. Since this is an infinite series, we truncated the calculation at 20 periods, at which point for $\gamma = 0.1$

$$\sum_{i=0}^{i=20} (1 - \gamma)^i = 0.89$$

(in our case the periods are semesters). In this case the values of γ were recalculated in order to make the previous sum equal to unity. For $i = 20$ the sum amounts to unity from $\gamma = 0.25$ upward (when $\gamma = 0.2$ this sum is 0.99).

11. Replacing U_t^{-1} with U_t^{-2} does not change the results, for the highest value of R_A^2 (0.76) for $\gamma = 0.7$ is maintained and the coefficient of ΔP_t^e is 1.249. The inclusion of U_t^{-1} and U_t^{-2}, however, introduces a high degree of multicollinearity.

12. In Canada, a more stable country with respect to both politics and prices, a maximum R^2 is also obtained when $\gamma = 0.7$. See Vanderkamp's (1972) analysis of the period 1949–1968.

13. At this point the limitations of an estimate model based on a single equation are seen more clearly. If we had estimated the following model of simultaneous equations: $\Delta W = f(\Delta P, X)$; $\Delta P = g(\Delta W, Y)$, where X and Y are other independent variables, then we would be in a position to see the effect of the changes in prices on wages, and subsequently of the latter on prices, in order to observe whether the rate of inflation tends toward equilibrium at a finite rate.

14. J.C. de Pablo (1972) has suggested that the reduction in the government deficit in the Krieger Vasena period was not undertaken as a method of attacking inflation through the demand side, but through its effects in the formation of inflationary expectations, given that many important sectors of the economy tend to associate a larger government deficit with higher rates of inflation. In this sense restrictive monetary and fiscal policy contribute to reduce inflation through their effects on expectations.

15. Another approach would be to estimate the wage equation for periods in which an incomes policy was applied and for those in which there was none, as well as for the whole period, and then to test the assumption that the wage equation remained stable during the entire period, independently of whether or not an incomes policy was applied. See Parkin, Summer, and Jones (1972).

16. For a detailed analysis of income distribution in this period see de Pablo (1974).

17. A detailed criticism of the use of the rate of change in the percentage of the labor force who are members of unions as an indicator of union militancy can be found in Purdy and Zis (1973).

18. "Conflictos de Trabajo," Ministerio de Trabajo, Dirección Nacional de Recursos Humanos, División Estadísticas Sociales, various annual issues.

19. The series on stoppages is expressed in man-hours lost, which were converted to working days on the basis of the assumption that a normal working day is equal to eight hours.

20. The variable ΔP_t^e corresponds to a value $\gamma = 0.7$. The replacement of ΔP_t^e with $\Delta P_t^{(2)}$ raises the coefficient DW to the area of indeterminateness at the 5 percent level.

21. When we replaced ΔS_t with S_t and S_{t-1} we obtained unsatisfactory results for the coefficients.

$$U_t = 0.18 + 0.0001 \, \Delta S_t \qquad R_A^2 = 0.15$$
$$(24.48) \ (1.93)$$

There is even more lack of dependence between the level of unemployment and the number of conflicts that occurred in the semester (S_t). The correlation coefficient is 0.05.

REFERENCES

Banco Central de la República Argentina, Centro de Estudios Monetarios y Bancarios, CEMYB-01. *Adaptación de las expectativas, Descripción y especificación para el uso del programa*, diciembre de 1970.

Mario S. Brodersohn. "Estrategias de política económica gubernamental en la Argentina, 1950-72." *Revista de Ciencias Económicas* (1974).

Carlos F. Díaz Alejandro. *Exchange-Rate Devaluation in a Semi-Industrialized Economy: The Case of Argentina, 1955-1961*. Cambridge, Mass.: MIT Press, 1965.

Milton Friedman. "The Role of Monetary Policy." *American Economic Review* (1968).

Leslie Godfrey and Jim Taylor. "Earning Changes in the United Kingdom, 1954-70: Excess Labor Supply, Expected Inflation and Union Influence." *Oxford Bulletin of Economics and Statistics* (1973).

A.G. Hines. "Trade Unions and Wage Inflation in the United Kingdom, 1893-1961." *Review of Economic Studies* (1964).

Richard G. Lipsey. "The Relation Between Unemployment and the Rate of Change of Money Wage Rates in the United Kingdom, 1862-1957." *Economica*, (1960).

D.I. Mackay and R.A. Hart. "Wage Inflation and the Phillips Relationship." *The Manchester School* (June 1974).

Richard D. Mallon and Juan V. Sourrouille. *Economic Policymaking in a Conflict Society: The Argentine Case*. Cambridge, Mass.: Harvard University Press, 1975.

Guillermo O'Donnell. *Modernización y autoritarismo*. Buenos Aires: Paidos, 1972.

Juan Carlos de Pablo. *Cuatro ensayos sobre la economía Argentina*, I: "Distribución del ingreso." FIEL, 1974 (mimeo).

———. *Política antinflacionaria en Argentina, 1967-70*. Buenos Aires: Amorrortu Editores, 1972.

M. Parkin, M. Summer, and R. Jones. "A Survey of the Econometric Evidence of the Effects of Incomes Policy on the Rate of Inflation," in M. Parkin and M. Summer (eds.) *Incomes Policy and Inflation*. Manchester: Manchester University Press, 1972.

Edmund S. Phelps. "Phillips Curves, Expectations of Inflation and Optimal Unemployment Over Time." *Economica* (1967).

A.W. Phillips. "The Relationship Between Unemployment and the Rate of

Change of Money Wages in the United Kingdom, 1861–1957." *Economica* (1958).

George L. Perry. "The Determinants of Wage Rate Changes and the Inflation-Unemployment Trade-off for the United States." *Review of Economic Studies* (1964).

D.L. Purdy and G. Zis. "Trade Unions and Wage Inflation in the UK: A Reappraisal," in M. Parkin and A.R. Nobay, (eds.) *Essays in Modern Economics.* London: Longman Group, 1973.

K.W. Rothschild. "The Phillips Curve and All That." *Scottish Journal of Political Economy* (1971).

Robert Solow. *Price Expectations and the Behavior of the Price Level.* Manchester: Manchester University Press, 1969.

Stephen Turnovsky and Michael Wachter. "A Test of the 'Expectations Hypothesis' Using Directly Observed Wage and Price Expectations." *The Review of Economics and Statistics* (1972).

John Vanderkamp. "Wage Adjustment, Productivity and Price Change Expectations." *The Review of Economic Studies* (1972).

Javier Villanueva. "Una interpretación de la inflación Argentina." *Revista de Ciencias Económicas, Temas de Economía* (1972).

R. Ward and G. Zis. "Trade Union Militancy as an Explanation of Inflation: An International Comparison." *The Manchester School* (1974).

8

SUSAN M.
WACHTER*

Structuralism vs. Monetarism: Inflation in Chile

1. INTRODUCTION

Inflation has plagued much of Latin America since the 1930s and Chile since the late nineteenth century. Two competing schools of thought have developed in Latin America to explain this chronic inflation. Latin American monetarism suggests that the factors causing inflation in Latin America are similar to those causing inflation elsewhere and are primarily a matter of excessive aggregate demand. The classic empirical study embodying monetarist assumptions is Arnold Harberger's analysis of Chilean inflation.[1] The second theory, structuralism, stresses that there are factors peculiar to Latin America's institutional structure that explain the region's predisposition to inflation.

One important argument of the structuralist school is that the roots of inflation can be found in bottlenecks of "inelastic supply" in the agricultural sector. This argument has been cited as particularly applicable to the Chilean economy. It is examined here and tested using Chilean data.

As might be expected, a consensus position exists in the literature that grants both structural and monetarist factors a role in the Latin American inflationary process: "Structural problems are considered

*The author wishes to thank Jere Behrman, David Belsley, Huston McCullogh, Stephen Ross, Geoffrey Woglam, and Michael Wachter for valuable suggestions.

227

to be at the root of inflation, but demand problems are clearly related to the propagation and persistence of the phenomenon."[2] However, although several econometric studies of inflation in Latin America have tested the significance of monetarist factors using Harberger's basic approach, little attempt has been made either to formulate rigorously or to test the structuralist theory based on a weak agricultural sector. The structuralist approach has lacked the theoretical underpinnings needed to compete with the monetarist hypothesis.

This chapter develops a statement of the structuralist hypothesis of the role of agricultural difficulties in inflation. The innovation of this model is that it does not rely on the assumption that prices adjust more slowly downward than upward, an assumption that is commonly felt to be necessary for the structuralist conclusions. The reformulated structuralist theory is incorporated into the Harberger model of inflation and is tested using quarterly Chilean data over the years 1940–1970.

The plan of the chapter is as follows. Section 1 summarizes salient aspects of the structuralist-monetarist dispute relevant to the agricultural weakness argument. In Section 2 this structuralist theory is critically examined. Section 3 develops an alternative formulation of the argument. In Section 4 the tests are performed, the empirical results analyzed, and the policy implications of the findings discussed.

1. SUMMARY OF THE STRUCTURALIST AND MONETARIST DISPUTE

The Latin American monetarist position is rooted in the belief that increases in money income occur in response to increases in aggregate demand. Inflation is the result of continued expansion of aggregate demand after real income approaches the capacity or supply constraints of the economy. According to Latin American monetarists, this inflation is generated by unjustified expansion both in government deficits (financed for the most part by increases in the money supply) and in central bank loans to the public and to commercial banks.[3] The policy prescription offered by monetarists is monetary and fiscal restraint since it it the lack of such restraint that leads to rising prices. If inflation is not contained, it is argued that a second best solution is to end or avoid price controls, although the result may be greater price level instability.

Harberger's "The Dynamics of Inflation in Chile," the best-known empirical study of Latin American inflation, provides and tests a

monetarist model of inflation.[4] The Harberger model uses the traditional liquidity preference function to express the demand for
money. In this view, the demand for money is a function of the price
level, the level of real income, and the cost of holding money. The
supply of money is assumed to be determined exogenously. In equilibrium, given the level of real income and the cost of holding
money, the price level will adjust to equate the demand for money to
an existing supply. The price level then is expressed as a function of
the quantity of money, the level of real income, and the cost of holding cash. The effects of increases in the money supply on the price
level are assumed to occur over time, and thus money supply enters
the equation in the form of a distributed lag. Since Harberger is interested in analyzing the inflation rate rather than the price level, he
takes percentage first differences of the above-described function and
arrives at the following inflation equation to be tested with quarterly
data:

$$P'_t = S'_t + \beta_1 Y'_t + \beta_2 M'_t + \beta_3 D'_t + \beta_4 A'_t \qquad (8\text{--}1)$$

where P'_t equals the percentage change in price level within each
quarter; Y'_t, the percentage change in real income from the past to
the current quarter; M'_t the percentage change in the money supply in the six months ending with the end of quarter t, and D'_t, a
distributed-lag weighted average of the three past values of M'_t.
A'_t equals the percentage change in the general price level in the year
ending at the beginning of the current quarter minus the percentage
change in the general price level in the year before that. This variable
does not include the change in the market rate of return realizable
from investment in nonmonetary assets because it is argued that past
changes in the inflation rate have the greatest impact on the change
in the expected costs of holding real cash. Finally, S'_t equals a seasonal constant. (A discussion of the results, broadly supportive of the
monetarist hypothesis, is postponed to Part IV.) Thus, in Harberger's
model, given full employment income and the predetermined cost of
holding cash, government-induced expansion in aggregate demand,
assumed to be the result of money supply growth, is responsible for
higher price levels.

Latin American structuralists will grant that the money supply
may increase along with the price level. Unlike monetarists, however,
they believe that the money stock is responding to inflation rather
than initiating it. The initiating or underlying factors, it is hypothesized, are not to be found in monetary and fiscal policies but rather
in the more basic weaknesses characteristic of the Latin American

economies. In general terms the source of rising prices is thought to be the pressure of economic growth on an underdeveloped social and economic structure. Specifically, the agriculture, foreign trade, and government sectors are regarded as suffering from institutional rigidities that cause prices to rise with economic development.[5] The structuralist factor that is cited as particularly applicable to the Chilean economy is a weak agricultural sector.[6] It is argued that, with economic growth and consequent industrialization, there is increased demand for food and raw material deliveries to the industrial sector; but agricultural output is sluggish and cannot keep pace with the demand at constant prices. The rural socioeconomic structure is most often held responsible for this.

Specifically, structuralists cite the land-tenure arrangement as the primary cause for low investment and for the relatively backward production techniques of Latin American agriculture. The land is divided predominantly into minifundia and latifundia; that is, small peasant plots and large estates. Both are seen as contributing to the problem of a relatively backward traditional agricultural sector. It is argued that large estates are inefficient because their owners are not "economic men" and thus are uninterested in maximizing their money profits. On the other hand, minifundia are not productive because they are too small to be efficiently cultivated and because their peasant owners lack the time and human resources to learn better techniques.[7]

A relatively backward agricultural sector is almost always one of the problems of developing economies. The distinguishing feature of the structuralist approach is the argument that this problem can lead to inflation. It is clear, however, that the absolute price level does not have to rise for the relative price of food to increase. A rise in the relative price of food can be accomplished through a decline in prices of other commodities with food prices constant. One additional and crucial assumption made by structuralists that turns relative price increases into overall inflationary pressure is the following: prices in the nonfood sectors of the economy are inflexible downward. It is the rise in the relative price of food combined with the rigidity of nonfood prices that results in an increase in the overall level of prices. In general, downward inflexibility of prices is ascribed to the pervasiveness of imperfect competition in those Latin American economies suffering from inflation. The existence of downward price inflexibility due to market power is accepted as an institutional constraint and is not given much attention. Yet it is as crucial to the structural analysis as is the assumption of bottlenecks in agriculture.

To summarize, there are two elements traditionally specified as necessary for structural inflation: first, excess demand in the agricultural sector due to the lack of sufficient technological change, bidding up relative prices in this sector; second, price and wage floors in the nonfarm sector.

If such factors are at the root of inflationary pressures, monetary and fiscal policies can slow inflation but only at a cost to economic development. With a stagnant agricultural sector, for example, growth elsewhere in the economy will increase the demand for agricultural products (due to an increase in income) while reducing the supply (by drawing away labor resources). This leads to an increase in prices that cannot be offset because prices are rigid elsewhere in the economy. Hence, the only way to prevent prices from rising is to curtail the increase in excess demand for agricultural goods. Without extensive structural change, this means stopping economic growth. Thus the structuralists argue that the preferred way to stop inflation is through structural reforms:

> The second sort of action, with a greater chance of success in Latin America than over-all restrictions upon demand, is the loosening of bottlenecks —that is, of particular insufficiencies in supply that are possible causes of inflationary spiral. Herein lies the role of investments bearing a rapid maturity, of food imports in the event of poor harvest, and of agrarian reforms, doubtless difficult to manage but the effect of which should eventually be the increase of food production and the simultaneous disappearance of both the largest landholdings, where there is no incentive to rational production, and the smallest whose lack of means restrains development.[8]

2. A CRITIQUE OF THE STRUCTURALIST MODEL

There are a number of problematical parts to the theory of structuralism. The structuralist explanation of inflation is criticized here on empirical and then on theoretical grounds. First, in the inflationary process that Chile has undergone, prices in the nonfarm sectors of the economy have not been merely rigid downward in the face of excess supply but rather they have continued to rise. The assumption of a floor to price changes is clearly inadequate to explain this.

Second, it is simply a matter of arithmetic that a rise in relative prices in agriculture, given a floor to prices in other sectors, requires a rise in the general price level. If prices advance due to excess demand in one sector and are not cut in response to excess supply, on the average prices increase. This combination of events offers an explanation for a once-and-for-all increase in the price level. A constant inflation rate, however, can only be explained within the structuralist framework if relative prices continue to advance.

Moreover, in Chile there has been a tendency for the rate of inflation itself to rise. For structuralist factors alone to lead to this result, relative food prices would not only need to rise, they would need to rise at an increasing rate. In Chile relative food prices have increased over the period 1940–1970. However, there has been no positive trend in the rate of change in relative food prices as required.

Third, structuralism does not provide a theoretical justification for the assumed downward rigidity of nonfood prices. Downward price rigidity and upward flexibility are attributed to the presence of oligopoly power in the manufacturing and service sectors; but theoretical doubts can be raised about ascribing this asymmetrical pricing response to oligopolistic factors. In particular the pricing behavior described by this assumption is not consistent with the maximization of an oligopolistic industry's long-run profits.

To see this point, assume that an oligopolistic industry is in equilibrium at its profit-maximizing price. Now assume that demand increases for just a short period and that this causes the short-run profit-maximizing price to rise. If oligopolies respond readily to the temporarily increased demand by raising prices, then when demand falls they have the wrong price. The original price now maximizes profits but by the assumption under question oligopolies hesitate to lower their prices again. It is quite likely that downward price changes do threaten industrywide pricing discipline. They may be interpreted as an attempt by one firm to increase its market share and so may spark a price war. To avoid this, firms may hesitate to cut prices. However, if firms are slow to lower prices, maximization of profits requires them to hesitate before raising prices as well. Since prices cannot be adjusted downward without cost, they should be raised only when conditions that call for a price rise clearly persist. Otherwise, firms may be committed to a pricing structure that is too high to maximize current profits. Hence, oligopolies may be slow to raise or lower prices in response to change in demand in order to preserve industrywide cooperation on pricing structure. If firms pursue this strategy the assumption that prices are more likely to move up readily but down slowly in organized sectors must be questioned.[9] However the assumption of asymmetrical price responsiveness is not necessary to a structuralist theory of inflation. In Section III below, where the structuralist model is reformulated, it is replaced with the assumption that, on average, firms in manufacturing and service markets are slower to adjust prices in either direction to changed market conditions than those in the agriculture sector.

Thus, the structuralist argument as it stands can be criticized on several specific grounds. More generally, the structuralist model is stated in an intuitive form. Consequently, it is unclear how one would go about testing it. Related to this is the fact that structuralism specifies no role either for inflationary expectations[10] or for aggregate demand elements, and so is incomplete as a model of inflation. The reformulated structuralist model, derived in Section III below, attempts to deal with this problem as well as to answer the specific criticisms of the traditional structuralist model raised in this section. Far from invalidating the basic point of the structuralist approach, once inflationary expectations and aggregate demand elements are included, it is possible to avoid the problems outlined above. In particular, structuralist factors can be linked to an ongoing inflation process without the need to assume a floor to price changes in the nonunionized, oligopolistic sector.

3. THE STRUCTURALIST MODEL REFORMULATED

The purpose of this section is to derive the structuralist hypothesis that relative prices affect the inflation rate from a clearly specified theoretical framework that provides refutable hypotheses and that answers the specific criticisms of the traditional structuralist approach raised in the previous section. The model is first briefly outlined and is then derived and stated in a more rigorous form.

In inflationary economies such as Chile's, where the annual rate of price change averaged 30 percent over the years 1940–1970, it is reasonable to assume that a positive future rate of inflation is anticipated. Thus it is likely that individuals use some model to formulate their expectations of future rates of price change. Now assume that in some way the government is able to increase monetary aggregate demand to validate the expected price increases (as discussed further below). Then in equilibrium real demand and supply of goods are in balance and prices increase at the expected rate of inflation. Monetarists would attribute a rise in the overall inflation rate to an increased rate of growth of aggregate demand. It would seem that if the expansion in money aggregate demand is kept equal to the real growth in output plus the expected growth in prices, inflation would continue at the equilibrium expected rate. This, however, is not necessarily the case. Overall demand may be kept in balance with an increase in demand in one sector balancing a decrease in another. Different sectors then may adjust their prices to changes in the level of demand at different speeds. Specifically, as was indicated above, competitive sectors may adjust their prices and wages in reaction to changed demand conditions faster than noncompetitive sectors. The rapidity with which prices adjust is also determined by the nature of the product. Those products with long- and fixed-contract periods for their inputs or outputs will have prices that adjust relatively slowly.

The assumption maintained here is that, for whatever reason, prices in agriculture react more rapidly to changed market conditions than do prices elsewhere. Then, if aggregate demand equals aggregate supply but the composition of excess aggregate demand is such that there is an exogenous increase in excess demand in agriculture and a corresponding decrease in excess demand elsewhere, the inflation rate in the short run will rise.

But this is just what the structuralists argue is occurring. The basic assumption of the structuralist view is that with industrialization and continued agricultural backwardness, the increasing demand for agricultural products overruns supply increases in that sector. The matching excess supply occurring in the nonfood sectors may not lead to a balancing decline in the rate of change in nonfood prices. Demand would be less than supply but prices would not fall elsewhere in the economy at the same rate that they are rising in the agricultural sector. The overall result in the short run is an increase in the inflation rate.

Furthermore, developing economies such as those of Latin America, to the extent that they are often subject to upward relative price pressure in the more traditional agricultural sector, would be more prone to inflationary pressures than developed countries where excess demand might not be expected to occur systematically in agriculture.

The Model Derived

To derive the model in a form suitable for hypothesis testing,[11] a linear price reaction equation is adopted such that:

$$\frac{\dot{P}_i}{P_i} = \frac{K_i X_i}{q_i^S} = \frac{K_i(q_i^D - q_i^S)}{q_i^S} \tag{8-2}$$

where $\dot{P}_i$ is the first derivative of the price of good i with respect to time, K_i, a positive constant, X_i, the level of excess demand, q_i^D, the quantity demanded, and q_i^S, the quantity supplied. The equation states that the relative rate of change in a price is directly proportional to the excess demand for the good expressed as a fraction of the quantity supplied. Excess demand equations take the following form:

$$X_i = X_i(P_1, \ldots, P_n; P_1^e, \ldots, P_n^e; A) \qquad (8\text{-}3)$$

where P_i^e indicates the expected price and A is a term representing the initial level and distribution of assets.[12]

The Laspeyres price index is then utilized to measure the inflation rate, $\dot{P}/P$. In a two-sector economy,

$$\frac{\dot{P}}{P} = \frac{\bar{q}_1 \dot{P}_1 + \bar{q}_2 \dot{P}_2}{\bar{q}_1 P_1 + \bar{q}_2 P_2} \qquad (8\text{-}4)$$

where $\bar{q}_1$ and $\bar{q}_2$ are base period quantities, and P_1 and P_2 and $\dot{P}_1$ and $\dot{P}_2$ are current prices and current changes in prices, respectively, the agricultural sector is indicated by subscript 1 and the rest of the economy by subscript 2. Substituting the price reaction Equation (8-2) into Equation (8-4) results in:

$$\frac{\dot{P}}{P} = \left(\frac{\bar{q}_1 P_1 K_1 X_1}{q_1^S} + \frac{\bar{q}_2 P_2 K_2 X_2}{q_2^S} \right) / (\bar{q}_1 P_1 + \bar{q}_2 P_2) \qquad (8\text{-}5)$$

$$\approx \frac{\displaystyle\sum_{i=1}^{2} P_i K_i X_i}{\displaystyle\sum_{i=1}^{2} \bar{q}_i P_i}$$

which holds precisely for the case where the quantity weights, $\bar{q}_i$, equal the quantities supplied, q_i^S.[13]

To interpret this result, use is made of Walras' law, which states that the total net monetary value of excess demand for goods is equivalent to the excess supply of money. In symbols,

$$\sum_{i=1}^{n} P_i X_i = -X_{n+1} \qquad (8\text{-}6)$$

where P_i is the price and X_i, the excess demand of the ith good. The

$n + 1$ commodity is money, and $P_{n+1} = 1$. When there is excess aggregate demand, by definition,

$$\sum_{i=1}^{n} P_i X_i > 0 \tag{8-7}$$

Equation (8-5) can then be rewritten, as follows,

$$\frac{\dot{P}}{P} = \frac{K_2 \sum\limits_{i=1}^{2} P_i X_i}{\sum\limits_{i=1}^{2} P_i \bar{q}_i} + (K_1 - K_2) \frac{P_1 X_1}{\sum\limits_{i=1}^{2} P_i \bar{q}_i} \tag{8-8}$$

to indicate that the inflation rate is positively related, first, to the current level of excess aggregate demand relative to output, and second, assuming $K_1 > K_2$, to excess demand in agriculture relative to overall output. This is so unless prices adjust quickly to clear markets. For example, if price reaction coefficients are sufficiently large, the entire price adjustment process could occur within the quarter. Then, even with $K_1 > K_2$, sectoral imbalances would not have any impact on the quarterly inflation rate since excess demand in each sector would return to zero within the quarter.

Equation (8-8) implies that inflation may occur in the short run, despite an absence of excess aggregate demand, if excess demand exists in agriculture. This follows because prices react more quickly in agriculture than elsewhere. Equation (8-8) also implies, *mutatis mutandis*, that when excess supply exists in agriculture, $P_1 X_1 < 0$, with $\sum\limits_{i=1}^{2} P_i X_i = 0$, the price level should fall in the short run, and the larger the excess supply in absolute value, the greater the decline in the price level.

Excess demand in agriculture, X_1, is not directly observable. Thus, the rate of change in the relative price of food, ψ, is substituted into equation (8-8) as follows: By definition

$$\psi = \frac{\dot{P}_1}{P_1} - \frac{\dot{P}_2}{P_2} \tag{8-9}$$

Substituting (8-2) into (8-9),

$$\psi = \frac{K_1 X_1}{q_1^S} - \frac{K_2 X_2}{q_2^S} \tag{8-10}$$

Using the identity $P_1 X_1 + P_2 X_2 = \Sigma\, P_i X_i{}^{14}$ to substitute for X_2 in (8-10) results in:

$$\psi = \left(\frac{K_1}{q_1^S} + \frac{K_2}{q_2^S} \frac{P_1}{P_2} \right) X_1 - \frac{K_2 \Sigma P_i X_i}{q_2^S P_2} \tag{8-11}$$

Then,

$$X_1 = \frac{1}{\dfrac{K_1}{q_1^S} + \dfrac{K_2}{q_2^S} \dfrac{P_1}{P_2}} \psi + \frac{K_2 / q_2^S P_2}{\dfrac{K_1}{q_1^S} + \dfrac{K_2}{q_2^S} \dfrac{P_1}{P_2}} \Sigma P_i X_i \tag{8-12}$$

Substituting (8-12) into (8-8) results in:

$$\frac{\dot{P}}{P} = h \frac{\Sigma P_i X_i}{\Sigma P_i \bar{q}_i} + g\psi \tag{8-13}$$

where

$$h = \frac{K_2 q_1 P_1}{K_1 q_2 P_2 + K_2 q_1 P_1} K_1 + \left(1 - \frac{K_2 q_1 P_1}{K_1 q_2 P_2 + K_2 q_1 P_1} \right) K_2 > 0 \tag{8-14}$$

which is a weighted average of each sector's price reaction coefficients with weights essentially made up of each sector's share of output; and where

$$\tag{8-15}$$

$$g = (K_1 - K_2) \frac{P_1 q_1 P_2 q_2}{K_2 (P_1 q_1)^2 + (K_1 + K_2) P_1 q_1 P_2 q_2 + K_1 (P_2 q_2)^2} \gtrless 0$$

Whether g, the coefficient of ψ, is positive or negative depends only on the size of K_1 relative to K_2. The absolute size of the coefficient of ψ approaches in the limit the share of sector 1 in the price index as K_2 approaches zero. Thus, Equation (8-13) indicates that the rate of change in the price level varies directly with the level of excess aggregate demand and, assuming $K_1 > K_2$ with ψ, the rate of change in the relative price of food.

In the estimation of an inflation equation, the coefficient of ψ may overestimate the impact of structural imbalances on inflation and may reflect to some extent the influence of excess aggregate demand variables since ψ, as indicated by Equation (8-11), is influenced by excess aggregate demand. This is discussed further below.[15] However, here it can be noted that this occurs only if price reaction coefficients are larger in agriculture than elsewhere. Only if K_1 is greater than K_2, which is all that is required for structuralist factors to have an impact on the short-run inflation rate, will the inflation rate vary directly with the rate of change in the relative price of food.

If X_1 is a sector in which prices adjust more slowly than elsewhere, K_2 will be greater than K_1 and the coefficient for ψ will be negative in an estimated inflation equation.[16]

Maintaining the assumption that $K_1 > K_2$, at a given level of excess aggregate demand relative to output, the inflation rate rises if excess demand increases in agriculture and falls elsewhere. The higher rate of change in prices in agriculture is not immediately matched by a decline in the rate of change in prices in the rest of the economy, and thus, when the relative price of food rises, the inflation rate is greater than if excess aggregate demand factors alone were considered. For this to be the case, in the short run the income velocity of money must rise. If the structural inflationary pressures persist, real output and the rate of employment will drop in the absence of expansionary monetary and fiscal policy.

Equations (8-8) and (8-13) state that the inflation rate varies directly with excess aggregate demand relative to output. Harberger's inflation equation indicates the potential extent of the excess supply of money or excess demand for goods and thus can be used to reflect $\Sigma P_i X_i$ in Equations (8-8) and (8-13).[17] However, it is implicitly assumed in the Harberger model that real income is always equal to full employment real income. This assumption, which implies that markets are always in equilibrium, is not required for the Latin American monetarist model, which argues only for the primacy of excess aggregate demand forces in inflation. If Harberger's assumption does hold, that is, if prices react quickly to clear markets in all sectors, no structural inflation is possible, as discussed above.

To use Harberger's variables in a test for structural inflation, Harberger's equation needs to be interpreted as representing the monetarist causes of inflation—that is, the growth in the money supply (since changes in fiscal policy are assumed to have relatively little impact) given the growth in full employment real income. More specifically, the real income term included in the Harberger equation must measure full employment income, Y_f, not actual income, Y. If prices do not clear markets continuously, actual quarterly income, Y, will often vary from full employment income, Y_f. Indeed, because of data limitations the income variable used by Harberger and also used here may well be closer to Y_f than to Y. Quarterly income data are not available and, therefore, annual data are interpolated to provide quarterly statistics.

To summarize the workings of a model of inflation that includes both structuralist and monetarist factors, assume that excess aggregate demand, as well as excess demand and excess supply in each sector and inflationary expectations, equal zero. The inflation rate then equals zero according to Equations (8-8) and (8-13). If monetary authorities increase the money supply so that there is an excess demand for goods, inflation results. The inflation rate varies with the amount of excess aggregate demand relative to output. Starting over again from a position of zero excess aggregate demand, structural imbalances may also provoke inflation in the short run. If $K_1 > K_2$ and if excess demand occurs in agriculture, balanced by equal excess supply elsewhere, in the short run inflation results. For this to be possible a temporary rise in the velocity of money is required. The greater the value of excess demand in agriculture, relative to overall output, and the greater $K_1 - K_2$, the greater is the short-run structural inflation. Thus both aggregate demand and structural factors can influence the short-run inflation rate.

An ongoing long-run inflation at a constant rate is also possible. This is the result if the government, through monetary and fiscal policy, maintains excessive aggregate demand. Eventually, expectations of a continuing inflation are likely to develop. If the government fulfills these expectations by expansionary monetary and fiscal policy, the inflation continues at the equilibrium expected rate.[18] A spurt (or decline) in the inflation rate is then possible if structural imbalances develop. However, structural factors alone will not lead to a permanently changed inflation rate unless fiscal and monetary policies respond in the appropriate direction. If structural pressures persist, then real output and the rate of employment may drop temporarily in the absence of an accommodating monetary and fiscal policy. To see this assume $\Sigma P_i X_i = 0$; then according to inflation equation (8-13), inflation occurs if excess demand arises in agriculture such that $P_1 X_1 > P_2 X_2$. Because $K_1 > K_2$, the price level rises. But since $K_2 > 0$, with $X_2 < 0$, eventually prices will fall in the non-food sector bringing the overall price level down. Furthermore, there is a wealth effect, since the rise in prices lowers real balances, a component of assets. With the fall in assets, excess demand in the ith sector, as (8-3) indicates, will decline. Then $\Sigma P_i X_i$ will be negative until the price level drops back to its initial position.

Structuralists usually grant that growth in aggregate demand plays some part in the process of inflation. Their essential differences with Latin American monetarists is their belief that monetary and fiscal authorities are reacting to a prior price increase.[19] Once the inflation rate increases due to structural factors, it is argued, monetary and fiscal authorities are disposed to raise the rate of growth of money supply to avoid cuts in government purchasing power and disruptions to the economy, such as increases in the unemployment rate and declines in output.

The monetarist hypothesis is that monetary and fiscal policies are active, or exogenous. Clearly, the potential for these policies to respond to inflation exists. The structuralist hypothesis that the relative price of food has an impact on the long-run inflation rate requires as a necessary condition that the monetary and fiscal policy implemented by the government be a passive variable. Although this is a crucial component of the structuralist theory, whether stated explicitly or left implicit, statistical tests to determine the hypothesis' validity for Latin American inflations have not yet been performed. Here, the Sims test[20] for the presence of a passive or active money supply is used to determine which of these hypotheses is tenable for the case of Chile. The test will be described and the results analyzed in Section IV.

4. THE TESTING OF LATIN AMERICAN STRUCTURALIST AND MONETARIST THEORIES

4.1 Results Using Harberger's Inflation Equation

In the Latin American monetarist model the inflationary process is ascribed to demand-pull factors. The Latin American structuralist hypothesis stresses the role of the relatively backward agricultural sector in inflation. In the structuralist model reformulated above, it is suggested that inflation may be related both to the level and distribution of excess aggregate demand, with inflation increasing, *ceteris paribus*, with the concentration of excess demand in agriculture. Thus, according to the price change equation derived from the reformulated structuralist theory,

$$\frac{\dot{P}}{P} = K_2 \frac{\Sigma P_i X_i}{\Sigma P_i \bar{q}_i} + (K_1 - K_2) \frac{P_1 X_1}{\Sigma P_i \bar{q}_i} \qquad (8\text{-}16)$$

As indicated above, monetarist pressures on prices are measured by Harberger's variables, and if Harberger's assumptions are correct, these variables should appear with the coefficients his model predicts and the coefficient of ψ should be insignificantly different from zero. On the other hand, if the reformulated structuralist hypothesis is correct, the coefficients of both the demand-pull variables and of ψ should be significant with the anticipated signs. Hence, to test for the existence of demand-pull and structural elements in the inflation process the Harberger equation is run without and then with the rate of change of the relative price of food, ψ.[21]

The results employing quarterly data[22] follow for the period 1940–1970 using only Harberger's variables. (Standard errors appear in parentheses; $m_{b_2 b_3}$ indicates the covariance of the coefficients M'_t and D'_t.)

$$P'_t = S'_t - \underset{(0.24)}{0.92} Y'_t + \underset{(0.06)}{0.26} M'_t + \underset{(0.06)}{0.12} D'_t \qquad (8\text{-}17)$$

$$\bar{R}^2 = 0.30$$
$$DW = 1.42$$
$$m_{b_2 b_3} = -0.00815$$

$$P'_t = S'_t - \underset{(0.23)}{0.39} Y'_t + \underset{(0.05)}{0.25} M'_t + \underset{(0.06)}{0.16} D'_t + \underset{(0.03)}{0.18} A'_t \qquad (8\text{-}18)$$

$$\bar{R}^2 = 0.47$$
$$DW = 1.66$$
$$m_{b_2 b_3} = -0.000580$$

These results broadly parallel those Harberger arrives at for the period 1940–1958. The demand-pull variables—current and lagged money supply, real income, and the change in the inflation rate—are significant with the expected signs in each equation, although the significance of the coefficient of the A'_t may represent the impact of omitted variables or additional lags on included variables as well as inflationary expectations. The sums of the coefficients of M'_t and D'_t in each equation are not significantly different from 0.5 as the theory predicts. The coefficient of the cost-of-holding-cash variable, A'_t, is significant with the anticipated position sign.[23]

4.2 The Importance of the Structuralist Variable

Harberger's equations are then augmented to include the rate of change of the relative prices of food with the following results:

$$P'_t = S'_t - 0.90Y'_t + 0.24M'_t + 0.16D'_t + 0.14\psi_t \qquad (8\text{-}19)$$
$$ (0.22) \quad (0.05) \quad (0.06) \quad (0.07)$$

$$\bar{R}^2 = 0.40$$
$$DW = 1.40$$
$$m_{b_2 b_3} = -0.000734$$

$$P'_t = S'_t - 0.45Y'_t + 0.23M'_t + 0.18D'_t + 0.13\psi_t + 0.16A'_t \qquad (8\text{-}20)$$
$$ (0.22) \quad (0.08) \quad (0.05) \qquad (0.06) \quad (0.03)$$

$$\bar{R}^2 = 0.53$$
$$DW = 1.58$$
$$m_{b_2 b_3} = -0.00631^{24}$$

The coefficients of the variables of Equations (8-17) and (8-18) remain substantially unchanged in the Equations (8-19) and (8-20) when the structuralist variable ψ is included. However, this variable is also significant and positive as predicted in the structuralist model.[25]

The Durbin-Watson statistics for Equations (8-17) to (8-20) are in the indeterminate range. This suggests the possibility that positive first-order linear correlation of the residuals exists. The equations can be reestimated making use of the Cochrane-Orcutt procedure to adjust for this possible problem. The results follow (ρ indicates the autocorrelation coefficient; $\bar{R}^2_u$, the variance explained by the independent variables not including ρ):

$$P'_t = S'_t - 0.79Y'_t + 0.22M'_t + 0.11D'_t \qquad (8\text{-}21)$$
$$ (0.28) \quad (0.06) \quad (0.08)$$

$$\bar{R}^2 = 0.36 \qquad \bar{R}^2_u = 0.30$$
$$DW = 2.01 \qquad \rho = 0.30$$
$$m_{b_2 b_3} = 0.0000004$$

$$P'_t = S'_t - 0.36Y'_t + 0.23M'_t + 0.15D'_t + 0.19A'_t \qquad (8\text{-}22)$$
$$ (0.25) \quad (0.05) \quad (0.07) \quad (0.03)$$

$$\bar{R}^2 = 0.48 \qquad \bar{R}^2_u = 0.47$$
$$DW = 1.93 \qquad \rho = 0.17$$
$$m_{b_2 b_3} = -0.000413$$

$$P'_t = S'_t - \underset{(0.26)}{0.69 Y'_t} + \underset{(0.06)}{0.21 M'_t} + \underset{(0.07)}{0.13 \psi_t} \qquad (8\text{-}23)$$

$$\bar{R}^2 = 0.46 \qquad \bar{R}^2_u = 0.39$$

$$DW = 2.06 \qquad \rho = 0.34$$

$$m_{b_2 b_3} = 0.000168$$

$$P'_t = S'_t - \underset{(0.24)}{0.38 Y'_t} + \underset{(0.05)}{0.22 M'_t} + \underset{(0.07)}{0.17 D'_t} + \underset{(0.06)}{0.13 \psi_t} + \underset{(0.03)}{0.17 A'_t} \qquad (8\text{-}24)$$

$$\bar{R}^2 = 0.55 \qquad \bar{R}^2_u = 0.53$$

$$DW = 1.95 \qquad \rho = 0.21$$

$$m_{b_2 b_3} = -0.000275$$

These results differ from those above in two respects: First, the co-efficient of the real income variable becomes insignificant in the Equations (8-22) and (8-24), where the A'_t variable is included. Second, in Equations (8-21) and (8-23) the coefficient of the lagged money supply variables are no longer significant. At least one money supply variable remains significant in each equation and the sum of the money supply variable's coefficients in each equation is insignif-icantly different from 0.5. The coefficient of ψ also remains signifi-cant with the positive sign predicted by the structuralist hypothesis.[26]

In sum, these regression results imply that the null hypothesis that excess aggregate demand variables as here constructed do not affect the inflation rate can be rejected. The rate of change of the relative price of food also enters significantly with the expected sign in each of the above equations so that the null hypothesis that the structur-alist variable does not influence the inflation can also be rejected.

4.3 The Direction of Causality Between Money Supply and Prices in Chile

In the Latin American monetarist framework inflation is the result of overly expansive fiscal and monetary policy. This implies that money supply increases lead to inflation. Structuralists do not neces-sarily deny that the supply of money grows along with the price level. However, they argue that the price level is exogenously determined by other factors such as excess demand conditions in agriculture and that the money supply responds. Sims offers a procedure to test for the direction of causality between two variables where the possibility of feedback in either direction exists. To derive this test, Sims shows that: "If and only if causality runs one way from current and past

244 Short Term Macroeconomic Policy in Latin America

values of some list of exogenous variables to a given endogenous variable, then in a regression of the endogenous variable on past, current, and future values of the exogenous variables, the future values of the exogenous variables should have zero coefficients."[27] That is, if causality runs from money supply to prices only, future values of money supply in a regression of prices on money should have zero coefficients. Similarly, if causality runs from prices to money supply only, future values of prices should have zero coefficients in a regression of money on prices.

Thus there are two null hypotheses to be tested. The first null hypothesis, $H_O{}^1$, is that future values of prices as a group have coefficients insignificantly different from zero in a regression of money on prices, past, current, and future. The second null hypothesis, $H_O{}^2$, is that future values of money supply as a group have coefficients insignificantly different from zero in a regression of prices on money, past, current, and future. These hypotheses are tested with an F-test on the coefficients of the future independent variables in regressions that include the past, current, and future independent variables along with a constant term and a linear trend term. Sims's testing procedure is followed. To avoid serial correlation in the residuals, all variables were prefiltered with the filter Sims uses. Thus, each variable in its log form $x(t)$ was replaced by $x(t) - 1.5\,x(t - 1) + 0.5625\,x(t - 2)$.

Regressions were run for the period 1940 through 1970 and for the subperiod 1960 through 1970. Table 8-1 shows the results of the regressions of money on prices and prices on money for the period 1940 through 1970, both with past and with past and future independent variables. Table 8-2 shows the results of these regressions for the subperiod 1960-1970.

The F-tests for the coefficients on the four future independent variables only, in the regressions including leading and lagging variables, are shown in Table 8-3. For the overall period, 1940-1970, and for the subperiod, 1960-1970, the strict monetarist hypothesis of one-way causality from money supply to prices can be rejected and the strict structuralist hypothesis of one-way causality from prices to money supply can be rejected. Passive money supply may exist. Therefore, the structuralist hypothesis, that is, that excess demand in agriculture has influenced the long-run inflation rate in Chile, cannot be rejected. These results also support the monetarist conclusion that money influences prices and thus that control over money can have an impact on prices.

In sum, the empirical results of this section support a broad model of inflation. The findings of significant coefficients with the anticipated signs for the demand-pull and expectational variables in the

Table 8-1. Chile: Regressions Between Past and Future Money Supply and Prices for the Period 1940–1970

	Coefficient on Lag of:									$\bar{R}^2$	DW
	-4	-3	-2	-1	0	1	2	3	4		
P on M: Past Only	0.194	0.038	0.189	0.258	0.225					0.9377	01.97
	(2.20)	(0.477)	(2.49)	(3.327)	(2.84)						
P on M: With Future	0.132	-0.042	0.160	0.248	0.215	0.168	0.041	-0.105	0.075	0.9415	1.93
	1.450	(-0.470)	(1.822)	(2.801)	(2.458)	(1.969)	(0.497)	(-1.272)	(.929)		
M on P: Past Only	0.146	0.005	0.218	0.351	0.406					0.9318	1.79
	(1.285)	(0.044)	(2.020)	(3.421)	(3.964)						
M on P: With Future	0.229	-0.031	0.047	0.122	0.097	0.181	0.099	0.074	0.272	0.9495	2.10
	(2.172)	(-0.297)	(0.444)	(1.133)	(0.845)	(1.90)	(1.046)	(0.805)	(3.88)		

Values of t-statistics appear in parentheses.

Table 8-2. Chile: Regressions between Past and Future Money Supply and Prices for the Period 1960–1970

	Coefficient on Lag of:									$\bar{R}^2$	DW
	-4	-3	-2	-1	0	1	2	3	4		
P on M: Past Only	0.337	0.173	-0.100	0.280	0.448					0.7927	1.82
	(2.256)	(1.021)	(-.605)	(1.814)	(3.487)						
P on M: With Future	0.171	0.082	-0.231	0.106	0.346	0.292	-0.041	0.005	0.171	0.8344	1.81
	(1.092)	(0.455)	(-1.278)	(0.596)	(2.477)	(2.043)	(-0.302)	(0.034)	(1.256)		
M on P: Past Only	0.261	0.016	0.195	0.485	0.345					0.8801	2.06
	(1.233)	(0.086)	(1.007)	(3.196)	(2.569)						
M on P: With Future	0.396	0.019	0.128	0.239	-0.002	0.091	-0.086	0.181	0.210	0.9095	2.21
	1.741	0.104	0.699	1.416	-0.014	0.750	-0.743	1.473	2.206		

Values of t-statistics appear in parentheses.

Table 8-3. *F*-Tests on Future Quarters' Coefficients

Regression Equation		*F*	*Degrees of Freedom*
1960–1970	*M* on *P*	3.89*	4,35
1960–1970	*P* on *M*	3.02*	4,35
1940–1970	*M* on *P*	4.45*	4,115
1940–1970	*P* on *M*	1.90**	4,115

F-tests are for the null hypothesis that all four future independent variables have zero coefficients.
*Significant at the 0.05 level.
**Significant at the 0.10 line.

Harberger inflation equations are consistent with the Latin American monetarist argument that excessive aggregate demand is responsible for inflation. Also, the Sims test for active and/or passive money supply does not refute the monetarist hypothesis that expansion of the money supply contributes to higher prices. However, the reformulated structuralist model is also substantially supported by the results here. First, the finding of the significant and positive coefficient for ψ (along with the significant coefficients with appropriate signs for the aggregate demand variables) in the estimation of the Harberger inflation equations is consistent with the reformulated structuralist model. Second, according to this model, if the concentration of excess demand in agriculture is to have an impact over the long run, the rate of monetary expansion must respond to the changed inflation rate. The null hypothesis that this in fact has occurred in the Chilean economy cannot be rejected by the Sims test for the existence of a passive and/or active money supply.

Thus there is evidence that inflation varies with excess demand in agriculture or with ψ, the rate of change in the relative price of food, as well as with overall excess aggregate demand. Since the relative price of food in Chile has increased over time (see Figure 8-1), this implies that ψ has been positive more often than negative and, therefore, that the inflation rate in Chile has been higher than would have been the case if purely excess aggregate demand variables were at work. In this sense the structuralist position on the predisposition of Latin American economies to inflation is supported by the evidence for Chile. The structuralist policy prescription of the need for land reform that increases agriculture's productivity is also validated by the evidence for this model. But the monetarist argument that the structuralist factors need not inevitably lead to increased inflation is

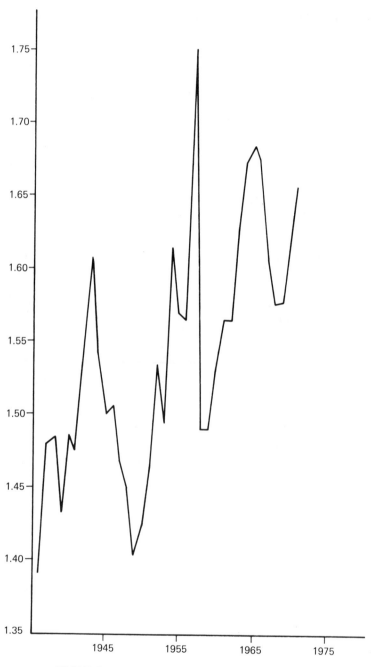

FIGURE 8-1. Chile-Food Price/CPI (1941–1975)

also supported. Money supply may, in fact, have been passive in Chile as the structuralists suggest. However, the importance of inflationary expectations suggests that if monetary and fiscal restraint is implemented, unemployment and a slowing of growth will ensue before inflation is brought completely under control. Furthermore, the results imply that the less flexible prices outside the agricultural sector are, the more agricultural difficulties will contribute to inflationary pressures. And, in spite of monetary and fiscal policies that keep aggregate demand in bounds, excess demand in agriculture can raise the short-run inflation rate. Thus policies that control inflationary expectations and that improve agricultural productivity will have an impact, along with the traditional policies of monetary and fiscal restraint, in limiting the inflationary process.

NOTES

1. Arnold Harberger. "The Dynamics of Inflation in Chile," in Carl Christ, ed., *Measurement in Economics: Studies in Mathematical Economics in Memory of Yehuda Grunfeld* (Palo Alto, Calif.: Stanford University Press, 1963), pp. 219–250.

2. Jorge Cauas, "Stabilization Policy—The Chilean Case," *Journal of Political Economy* (July-Aug 1970) p. 816.

3. Due to the weakness of government bond markets, in Latin America little expansion in aggregate demand occurs without concomitant growth in the money supply. Thus, increases in the money supply accompany expansionary fiscal policy as well as expansionary monetary policy. This may explain the origin of the use of the term "monetarist" in Latin America to refer to those who see excess aggregate demand as the cause of inflation. It should be noted that Latin American monetarists, unlike those identified as monetarists in the United States, do not take a position on the question of whether money supply growth to finance government spending has a greater impact on nominal income than money supply growth to finance central bank loans to the public. Hence, Latin American monetarists do not take a position in the debate over whether, in theory, only money matters. In this respect they can be distinguished from U.S. monetarists. Since the Latin American monetarist viewpoint stresses the role of aggregate demand, U.S. monetarist theory is a subcategory of this broader approach.

4. Op. cit., Harberger.

5. See W. Baer, "The Inflation Controversy in Latin America: A Survey," *Latin American Research Review* (Spring 1967) for a summary of the structuralist theory and D. Seers, "A Theory of Inflation and Growth in Underdeveloped Economies," *Oxford Economic Papers*, No. 1, 1964, for a discussion of its historical development.

6. D. Seers, "A Theory of Inflation and Growth in Underdeveloped Economies," p. 195.

7. Thus, according to David Felix (1965), Julio Olivera (1967), and Dudley Seers (1962) among others, it is the deficient institutional structure in the countryside that limits food production and renders it rigid and unresponsive to demand pressures. In their broad use of the term, supply is "inelastic." However, as shown in "Aggregate Market Responses in Developing Agriculture: The Postwar Chilean Experience" by Jere Behrman, Chapter 2 in *Analysis of Development Problems: Studies of the Chilean Economy*, edited by R. Eckaus (New York: Elsevier, 1973), the agriculture sector in Chile is not unresponsive to economic signals. The explanation for low land productivity is, therefore, obviously more complicated. Theordore Schultz, *Transforming Traditional Agriculture* (New Haven: Yale University Press, 1964), argues that the missing factor is public infrastructure investment. It may be that the holders of land in Chile do not demand such an infrastructure and the increase in taxes that would go with it. The desire for bringing the government into the promotion of agricultural growth in this way may be correlated with the rural class structure so that, for example, the Mexican Revolution brought a new class of landowners who sought and obtained more growth and more government involvement in agriculture. Not all structuralists hold government policy blameless for agriculture's backwardness in Latin America. See, for example, Geoffrey Maynard, *Economic Development and the Price Level* (London: Macmillan, 1962).

8. Pierre Uri with Nicholas Kaldor, Richard Ruggles, and Robert Triffin, *A Monetary Policy for Latin America* (New York: Praeger, 1968), p. 85.

9. There is another explanation for a lagged adjustment of prices to excess demand conditions in organized and, to a lesser extent, in competitive industries. In unionized firms and even in many nonunion firms, wages of employees are altered only at discrete intervals—generally once a year, but occasionally longer. The explanation for this wage-setting process in unionized firms is related to the fixed-term wage contract. Even where escalator clauses are present, the wage rate is adjusted with a time lag, again at regular time intervals fixed by the contract. One reason for this behavior is that it is costly for employers to inform employees of pay changes and to make such changes at short intervals. This involves the direct pecuniary costs of setting the wage and notifying workers of the changes and the indirect or nonpecuniary costs related to the inevitable morale problems that arise whenever wages are changed. Prices may then be set to some extent as a markup on wages. In many nonunionized firms the same process may be observed. One might expect, however, that wages and prices are set more frequently in competitive firms, and thus also on these grounds prices are more flexible in competitive than in organized sectors. The existence of unions may explain wages and prices that move upward easily, but are rigid downward. However, union power has not been pervasive in the Chilean economy over the years 1940–1970.

10. It has been suggested by some structuralists (see Mueller [1965, p. 153], Uri [1968, p. 83], and Seers [1962, p. 189]) that the fact that when monetary authorities restrict growth in credit, the decline in inflation that occurs is accompanied by a decline in economic growth disproves the neoclassical monetarist theory. Once expectations and discrete price changes are included in an inflation

model, it is clear that prices would not adjust immediately to a decline in aggregate demand and that output would fall as well.

11. The framework used here is similar to one evolved originally by A. Enthoven in his "Monetary Disequilibria and the Dynamics of Inflation," *Economic Journal* (June 1956), which derived necessary and sufficient conditions for a price rise under a variety of price reaction assumptions.

12. Hence, X_i depends on expected prices as well as actual prices and assets. It is possible to separate out the influence of expected prices and have $\dot{P}_i/P_i$ be a function of the expected inflation rate, $\dot{P}_e/P$, and a redefined excess demand variable, Z_i, which excludes the impact of expectational elements. Thus each sector's prices will vary with excess demand and the expected inflation rate; and, aggregating, it can be shown that the overall inflation rate varies with the anticipated rate of inflation and excess aggregate demand. To see this, the definition of X_i is rewritten to isolate the influence of expectations so that,

(i) $\quad X_i = f_1^i (P_1, \ldots, P_n; A) + f_2^i (P_1^e, \ldots, P_n^e)$

substituting (i) into the price reaction Equation (8-2), the result is

(ii) $\quad \dfrac{\dot{P}_i}{P_i} = \dfrac{K_i f_1^i (P_1, \ldots, P_n; A)}{q_i^S} + \dfrac{K_i f_2^i (P_1^e, \ldots, P_n^e)}{q_i^S}$

Let

(iii) $\quad Z_i = f_1^i (P_1, \ldots, P_n; A)$

Then, since it will be assumed that when $Z_i = 0, \dfrac{\dot{P}_i}{P_i} = \dfrac{\dot{P}_e}{P}$,

(iv) $\quad \dfrac{\dot{P}_i}{P_i} = \dfrac{K_i Z_i}{q_i^S} + \dfrac{\dot{P}_e}{P}$

For now, however, the expected inflation rate is assumed to be zero.

13. This assumption, which essentially requires the quantity weights to equal the current quantities supplied, is maintained throughout. The assumption simplifies the exposition but is not necessary for the testing of the model.

14. Hereafter the range of indexation is suppressed. It should be assumed to be 2 unless otherwise indicated.

15. The circumstances under which the coefficient of ψ overestimates the influence of structural imbalances on the inflation rate are discussed in footnote 24.

16. The results of estimating an inflation equation with X_1 chosen as a sector with relatively sticky prices are described below.

17. Harberger's equation can be seen as giving the inflation rate as a function of $\dot{M}_S/M - \dot{M}_D/M = (\dot{M}_S - \dot{M}_D)/M = \Sigma P_i X_i/M$. That is, for Harberger, the excess

supply of money in the current period is determined by the rate of change in the money supply in the current and preceding periods minus the rate of change in the variables determining the demand for money in the current period. (Current excess supply of money does not depend on rates of change in money demand and supply lagged additional periods because of the assumed rapid adjustment of prices.) The variables that Harberger uses are included in one test of (8-13) along with ψ. So the regression performed is:

$$\frac{\dot{P}}{P} = \alpha \frac{\Sigma P_i X_i}{M} + \beta \psi + u$$

Then, in terms of Equation (8-13), α measures $hM/\Sigma P_i q_i$ and β measures g. In the case when $K_1 = K_2 = K$, α equals $KM/\Sigma P_i \bar{q}_i$ and $\beta = 0$. In this case, the price reaction coefficient, K, indicates according to (8-8) and (8-13) to what extent excess aggregate demand relative to output gives rise to inflation. The inflation equation (8-13) developed here is meant to be consistent with Harberger's model when it is assumed that the income variable used reflects full employment income and that monetary policy is the important determinant of excess aggregate demand. Therefore, $K = V = \Sigma P_i \bar{q}_i/M$, so that $\alpha = \Sigma P_i \bar{q}_i/M \ M/\Sigma P_i \bar{q}_i = 1$, and in testing (8-13), one would expect the same coefficients that Harberger finds. However, to the extent annual real income is an endogenous variable, the Harberger prediction of a negative (and insignificantly different from minus one) coefficient for this variable would not be found.

18. In the case of inflationary expectations, market conditions of excess aggregate demand are not necessary for inflation. As indicated in note 12, the impact of inflationary expectations on price changes can be separately added to the sectoral or aggregate price change equations to reflect this.

19. Although Harberger's study, "The Dynamics of Inflation in Chile," focuses on and supports the impact of money supply on pricing, he suggests the possibility in the conclusion of the study that monetary authorities are adjusting the money supply in response to inflation.

20. Chris Sims, "Money, Income, and Causality," *American Economic Review* (September 1972).

21. The rate of change in the price of food relative to other prices will move with the rate of change in the price of food relative to *all* prices. In the estimation of an inflation equation this latter variable is used to measure ψ. That is, *FPI/CPI* is found by dividing the food price component, *FPI*, of the *CPI* by the *CPI*. $\psi(t)$ is then proxied by taking the quarterly rate of change in the price of food relative to all prices; that is,

$$\psi(t) = \frac{\dfrac{FPI}{CPI}(t) - \dfrac{FPI}{CPI}(t-1)}{\dfrac{FPI}{CPI}(t)}$$

22. Data on prices, money supply, and income are obtained from the Boletin Mensual of the Banco Central de Chile. Data on prices are derived from the consumer price index for Santiago. The food price component of the *CPI* is used to derive the relative price of food. The series used for money supply is that for the "total del dinero circulante." Since 1948 this series includes currency outside of banks, demand deposits in commercial banks (including float and government deposits and excluding interbank deposits), and deposits of the government and semifiscal agencies in the central bank. The definition of the money supply differed slightly before 1948. In periods of overlap the latest data is used. Data on prices and money supply are provided in monthly form. An averaging procedure is used to calculate a quarterly series. Quarterly real national income statistics are found through linear interpolation of the annual data in a manner suggested by Adolofo Diz in his study, "Money and Prices in Argentina," in *Varieties of Monetary Experience,* David Meiselman, ed. (Chicago: University of Chicago Press, 1970).

23. For purposes of comparison, the results Harberger arrives at when estimating these equations for 1940 through 1958 are reproduced here:

(i) $\quad P'_t = S'_t - 0.63Y'_t + 0.32M'_t + 0.27D'_t \qquad\qquad R^2 = 0.52$
$\qquad\qquad\ (0.22) \quad\ (0.09) \quad\ (0.10)$
$\qquad\qquad\qquad\qquad\qquad\qquad\qquad\qquad\qquad\quad R^2 = 0.54$
(ii) $\quad P'_t = S'_t - 0.49Y'_t + 0.33M'_t + 0.26D'_t + 0.05A'_t$
$\qquad\qquad\ (0.24) \quad\ (0.09) \quad\ (0.10) \quad\ (0.03)$

The results obtained for the longer period, 1940-1970, differ in that the cost-of-holding variable, A'_t, is significant. As in Harberger's estimation of these equations when A'_t is included, the coefficient of real income is smaller than unity and so does not conform in this respect to the model's predictions. Harberger attributes this to the possibility that the level of real income affects the inflation rate over time as does the rate of monetary expansion. He does not attempt to correct for this by including income in the form of a distributed lag because the quarterly real income data is a constructed series, arrived at, in the first place, by interpolating the annual data. An alternative explanation for the size of the coefficient of Y and for its lack of significance at even the 10 percent level in several of the estimated equations reported below is that, as suggested above, this variable does not reflect full employment real income but actual real income that is not exogenous but rather is determined simultaneously with the inflation rate.

24. The seasonal constants are insignificant in all these equations estimated over 1940-1970 except for a positive coefficient for the second quarter of the year in Equations (8-17) and (8-18), which include only the money supply variables and real income.

25. There is a difficulty in interpreting the size of the coefficient of ψ, the rate of change in the relative price of food. Since, as indicated by Equation (8-11), ψ is itself a function of excess aggregate demand, its coefficient may, to some extent, reflect the influence of excess aggregate demand variables. If, as is assumed, agriculture prices adjust more rapidly than other prices, ψ will be a

leading indicator. That is, in an excess aggregate demand-caused spurt in inflation, food prices will go up first. The relative price of food will then rise, and there will be a positive correlation between the rate of change in relative food prices and the inflation rate. However, if excess aggregate demand continues at the same level, the inflation rate will persist at the new level, but the relative price of food will drop to its original level. The higher level of inflation will then be correlated with a negative rate of change in the relative price of food. Thus, on balance, no positive correlation results between ψ and the inflation rate because agriculture is a leading sector unless increases in aggregate demand and the inflation rate are reversed *before* relative food prices can adjust back to their original level. Under this circumstance of a gyrating excess aggregate demand and inflation rate, the size of the independent influence of the distribution of excess aggregate demand on inflation will be overstated by the coefficient of ψ in the inflation equation. But agriculture can be a leading sector only if prices adjust more rapidly in agriculture than elsewhere. The attribution of a positive coefficient of ψ to the influence of excess aggregate demand on both the inflation rate and the rate of change in the relative price of food is based on the assumption that prices in agriculture are more flexible than other prices. If this assumption is correct, the distribution of excess aggregate demand will have an impact on the inflation rate, as the structuralists claim, although the impact will be overstated by the coefficient of ψ.

26. The equations described above also were estimated with ψ defined as the rate of change in the relative price of housing. To construct ψ, the consumer price index housing (*vivienda*) component available since 1958 was used. Following the comments made above, a negative coefficient should be found for this term. The equations were estimated for the period 1958-1970 with results similar to those updated above except that the coefficients of ψ are all negative and significant as predicted. The results are available from the author.

27. Chris Sims, op. cit., p. 541.

REFERENCES

Baer, Werner. "The Inflation Controversy in Latin America: A Survey." *Latin American Research Review* II: 2 (Spring 1967).

Behrman, Jere. "The Determinants of the Annual Rates of Change of Sectoral Money Wages in a Developing Economy." *International Economic Review* (1971).

———. "Short-Run Flexibility in a Developing Economy." *Journal of Political Economy* (1972), 292-313.

———. "Aggregative Market Responses in Developing Agriculture: The Postwar Chilean Experience," in R. Eckaus, ed. *Analysis of Development Problems: Studies of the Chilean Economy.* New York: Elsevier Scientific Publishing Company, 1973, ch. 2.

Campos, Roberto de Oliviera. "Two Views on Inflation in Latin America," in A.O. Hirschman, ed. *Latin American Issues.* New York: Twentieth Century Fund, 1961, 69-73.

———. "Monetarism and Structuralism in Latin America," in G.M. Meier, ed. *Leading Issues in Economic Development: Studies in International Poverty*. New York: Oxford University Press, 1970, 241–247.

Deaver, John. "The Chilean Inflation and the Demand for Money," in David Meiselman, ed. *Varieties of Monetary Experience*. Chicago: University of Chicago Press, 1970.

Díaz Alejandro, Carlos F. *Essays on the Economic History of the Argentine Republic*. New Haven: Yale University Press, 1970.

Diz Cesar, Adolfo. "Money and Prices in Argentina." in David Meiselman, ed. *Varieties of Monetary Experience*. Chicago: University of Chicago Press, 1970.

Edel, Matthew. *Food Supply and Inflation in Latin America*. New York: Praeger, 1969.

Enthoven, Alain. "Monetary Disequilibria and the Dynamics of Inflation." *The Economic Journal* (June 1956), 256–270.

Felix, David. "Monetarists, Structuralists and Import-Substituting Industrialization: A Critical Appraisal." *Studies in Comparative International Development* I: 10 (1965).

Harberger, Arnold. "The Dynamics of Inflation in Chile," in Carl Christ, ed. *Measurement in Economics: Studies in Mathematical Economics in Memory of Yehuda Grunfeld*. Palo Alto, Calif.: Stanford University Press, 1963, 219–250.

Mamalakis, Markos, and C.W. Reynolds. *Essays on the Chilean Economy*. Homewood, Ill.: Irwin Publishing Co., 1965.

Maynard, Geoffrey. *Economic Development and the Price Level*. London: Macmillan, 1962.

Mueller, Marnie W. "Structural Inflation and the Mexican Experience." *Yale Economic Essays* E, No. 1 (Spring 1965).

Olivera, Julio H.G. "Aspectos Dinámicos de la Inflación Estructural." *Desarrollo Económico* (October 1967).

Prebisch, Raul. "Structural Vulnerability and Inflation," in G.M. Meier, ed. *Leading Issues in Economic Development: Studies in International Poverty*. New York: Oxford University Press, 1970, 238–241.

Reichmann, Thomas. "Persistent Inflation and Macroeconomic Equilibrium— The Case of Chile: 1960–1969." Ph.D. dissertation, Harvard University, 1973.

Seers, Dudly. "Normal Growth and Distortions: Some Techniques of Structural Analysis." *Oxford Economic Papers* XVI:1 (1964).

———. "A Theory of Inflation and Growth in Underdeveloped Economies Based on the Experience of Latin American." *Oxford Economic Papers* XIV:2 (1962).

Sims, Chris. "Money, Income, and Causality." *American Economic Review* (September 1972).

Sunkel, Osvaldo. "Inflation in Chile" An Unorthodox Approach." *International Economic Papers*, #10.

Uri, Pierre with Nicholas Kaldor, Richard Ruggles, and Robert Triffin. *A Monetary Policy for Latin America*. New York: Praeger, 1968.

Vogel, Robert. "The Dynamics of Inflation in Latin America, 1950–1969." *American Economic Review* (March 1974).

9

GEORGE H.
BORTS
and
JAMES A.
HANSON

The Monetary Approach to the Balance of Payments with an Empirical Application to the Case of Panama*

The monetary approach to the balance of payments explains the elimination of payments disequilibrium in terms of factors bringing the demand and supply of money into equality. It treats the supply of money as endogenous by assuming a feedback from the balance of payments through changes in international reserves to changes in the monetary liabilities of the central bank and government.

One of the important questions of monetary policy is the extent to which the monetary authority of an open economy can affect the price level or the other arguments of the demand for money, such as the level of real output and the interest rate. If it were the case that these could not be changed, then any increase in monetary liabilities

*This work was partially supported under Contract No. 1005-4000726 U.S. Dept. of State and U.S. Treasury. The authors would like to thank Jere Behrman, Roque Fernandez, and Cyrus Sassanpour for comments on an earlier draft. However, the opinions expressed in this study are the exclusive responsibility of the authors and may not coincide with those of the sponsoring organizations.

of the authority would be met by an equal and offsetting outflow of international reserves (or an equiproportionate rise in the price of home goods and foreign exchange), and one would have to argue that monetary policy had no influence on the real responses of the system.

We argue below that monetary policy will have real effects since it produces changes in relative prices. An example of such a change would be a rise or fall of prices of nontraded or home goods relative to world prices in a regime of either fixed or flexible exchange rates. Thus the effectiveness of monetary policy in an open economy may depend on the existence of a group of commodities whose relative prices can be influenced by domestic conditions of demand and supply. The simple monetarist models do not allow such commodities but focus on a world in which prices are given to each trading country. One of the purposes of this chapter is to widen these assumptions, to allow for nontraded goods, and implicitly to bring monetary policy back into the monetarist model.

A second purpose of the chapter is to clarify the effects of external shocks on the balance of payments. The simple monetarist model may provide an incorrect answer to the question: "What is the impact effect of an increase in particular world prices on the balance of payments of a small country?". The simple model tells us that the balance of payments will temporarily improve as the higher prices produce an increase in the demand for the stock of money. But we shall see that the answer is far more complex. Indeed the effects on the balance of payments depend on whether it is import or export prices that have risen and on a more traditional consideration of elasticities of demand.

This chapter is organized into five sections. Section 1 will discuss the small country model in which the price level and other determinants of the demand for money are exogenous. Section 2 will develop a small country model in which the price level is endogenous. Section 3 will discuss some of the issues involved in empirical testing of the model, and an Appendix treats a more complicated version of the model. Finally, Section 4 discusses some empirical estimates for the case of Panama and Section 5 summarizes the results.

1. SMALL COUNTRY MODEL—
EXOGENOUS PRICE LEVEL

One of the first methodological approaches in the area of monetary models of the balance of payments was the specification and testing of the simple, small country model.[1] In such a model the balance of the payments of the country is shown to be positively related to the demand for money and negatively related to the domestic sources of the supply of money, the latter being exogenous to the former.

To see how these results may be obtained, assume that because of fixed effective exchange rates the local price level is fully determined in the world market; that all goods are transportable and markets are perfect so that only one price prevails; and that the country is too small for its quantities purchased and sold to have an effect on world prices, or for its balance of payments deficits and surpluses to have an effect on the world money stock, so that there is no lack of effective demand and aggregate output is supply determined.

Next assume that the country is in equilibrium in the sense that the demand for the money stock, M_d, is continuously equal to the supply of the money stock, M_s. In the simple model, neglecting the commercial banking system, the supply of the money stock is definitionally equal to two sets of liabilities, those of foreign governments, R, and those of the locals, D.[2] The condition of stock equilibrium may then be written:

$$M_d = R + D \qquad (9\text{-}1)$$

Noting that the three terms are subject to change over time, the theory implies that ΔR may be written as follows:

$$\Delta R = \Delta M_d - \Delta D \qquad (9\text{-}2)$$

Note that ΔR is the balance of payments.

The empirical implications of Equation (9-2) are that exogenous factors increasing the demand for the money stock (increased prices or output and decreased costs of money holding) will yield a surplus in the balance of payments, while *ceteris paribus* increases in the supply of local monetary liabilities will yield a deficit.[3] In a statistical regression with ΔR the endogenous dependent variable, the theory would lead one to expect a coefficient on ΔD of minus unity, positive coefficients on the (exogenous) changes in the price level and real output.[4]

Empirical tests of the small country model have been carried out by fitting the balance-of-payments function, Equation (9-2), to the right-hand variables (ΔD, and the arguments of ΔM_d) on the assumption that they are all exogenous and the error term results from the M_d equation. The results have been mixed. Some investigators have reported a coefficient on ΔD of minus unity; others obtain a smaller absolute coefficient. Almost all investigators obtain positive coefficients for real income and the price level (which increase M_d), but the coefficients are often different, suggesting that the price level may play a different role from real output in affecting the demand for money. Many of the tests are statistically significant, and the goodness of fit is taken as confirmation of the empirical validity of the model.[5]

This methodology does not permit a definitive test of the proposition that under fixed exchange rates domestic prices are unaffected by monetary policy (most of the tests were carried out for countries with fixed rates). While the data generally do not reject the implications of the small country assumptions, the tests may be insensitive to the possibility that the assumptions are false. What is needed then is a model that is so specified that local prices may be identified as either endogenous or exogenous, depending on the values of certain empirically estimable parameters or on certain statistical relationships that hold in one case and not the other. In Section 4 we make a direct test of the model's underlying hypotheses that local prices move proportionately to world prices and that domestic credit expansion does not affect local inflation.

Before such a model is presented, however, it is useful to look more carefully at the assumptions underlying Equation (9–2). Some of these assumptions may be retained in the later model. Others require considerable exploration and change, particularly if the model is to be applied to a wider variety of country experiences.

1. One problem with Equation (9–2) is definitional: in a developed banking system with a central bank the authority issues high-powered money, H, that is, $H = R + D$, and the relevant measure of D comes only after an examination of the combined financial operations of the central bank and the Treasury; while R consists not simply of gold reserves, SDRs and deposits of foreign exchange, but must be corrected for official holdings of the short-term liabilities and assets. There are a number of possible institutional settings in which correct measurement of ΔH, ΔR, and ΔD will not occur by looking only at the balance sheet of the central bank. A few of these are international reserves are held by more than a single government department, or held by the Treasury alone; high-powered money is issued by both Treasury and central bank; the government's short-term liabilities are held by foreign governments and central banks. For these reasons we would submit that the correct way to measure changes in D is through the flows over time in the government–central bank budget constraint. In this definition the sources of government funds consist of tax revenues, t, the net

issuance of debt, i_g, and the issuance of high-powered money, h. (Henceforth flows are denoted by small letters.) The uses of government funds are the net acquisition of international reserves, r, and the purchase of goods and services, y_g. This definition may then be used to express the components of $\Delta H = \Delta D$ as

$$h = r + (y_g - t - i_g)$$

(9-3)

The last three terms thus constitute the ΔD that must be measured.

2. A second question relating to Equation (9-2) is the appropriate time period over which it holds. Actual money holdings may differ substantially from desired stocks over long periods of partial adjustment, implying expansions in domestic credit do not immediately "leak out" and over relevant time horizons the sum of coefficients of lagged values of ΔD sum to less than unity. However, there are greater difficulties with the simple model than the appropriate lag structure.

3. Perhaps the strongest assumption underlying Equation (9-2) is that the determinants of the demand for money are exogenous, and therefore, unaffected by the supply of money. To see how extreme this assumption is, consider what it implies for the price level. While foreign prices may be independent of the money supply can the same be true of prices of nontraded goods? To make a case for such a proposition, one would have to argue that the price of nontraded goods is strictly proportional to export and import prices. However, to satisfy equilibrium conditions these prices also must bear a determinate relation to each other, which depends on the production transformation function and the state of demand, a relation that would be proportional only under very specific assumptions. Thus the assumption of independence of money demand and supply is broken once nontraded goods are allowed into the picture. In the next sections we explore the implications of such a more complicated model.

Once we do assume that all prices are fixed in the world market, then it is easy to see why the level of output and employment are independent of monetary policy. Why should anyone close down a factory or lay off workers if he can see all his output at a fixed price in the world market? One would have to assume institutionally fixed wages to have unemployment in such an economy; and even then the output level would be exogenous in the sense that producers can sell what they wish, abroad if not at home, and cannot be influenced by domestic manipulation in aggregate demand.

While the assumption of exogenous output is therefore logically consistent with the small country hypothesis, it seems unsatisfactory as a maintained hypothesis. Even small countries seem to have experienced periods of Keynesian unemployment and less than desired output by producers. Moreoever, imports appear to have a positive statistical association with short-run variations in real output in a manner contrary to that implied by Equation (9-2). Thus a more theoretical structure is needed to understand why the overall balance of payments appears explainable in a model that does not attempt to explain variations in output. This problem also will be explored below.

2. A SMALL COUNTRY WITH ENDOGENOUS PRICE LEVEL

To keep the presentation simple, we will assume that the government issues money, there are no banks, and no market in securities. Later in the chapter these institutions will be introduced, but the logic of the model may be seen by abstracting from them.

It is assumed that the household earns income from the production of an export good, x, and a home good, y. Income is disbursed on the home good, y_h, an imported good, v, on the flow accumulation of cash balances, m, and on the payment of taxes, t.[6] All the symbols are in nominal money units. Thus we have

$$x + y \equiv y_h + v + m + t \qquad (9\text{-}4)$$

It is assumed that government finances its expenditure through taxation, t, and the issuance of money, m^s. These funds are spent on the net purchase of international financial assets, r, and on the purchase of the home good.[7] We have

$$t + m^s \equiv r + y_g \qquad \text{or} \qquad (9\text{-}5)$$
$$m^s \equiv r + y_g - t = r + d$$

The excess demand for home goods may then be written:

$$E(y) \equiv y_h + y_g - y = x - v - m - t + y_g$$

When the definitions of the balance of payments ($r = x - v$) and of the government budget constraint are introduced, we have

$$E(y) \equiv m^s - m$$

Looking behind the definitions to the economic determinants of m^s and m, we shall demonstrate that excess demand for home goods is a function of P_y and the money stock M_s. We shall then assume that the home good market is cleared by the movement of that price.[8]

This model stands in contrast with the simple one-country model presented earlier, where the only endogenous variable is r, determined by a structural equation (9-2). As we saw earlier, that relation implied a positive relation between r and prices. But in the present model, P_y is endogenous, related to d, and is not fixed; thus (9-2) is not sufficient to determine r. An additional relation in which the home goods market clears is necessary. It will be seen that the second relation, which also implies a relation between r and P_y, can be interpreted as the "conventional wisdom" on the balance of payments and underlies the usual "micro" approach to balance-of-payments analysis.

To put it another way, in the short run with the money stock fixed a determinate price of y brings $E(y)$ to zero in a stable fashion. In addition, in the short run the flow of reserves, r, simultaneously adjusts the flow rate of increase in the money supply toward flow money demand. Thus to repeat, in the short run the model has two endogenous variables, r and P_y.

In the long run, M_s constitutes a third endogenous variable. In the long run, with the money stock determined by government budget activities and reserve increments, the money stock, r, and P_y all attain stable equilibrium values.

2.1. The Determinants of m^s: As shown in the government budget constraint (9-5), the growth of the money supply consists of two terms—r, the net growth of international financial assets, and a composite term $y_g - t$, which, in the simplified institutional setting assumed here, is the growth of domestic liabilities of the government, d. We shall assume that d is exogenous, but that r depends on the factors influencing exports and imports. Two factors stand out—P_y and M_s. It is assumed the prices of exports and imports are exogenous. When P_y rises, there will be two effects—a substitution of consumer spending away from y and toward imports and a substitution of production away from exports and toward y. Both effects will lead to an excess supply of y.[9] The two effects, also by assumption, lead to a reduction in the excess of exports over imports.

The balance of payments also depends on M_s, the money stock. Holding everything else constant, a higher level of M_s would lead to an increase of household expenditures and thus an increase of imports and a decline in the balance of payments position. To summarize, the determinants of m^s may be written:

$$m^s \equiv r\,(P_y, M_s) + d, \quad \text{where } r_1, r_2 < 0 \qquad (9\text{-}6)$$

The $r\,(\cdot)$ function, which constitutes the traditional wisdom about the balance of payments, implies a negatively sloped relation between r and P_y for a given money stock, as shown in Figure 9-1. The function shifts downward for larger values of M_s.

2.2. The Determinants of m: We shall assume that the desired flow rate of hoarding responds to the stock disequilibrium. If households wish to hold more money than they have at present, then they will hoard, and conversely, if they wish to hold less. Thus it is immediately evident that the flow rate of hoarding is negatively related to M, the stock of money. But what determines the desired level of money stock; and will households move immediately to the desired level, or will they adjust fractionally and with a lag? We shall adopt the approach that households use money as a shock absorber to even out the flow of real consumption in the face of short-run variations in prices.[10] This role of money may be seen by rewriting the consumer budget constraint:

$$m \equiv x + y - y_h - v - t$$

An increase in the price of exports would raise the household's income. So would a rise in the price of the domestic goods since $y > y_h$. Assume that the household expects such increased income to be temporary and holds real consumption constant. This assumption implies that households engage in short-run hoarding or saving of money in the face of the expectation that real income will fall to

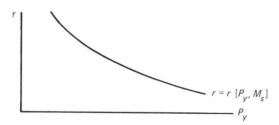

FIGURE 9-1. Graphical Relation Between Prices and the Balance of Payments—Monetarist View

its original level at a later date. Thus the holding of money as a shock absorber will be positively related to the price of y and price of exports. Import prices may also affect hoarding, though the direction of the relation is ambiguous.[11] It is also reasonable to assume that the demand for money as a shock absorber is negatively related to the amount of money so held.

Households also store wealth in the form of money. This part of the demand dominates in the long run but presumably changes more slowly and will not be discussed in detail in the theoretical model. However, in any econometric estimation involving changes over time one would expect long-run demands for wealth to play a role.

We shall then write m in terms of its determinants:

$$m = f(P_y, M_s) \qquad f_1 > 0, f_2 < 0 \qquad (9\text{-}7)$$

Combining (9-6) and (9-7), the market clearing of the price of domestic goods can be written as a single equation:

$$\dot{P}_y = g(E[Y]) = g(m^s - m) = g(r[P_y, M_s] + d - f[P_y, M_s]) \qquad (9\text{-}8)$$

For a given level of the money stock and of d, Equation (9-8) implies a stable market clearing process since $r_1 < 0$ and $f_1 > 0$.

Over time the money supply will also change, as a consequence of the government budget and balance of payments flows, and a second equation is added:

$$\dot{M}_s = m^s = r(P_y, M_s) + d \qquad (9\text{-}9)$$

For a given level of d, the money stock and price level reach equilibrium through a stable process at which $m^s = 0; m = 0, r = -d$.[12]

2.3. Equilibrium with Fixed and Variable Money Supply.

The approach to short-run equilibrium may be depicted graphically by imposing on Figure 9-1 the representation of the flow money market equilibrium condition $m^s = m$. Writing this as $r = -d + f(P_y, M_s)$ we may plot the relation as an upward sloping function in the r, P_y plane. This is shown in Figure 9-2, together with the negatively sloped "micro" relation $r = r(P_y, M_s)$.

As mentioned earlier, the upward sloping relation is an implication of the simple, small country approach discussed at the beginning of the chapter. If P_y were exogenous, as claimed in that model, then there would be no need for the graph. The flow of reserves would be determinate, as only one r satisfies the flow equilibrium relation,

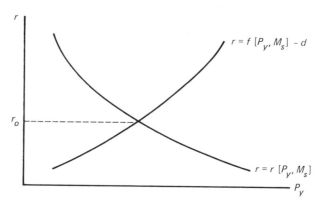

FIGURE 9-2.   Joint Determination of the Balance of Payments and Home Goods Prices

$r = f(P_y, M_s) - d$, for the given values of P_y and M^s. However, in the present model P_y is endogenous, and the short-run, flow equilibrium pair, P_y, r, are found at the point on the $r(P_y, M_s)$ function that implies equilibrium in both the home goods and money markets.

The approach to equilibrium with a variable money supply may also be described in Figure 9-2. Suppose for the sake of example that the intersection, r_0, is a positive balance of payments, and $d = 0$. Then the money stock will increase. The negatively sloped $r(\ )$ function will shift back to the left, and the positively sloped $m = m^s$ function will shift down to the right. The net effect is to eliminate the balance-of-payments surplus and change the money supply at full long-run equilibrium when stock as well as flow demands equal supplies.

We can now see the short-run and long-run effects of changing d. Begin at full equilibrium with $d = 0$. Then raise d to some positive number. In the short run, holding M^s constant this yields an increase of P_y equal to $-1/(r_1 - f_1)$ and a reduction of r equal to $-r_1/(r_1 - f_1)$. This increase of d will yield money supply growth because $\Delta r/\Delta d + 1 > 0$.

In the new full equilibrium, when the money supply stops growing the flow value of r equals the negative of d while P_y has risen (from the original $d = 0$ equilibrium) by $-f_2/r_2(r_1 - f_1) - r_1(r_2 - f_2)$. Whether P_y rises more in the long run than the short run depends on the difference $r_2 - f_2$.

Note that this long run does not imply homogeneity of degree zero; that is, the equilibrium real money stock is not necessarily invariant to changes in the flow rate of domestic credit creation, d.

Unlike the result of the simple model, all domestic credit creation does not leak out through corresponding losses in reserves. The reason is that the creation of domestic credit raises the demand for home goods and household's perception of their long-run incomes since $y > y_h$. Households, by assumption, are unaffected by the falling relation of reserves to domestic credit in the equilibrium money stock that this credit creation implies.

In a more realistic world, where international reserves are limited, households might use the change in the composition of the money stock in forming their expectations about the future course of relative prices and react accordingly. In other words, the composition of the money stock would enter the behavioral functions. However, in such a world governments also would act to stem the reserve loss by either reducing credit expansion or varying the effective exchange rate. Of course, the latter policy might include variations in tariffs and other limitations on international commerce and finance as well as straightforward variations in the exchange rate. The discussion of these reactions by households and governments goes far beyond the scope of this chapter and will be treated in the authors' future work.

2.4. The Shock Absorber Hypothesis. The shock absorber hypothesis is derived from the permanent income theory of consumption. It underlies the preceding discussion of the hypothesis that cash hoarding and dishoarding are used to maintain a constant level of utility in the face of expected but temporary variations in real income. Deeper examination of this hypothesis reveals more clearly the nature of the $r(P_y, M_s)$ and $f(P_y, M_s)$ functions discussed earlier and permits a closer identification of the exogenous elements of the government budget constraint. Look again at the household budget constraint and rewrite it in terms of prices and quantities.

$$m \equiv x \cdot P_x + y \cdot P_y - y_h \cdot P_y - v \cdot P_v - t$$

where x, y, y_h, and v all now represent quantities rather than nominal values. Now assume that t, P_x, and P_v are fixed and derive $f_1 = \delta m / \delta P_y$.

$$\delta m / \delta P_y = \left[P_x \cdot \frac{\delta x}{\delta P_y} + P_y \frac{\delta y}{\delta P_y} \right] - \left[P_y \cdot \frac{\delta y_h}{\delta P_y} + P_v \frac{\delta v}{\delta P_y} \right] + y - y_h \quad (9\text{-}10)$$

Assuming competitive equilibrium in the production of x and y, the first bracketed term is zero. Assuming consumer utility maximization and a fixed level of utility, the second bracketed term is zero. Thus the effect on hoarding of a change in P_y is

$$\delta m/\delta P_y = y - y_h > 0 \qquad (9\text{-}10')$$

Now look at the balance-of-payments relation implied by the shock absorber demand for hoarding. Rewrite the budget constraint and derive $r_1 \equiv \delta r/\delta P_y$.

$$r \equiv x \cdot P_x - v \cdot P_v \equiv m - y P_y + y_h P_y + t \qquad (9\text{-}11)$$

$$\delta r/\delta P_y \equiv \delta m/\delta P_y - y + y_h - P_y \frac{\delta y}{\delta P_y} + P_y \frac{\delta y_h}{\delta P_y}$$

Substituting from above, we see

$$\delta r/\delta P_y = - P_y \frac{\delta y}{\delta P_y} + P_y \frac{\delta y_h}{\delta P_y} < 0 \qquad (9\text{-}11')$$

Note that $\delta y_h/\delta P_y$ is negative for a constant level of utility. Thus the negative slope $\delta r/\delta P_y$ depends only on substitution effects in the production and consumption of y.[13]

It may also be seen that m and r depend negatively on the actual amounts of cash held. Assume that the consumption levels y_h and v depend on cash holdings. Then

$$\delta m/\delta M_s = - P_y \cdot \delta y_h/\delta M_s - P_v \cdot \delta v/\delta M_s \qquad (9\text{-}12)$$

and

$$\delta r/\delta M_s = - P_v \cdot \delta v/\delta M_s \qquad (9\text{-}13)$$

We may now see more clearly the $r(P_y, M_s)$ and $f(P_y, M_s)$ functions underlying the equilibrium depicted in Figure 9-2. The $f(\ )$ function depicts the behavior described in (9-10) and (9-12); the $r(\ )$ function depicts that described in (9-11) and (9-13). The condition of equilibrium that implies $m^s = m$ may again be written as the upward sloping function.

$$r = m - d = f(P_y, M_s) - d \qquad (9\text{-}14)$$

While the downward sloping r function may be written

$$r(P_y, M_s) = m - yP_y + y_g P_y + y_h P_y + t = f(P_y, M_s) \atop - E(y) - d \qquad (9\text{-}15)$$

Exogenous shifts in the two functions may be seen by rewriting them with the d term made explicit:

$$r = (xP_x + yP_y - y_h P_y - vP_v - t) - (y_g P_y - t) \qquad (9\text{-}14')$$

$$r = (xP_x + yP_y - y_h P_y - vP_v - t) - (yP_y - y_h P_y - y_g P_y) \atop - (y_g P_y - t) \qquad (9\text{-}15')$$

It may be seen that a shift of d that occurred through a rise of government demand for y, holding t constant would shift (9-14′) but not (9-15′). On the other hand, a change in d that occurred because of an exogenous change in the level of tax collections would have *no* effect on either function because it would change the demand for hoarding by an equivalent amount. This rather extreme result is due to the shock absorber assumption that the household views changes in the determinants of its cash flow as temporary, maintaining a consumption level that yields a constant level of utility. There is no question that if a change in t were expected to be permanent, there would be a smaller effect on m because the household would change its long-run consumption level.

2.5. An Expanded Model. It is possible to increase the range of the model by introducing the commercial banking system and a central bank. The government–central bank will issue high-powered money to be used exclusively as a reserve by the commercial banks. There will be a securities market in the liabilities of government, business, and households, all assumed to pay the same interest rate, n. Securities will be purchased by foreigners, by households, and by banks. Security sales by businesses will be used to purchase the domestic good for capital construction.

The new assumptions lead to a new set of budget constraints, an additional market, and an additional dependent variable, the interest rate n. Whereas the simpler model was solved by finding an equilibrium price level and money stock, this expanded system also has an equilibrium interest rate. That is, we assume there are no small countries in the world capital market; additional borrowings require payment of higher interest rates.

Budget Constraints

a. Government–Central Bank

Sources of funds are $h + t + i_g$, respectively, the issuance of high-powered money, tax receipts, and net sales of debt. Uses of funds are $r + y_g$ as before, the net acquisition of international reserves and the nominal purchase of goods and services. This implies that $h = r + (y_g - t - i_g)$. We shall now denote the parenthesized term as d.

b. Commerical Banks

Sources of funds are m^s, the net issuance of new deposit liabilities. Uses of funds are $h + i_B$, respectively, the acquisition of high-powered money and the acquisition of securities.

c. Households

As before, sources of funds are $x + y$, the income generated from production of exports and home goods. Uses of funds are $y_h + v + m + t + s$, the same as before, but with the addition of s, the net purchase of securities.

The Securities Market

It will be assumed that the interest rate equilibrates the flow demand and supply of securities. The demand for securities consists of foreign demand b_k, plus the sum of household and bank demand, $s + i_B$. The supply consists of the sum of security issuance by government and businesses, $i_g + y_B$. When the securities market is thus in equilibrium, the balance on capital account is the net foreign purchase of securities.

$$b_k = i_g + y_B - i_B - s \qquad (9\text{--}16)$$

Additional Behavior Assumptions

The cash hoarding demand m will now depend on P_y, M_s, n, and W, nonmonetary wealth, consisting of the net sum of securities owned by households. It will be assumed that cash hoarding will depend positively on W and negatively on n. It will also be assumed that the level of business investment depends negatively on n and that foreign purchases of securities depend positively on n.

Solution for P_y, M_s, and n

The new budget constraints again lead to the definition of excess demand for y equal to $m^s - m$.[14]

$$y_h + y_g + y_B - y \equiv m^s - m \qquad (9\text{--}17)$$

Assuming that P_y brings the excess demand for y to zero, we may write:

$$m^s = f(P_y, M, n, W)$$

Furthermore, assume that the growth of the money supply bears a fixed ratio, ϕ, to the growth of high-powered money:

$$m^s \equiv \phi(r + d)$$

Then equilibrium in the market for home goods implies the relation

$$\phi(r + d) = f(P_y, M_s, n, W) \tag{9-18}$$

For fixed levels of d, n, M, and W, this may again be represented as a positive relation between r and P_y.

When we do not impose the condition $m^s = m$, the definition in (9-17) again implies a negatively sloped relation between r and P_y. This may be seen by rewriting (9-17)

$$\phi(r + d) = m + y_h + y_g + y_B - y \tag{9-19}$$

thus

$$r = r[P_y, M, n] \tag{9-19'}$$

The arguments given earlier indicate that in (9-19) $\delta r/\delta P_y < 0$ since $\delta r/\delta P_y$ depends on the substitution responses of the households and firms to the change in P_y. It may also be seen that in (9-19') r depends on n because both m and y_B will decline if n increases.[15]

The system is closed by noting that equilibrium in the securities market determines a relation between m and h; and therefore, there is a second relation between n and r. This may be seen by rewriting (9-16), noting that b_k and y_B depend on n, s depends on W, and i_B depends on h.

Thus we have

$$b_k(n) = i_g + y_B(n) - s(W) - i_B$$

Substituting the identity

$$i_B \equiv m^s - h = h(\phi - 1)$$

we have

$$b_k(n) = i_g + y_B(n) - s(W) + h(1 - \phi)$$
$$= i_g + y_B(n) - s(W) + r(1 - \phi) + d(1 - \phi)$$

So we may write

$$r = b(n, W) \qquad\qquad (9\text{-}20)$$

To recapitulate, with a fixed level of the money stock M_s, and wealth W, Equations (9-18), (9-19), and (9-20) determine equilibrium levels of P_y, n, and r. When we allow the money supply to change as a result of the solution for r, a long-run equilibrium will be reached at which an equilibrium money stock is found. This solution implies $r + d = 0$. Thus in the long run, we have a solution for P_y, n, and M_s.

2.6. Floating Exchange Rates. Up to now the model has been applied to a fixed exchange environment in which the government purchased all the foreign exchange presented to it. It is possible to weaken this assumption so that one may simultaneously determine the price of home goods, the money supply, and the exchange rate. A free exchange rate system is usually conceived to be an environment in which the government fixes the money supply independently of the state of the balance of payments and allows the exchange market to set the price of foreign exchange. If the government allowed the money supply to be influenced directly by the state of the balance of payments, there could be no variation in the price of foreign exchange.

One can see the impossibility of simultaneous determination of the price of home goods, money supply, and exchange rate by writing the following market-clearing system. Note that p is the price of foreign exchange. (For the sake of simplicity, the discussion of this section ignores the capital market and returns to the model of Section 1.

$$\dot{P}_y = (r(P_y, p, M_s) + d - f[P_y, p, M_s]) \qquad\qquad (9\text{-}21)$$

$$\dot{M}_s = r(P_y, p, M_s) + d \qquad\qquad (9\text{-}22)$$

$$\dot{p} = -\theta\,(r[P_y, p, M_s]) \qquad\qquad (9\text{-}23)$$

The determinant of this system would be zero. However, it is possible to model the three variables if one imagines government intervention in the exchange market that leans against movements in the exchange rate, but does not attempt to fix the rate. If, for example, the government purchased foreign exchange when the price fell and sold foreign exchange when the price rose, then an additional functional relation would be added to the model. It would link changes in the money supply to changes in the exchange rate. Moreover, the exchange rate would now bring the net sum of all international financial transactions to zero. Those transactions that the government chose not to clear through its own foreign exchange stabilizing operation would be brought to equality with those transactions carried out for stabilization purposes. An important result of this section is that the government demand for foreign exchange must be price elastic. That is, the government must increase the domestic currency value of foreign exchange purchases when the price of foreign exchange falls. An inelastic demand for foreign exchange would destabilize the model.

The assumed type of reaction function is not unrealistic. Most governments intervene in the exchange market even when there is no stated par value for foreign exchange. The problem with modeling such an assumption, however, is that the target level of p that triggers off such intervention will itself change from one period to another. In the conceptual model, this issue will be ignored, and the target level will be assumed a constant. The problem would surface, however, if an econometric specification were considered.

Government intervention in the exchange market requires a redefinition of variables. In particular, r will now denote the net excess supply of foreign exchange, consisting of the sum of two elements, r^o, the private supply, and r^1, the government demand.[16] Note that both r^o and r^1 are measured in the domestic currency. The term r^1 denotes government purchase (or sale) of foreign exchange. It will be assumed that

$$r^1 = j(p) \qquad j' < 0$$

Government buys foreign exchange when its price falls, and sells foreign exchange when its price rises. The government budget constraint is then $m^s = r^1 + d$.

The new model is now written as follows:[17]

$$\dot{P}_y = r^o(P_y, p, M_s) + d - f(P_y, M_s) \qquad (9\text{-}21')$$

$$\dot{p} = -\theta \left(r^o(P_y, p, M_s) - j[p] \right) \tag{9-22'}$$

$$\dot{M}_s = j(p) + d \tag{9-23'}$$

It is assumed that P_y and p quickly reach equilibrium for a fixed level of the money supply. The determinant of the system in P_y and p is positive if $j' < 0$, as assumed. The value of this determinant is $j'(r_1^o - f_1) + f_1 r_2^o$. Also note that a higher level of the money stock implies a higher price of foreign exchange. Over time the money stock will change if $j + d \neq 0$, and the money stock will reach a stable equilibrium if $\delta M_s / \delta M_s \equiv j'(\delta p / \delta M) < 0$. This is assured if $j' < 0$. It is clear then how important the assumption of exchange rate intervention $(j' < 0)$ is to determine this hybrid system. Note that both the exchange rate and money supply are determinate and that the exchange rate brings r^o (the portion of the excess demand for foreign exchange that the government does not accommodate) into equality with $-r^1$.

3. SOME ASPECTS OF ECONOMETRIC ESTIMATION: A MODEL INVOLVING HOME GOODS, NO SECURITIES, NO BANKS, FIXED EXCHANGE RATES

We shall derive reduced form estimating equations for the preceding models on the assumption that the data satisfy short-run but not necessarily long-run equilibrium. Thus it is assumed that $m = m^s$ (the demand for hoarding equals the flow of new cash), but that the money stock continues to change as a result of new shocks to its exogenous component d. The statistical implications of this hypothesis will be contrasted with rival hypotheses about the determinants of the money supply.

The model may be written as a set of linear equations and put into the reduced form. It is also possible to include M as an endogenous variable, changing over time in response to the identity $m^s \equiv r + d$. In that case the final reduced forms involve distributed lags of exogenous variables—the government deficit, d, and the export and import prices, P_x and P_v.

The hoarding function $f(P_y, M_s)$ can be written

$$m = a_o + a_1 P_y - a_2 M + a_3 P_x - a_4 P_v \tag{9-24}$$

The equality of m^s and m may then be written:

$$r = -d + a_o + a_1 P_y - a_2 M + a_3 P_x - a_4 P_v{}^{18} \qquad (9\text{-}25)$$

The balance of payments equation $r = r(P_y, M_s)$ will be written:

$$r = u_o - u_1 P_y - u_2 M + u_3 P_x + u_4 P_v \qquad (9\text{-}26)$$

The coefficients of P_x and P_v reflect the assumptions that a rise of P_x will increase m and r, a fall of P_v will increase m, and has an ambiguous effect on r.

Equations (9-25) and (9-26) can be solved for r by eliminating P_y.

$$r = B_o - B_1 d - B_2 M + B_3 P_x - B_4 P_v \qquad (9\text{-}27)$$

where the Bs are functions of the as and us. Unfortunately, this system is not identified, that is, if Equation (9-27) is estimated we cannot obtain the original values of the as and us. However, if we assume that P_v does not affect the demand for money, as discussed earlier, the system is just identified.

If it seems desirable to incorporate M as an endogenous variable, we note that $M_T = M_o + \sum\limits_{0}^{T} (r_T + d_T)$. When this definition is substituted in (9-27) a difference equation may be formed:

$$
\begin{aligned}
r_T = {} & v_1 r_{T-1} - v_2 d_T + v_3 d_{T-1} + v_4 P_{xT} - v_4 P_{xT-1} \\
& - v_5 P_{vT} + v_5 P_{vT-1}
\end{aligned}
\qquad (9\text{-}28)
$$

This difference equation may be expressed as r_T equal to a sum of weighted lagged terms in d_T, P_{xT}, and P_{vT} where the weights decline to zero. That is,

$$r_T = \sum_{0}^{T} \delta_T d_T + \sum_{0}^{T} \epsilon_T P_{xT} + \sum_{0}^{T} \theta_T P_{vT} \qquad (9\text{-}29)$$

where the coefficients of the lagged exogenous variables represent weights that decline to zero. A least squares estimation procedure may be used by truncating the length of the lags. Once an estimate of r_T is obtained, it can be used to estimate M_T, and P_y may be estimated in the second stage from either (9-25) or (9-26). The discussion of the shock absorber hypothesis suggests that d might be replaced by y_g in (9-25).

4. SOME EMPIRICAL RESULTS: THE CASE OF PANAMA

Panama represents an interesting test case for the monetary model of the balance of payments. In addition to being physically small, which should tend to reduce the relative size of the home goods sector, it is one of the few countries in which foreign and domestic currency circulate side by side. The rate of exchange has been maintained at par with the dollar and is unlikely to change although there may have been some variations in the effective rate of exchange.[19] Thus it seems that the simple monetary theory should be quite appropriate in the case of Panama.

The simple monetary model yields two directly testable hypotheses—that local prices move in proportion to international prices and that domestic credit expansion has no effect on the rate of change of prices. To test the first hypothesis the growth rate of local prices, as measured by the consumer price index, was regressed on the growth rate of import prices, yielding the following equation:[20]

Growth rate of consumer prices

$$= 0.19 + 0.47 \text{ Growth rate of import prices}$$
$$(0.10)$$

$R^2 = 0.97 \; SEE = 1.33 \; DW = 1.55 \text{ (no serial correlation)}$

That is a 10 percent growth in import prices causes a growth in consumer prices of between 2.7 and 6.7 percent, but *not a 10 percent* growth as the simple model predicts. Regressions of the logarithms of consumer prices on import prices or import and export prices yield elasticities significantly less than one.[21] This result would reject the applicability of the simple model.

To test the second hypothesis, domestic prices were regressed on domestic credit creation, changes in reserves, real growth, and import prices. The influence of domestic credit was found to be significantly positive although quite small. Import prices had an insignificant effect on the growth of domestic prices when domestic credit was included. Thus this direct test also rejects the applicability of a simple model.

The effect of reserve growth on prices was generally insignificant. Since there is a high inverse correlation (−0.81) between reserves and import prices one might imagine that to some extent reserves act as a buffer to import price changes and at the same time buffer the effect of import prices on the domestic price index.[22]

As a preliminary test of the model of the balance of payments described in Section 2 we linearize equations (9-6) and (9-8), shown in Figure 9-2, and add an error term.[23]

$$r = a_o + a_1 P_y + a_2 P_x + a_3 M + \alpha_4 d + u_I$$
$$\ (+) \quad\ (+) \quad\ (-) \quad\ (-)$$

$$r = b_o + b_1 P_y + b_2 P_x + b_3 M + b_4 P_v + u_{II}$$
$$\ (-) \quad\ (+) \quad\ (-)$$

where the expected signs of the coefficients are shown in parentheses. These structural equations are just identified[24] but were estimated with two stage least squares to facilitate hypothesis testing.

The estimated structural equations, using the estimated values of r and P_y, respectively, are:

$$P_y = 91 + 0.06\ d + 0.04\ \hat{r} + 0.06\ M_{t-1} + 0.04\ P_x$$
$$\ (0.02)\quad (0.03)\quad (0.01)\quad\quad (0.02)$$
$$R^2 = 0.99\ SEE = 0.68\ DW = 1.03$$

$$r = 2199 - 29.9\ \hat{P}_y + 1.51\ M_{t-1} + 1.69\ P_x + 4.9\ P_v$$
$$\ (7.0)\quad\quad (0.44)\quad\quad (0.50)\quad (1.51)$$
$$R^2 = 0.91\ SEE = 10.7\ DW = 2.6$$

All variables are significant at the 95 percent level and of the correct sign except r, which is significantly positive at only the 90 percent level in the first equation, and M which is significantly positive in the second. As the hypothesis suggests, the coefficients of d and r are essentially the same (actually 0.056 and 0.042).[25] Imports appear to be highly elastic, that is, a rise in import prices reduces both import quantity and expenditure on imports substantially. Exports appear to be in elastic supply.

5. CONCLUSION

This paper develops an extended version of the monetary model of the balance of payments in which home goods provide some monetary independence in a fixed exchange rate economy. That is, an expansion of domestic credit does not fully leak out through an exactly equal loss of international reserves, but is partially absorbed by an increased demand for money, brought about by an increased relative and absolute price of domestic goods. The increased price of domestic goods occurs because government (flow) monetary creation (in excess of monetary demand at stable prices) represents an excess of purchasing power, relative to production, that must fall partially on home goods. Within this home goods model the extent of the reserve loss and local price change can be shown to be interdependent and to depend partially upon the traditional elasticities. The analysis can be extended to analyze the effect of exogenous changes in foreign prices and to include trade in securities as well as goods. In the latter case a local interest rate as well as a local price level is determined.

This analysis should not be interpreted to mean that "excess" domestic credit creation will leave international reserves intact. In fact, as we show, the quasi-equilibrium is one in which the flow loss of reserves equals the constant flow expansion of domestic credit although the total loss in reserves will be less than the expansion of credit. Clearly such a flow loss would be untenable in the long run and any country suffering such a loss would be forced to initiate some sort of corrective action.

In the last section of the paper we perform some econometric tests using data from Panama, which allow us to distinguish between the extended and simple monetary model. Panama was selected owing to the openness of its economy and the fact that U.S. currency circulates freely.

We show that even in an economy as open as Panama foreign and local prices do not move proportionately, as the simple model would predict, and that domestic credit does influence the local price level, contrary to the simple model. These results suggest that the extended model, involving the simultaneous determination of reserve loss, and the price level, is more appropriate. This model was then estimated using two-stage least squares and yielded satisfactory results, while the straightforward estimate of the reserve loss as a function of domestic credit expansion, assuming domestic prices exogenous as implied by the simple model, performs poorly.

NOTES

1. For example, see Johnson (1961) and Mundell (1968) for representations of such a model. Collery discusses how Hume's price specie flow model differs from the modern monetary theory of the balance of payments, elements of which are found in Johnson (1973) and Mundell (1971). A recent summary of the monetary model can be found in Whitman.

2. If we include a commercial banking system, then the money stock consists of net domestic and foreign assets of the consolidated banking system.

Under fractional reserve banking, domestic assets would be related to member bank reserves, which would in turn depend upon loans and foreign assets of the central bank. See note 3.

3. It is assumed implicitly or explicitly that demand for local money is independent of the ratio $R : D$ and, if asset markets are also considered, the interest rate is independent of the same ratio.

4. Assuming fractional bank reserves of $RR\%$, that currency is a liability of the central bank and a constant fraction, c, of bank reserves, and that either foreign exchange reserves of commercial banks are zero or count as bank reserves, we have

$$M_d = Demand\ Deposits + Currency$$
$$= MBR/RR \qquad\qquad + cMBR$$
$$= \frac{(D + R)}{1 + c} \left(\frac{1}{RR} + c\right) = (D + R)\ \frac{1 + c\ RR}{(1 + c)\ RR}$$
$$\Delta R = -\Delta D + \Delta M^d\ \frac{(1 + c)\ RR}{1 + c\ RR}$$

and the hypothesized coefficient of ΔD remains unity, with ΔR = the change in the banking system's holdings of reserves.

5. In an unpublished paper written in April 1974, Hans Genberg noted twenty-five studies of the empirical aspects of the monetary approach to balance of payments.

6. The general nature of the results does not change if exportables are consumed or importables produced. See Jones for a discussion of the real interactions of production and consumption where all three goods may be produced and consumed.

7. For the results of the model it is only necessary that the government buys some of the nontraded good although the above representation may be a reasonable approximation of behavior.

8. Thus there is no lack of demand because of the possibility of fixed prices in the home goods sector. For a similar model in which lack of demand and unemployment may result from a fixed wage price vector see Grossman, Hanson, and Lucas.

9. Rudiger Dornbusch analyzes a micromodel of devaluation in which the excess demand for the home good is offset by fiscal policy. This chapter assumes instead that excess demand for the home good is corrected in the short run by changes in its price and in the balance of trade (P_y and r); and in the long run it is corrected by changes in its price and in the money stock (P_y and M).

10. See Michael Darby's paper for a statement of this theory applied to the demand for consumer durables. Except for the results on the price of imports, all the results of this chapter can be obtained using the usual demand for money function.

11. A change in import prices that was known to be permanent would seem to have no affect on long-run money holdings since it does not cause a change in

the division of expenditures between present and future. A permanent rise (fall) in import prices would lower (raise) the real value (in terms of utility) of present consumption and saving-wealth-future consumption in exactly the same proportion. Therefore, there would be no incentive to vary hoarding. See Kemp for a discussion of this point.

A change in import prices that is not known to be permanent could affect hoarding either positively or negatively. When import prices fall temporarily, there is a tendency to spread the potentially higher level of consumption over the future by using cash balances as a shock absorber. On the other hand, if imports are durables, which may be an important case in developing countries, then there will be some tendency to take advantage of abnormally low prices by substituting holdings of goods for cash. See also note 13. Notice that both the income and speculative effects work in the same direction for home goods, as $y > y_h$.

12. It is assumed that P_y reaches an equilibrium for a given level of M_s and then is displaced by changes in the level of M_s. The stability of this process thus depends on sign $dM_s/dM_s = r_1(P_y/M_s) + r_2 = (r_1f_2 - r_2f_1)/(r_1 - f_1)$. Under the sign assumptions in the text this derivative is negative.

13. These relations may also be used to identify the effect of an exogenous increase in P_v, the price of imports. Using the same arguments as above we see that $\delta m/\delta P_v \equiv f_3 = -v$; while $\delta r/\delta P_v \equiv r_3 = -v - P_v(\delta v/\delta P_v)$. Thus, both of the curves shift in Figure 9-2 as a consequence of the increase in the price of imports. The upward sloping $f[\ ] - d$ function shifts downward while the downward sloping $r[\ ]$ function may shift in either direction, depending on the (utility constant) price elasticity of demand for imports. The impact on P_y is unambiguously positive since $\delta P_y/\delta P_v = (f_3 - r_3)/(r_1 - f_1) > 0$. The impact on r the balance of payments function is ambiguous since $\delta r/\delta P_v = (r_1f_3 - r_3f_1)/(r_1 - f_1)$. Note, however, that even if expenditures on imports are unchanged ($r_3 = 0$), the balance-of-payments effect will be negative since the higher P_y draws resources out of export production.

14. A series of substitutions lead to this result:

$$E(y) \equiv y_h + y_g + y_B - y \equiv x - v - m - s - t + y_B + y_g.$$

Substitute $\quad b_k = i_g + y_B - s - i_B$

$$E(y) \equiv x - v - m - t + y_g + b_k - i_g + i_B.$$

Substitute $\quad m^s \equiv h + i_B$

$$E(y) = x - v - m - t + y_g + b_k - i_g + m^s - h.$$

Note the definition of the balance of payments

$$r \equiv x - v + b_k$$

and substitute the government budget constraint.

15. As in the case discussed in Section 3, the two functions (9-18) and (9-19) shift asymmetrically with a change in d. This may be seen by rewriting (9-18) and (9-19) explicitly

$$\phi r = m - \phi d = x + y - y_h - v - t - s - \phi(y_g - t - i_g) \qquad (9\text{-}18')$$

$$\phi r = m - y + y_h + y_B + y_g - \phi(y_g - t - i_g) \qquad (9\text{-}19')$$

A number of variations of d are possible. If t and i_g are constant and y_g varies, then

$$\delta r/\delta d = -1$$

$$\delta r/\delta d = (1 - \phi)/\phi < 0$$

If y_g and i_g are constant, and t varies,

$$\delta r/\delta d = (1 - \phi)/\phi$$

$$\delta r/\delta d = -1$$

If y_g and t are constant, and i_g varies,

$$\delta r/\delta d = -1$$

$$\delta r/\delta d = -1$$

Those differences can play a role in identifying the econometric counterparts of (9-18) and (9-19).

16. The net private supply of foreign exchange $r^o = r^o(P_y, p, M_s)$ is derived from the function $r = r(P_y, M_s)$ described earlier in equation (9-6). It is assumed that $r_1^o < 0, r_2^o > 0$, and $r_3^o < 0$.

17. The function f would depend on the exchange rate if the demand for hoarding rises when foreign prices rise. In fact, under the shock absorber hypothesis m is independent of p since a change in traded goods prices changes the money value of exports and imports equiproportionately. Starting the analysis at a current account equal to zero, the change in p leaves m unchanged.

18. Notice that Equation (9-25) precludes a long-run demand function for money that is homogeneous of degree zero. While we have previously hypothesized homogeneity, it would be useful to test the hypothesis. Unfortunately, this would require a flow money demand equation that is nonlinear in P_y, yielding inconsistent estimators in the reduced forms. This problem might be solved through an iterative estimating procedure, but at present we have decided to use the linear forms.

19. Tariffs for purposes of import substitution have risen. The physical growth of the Free Zone of Colon vis-à-vis the rest of the country also tends to act as an effective devaluation.

20. All data have been taken from IMF International Financial Statistics (IFS). Monetary data for June were taken directly from the monetary survey for the following years: 1953-1954, IFS, December 1955, 1955-1956, IFS, December 1957, 1957-1962 IFS Summary, 1963-1964, 1967, 1965-1966, 1968, 1967-1968, 1970, 1969-1971, IFS, January 1973, 1972-1973, IFS, July 1975. Reserves = Foreign Assets (net) - Foreign Deposits, Domestic Credit = Money - Reserves. Money includes quasi-money but excludes currency. Most of the currency consists of U.S. bills, and there are no estimates of the amount circulating. The assumption used here is that the relationship between currency and quasi-money is stable.

Consumer prices were used to represent home goods prices as they contain a larger element of service prices than wholesale prices. The GNP deflator was not used, owing to the problem of a variable base. Import prices shown in the IFS are U.S. export prices; import unit values, shown in various issues of *Ingreso Nacional*, yield similar results. Presuming that the effective exchange rate, including transport costs, that is applicable to imports has risen more rapidly than U.S. export prices, the responsiveness of local consumer prices to import prices in Panama would be even lower than shown here.

21. Log consumer prices = 1.88 + 0.59 log import prices

$$(0.03)$$

$$R^2 = 0.98 \; SEE = 0.02 \; DW = 0.72$$

Log consumer prices = 1.43 + 0.58 import prices + 0.11 log export prices

$$(0.02) \qquad\qquad (0.03)$$

$$R^2 = 0.99 \; SEE = 0.01 \; DW = 1.09$$

Part of the slight difference in coefficients is attributable to the use of logarithms rather than percentage growth rates.

22. The revelant regressions are:

Growth rate of domestic prices = -0.92

+ 0.13 Growth rate of money due to domestic credit
(0.04)

+ -0.01 Growth rate of money due to reserve changes
(0.04)

+ 0.09 Growth rate of import prices
(0.12)

- 7.8 Growth rate of income
(9.4)

$$R^2 = 0.90 \; SEE = 0.99 \; DW = 1.75$$

Growth rate of domestic prices = -0.61

+ 0.03 Change Domestic Credit -0.03 Change in reserves
(0.01)   (0.01)

- 0.11 Growth rate of import prices
(0.08)

+ 11.5 Growth rate of income
(5.7)

$$R^2 = 0.96 \; SEE = 0.59 \; DW = 1.49$$

Growth rate of domestic prices = 0.02

+ 0.04 Change Domestic Credit
(0.01)

- 0.11 Growth rate of import prices
(0.10)

$$R^2 = 0.94 \; SEE = 0.70 \; DW = 1.85$$

23. Recall the linearization implies that the flow money demand function cannot be homogeneous of degree zero.

There is also a question of the appropriate point at which to measure prices and money for flows over a period. In this preliminary work the money stock is measured at the end of June, and prices at the year end. It could be argued that the appropriate measure of prices over the period and money stock would be centered at the middle of the period, that is, December from the year June to June. However, this presents certain problems due to seasonality and because the mid-period money stock is not completely independent of the flows. These problems will be investigated in later work.

24. Recall this depends upon our assumption that import prices do not enter the money demand function. However, we have just seen that import prices do not significantly influence domestic prices when domestic credit is included.

25. In the direct regression of r on d, allowing for nonlinearities in the demand for money, the coefficient of d was not significantly different from zero as opposed to the coefficient of one predicted by the monetary theory.

$$r = -7.6 + 0.01 \, d + 0.96 \, (\text{growth of income} \times M)$$
$$ (0.22) \quad (0.58)$$

$$- 3.83 \, (\text{growth of price} \times M)$$
$$(1.26)$$

$$R^2 = 0.94 \; SEE = 8.1 \; DW = 2.34$$

26. Equations (9–30) and (9–32) are derived in the text as (9–18) and (9–20). Equation (9–31) goes back to Equation (9–6).

27. Foreign purchases of domestic securities may also depend on the exchange rate for two reasons. First, because of speculative anticipations of future changes in the exchange rate, and second, because foreign demand perhaps should be measured in the foreign unit of currency and then converted to domestic currency at the going exchange rate.

REFERENCES

Collery, A. *International Adjustment, Open Economies and the Quantity Theory of Money.* Princeton Studies in International Finance No. 28, Princeton University, 1971.

Darby, M. "The Allocation of Transitory Income Among Consumer's Assets." *American Economic Review* 62:5 (December 1972), 928-941.

Dornbusch, R. "Devaluation, Money, and Nontraded Goods." *American Economic Review* 63:5 (December 1973), 871-880.

Genberg, H. "A Summary of Some Recent Research on the Monetary Approach to Balance of Payments Theory." Geneva: April 1974 (unpublished).

Grossman, H., Hanson, J., and Lucas, R. "The Effects of Demand Disturbances Under Alternative Exchange Rate Regimes." Brown University Working Paper No. 76-12.

Johnson, H. "Towards a General Theory of the Balance of Payments." In *International Trade and Economic Growth.* Cambridge, Mass.: Harvard University Press, 1961, 153-161.

——. "The Monetary Approach to the Balance of Payments," in M. Connolly and A. Swoboda, eds. *International Trade and Money.* Toronto: 1973, 206-224.

Jones, R. "Trade With Non-Traded Goods: The Anatomy of Interconnected Markets." *Economica* (May 1974).

Kemp, M. *The Pure Theory of International Trade.* Englewood Cliffs, N.J.: Prentice-Hall, 1964.

Mundell, R. *International Economics.* New York: Macmillan Publishing Co., 1968.

——. *Monetary Theory: Inflation, Interest and Growth in World Economy.* Los Angeles: Goodyear 1971.

Appendix 9

Some Additional Aspects of Econometric Estimation in More Complicated Models

Add securities, banks, and the rate of interest to the model of Section 3, but keep the exchange rate fixed. The reduced form of this system may be derived by looking back at Equations (9-18) to (9-20) and changing the specifications slightly. We shall split the balance of payments r into its components b_c, the balance on current account, and b_k, the balance on capital account. The actual solutions will not be presented because of their length, but the solution will be described heuristically. There are now five equations in this system:[26]

Equilibrium in the market for home goods

$$\phi(r + d) = f(P_y, M, n, P_x, P_v, W) \tag{9-30}$$

The balance on current account

$$b_c = r(P_y, M, P_x, P_v) \tag{9-31}$$

The balance on capital account

$$b_k = i_g + y_B(n) - s(W) + r(1 - \phi) + d(1 - \phi) \qquad (9\text{-}32)$$

where

$$b_k = b_k(n) \qquad (9\text{-}33)$$

$$r \equiv b_c + b_k \qquad (9\text{-}34)$$

The endogenous variables in this system are r, b_c, b_k, P_y, and n. The procedure followed is to note that we may transform (9–31) into

$$b_c = f(P_y, n, E) \qquad (9\text{-}31')$$

by substitution from (9–33) and (9–34). The term E denotes the exogenous variables. In addition, (9–32) may be transformed into

$$b_c = h(n, E) \qquad (9\text{-}32')$$

by substitution from (9–33) and (9–34). We may then solve (9–32′) for n as a function of b_c; solve (9–33) for P_y as a function of b_c, and substitute into (9–30′), deriving a reduced form for b_c as a function of the exogenous variables.

$$b_c = j(E) \qquad (9\text{-}35)$$

This reduced form may be estimated. The estimates b_c will be employed to derive a second-stage estimate of r as a function of b_c and the other exogenous variables. The vehicle for this procedure is Equation (9-32), which may be written as follows:

$$r(1 - \phi) = b_k(n(b_c, E)) - y_B(n(b_c, E)) - i_g - s(W) - d(1 - \phi) \qquad (9\text{-}36)$$

All of the right-hand side variables are now exogenous, and we may estimate (9-36). It should, therefore, be possible to find the effects of exogenous variables on the current account as well as on the capital account.

Ad Hoc Assumptions about Central Bank Behavior

At the beginning of the paper, it was suggested that h may not be an endogenous variable. The Central Bank may fix the level of the increase in high-powered money h, or it may vary h in response to variations into the interest rate.

If the Central Bank fixes the level of h independently of the other variables in the system, then h will be independent of r, the predicted level of the balance of payments. This hypothesis may be tested once r is estimated.

If h is a function of the interest rate, then equation (9–32) could be estimated directly with n as a function of W and the other exogenous variables in that equation. Then $\hat{h}$ could be estimated from $\hat{n}$, and $\hat{M}$ could be estimated from $\hat{h}$. These estimates could be compared with h and M derived from the earlier procedures. An additional test would be available from alternative estimates of (9–30). If h is a function of n, then P_y can be estimated as a function of present and past values of n and values of P_x, P_v, and W. These estimates of P_y could be compared with those derived above for, if h is independent of r, then P_y should be independent of r.

Add Floating Exchange Rates

Assume that government transactions in foreign exchange are a function of the exchange rate, as described earlier in Section 2.5. Again we shall write government purchases of foreign exchange as $r^1 = j(p, \overline{p}), j_1 < 0$. We shall also assume that the government has a target value of the exchange rate in mind. This target value is not a rate that they wish to achieve, but a benchmark that serves to define the further range of government exchange operations. When this benchmark changes, as it is likely to do from time to time, the whole function will shift. The exchange rate brings the total volume of exchange market transactions into equilibrium, that is, $j = b_c + b_k$. Thus floating exchange rates may be introduced into the preceding model by expanding the system to six equations. As before we have equilibrium in the market for home goods:

$$\phi(r^1 + d) = f(P_y, n, E) \tag{9–37}$$

As before we assume that the exchange rate does not affect the demand for cash hoarding. E denotes the exogenous variables.

The balance on current account:

$$b_c = r(P_y, p, E) \tag{9–38}$$

The exchange rate does affect the current account.

The balance on capital account:

$$b_k = i_g + y_B(n) - s(W) + r^1(1 - \phi) + d(1 - \phi) \tag{9–39}$$

Foreign purchases of domestic securities:[27]

$$b_k = b_k(n) \tag{9-40}$$

The government's decision function for purchasing foreign exchange:

$$r^1 = j(p, \bar{p}) \tag{9-41}$$

Finally the exchange market equilibrium condition

$$r^1 = b_c + b_k \tag{9-42}$$

Conceptually, this system can be reduced to four equations and then solved for b_c as a function of the exogenous variables. By substituting from (9-42) and (9-40), equation (9-37) may be written as

$$b_c = f(P_y, n, E) \tag{9-37'}$$

By substituting from (9-40) and (9-42), Equation (9-39) may be written as

$$b_c = g(n, E) \tag{9-39'}$$

By substituting (9-38), (9-39), and (9-41) into (9-42) we have

$$p = p(P_y, n, E, \bar{p}) \tag{9-42'}$$

This system of four equations may then be solved for b_c as a function of the exogenous variables. The econometric procedures would then follow those described for the fixed exchange rate case. Note that the measurement of $\bar{p}$ is not possible so that it may be necessary to use dummies for specific periods when it is known from other information that $\bar{p}$ has changed.

10

GABRIEL SIRI | A Minimodel of External Dependence of the Central American Economies*

1. INTRODUCTION

This chapter describes a small econometric model showing the high degree of dependence of the Central American economies on external factors that are beyond the control of internal policy measures, such as world prices of the principal export commodities. The model is composed of extremely simple submodels of the five Central American countries that are interrelated by equations of intraregional trade.[1]

Given the prices of the main export commodities, the model "forecasts" GDP, starting from the first year of the sample period 1966–1975, with an average margin of error of 2 percent (dynamic simulation generating its own endogenous variables, given the exogenous ones). On the basis of this small model it is possible to anticipate the

*Juan Rafael Vargas, and Ana Rosa de Osorio of the Permanent Secretariat of the General Treaty for Central American Integration, SIECA, cooperated in the quantitative analysis. Federico Sanz, also of SIECA, offered some suggestions regarding the conceptual aspects of the model. Some of the suggestions made by James A. Hanson were also incorporated. The study presented here is, however, the exclusive responsibility of the author.

short-term evolution of Central America's intraregional trade, its exports to the rest of the world, and the gross domestic product of each country, provided projections are available for the prices of the main export commodities. Although of minimum size, the model yields interesting results, notwithstanding the fact that its simplicity seriously limits its explanatory capacity. By definition, the model analyzes only the performance of exports and the domestic product of each country.

The analysis implicitly assumes that the economic system will continue to behave as it has in the past without incorporating internal economic policy measures that might alter either the countries' pattern of economic growth or possibilities of structural change. An effort has been made to present this paper in clear didactic terms. In particular, the description of the model has been kept as simple as possible, omitting some of its theoretical underpinnings.

2. STRUCTURE OF THE MODEL

The flow chart (Figure 10-1) shows the assumed system of operation of economic activity for a sample economy (Nicaragua). Basically, the model for each country is composed of the following six behavioral equations:

$$
\begin{array}{ll}
\begin{matrix} \text{Annual Growth} \\ \text{of the GDP} \end{matrix} \quad \begin{matrix} \text{Function of} \\ \text{= the Growth of} \end{matrix} & \begin{bmatrix} \text{Main Exports} & \text{Exports to} \\ \text{(Coffee, Cotton,} & \text{Central} \\ \text{Bananas, etc.} & \text{America} \end{bmatrix}
\end{array} \qquad (10\text{-}1)
$$

$$
\begin{array}{ll}
\begin{matrix} \text{Exports to} \\ \text{Central} \\ \text{America} \end{matrix} \quad \begin{matrix} \text{= Function} \\ \text{of} \end{matrix} & \begin{bmatrix} \text{Total Exports from} & \text{Obstacles to} \\ \text{``Other'' Central} & \text{Intraregional} \\ \text{American Countries} & \text{Trade} \end{bmatrix}
\end{array} \qquad (10\text{-}2)
$$

$$
\begin{bmatrix} \text{Honduras-} \\ \text{El Salvador} \\ \text{Conflict} \\ (1969) \end{bmatrix}
$$

$$
\begin{array}{ll}
\begin{matrix} \text{Exports of} \\ \text{Coffee, Cotton,} \\ \text{Bananas, etc.} \end{matrix} \quad \begin{matrix} \text{= Function} \\ \text{of} \end{matrix} & \left[\dfrac{\text{World Prices of Coffee, Cotton, etc.}}{\text{Domestic Price Level}} \right]
\end{array} \qquad
\begin{matrix} (10\text{-}3) \\ (10\text{-}4) \\ (10\text{-}5) \\ (10\text{-}6) \end{matrix}
$$

The models for each country include equations for their four most important export commodities. The products analyzed constitute a

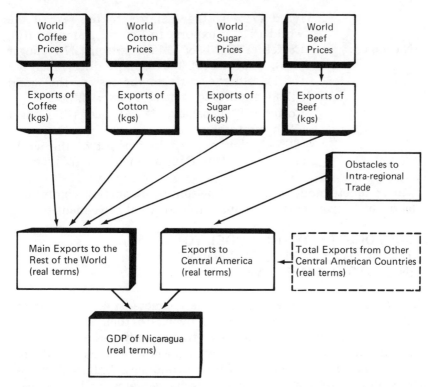

FIGURE 10-1. Flow Chart of the Minimodel of External Dependence of the Central American Economies (chart for Nicaragua, as an example)

substantial part of the total exports of each country, as is evidenced by the percentages listed below, corresponding to the years 1971–1975:

Guatemala: Coffee (30%), bananas (5%), cotton (11%), sugar (9%); subtotal of the four products analyzed (55%); other exports to the rest of the world (14%); exports to Central America (31%).

El Salvador: Coffee (45%), sugar (6%), cotton (12%); subtotal of the three products analyzed (64%); other exports to the rest of the world (8%); exports to Central America (28%).

Honduras: Coffee (18%), bananas (31%), timber (16%), beef (7%); subtotal of the four products ana-

	lyzed (72%); other exports to the rest of the world (21%); exports to Central America (7%).
Nicaragua:	Coffee (13%), beef (11%), cotton (27%), sugar (5%); subtotal of the four products analyzed (56%); other exports to the rest of the world (21%); exports to Central America (23%).
Costa Rica:	Coffee (26%), bananas (27%), beef (8%), sugar (5%); subtotal of the four products analyzed (66%); other exports to the rest of the world (14%); exports to Central America (20%).

The complete model utilized in the simulation analysis comprises a total of thirty-five behavioral equations and twenty-five identities.

3. CONFORMITY OF THE MODEL TO THE ACTUAL CONDITIONS FOUND IN CENTRAL AMERICA

The openness of their economies is a characteristic feature of the Central American countries, which, owing to their size and geographical position, have remained traditionally oriented toward external trade. The economic policy of the governments has adapted itself to this natural tendency of these economies. With rigid and relatively low tariff barriers,[2] stable exchange rates, and, moreover, restricted international liquidity, the growth of the Central American economies has tended to fluctuate in accordance with the increases and decreases in exports.

Balance-of-payments deficits tend to contract money supply and thus aggregate demand. In addition, the Central American countries, when faced with balance-of-payments deficits, often have played by the rules of the gold standard game contracting aggregate demand and restricting imports by means of monetary and fiscal policies designed to reduce consumption and investment. Recently, however, the governments have shown some reluctance to continue this traditional pattern of contraction of the economies in the face of trade imbalances.[3] Nevertheless, the economies continue to be very open and dependent upon exports for their growth.

Equation (10-1) reflects the hypothesis that exports constitute the driving force behind Central American economic growth. Beneath the simplistic formulation of this equation are hidden the multiple interrelationships that exist between exports and the whole economic apparatus of a country as well as the causal process through which they exert their influence.

Increases in exports represent increases in production, which generate more income in the form of profits and wages. These in turn are channeled into investment and consumption. At the same time, and perhaps even more important, exports provide foreign exchange, which permits more imports of consumer goods, raw materials, intermediate products, and capital goods, the latter largely determining the countries' future productive capacity. Thus a rise in exports has effects that spread to all sectors of the economies with direct and indirect influences on product, not only immediately, but also in subsequent years.

Equation (10-2) describes the performance of the exports of each country to the rest of Central America in terms of "the capacity to import of other countries" and the establishment of the Common Market. The equation could also have been expressed in terms of "income of other countries" (the goodness of fit of the regression coefficients is equally satisfactory). It was considered, however, that the explanatory variable "total exports of other Central American countries" in this quasi-reduced form of the equation represents not only income or purchasing power, but also the availability of foreign exchange, both of which are factors determining the capacity to import.

Equation 10-2 is a typical demand equation and should, in theory, include relative prices as an independent variable in addition to the variable representing purchasing power.[4] Unfortunately, sufficiently reliable statistical series are not available to establish the price relationships between the countries. In any case, since most of Central America's trade is "intrasectoral," this equation would have to be disaggregated into a large number of products in order to adequately measure the effect of prices.[5]

The variable representing the establishment of the Common Market is composed of the sum of the levels of customs tariffs between the countries plus the transport costs involved; both factors affecting the price of the products traded within the region.[6] Intra-area trade has grown at an accelerated pace since 1961 as a result of the elimination of the tariff barriers between the countries and the simultaneous reduction in the cost of highway transportation. Intra-area trade currently represents more than one-quarter of the total exports of the countries.

The variable DUM 1969 is a dummy variable representing the conflict between Honduras and El Salvador and, by definition, covers the years after 1969. Equations (10-3), (10-4), (10-5), and (10-6) for each country are based on the hypothesis that exports of the major commodities (coffee, cotton, bananas, sugar, beef, and timber) to third countries depend on present and past external prices of those commodities. They are supply functions describing a situation in which small producer countries are faced with prices established externally that they cannot influence by production decisions. The specific description for each equation is presented together with the results of the statistical analysis in Section 4.3.

The model would be more realistic if production for domestic consumption were separated from that destined for export. However, as a first approximation, it has been decided to keep the model simple, taking into account that these are goods produced mainly for export, whose domestic prices mainly depend on external prices.

4. RESULTS OF THE STATISTICAL ANALYSIS

The equations in the model, with the exception of those pertaining to the supply of export products, are formulated in linear terms and were estimated, in the first instance, by the simple least-squares technique. In those cases where strong autocorrelation in the errors was suspected, the equations were estimated by the Cochrane-Orcutt iterative technique.

The dependent variables of the model form a triangular matrix that can be divided into recursive blocks. In particular the estimated model can be divided into three "completely contained" subsystems (consistent and with a single solution). The three submodels may be estimated consecutively in the following order:

(i)   Exports of the main products (Equations [10-3] to [10-6]) constitute a diagonal matrix that can be divided into five small independent national models, each "completely self-contained".

(ii) Given the exports to countries outside Central America, estimated in the above model, exports to Central America can be calculated as an independent model (Equation [10-2]).

(iii) Once the results of the second model are obtained, the GDP can be calculated for each of the countries concerned (Equation [10-1]).

The results of the simultaneous simulation of the three subsystems, using the estimated equations described in Sections 4.1–4.3 are given in Table 10-1. The model has been simulated dynamically using the Gauss-Seidel iterative procedure, and as shown in Table 10-1, tracks quite well.

The remainder of this section analyzes the estimated equations. In

Table 10-1. Results of Dynamic Simulation of the Model for the Period 1966-1975

	Total Exports (in real terms)			Exports to Central America (in real terms)			Gross Domestic Product (in real terms)		
	Historical	Estimated	% Error	Historical	Estimated	% Error	Historical	Estimated	% Error
Guatemala									
1966	236.9	232.2	2.0	57.1	57.4	-0.5	1429.9	1515.5	-6.0
1967	210.7	211.6	-0.4	67.9	68.6	-1.0	1488.6	1556.0	-4.5
1968	235.4	241.6	-2.6	78.6	73.2	6.9	1619.2	1650.7	-1.9
1969	255.1	270.5	-6.0	86.2	87.8	-1.9	1695.9	1749.4	-3.2
1970	277.1	286.4	-3.4	101.1	98.8	2.3	1792.8	1839.7	-2.6
1971	273.8	265.3	3.1	92.4	82.9	10.3	1892.8	1898.1	-0.3
1972	323.9	311.8	3.7	103.6	87.0	16.0	2031.6	2020.6	0.5
1973	368.3	377.4	-2.5	117.3	110.3	6.0	2169.4	2161.8	0.4
1974	417.6	391.0	6.4	127.5	126.2	1.0	2307.7	2255.6	2.3
1975	402.3	400.3	0.5	119.3	128.3	7.5	2352.7	2293.3	2.5
El Salvador									
1966	184.8	200.5	-8.5	56.2	57.6	-2.5	825.4	816.4	1.1
1967	203.5	189.3	7.0	73.8	65.9	10.7	870.3	847.4	2.6
1968	207.5	202.5	2.4	83.2	65.7	21.0	898.4	882.7	1.7
1969	197.2	198.2	-0.5	70.0	66.7	4.7	929.8	908.5	2.3
1970	219.9	214.4	2.5	69.8	68.6	1.7	957.4	945.2	1.3
1971	225.2	224.7	0.2	74.2	70.9	4.4	1001.7	980.1	2.2
1972	277.0	254.7	8.1	78.2	70.2	10.2	1058.4	1027.8	2.9
1973	297.4	297.1	0.1	88.7	85.2	3.9	1103.6	1084.3	1.7
1974	343.3	322.4	6.1	105.6	98.8	6.4	1169.7	1145.4	2.1
1975	342.9	376.6	-9.8	80.6	98.9	-22.7	1219.6	1216.3	0.3
Honduras									
1966	142.0	139.8	1.5	19.0	20.9	-10.0	550.0	555.8	-1.1
1967	148.9	140.2	5.8	20.2	22.2	-9.9	579.8	584.2	-0.8
1968	162.9	151.3	7.1	26.3	21.9	16.7	616.2	612.4	0.6
1969	152.2	148.5	2.4	19.6	16.4	16.3	621.3	629.2	-1.3
1970	150.2	147.1	2.1	15.0	11.3	24.7	638.0	633.3	0.7

Table 10-1. continued

	Total Exports (in real terms)			Exports to Central America (in real terms)			Gross Domestic Product (in real terms)		
	Historical	Estimated	% Error	Historical	Estimated	% Error	Historical	Estimated	% Error
1971	160.3	144.9	9.6	4.2	3.0	28.6	666.5	637.5	4.4
1972	164.6	174.6	-6.1	5.4	9.1	-68.5	702.5	650.5	7.4
1973	191.1	218.2	-14.2	9.5	13.4	-41.1	732.0	694.2	5.2
1974	177.5	166.7	6.1	17.3	16.0	7.5	739.0	690.8	6.5
1975	206.3	215.9	-4.7	18.0	17.3	3.9	743.0	695.0	6.5
Nicaragua									
1966	133.8	148.4	-10.9	13.7	15.4	-12.4	570.8	590.8	-3.5
1967	140.9	152.3	-8.1	16.8	20.5	-22.0	610.6	635.9	-4.1
1968	144.3	145.5	-0.8	23.4	19.8	15.4	618.8	656.9	-6.2
1969	139.5	153.6	-10.1	26.5	30.4	-14.7	657.4	681.4	-3.7
1970	153.4	157.7	-2.8	41.8	39.0	6.7	671.0	695.2	-3.6
1971	158.7	163.9	-3.3	40.3	41.3	-2.5	703.4	725.7	-3.2
1972	204.2	204.8	-0.3	45.2	41.2	8.8	728.3	762.5	-4.7
1973	191.9	209.0	-8.9	41.6	37.8	9.1	750.1	796.1	-6.1
1974	215.7	221.0	-2.5	47.1	51.1	-8.5	855.8	864.8	-1.1
1975	205.6	185.2	9.9	57.6	52.1	9.5	868.6	879.4	-1.2
Costa Rica									
1966	135.5	137.4	-1.4	24.6	26.2	-6.5	647.3	653.9	-1.0
1967	140.6	150.4	-7.0	28.9	25.1	13.1	683.9	703.8	-2.9
1968	163.8	162.3	0.9	34.4	28.2	18.0	741.8	755.7	-1.9
1969	173.9	167.5	3.7	31.6	32.8	-3.8	782.6	804.4	-2.8
1970	197.4	172.5	12.6	39.6	38.0	4.0	841.2	851.3	-1.2
1971	196.0	183.5	6.4	38.4	37.6	2.1	898.3	898.1	0.0
1972	243.5	230.1	5.5	41.4	46.7	-12.8	971.8	952.4	2.0
1973	266.0	283.3	-6.5	50.9	56.4	-10.8	1046.7	1017.3	2.8
1974	305.3	305.7	-0.1	65.6	56.4	14.0	1103.8	1084.4	1.7
1975	292.3	263.0	10.0	53.7	55.9	-4.1	1140.5	1134.3	0.5

general, the series of observations used cover fifteen to twenty-five years; that is, at least the period 1960–1975. In some cases the sample periods are shorter, owing to lags in the independent variables. Moreover, some of the series have been shortened in order to analyze their most recent behavior.

The data on the GDP and export commodity prices were taken from the publications of the central bank of each country. The source of foreign trade figures is the Department of Statistics of SIECA.

The following abbreviations are used throughout the presentation of the statistical results:

( )   "t" coefficient

R^2 Multiple correlation coefficient of the regression

SE   Standard error

DW   Durbin-Watson coefficient

DF   Degrees of freedom

*   Equation that has been estimated by the Corchrane-Orcutt iterative method because high serial correlation of the error term was suspected (unsatisfactory Durbin-Watson statistic). All other equations were estimated by ordinary least squares. To simplify the presentation, the coefficients of the Corchrane-Orcutt adjustment are omitted in the description of the regression analyses.

4.1 Annual Change in the Gross Domestic Product—Estimates of Equation (10-1)

$$
\begin{bmatrix} \text{Annual} \\ \text{Change} \\ \text{in Real} \\ \text{GDP} \end{bmatrix} = \alpha \begin{bmatrix} \text{Annual} \\ \text{Change} \\ \text{in Total} \\ \text{Exports} \end{bmatrix} + \beta \begin{bmatrix} \text{Annual} \\ \text{Change} \\ \text{in Total} \\ \text{Exports} \end{bmatrix}_{-1} + \delta \begin{bmatrix} \text{Annual} \\ \text{Change} \\ \text{in Total} \\ \text{Exports} \end{bmatrix}_{-2} + \text{Constant}
$$

		R^2	*SE*	*DW*	*DF*
$\Delta(\text{GDP})$ * (Guatemala)	$= 1.04\ \Delta(X/po)$ (4.9) $-\ 42.58\ DM60 + 65.0$ (−2.1) (7.2)	0.64	22.1	1.78	17
$\Delta(\text{GDP})$ * (El Salvador)	$= 0.38\ \Delta(X/po)$ (2.5) $+\ 0.32\ \Delta(X/po)\text{-}1$ (1.9)	0.61	11.6	1.85	16

$$+ 0.36\ \Delta(X/po)\text{-}2$$
$$(1.9)$$
$$-\ 33.1\ DM58 + 27.2$$
$$(-2.7) \qquad (8.8)$$

$\Delta(GDP)$ = $0.67\ \Delta(X/po)$ 0.67   6.8   2.32   10
(Honduras)   (4.8)
$$+ 0.18\ \Delta(X/po)\text{-}1$$
$$(1.0)$$
$$+ 0.26\ \Delta(X/po)\text{-}2$$
$$(1.6)$$
$$+ 0.16\ \Delta(X/po)\text{-}3$$
$$(1.1)$$
$$-\ 21.7\ DM74 + 12.8$$
$$(-2.4) \qquad (4.6)$$

$\Delta(GDP)$ * = $0.30\ \Delta(X/po)$ 0.66   13.8   2.0   18
(Nicaragua)   (1.5)
$$+ 0.16\ \Delta(X/po)\text{-}1$$
$$(.7)$$
$$+ 1.11\ \Delta(X/po)\text{-}2$$
$$(4.4)$$
$$-\ 30.2\ DM58.9 + 18.9$$
$$(-2.9) \qquad (4.3)$$

$\Delta(GDP)$ = $0.65\ \Delta(X/po)$ 0.61   13.3   1.61   7
(Costa Rica) (1.4)
$$+ 0.81\ \Delta(X/po)\text{-}1$$
$$(1.8)$$
$$-\ 36.9\ DM64$$
$$(-2.4)$$
$$-\ 40.4\ DM72 + 27.2$$
$$(-2.3) \qquad (2.5)$$

where

$\Delta(GDP)$ Annual change of GDP in millions of \$CA (approximately equal to one U.S. Dollar) at constant prices.

$\Delta(X/po)$ Annual change in total exports in millions of \$CA divided by the GDP deflator.

$\Delta(X/po)$-1, $\Delta(X/po)$-2, $\Delta(X/po)$-3 Annual change in total exports of previous years.

$DM60$ Dummy variable representing political disturbances in Guatemala in the year 1960.

*DM*58   Dummy variable representing the political disturbances in El Salvador in the year 1958.

*DM*74   Dummy variable representing Hurricane Fifi, which devastated the Atlantic coast of Honduras in September 1974.

*DM*64   Dummy variable representing the eruption of the Irazú volcano in Costa Rica in 1964.

*DM*72   Dummy variable representing the eruption of the Arenal volcano in Costa Rica in 1972.

The *t*-values for most of the variables are acceptable. The low multiple correlation coefficients obtained in some cases, however, suggest the omission of additional explanatory variables.

An estimate of the total effect of a change in the value of exports on the growth of the GDP can be calculated by adding the regression coefficients α, β, and δ. The total obtained represents a measurement of the increase in the GDP (in $CA) that may be expected as the result of a permanent increase of one unit ($CA) in exports: The results for the individual countries are: Guatemala 1.0, El Salvador 1.1, Honduras 1.3, Nicaragua 1.6, Costa Rica 1.5.

Obviously, the coefficients obtained from this type of reduced-form equations, with highly aggregated components, must be treated with great caution. One of the most difficult problems to overcome lies in the possibility of omitted explanatory variables that may be collinear with those included in the equations, which would introduce a bias in the estimates of the regression coefficients. Since in this case, however, the "changes in exports" fluctuate substantially from year to year, it is unlikely that this variable will be strongly correlated with other variables that may affect the domestic product (such as productivity increases).

4.2 Exports to Central America—Estimates of Equations 10–2

$$\begin{bmatrix} \text{Exports to} \\ \text{Central} \\ \text{America} \end{bmatrix} = \alpha \begin{bmatrix} \text{Sum of Total} \\ \text{Exports of} \\ \text{"Other" C.A.} \\ \text{Countries} \end{bmatrix} + \beta \begin{bmatrix} \text{Cost of} \\ \text{Intra-} \\ \text{Regional} \\ \text{Trade} \end{bmatrix} + \delta \begin{bmatrix} \text{Dummy} \\ \text{Honduras-} \\ \text{El Salvador} \\ \text{Conflict} \end{bmatrix} + \text{Constant}$$

		R^2	*SE*	*DW*	*DF*
X CA (*G*) *	= 0.165 *XOTH*-1 -3.26 *CACM*	0.95	8.8	1.79	10
(Guatemala)	(9.6) (-1.9)				

$$+ 19.8 DM69 \qquad - 10.4$$
$$(2.2) \qquad (-0.6)$$

$X\,CA\,(S)\,*$ $= 0.095\,XOTH\text{-}1$ 0.86   10.7   1.62   12
(El Salvador)   (3.2)

$- .76\,CACM - 6.5\,DM69$
$(-2.1) \qquad\quad (-0.5)$
$+ 11.3$
(0.6)

$X\,CA\,(H)\,*$ $= 0.017\,XOTH\text{-}1$ 0.80   2.8   1.76   12
(Honduras)   (2.8)

$- 2.2\,CACM - 12.5\,DM69$
$(-3.7) \qquad\quad (-3.6)$
$+ 12.0$
(2.9)

$X\,CA\,(N)\,*$ $= 0.067\,XOTH\text{-}1$ 0.99   2.2   1.55   11
(Nicaragua)   (39.2)

$+ 13.2\,DM69 - 25.2$
$(13.0) \qquad\quad (-20.5)$

$X\,CA\,(CR)\,*$ $= 0.64\,XOTH\text{-}1$ 0.96   3.7   1.90   11
(Costa Rica)   (8.6)

$- 0.15\,CACM + 5.1\,DM69$
$(-1.9) \qquad\qquad (1.8)$
$- 16.9$
(-2.7)

where the value of exports to Central America and the sum of total exports of the "other Central American countries" are in millions of $CA and have been divided by the implicit price of the GDP. Total exports of the "other" countries comprise exports to Central America plus exports to the rest of the world of the four main products considered for each country, plus a residual comprising other exports to the rest of the world (all divided by the GDP deflator of the corresponding country). The Common Market variable, CACM, comprises the incidence of tariffs on the price of the traded goods, plus the incidence of transportation costs. The dummy variable represents the period following the Honduras–El Salvador conflict in August 1969.

The results of the regression analysis are satisfactory. The goodness of fit coefficients are adequate and appear to confirm the hypotheses that served as a basis for formulating the equations. The average standard error of the estimated values obtained through the dynamic simulation of the model in the ten-year sample period is approximately 9 percent.

The following average elasticities are derived from the estimated coefficients (percentage change in exports to Central America, resulting from a percentage change in total exports of the "other" Central American countries): Guatemala 1.38, El Salvador 1.01, Honduras 0.83, Nicaragua 1.83, Costa Rica 1.47. As may have been expected, Honduras has a lower coefficient because its industrial park is much less developed than that of the rest of the countries.

The DUMMY 1969 coefficient is negative for El Salvador and Honduras and positive for the other countries, which reflects the fact that the other countries, particularly Guatemala, have partially absorbed the reduction of the flow of trade between Honduras and El Salvador.

4.3 Main Exports to the Rest of the World-
Estimates of Equations (10–3) to (10–6)
4.3.1 Exports of Coffee

$$\log \begin{bmatrix} \text{Export of} \\ \text{Coffee} \end{bmatrix} = \alpha \log \begin{bmatrix} \dfrac{\text{Price Coffee}}{\text{GDP Deflator}} \end{bmatrix}_{-i} + \beta \log \begin{bmatrix} \dfrac{\text{Price Coffee}}{\text{GDP Deflator}} \end{bmatrix}_{-j} + \delta \text{ Time} + \text{Constant}$$

	R^2	SE	DW	DF
X COFFEE = 0.306 PC - 2 (Guatemala) (2.1)	0.88	0.068	2.07	15

X COFFEE   = 0.306 *PC* - 2
(Guatemala)   (2.1)
          0.396 *PC* - 9
          (3.6)
          0.040 TIME
          (8.8)
          - 0.176 *D67* + 3.76
          (-2.5)   (42.8)

X COFFEE* = 0.789 *PC* - 3
(El Salvador) (5.5)
          + 0.170 *PC* - 9
          (1.3)
          + 0.293 *PC* - 10
          (4.9)
          + 0.109 *PC* - 11
          (1.1)

	R^2	SE	DW	DF
X COFFEE* (El Salvador)	0.79	0.071	2.47	10

$$+ 2.25 \text{ AREA} - 9 \quad - 6.34$$
$$(11.1) \qquad\qquad (-7.3)$$

X COFFEE* (Honduras)	$= 0.491 \, PC - 2$ (3.1)		0.91	0.112	2.28 12

$$+ 0.173 \, PC - 9$$
$$(1.1)$$
$$+ 0.167 \, PC - 10$$
$$(2.5)$$
$$+ 0.305 \, PC - 11$$
$$(5.4)$$
$$+ 0.208 \, PC - 12$$
$$(4.3)$$
$$+ 2.51 \text{ AREA} - 9 \quad - 7.36$$
$$(6.8) \qquad\qquad (4.1)$$

X COFFEE (Nicaragua)	$= 0.335 \, PC - 1$ (4.2)		0.92	0.062	2.31 14

$$+ 0.199 \, PC - 7$$
$$(2.0)$$
$$+ 0.050 \text{ TIME}$$
$$(10.1)$$
$$- 0.223 \text{ D59} + 2.37$$
$$(-3.5) \qquad\quad (25.5)$$

X COFFEE (Costa Rica)	$= 0.362 \, PC - 2$ (1.7)		0.93	0.055	2.16 11

$$+ 0.373 \, PC - 8$$
$$(3.1)$$
$$+ 1.44 \text{ AREA} - 8$$
$$(11.2)$$
$$- 0.0039 \text{ CYCLE}$$
$$(-2.1)$$
$$- 0.299 \, D64 - 1.67$$
$$(-6.9) \qquad\quad (-3.4)$$

where exports of commodities are the natural logarithm of variables in thousands of metric tons, the prices of export products are the natural logarithm of the commodity price actually accruing to each country in thousands of $CA per metric ton, the GDP deflator is the index relating the GDP at current prices with the GDP at constant prices (1962 = 100), time is the series of consecutive cardinal members corresponding to the year of the sample period, and where called for, weather dummies were included in the equations.

These supply equations, as specified, assume that world prices affect short- and long-term exports:

In the first place, recent prices influence the intensity of the production of the crop (amount of fertilizer and insecticides, care in pruning, etc.). It should be noted that coffee is exported no earlier than the year following the harvest year, which helps to explain the lag observed in the first independent variable.

Moreover, in view of the fact that coffee is a perennial crop and the bush takes from four to six years to reach maturity, it is reasonable to expect that prices of seven to twelve years ago affect current output. Former prices affect both the intensity of cultivation and the planting of new trees. The natural logarithm of this last variable (AREA) is included in some regressions as a separate variable.

Coffee exports to Costa Rica are assumed to depend on two additional variables: a dummy corresponding to the eruptions of the Irazú Volcano during the period 1964–1966, and the often cited two-year coffee cycle. No evidence of the existence of this cycle was found for the other countries.

The results of the regression analysis indicate that coffee exports tend to increase (or decrease) as follows, in line with the stimulus of prices:

	Export-price Elasticity Corresponding to Recent Prices	*Export-price Elasticity Corresponding to "Former" Prices*
Guatemala	0.31	0.40
El Salvador	0.79	0.98
Honduras	0.49	0.45
Nicaragua	0.34	0.20
Costa Rica	0.36	0.37

Exports of Cotton

$$\log \left[\begin{array}{c} \text{Exports of} \\ \text{Cotton} \end{array} \right] = \alpha \log \left[\frac{\text{Price of Cotton}}{\text{GDP Deflator}} \right]_{-i} + \beta \text{ Weather Dummies} + \text{Constant}$$

	R^2	SE	DW	DF

X COTTON* = 0.851 *PA* - 1   0.93 0.157 1.04 13
(Guatemala)   (1.6)
                    -0.484 *DM*67/71 -5.52
                    (-4.0)   (12.9)

X COTTON* = 1.593 PA - 1   0.64   0.219   2.16   15
(EL Salvador) (3.0)
                -0.567 $DM67/9$ + 4.81
                (-3.2)   (15.5)

X COTTON* = 0.945 PA - 2   0.86   0.140   2.07   12
(Nicaragua)   (2.0)
                -0.343 $DM70/1$ + 5.51
                (-3.0)   (14.8)

Except in the case of El Salvador, the supply response to price changes appears to be low. The function requires further study to discover the determinants of export supply. It would be useful to analyze not only the effect of prices, but also that of the costs of factors of production and inputs and, in particular, of fertilizers and pesticides.

The dummy variables referring to the years following 1967 correspond to the decline in the area sown in Guatemala and El Salvador as a result of agricultural plagues in both countries. Both insect plagues and a heavy drought explain the sharp drop in production of cotton in Nicaragua during the period 1970–1971.

Exports of Bananas

$$\log \begin{bmatrix} \text{Exports of} \\ \text{Bananas} \end{bmatrix} = \alpha \log (\text{GNP/Capita USA}) + \text{Constant}$$

	R^2	SE	DW	DF

X BANANA* = 3.39 Y US   0.85   0.283   2.20   12
(Guatemala)   (3.2)
               -1.24 $DM65/7$ -23.51
               (-5.7)   (-2.6)

X BANANA* = 3.07 Y US   0.89   0.133   2.18   12
(Honduras)   (12.3)
               -0.43 $DM63/4$
               (-4.7)
               -0.59 $DM74/5$ - 19.29
               (-6.3)   (-9.2)

X BANANA* = 5.12 Y US - 36.93   0.92   0.172   1.52   15
(Costa Rica) (6.6)   (-5.6)

Since the foreign companies that transport and market bananas are generally also producers, the export prices have often been internal to the firms and therefore not treated as determinants of supply decisions. It is interesting to note that local producers receive barely over 10 percent of the final price of the product.[7]

The equations, as specified, show the high supply elasticity that exists with respect to GNP per capita of the United States, Central America's main export market (the variable is given in natural logarithms). The dummy variable DM 74-75 corresponds to the years following Hurricane Fifi, which devastated the Atlantic coast of Honduras in October 1973.

Exports of Sugar

$$\log \begin{bmatrix} \text{Exports of} \\ \text{Sugar} \end{bmatrix} = \alpha \log (\text{GNP/Capita USA}) + \text{Constant}$$

		R^2	SE	DW	DF
X SUGAR* (Guatemala)	= 3.42 *Y* US (2.7) + 1.24 *DM*75/6 – 24.77 (5.0) (–2.3)	0.87	0.258	1.64	11
X SUGAR* (El Salvador)	= 7.36 *Y* US (15.7) – 1.36 *DM*65 – 58.24 (–5.5) (–14.7)	0.93	0.239	2.21	12
X SUGAR* (Nicaragua)	= 2.90 *Y* US (5.3) – 1.06 *DM*66 + 0.40 *DM*75/6 (–6.1) (2.3) D75/6 – 20.43 (–4.5)	0.91	0.185	1.92	15
X SUGAR*	= 5.76 *Y* US (13.0) –0.38 *DM*75/6 –44.68 (–2.1) (–12.0)	0.87	0.250	1.72	14

Preliminary results of statistical analyses indicated a low *t*-value for sugar prices. The reason for this may be that part of the sugar crop is consumed locally under a price system that is not the same as that of the world market. Perhaps more important is the fact that the international sugar market is highly regulated and fragmented, and exports from the Central American countries have been very dependent for most of the period under consideration on a quota system established by the United States.

The results of the statistical analyses presented show a high elasticity of exports of sugar to variations of GNP per capita of the United States, the countries' main export market.

Exports of Beef

$$\log \begin{bmatrix} \text{Exports} \\ \text{of Beef} \end{bmatrix} = \alpha \log \begin{bmatrix} \dfrac{\text{Price of Beef}}{\text{GDP Deflator}} \end{bmatrix}_{-i} + \text{Constant}$$

		R^2	SE	DW	DF
X BEEF* (Honduras)	= 2.12 *PB* – 1 (4.4) + 0.137 TIME (16.1) – 1.05 *DM*74/5 + 0.54 (–7.1) (1.8)	0.96	0.111	2.36	9
X BEEF* (Nicaragua)	= 0.70 *PB* – 1 (2.7) + 1.65 *PB* – 3 – 0.44 *DM*65 (6.4) (–3.4) –0.56 *D*74/5 + 3.50 (–2.3) (38.6)	0.81	0.177	1.79	10
X BEEF* (Costa Rica)	= 1.70 *PB* – 1 (2.9) + 1.51 *PB* – 2 (2.7) – 0.55 *DM*65 + 3.24 (–2.3) (18.2)	0.85	0.259	1.52	12

The results of the regression analysis generally indicate high short-term supply price elasticity for exports of beef: Honduras, 2.1; Nicaragua, 2.3; Costa Rica, 3.2. In the case of Honduras the regression results also show a steady trend of export growth (14 percent per year), which appears to be independent of price variations.

Exports of Timber

$$\log \begin{bmatrix} \text{Exports} \\ \text{of Timber} \end{bmatrix} = \alpha \text{ Time} + \text{Constant}$$

$$
\begin{array}{cccc}
R^2 & SE & DW & DF
\end{array}
$$

X TIMBER = 0.094 TIME $\quad$ 0.95 0.090 1.66 12
(Honduras)   (15.8)
              − 0.606 *DM*76 + 3.74
              (−5.9)   (33.2)

Regression analysis does not indicate a positive supply price elasticity of exports of timber. This result probably reflects the efforts of the Government of Honduras to regulate the excessive exploitation of conifers in the past decade, particularly since the establishment of the Honduran Forest Development Corporation (COHDEFOR) in 1973. In particular, measures of export control explain the sharp drop in exports of timber in 1976. The TIME variable represents the historical growth trend of exports (about 9 percent) and dominates price effects.

5. CONSIDERATIONS ON THE POSSIBLE USE OF THE MODEL IN SHORT-TERM PLANNING

The model basically illustrates the situation of vulnerability that characterizes the Central American economies with respect to fluctuations in world prices of a few export commodities. Given this situation, the most desirable objective that could be achieved would be for the model (with the simplistic structure with which it is conceived) to function less accurately in the future.

However, in spite of the success that may have been obtained toward reducing the degree of external dependence of the economies through the integration process, the Central American countries are certainly not becoming less open. On the contrary, situations such as the deterioration in the terms of trade, the sudden rise in oil prices, and the increasing imports of raw materials required for the industrial development process may well have accentuated the vulnerability of the economies.

The model presented illustrates the magnitude of the dependence of the economies, and in particular, it analyzes in quantitative terms the effects of fluctuations in world prices. In this respect, the model could—until the time that more complete models become available—provide some general guidelines for the formulation of operative plans.

There is a series of measures that the Central American Governments can adopt—and in fact are adopting—to counteract the fluctuations deriving from the external sector. In view of the fact, however, that policy measures such as those affecting public investment, the production of "importable commodities," export diversification, external indebtedness, and so on, produce results in the medium term, any possibility of forecasting the fluctuations of economic activity some years in advance—if only roughly—is obviously useful.

To sum up, these are small economies that are highly dependent on an eminently unstable external sector; they are also characterized by their limited capacity to mitigate the fluctuations in world prices of their main export commodities and to effect the necessary internal adjustments as rapidly as might be desired. Econometric models that relate the external sector to the product of the economies are useful in that they make possible the forecasting of the effects of sharp drops in exports and, consequently, the formulation of timely measures that can attenuate recessions in economic activity.

NOTES

1. The specification of the model is based on the experience acquired in the formulation of a much more comprehensive model currently being developed by the author for SIECA's Study Unit for Integration and Development.

2. See *La revisión de la política arancelaria centroamericana*, SIECA/75/FIA/24/I/A. June 3, 1975.

3. The governments have adopted the following internal measures designed to reduce the countries' external dependence:

(i) Progressive reduction of the fiscal system's dependence upon the tariff revenue accruing to the governments, which favors the adoption of anti-cyclical public investment policies in periods of contraction of the external sector. The share of tariffs in total tax income has dropped from 49.6 percent in 1960 to 23.6 percent in 1974. See SIECA, *La revisión de la política arancelaria centroamericana*, op. cit.

(ii) Attempts to attain some degree of self-sufficiency in basic grains.

(iii) Import substitution of manufactures (one of the primary objectives of the integration process).

Moreover, the governments have not confined themselves to the adoption of internal measures, but have made use of external measures and those related to international liquidity.

(i) An increase of approximately 30 percent in the Central American common external tariff (San José Protocol for the Defense of the Balance of Payments, 1968).

(ii) Increase in external loans to finance public investment (the annual amount of external loans increased fivefold during the period 1969-1974).

4. There is no reason to assume at first glance that the variable representing "exports of other countries" is correlated with the excluded "relative prices" variable, thus causing errors in the estimated coefficients.

5. It can be pointed out here that in open economies such as those of the Central American countries, domestic prices are largely determined by world prices. Therefore, the inclusion of price equations in the model would probably confirm even further the high degree of external dependence of the Central American economies.

6. G. Siri, *El precio del transporte como arancel implícito en el comercio centroamericano*, SIECA/Brookings, 1974.

7. UNCTAD, *Sistema de comercialización y distribución del banano*, Committee on Commodities, eighth session, February, 1975, Tables 7 and 8.

11

DANIEL M.
SCHYDLOWSKY

Capital Utilization, Growth, Employment, Balance of Payments, and Price Stabilization*

1. CAPITAL IDLENESS IN THE MIDST OF CAPITAL SCARCITY

Latin American countries are unanimously regarded as being well endowed with labor and scarce of capital. In such a situation, common sense leads to the conclusion that existing capital should be intensively used and existing labor should be extensively applied. Yet casual empiricism and as well as more careful research indicates that this natural expectation does not correspond to reality; capital,

*An earlier version of this paper was presented at the Conference on Planning and Short Run Macroeconomic Policy organized jointly by the Instituto Latino Americano de Planificación Económica y Social, the Ministry of Planning and Economic Policy of Panama and the NBER, held at the Isla Contadora, Panama, October 31 to November 2, 1975. The author wishes to thank the participants of that conference especially Drs. J. Hanson, L.E. Rosas, J. Behrman, and M.I. Nadiri for their comments. He is also indebted to Mr. Jorge Rodriguez for valuable computational help.

despite its scarcity, is underutilized.[1] In parallel, large-scale unemployment exists. Hence a situation reminiscent of Keynes pervades the Latin American economic scene—the coexistence of unemployed labor and unemployed capital. What is more, this underutilization of capital appears not be a temporary phenomenon, the result of short-term fluctuations in aggregate demand or of building ahead of future need, but rather it appears to be a permanent situation, where the low rate of utilization of capital reflects the fundamental characteristics of the economic environment. A further element in the picture, which introduces a decidedly non-Keynesian note, is the foreign exchange constraint affecting most of these economies. As a consequence, it is not feasible to employ the existing capital and labor simply by expanding aggregate demand. Output might well go up with such a policy, but only for a time, since the import requirement generated by such an increase in industrial production would soon exhaust the international reserves of any of the countries in the hemisphere and hence the policy would abort on its own accord. At the same time, it is true that without additional demand, additional product could not be absorbed. Hence, Latin American capital and labor idleness may well be called quasi-Keynesian.

Capital idleness takes a number of forms. The most important is the short number of hours that machines are used during the day. Indeed, one would expect that under the existing conditions of scarcity, a very large number of firms would work two and three shifts. Yet the overwhelming number of enterprises work only a single shift. Although there are significant differences between firm's behavior in this regard, the widespread practice of single shifting is the most important contributor to underutilization of capital in the region. Second in line stands the large number of days when activities shut down. These comprise Saturdays, Sundays, holidays, and collective vacations. Again, one would think that the capital scarcity and labor plenty would dictate the use of machines and equipment 365 days a year. Yet this does not occur. Finally, there is a significant amount of underutilization of capacity within both shifts and days actually worked. In some cases machines are idle for large parts of the working day; in other instances intensity of utilization is lower than it might be.

A more detailed picture of the empirical situation than was heretofore available emerges from the research on capacity utilization in six Latin American countries, coordinated at Boston University's Center for Latin American Development Studies. The countries studied are Brazil, Chile, Colombia, Costa Rica, Peru, and Venezuela. Table 11-1 shows the percentage of firms working one, two, or three

Table 11–1. Percentage of Firms by Number of Shifts Worked

		1	2	3
Brazil	1974	35.60	25.00	39.40
Colombia	1973	58.79	20.46	20.75
Costa Rica	1974	66.56	11.00	22.44
Peru	1971	63.70	16.50	19.80
Venezuela	1974	73.80	12.70	13.50

Source: Country studies.

shifts with the percentage of labor employed and value added gen-about two-thirds of the firms typically work one shift, another 15 percent work two shifts, and the remaining 20 percent work three shifts. The country variations around this average are significant with Venezuela showing more single-shift and fewer three-shift firms and Brazil the opposite.[3]

The pattern inside different industrial groups, of course, varies both across industries and across countries, as can be seen from Table 11–2. It is very significant that there are some single shifters and some triple shifters in each industrial category, thus the products produced do not seem to be a determinant of the pattern of utilization. Whereas this might appear to be a phenomenon of aggregation, it also holds true at the more disaggregated level. The implications of this finding are very interesting. On the one hand, it would appear that the different behavior patterns of different enterprises would reflect a combination of different preferences and different environments; on the other hand, it indicates that it is not impossible to work more shifts in any sector as some of the single-shifting firms allege.

Table 11–3 tabulates the number of days worked in Peru. It is significant that the median firm works a six-day week throughout the year. On the other hand, relatively few firms are true "continuous process" firms, where the costs of stopping or starting the factory are tremendously large and where round-the-clock and round-the-year operation would thus appear to be indispensable.

An equally interesting view is offered by Table 11–4, which shows the percentage of capital stock that operates one, two, and three shifts with the percentage of labor employed and value added generated in plants working different number of shifts. It can be deduced from this table that the more capital-intensive firms operate a greater number of shifts. A similar conclusion is reached by cross-classifying firms by shifts worked and capital/labor ratios.[4] Further

Table 11-2. Distribution of Plants by Sector and Shifts Worked

ISIC	Colombia 1973			Costa Rica 1974			Peru 1971			Venezuela 1974			Brazil 1974		
	1	2	3	1	2	3	1	2	3	1	2	3	1	2	3
31 Food, beverage, and tobacco industries	45	25	30	60	17	23	51	20	29	66	18	16	47	29	24
32 Clothing and leather	65	19	16	59	12	29	55	22	23	74	13	13	36	19	45
33 Wood and woodwork	100	–	–	92	–	8	92	4	4	89	8	3	37	16	47
34 Paper, printing, and publishing	44	26	30	64	22	14	59	23	18	59	25	16	–	–	–
35 Chemicals and coal	53	18	29	66	13	21	66	10	24	62	10	28	35	15	50
36 Nonmetalic mineral	57	20	23	55	9	36	70	11	19	79	9	12	24	11	65
37 Basic metals	43	14	43	50	–	50	42	29	29	71	10	19	28	27	45
38 Metal working	66	24	10	28	4	18	83	15	2	83	11	6	36	42	22
39 Miscellaneous	72	14	14	86	–	14	54	15	31	85	12	3	28	36	36

Table 11-3. Peru 1971: Number of Days Worked per Year in Manufacturing Plants

Number of Days	One Shift	Two Shifts	Three Shifts	Total
Less than 100	8	–	–	8
100 to 150	18	5	1	24
151 to 200	31	7	6	44
201 to 250	104	15	16	135
251 to 270	95	15	17	127
271 to 290	113	50	55	218
291 to 310	317	71	62	450
311 to 330	48	9	22	79
331 to 360	13	2	28	43
361 to 365	22	18	24	64

Mean = 282
Median = 298
Mode = 302
Source: Ministry of Industry and Commerce, Industrial Statistics for 1971.

Table 11-4. Comparison of Shift Work Measures—Peru and Venezuela

	Single-Shift Firms	Double-Shift Firms	Triple-Shift Firms
Peru			
% of firms	63.7	16.5	19.8
% of employment	46.0	17.5	36.5
% of capital stock	21.9	13.9	64.2
% of value added	33.1	18.3	48.6
Venezuela			
% of firms	73.8	12.7	13.5
% of employment	50.5	16.3	33.2
% of capital stock	24.8	10.0	65.1
% of value added	41.8	15.3	42.9

confirmation is obtained from logistic regression analysis.[5] This result is encouraging since it indicates a lower degree of capital idleness than appears from looking at the number of firms working multiple shifts. It should be borne in mind, however, that low capital-intensive processes have high output/capital ratios and high labor/capital ratios, which means that the amount of output and employment forgone by low capital use in low capital-intensive firms is very much higher than would occur if it were the capital-intensive firms that were underutilizing their capital stock.

Table 11-4 also illustrates how crucial the aggregation scheme is to the average rate of utilization. Whereas two-thirds of the capital stock is in multiple shift firms, about half of employment is in single shift firms and such firms produce a little more than one-third of value added. A capital weighted index will therefore show high average utilization, an employment weighted or value-added weighted index will show lower utilization. Since what is of interest is the potential generation of employment and output, it is clearly the latter weighting schemes that are of interest.

The size of the establishment can also be seen to have an effect on the utilization of capital. Analysis of this variable must proceed with caution, however, since firms that work more shifts will simply by that fact be larger, thus output and employment must first be standardized at the single shift level before the impact on utilization can be derived. In the absence of this adjustment, one would pick up the impact of shifting on size and not the impact of size on shifting. Nonetheless, with this correction made, size continues to show an impact on utilization. This can be seen in summary form in Table 11-5, which shows data from Colombia, Costa Rica, Peru, and Venezuela on utilization by size of firms.[6] The Abusada logistic regressions also bring out size as a significant determinant of utilization in a multiple regression framework.[7]

The quality of organization is obviously also an important element affecting the level of utilization. The Chilean data show that family firms do not multiple shift nearly as much as do corporations. Indeed, when firms are classified by their form of legal organization (i.e., between corporations and noncorporations) it is found that corporate firms work more shifts than noncorporate ones. A similar variable also helps explain utilization in Colombia. Finally, a related variable, that of foreign participation, appears to have a positive correlation with utilization in both Peru and Costa Rica.

A further major variable that affects utilization is the extent to which a firm's output is exported. In the presence of economies of scale, protected domestic markets tend to develop oligopolistic structures, which hamper expansion of sales and multiple shifting. Exporting provides a "vent for surplus" for the production of additional shifts while not upsetting the domestic oligopolistic structure. Exports seem to be related to utilization in the Costa Rican and Peruvian data, but less so in the Colombian data.

The utilization picture is thus both varied and complex and its

Table 11-5. Shift Work by Size of Firm

Number of Workers per Shift:	1-20			21-50			51-100			>100		
Shifts Worked	1	2	3	1	2	3	1	2	3	1	2	3
						Percent of Firms						
Colombia	73	18	9	71	21	8	47	29	24	36	16	48
Costa Rica	73	9	18	73	6	20	50	15	35	67	20	14
Peru		n.a.		61	18	21	68	15	17	67	12	21
Venezuela		n.a.		75	13	12	77	11	12	67	15	18

explanation requires a multidimensional framework. The next section surveys some recent thinking in this regard.

2. THE PRIVATE AND THE PUBLIC CALCULUS OF CAPITAL UTILIZATION

The commonsense notion that when capital is scarce and labor is plenty the former should be used very intensively withstands rigorous analysis. At the same time, it rapidly becomes evident that there may be circumstances when it is preferable to use more capital than to work longer hours. Essentially, one is confronted with a tradeoff between working at less desirable hours, that is, using higher cost labor and using expensive capital. Such tradeoffs are imminently amenable to economic analysis, and indeed a number of models have been developed to analyze the optimality of different levels of capital utilization under varying conditions.[8] All these models maximize an objective, generally profits, but in a few instances the average income of labor, subject to the constraints imposed by a production function and the conditions in the factor and product markets. It turns out that the desirability of an intensive utilization of capital, that is, shift work, depends essentially on six elements: (1) factor intensities; (2) relative factor prices and particularly, the cost differential between different shift labor, that is, the shift premium; (3) the extent of the economies of scale; (4) the elasticity of substitution between the inputs; (5) the price elasticity of demand; and, (6) the price and availability of working capital.

A high shift premium by itself can make it optimal to keep capital idle. This is intuitively plausible since if the cost of higher shift labor is sufficiently expensive, it pays to buy additional capital for use with more first-shift labor rather than incurring the higher labor cost and using the existing capital more intensively. Strong economies of scale may also make single shift work optimal, since the cost savings due to greater volume of output per hour may more than outweigh the cost of keeping the capital idle part of the time. The price and availability of working capital may also make single shifting optimal whenever the cost of such capital is either very high or alternatively is tied in some fashion to the fixed assets owned by the firm. Even if the existence of each of these factors is sufficient to generate single shifting, the precise way in which they each affect optimal utilization is naturally the result of interaction between all of the six elements mentioned.

The tradeoffs entering the private and the public calculus on capital utilization are the same. Hence, in a perfectly functioning competitive economy, both would yield the same result, and the market mechanism would automatically bring about socially optimal rates of capital utilization. In Latin America we observe actions of entrepreneurs that apparently fly in the face of *prima facie* desirable social behavior. Thus either entrepreneurial behavior is optimal and our *prima facie* impression of socially optimal capacity utilization is wrong; or the *prima facie* impression of socially optimal behavior is right and entrepreneurs are irrational; or yet again the socially optimal capacity utilization is a high level of utilization *and* entrepreneurs are rational, but there are distortions in the markets facing entrepreneurs that explain the shortfall of the private from the social optimum.

Three kinds of factors cause divergence between the private calculus and the public good: (1) the prices at which entrepreneurs maximize; (2) the objective function maximized by entrepreneurs; and (3) nonprice factors.

It is well known that for private profit and the public good to coincide in a profit and utility maximizing society, prices must accurately measure marginal social utilities and marginal social costs. Unfortunately, a number of distortions exist in the Latin American price systems that systematically lead privately optimal capital utilization to fall short of the corresponding social optimum. The best known of these distortions relates to the wage rate, which is maintained above the social opportunity cost of labor by a combination of legislation and trade union pressure. The social calculus done at the shadow wage rate will thus naturally lead to higher utilization of labor and therefore a higher preference for more hours worked as opposed to more capital bought when compared to the private calculus. In addition to the divergence between the market wage and the shadow price of labor, the legislation of wage premiums reinforces the distortion against extensive use of existing manpower. Rules on overtime pay and nighttime pay are derived from precedents in the developed world, international custom, and political pressures and appear to have no relationship to the preferences of the work force to which they apply. An excess of a market night premium over the shadow night premium would by itself lead to underutilization of capital; in combination with a basic market wage in excess of the basic shadow wage, that effect is multiplied.[9]

Distortions also exist on the side of capital. The most well known of these distortions refers to the ceiling on interest rates, which are held below equilibrium level by a combination of government regulation and rationing. Equally important, however, are the tariff exemptions for the import of capital goods, which lower the private price of these goods below the social opportunity cost of either the savings or the foreign exchange. Further reinforcing this lowering of the price of capital are the tax provisions that allow deduction from the corporate income tax base of part or all of reinvested funds, provided these are put in real assets. Such deductions are equivalent to lowering the purchase price of new equipment to the private buyer, thus creating a further understatement of the cost of capital. As a final twist, many tax legislations specify depreciation of equipment in relation to a fixed lifetime, rather than proportional to use. This implies that profits derived from second- and third-shift output pay a higher effective tax rate than profits from first-shift operations, thus distorting the choice between producing an additional shift and expanding the plant.

It is evident that as the private price of capital diverges on the low side from its social opportunity cost, the private decision will tend toward the utilization of more capital-intensive processes and more machines utilized fewer hours compared to what could occur at the proper scarcity prices. Hence on this account also the private decision deviates from the public welfare toward low utilization.

A further element affecting the utilization decision relates to the availability of working capital. Typically, loans are plentiful and cheap for the purchase of capital equipment but expensive and few for the funding of working capital. What is more, in many instances loans are tied to the pledging of real assets. The net effect is to make the intensive utilization of capital either very expensive or impossible and to bias the private decision further toward the expansion of plant and equipment in preference to its utilization.[10]

Finally, the international trade policy of the Latin American countries with their well-known import-substitution and antiexport biases lead to relatively small domestic markets, often served by tight oligopolies, in which the economies of scale cannot be appropriately exploited. In this situation, the marginal social utility of export sales is well above the marginal private revenue. As a result, exports do not take place, and the rate of utilization is artificially depressed compared to the social optimum.

In summary, private profit maximization cannot lead to the maximization of social welfare and to a socially optimal utilization of existing capital stock nor of new, to be installed, capital stock, in view of the major distortions that exist in the price system—the overpricing of labor, the underpricing of capital, the discriminatory taxing of intensive utilization of capital, and the artificial limiting of the size of the market with the consequent underutilization of economies of scale.[11]

Consider now the possibility of entrepreneurs not maximizing profits. In this case, naturally the coincidence between the private and the public good, even at the optimal prices, need no longer hold. The principal nonprofit variables that entrepreneurs appear to be concerned with are two: (i) control over their enterprise and (ii) "tranquillity."

Concern with control arises out of two situations. The first of these is concerned with the explicit loss of property rights, the second with loss of quasi-rents. Fear of loss of property has affected utilization in Peru and in Chile. In the former, industrial law specifies a gradual transfer of shares to firms' workers with the consequence of participation of these in management. Under the provisions of the law, reinvestment postpones the time when workers achieve a 50 percent shareholding. As a result, entrepreneurs have great interest in expanding capital stock in order to postpone the day when their workers will be equal owners. The results in the acquisition of new fixed assets in lieu of utilization of existing assets. Furthermore, the incentive to adopt very capital-intensive processes of production within shifts is extremely strong. Finally, the workers themselves prefer expansion of fixed assets and greater capital intensity to expansion of the labor force, since every new worker dilutes the equity of the previously employed. A similar situation arose in Chile under Allende, where firms with larger work forces perceived themselves as being more liable to early takeover than firms with smaller work forces. In consequence, entrepreneurs preferred not to use their capital intensively in order to avoid provoking takeovers.

The second kind of control issue arises in fairly small owner-managed firms in which the technology of production or management is essentially the scarce asset. A good example is shoe production. In these situations, the entrepreneur perceives a continuous danger that his better foremen will set themselves up in business as rivals, and he thus wishes to minimize the amount of information his workmen have access to. This implies an obstacle to decentralization and growth of the firm and naturally an obstacle to multiple shift work since the night shift labor cost of the entrepreneur himself or of his family members is extremely high.

The concern with tranquillity arises essentially from labor-management relations. Depending on the institutional framework and the labor climate, entrepreneurs often prefer to keep their firms small and their labor forces decentralized. Thus it appears preferable to a good many of them to have 150 workers spread over three firms with three plants of 50 workmen each, working one shift in each plant, rather than having a single firm with a single plant working three shifts and having the same 150 workers. In the first case, there will be three different unions, each of which can be bargained with separately, whereas in the second case there will be one much more powerful and larger union. The entrepreneur decentralizes his risk and increases his "tranquillity" by fragmenting his labor force.

Nonprice factors are also at work in the utilization decision and may well contribute a significant explanatory element to the observed situation. A major nonprice factor is the problem of minimum scale plants. In many cases it is simply not possible to buy a plant small enough to serve the domestic market on a three-shift basis. (In other cases the alternative is between a second-hand large plant that is inexpensive and a new small plant that is significantly more expensive. In this case, to buy the large one and underutilize it is better both from a social as well as from a private point of view. It would be even better, however, to buy the large plant and use it intensively, which would require a change in trade policy; exports would have to be profitable. In these situations, however, it is price that is at work). Another nonprice element that appears to be important is sheer imitation of the way plants are organized in the more industrial countries. The simple fallacy of "what is good for the industrialized countries is good for us" leads not only to factor proportions inappropriate to the factor endowments of developing countries but also to patterns of utilization that are more appropriate to capital-rich labor-scarce countries than to the reality of Latin America. Product diversification contributes a causal element as well. Rather than having long production lines of standardized product, small production lines of many products lowers the output obtainable per unit of time. Whereas capital is not idle longer because it produces a more diverse output, it nonetheless is underutilized in the sense that production falls short of the potential. Again, trade policy may well be part of the problem because greater specialization would be possible only if a greater integration through world trade were achieved.

Social "custom" also hampers night work because transportation systems and other amenities may not be geared for round-the-clock operation. Evidently, if industry moved massively toward multiple shifting, these services would appear, thus we have here a classic case of pecuniary external economies. Finally two additional nonprice factors should be mentioned. The first of these is the phenomenon of building ahead of demand, which indicates a rational decision both in the private and in the public calculus, but where divergencies in both will still arise due to the distortions discussed previously as well as in the discount rate. The second element relates to the transition from the present pattern to one of greater shifting and refers to the risk inherent in a multiple shift operation. This risk takes two forms, one refers to the physical risk of breakdown of the machines, which is much more costly if there are fewer machines that produce more output than if there are many machines each of which produces little output. The second relates to the labor problems inherent in having larger work forces and even more to expanding the labor force through the addition of a shift under conditions where firing of labor may be hard or impossible. Under some Latin American regimes that have legislated labor tenure, the choice of a second shift in an existing enterprise versus the creation of a new first shift in a new enterprise entails taking on very different risks. Were the expansion of output not to be sustainable, it would be impossible to fire the second shift work crew; however, a new firm could be closed down and go out of business. Had the existing firm added a second shift, its first shift profits would be compromised and perhaps the existence of the whole firm would be in question; had it decided to create a subsidiary starting a new first shift, its liability would have been limited due to the normal protection of corporate liability.

The preceding discussion has brought out the wide variety of causal elements that enter into the underutilization of capital in Latin America. It is not surprising that many of the causal factors are there at the same time. Nor is it suprising that there is excess causation of underutilization. After all, for single shifting to occur it is sufficient that it be more profitable than multiple shifting. It is not necessary that it be more profitable by, say, a factor of five; nor is it necessary that in addition to being unprofitable it be risky, not consistent with "tradition," and not conducive to entrepreneural "tranquillity." Once the scales are tipped against the intensive utilization of capital, additional causes do not change the decision; they merely generate overcausation.

The existence of overcausation causes significant difficulties both in identfying the causal structure of idle capital as well as in designing the policy to cope with it. When more than enough causes are present, no single cause or cluster can be identified as "the" cause or causes; we simply know that there are a set of alternatively necessary and collectively oversufficient causes, many of which are present simultaneously. For policy design, the implication is that as many as possible of the causes should be neutralized by policy because we do not know which one would be residually operative and sufficient to cause the underutilization. Such a situation can certainly compound the policy design problem.[12]

3. NECESSARY CONDITIONS FOR THE FULL UTILIZATION OF INSTALLED CAPITAL

Given the fact that capital is now underutilized, what conditions must be fulfilled in order to make full utilization of existing installed capacity possible and, further, to enable newly installed capital to be used more fully as well? The answer involves macroeconomic factors as well as microeconomic firm theoretic factors because the purpose is to move not just individual enterprises but the whole industrial sector and perhaps some of the service sectors to multiple shifting. Furthermore, there is a distinction to be made between the short run, which involves increasing the utilization of already installed capital, and the longer run, which implies a change in behavior for newly added capital stock.

At the macroeconomic level, three necessary conditions must be fulfilled for making the utilization of existing capital possible: (a) demand must be available; (b) imported inputs complementary to domestic production must be available, (c) credit for working capital to finance the period of production must be available.

The availability of demand seems an obvious necessary condition because without a market additional output could not be sold. At the microeconomic level it could be argued that competitive firms face no market problems. Minimal price reductions would create a market. Alternatively, if markets are not competitive then the microeconomic solution is still price reduction.

At the macroeconomic level, however, increased output of a major part of the economy is at issue; hence price elasticities may be low. Furthermore, cost reductions would not be more than the per unit reduction of depreciation attendant to multiple shifting. Therefore the increase of demand for industrial output produced by price reduction will perforce be low. On the other hand, it is true that where multiple shifting is massively implemented, the new supply will generate some of its own demand, via the so called "Nurkse effect." In other words, additional output arising from multiple shifting will be accompanied by increases in income that will generate increases in demand, some of which will be for precisely those products of which additional output has become available. Whereas in the aggregate expenditure will equal additional income, except for the amounts flowing into monetary savings, such balance does not hold at the sectoral level. There will be excess supply of those items produced by sectors with newly increased utilization of capital, that is, industry, and there will be excess demand in the sectors for which output has not gone up, principally agriculture (it can be argued that services have a very highly elastic supply curve and hence will respond rapidly to the increased demand). These imbalances in sectoral demands and supplies can best be dealt with if recourse is had to the international market, the excess supplies are exported, and excess demands lead to competitive imports. In turn, such a solution requires export subsidization to compensate for the high cost of industrial products in most Latin American countries as well as liberalization of import regulations to allow in the goods necessary to satisfy the excess demand. Since exports as well as imports expand, a balance of payments deficit does not necessarily have to result.[13]

The availability of imported complementary inputs is an equally obvious necessity for the more intensive utilization of the existing installed capital since without indispensable raw materials it is not possible to produce. The question becomes one of paying for these imports, and it is clear that the most immediate and easily available source of such foreign exchange is the sale abroad of part of the output to be produced with those inputs. Hence the need to find a foreign market for the output dovetails very neatly with the need to earn the foreign exchange to pay for the inputs to produce that output. Both supply of output and demand for inputs lead naturally to a very active participation in international trade.

The need of credit for working capital results from the fact that production is not instantaneous, and hence firms hold inventories of embodied factors and raw materials as goods in process. Such goods in process involve the investment of national savings in inventories, and rapid increases in their size would ordinarily not be directly financiable by the producing firms themselves. At the same time, the higher level of output will generate higher demand for monetary balances, thus generating national savings in the form of money holdings. The creation of the respective money supply can take place through the extension of credit for working capital, thus neatly transferring the monetary savings to the firms that require those savings for investment in the working capital needed to make increased output possible.

The macro conditions that hold for the short run also hold for a new investment. Unless the foreign exchange constraint is removed through a trade policy aimed at active participation in the world markets, particularly one supporting export expansion, it will not be very helpful to depress the capital/output ratio through higher utilization of the investment. The only thing that would happen is that the trade constraint would become even more binding and no change in output would occur, just a shuffling around of the excess capacity from one sector to another. With the elimination of the trade constraint through an appropriate trade policy, however, the full benefits of a lower capital/output ratio and possibly a higher savings ratio can be realized. A shift in investment toward inventories (working capital) is also required for the longer run.[14]

On the microeconomic side, two conditions for full utilization of capital are necessary: (a) the profitability of such utilization; and (b) the relative unimportance of the nonprice factors restricting utilization.

With regard to profitability, in the short run all that is needed is that the revenue from increased output exceeds the costs. This is usually a condition that is easily achieved, particularly if the necessary macroeconomic conditions have been met. The longer run condition is more difficult to achieve, since any expansion of utilization in the short run can be substituted in the long run by a reduction of utilization and an expansion of capital stock. For the long run, therefore, it is necessary to eliminate the distortions that now make expansion of capital stock more desirable than utilization, that is, the relative profitability of working one, two, and three shifts has to be shifted sufficiently to make two and three shifts more profitable than single shifting. Under the prevalent condition of overcausation, it may not be necessary to remove all the separate incentives for single shifting, but enough of them need to be dealt with so that the scales are tipped in favor of multiple shifting.

Some of the nonprice factors are dealt with automatically through the side effects of the macroeconomic requirements for utilization. For example, product diversification and a minimal sized plant are dealt with automatically by the increased participation in the world market; externalities are dealt with by the simultaneous introduction of multiple shifting in all of industry. Risk is still a serious problem, however, and may require special treatment, particularly where labor legislation hampering the flexibility of hiring and firing is involved.

Surveying the macroeconomic and microeconomic necessary conditions for full utilization of installed capital brings out the manner in which the existing idleness of capital and labor in Latin America is non-Keynesian. The trade constraint must be removed and domestic price distortions must be dealt with. At the same time the similarity with the Keynesian analysis is also striking. Demand must be created, albeit foreign demand, fiscal and tax measures are appropriate, and an expansion of the money supply is part of the package. The characterization of the situation as quasi-Keynesian seems indeed appropriate.

4. THE GROWTH POTENTIAL OF CAPITAL UTILIZATION

Capital utilization provides two kinds of growth effects—a once and for all effect, arising from the intensive utilization of already ininstalled capital, and a continuous growth effect, arising from a lower capital/output ratio on new investments planned to work more shifts.[15]

The mechanism by which the once and for all effect takes place can be very simply stated. The more intensive utilization of existing industrial capital raises industrial output and incomes. The additional output obviously constitutes new supply, whereas the increase in incomes generates increased demand for agricultural and industrial goods and for services. In the absence of a positive and high short-run supply elasticity of agriculture goods, the increased demand for such goods translates directly into demand for imports. The increased demand for industrial goods can be satisfied in part by the increased industrial output, but sectoral differences in the composition of supply and demand will lead to net export supply in some industrial sectors and net import demands in others. Finally, the demand for services must be satisfied domestically, thus leading to another round of income, output, and demand creation. The excess supply of some industrial goods will require government support for sale abroad, thus causing some fiscal expenditure. On the other hand, additional imports will signify the collection of new import duties, and the higher levels of domestic income and output will signify higher payments of domestic taxes, both thus offsetting the export subsidies required to make selling abroad possible. The output and income increases that begin in the industrial sectors thus spread very rapidly to the rest of the economy, causing secondary income increases wherever supply elasticities are high, principally in services.

A higher level of utilization of new investment does not have a similarly complex set of macroeconomic interactions; however that higher level of capital utilization may well shift the comparative advantage of the economy since capital costs are lower under multiple shift operation. Such changes in comparative advantage, if they do occur, may well signify major structural changes in the economy over the long run. Furthermore, the policies adopted to achieve the higher level of utilization (e.g., export promotion) will by themselves change the growth path of the economy, bringing it closer to that dictated by the underlying comparative advantage of the country.

In order to obtain a sense of the magnitudes of the static, once and for all contribution to growth that the utilization of capital can make, it is useful to derive a simple GNP projections model. This model is developed in the following paragraphs and applied to six Latin American countries: Brazil, Chile, Colombia, Costa Rica, Peru, and Venezuela.

We begin by defining the GNP increase (V) as composed of increases in three sectors: increase in agricultural value added (V_A) increase in industrial value added (V_I) and, increase in service value added (V_S).

$$V \equiv V_A + V_I + V_S \tag{11-1}$$

The characteristics of the agricultural sector imply that a significant increase in output in the short run without substantial investment is highly implausible, that is, its "installed capacity" is fully utilized.

$$V_A = 0 \tag{11-2}$$

The increase in value added of the industrial sector is related to the amount of additional shift work as well as to the amount of initial value added being produced under current levels of utilization of capital. Equation 11-3 specifies the increase in industrial value added as a linear function of the existing level of value added and a proportional increase in shifts (S).[16]

$$V_I = \overline{V}_I \cdot S \tag{11-3}$$

In the service sector, it is assumed that any increase in demand must be satisfied from domestic supply since imports are not usually possible. On the other hand, the supply response to an increase in demand is assumed to be high. Indeed, to the extent that personal services or other highly labor intensive output is involved, high unemployment implies a supply curve of services that is infinitely elastic for a range. Even where some investment is required, it is often possible to raise output by a multiple very rapidly. Such is the case, for example, in construction. On the other hand, for some subsectors of the service sector, such as the generation of electricity, the elasticity of supply is rather low. For the purpose of the model, it has been assumed that the elasticity of supply of the service sector taken as a whole is infinitely elastic. This implies that some investment in this sector will be required to offset the low short-run supply elasticity of some of the subsectors. Equation (11–4) specifies this behavior and also note that services have an import component.

$$V_S(1 + m_S) = E_S \tag{11-4}$$

$$V_S = \frac{1}{1 + m_S} E_S \tag{11-4a}$$

where E_S is the new private expenditure on services, and m_s is the part of that expenditure that covers the import component of services expressed as a proportion of the respective national component.

We can now rewrite the increase in total value added as a function of the increases in value added in the industrial and service sectors:

$$V = V_I + V_S = \overline{V}_I \cdot S + \frac{1}{1 + m_S} E_s \tag{11-5}$$

The increase in total of private consumption and investment expenditures is taken to equal the increase in private disposable income, that is, the increase in total income minus domestic taxes.[17] In turn, the new private expenditure can be disaggregated into its sectoral components, and the distribution of expenditure takes place in accordance with the respective marginal propensities to spend.

$$E = V(1 - t_1) \tag{11-6}$$

$$E \equiv E_A + E_I + E_S \tag{11-7}$$

$$E_A = e_A E = e_A V(1 - t_1) = c_A V(1 - t_1) \tag{11-8}$$

$$E_I = e_I E = e_I V(1 - t_1) = (c_I + i_I)V(1 - t_1) \tag{11-9}$$

$$E_S = e_S E = e_S V(1 - t_1) = (c_S + i_S)V(1 - t_1) \tag{11-10}$$

$$e_A + e_I + e_S \equiv 1 \tag{11-11}$$

Note that in these equations the marginal propensities to spend (e_i) are composed of the marginal propensities to consume and to buy for investment purposes the goods originating in the respective sectors. Thus, for example, the expenditure on industrial goods (E_I) is determined by the propensity to consume industrial goods (c_I) and by the propensity to use industrial goods for investment purposes (i_I). The same holds for expenditure on services since investment has a component originating in the service sector, particularly when construction is involved. On the other hand, the demand for agricultural goods does not include an investment component, owing to the particular nature of the goods involved.

Inserting Equation (11–10) in Equation (11–5), collecting terms and solving for the increase in GNP, shows the total increase in value added arising from the more intensive use of existing installed capacity as depending on the initial level of industrial value added, the amount of increased shifting, and a multiplier that reflects the proportion of the new income spent on domestic services. Equations (11–12) to (11–13) portray this outcome symbolically.

$$V = \overline{V}_I \cdot S + \frac{1}{1 + m_S} e_S V(1 - t_1) \qquad (11\text{--}12)$$

$$V = \frac{1 + m_S}{1 + m_s - e_S(1 - t_1)} \overline{V}_I \cdot S \qquad (11\text{--}13)$$

In empirical applications, it is often difficult to determine the imported input into services and thus it is useful to simplify the formula with the assumption that no complementary imports exist in the service sector.[18] This leads to the expression shown in Equation 11–14.

$$V = \frac{1}{1 - e_S(1 - t_1)} \overline{V}_I S \qquad (11\text{--}14)$$

It is worth pointing out that the multiplier in this expression has the same rationale as the conventional Keynesian macro multiplier. In Keynesian theory we subtract the marginal propensity to consume because it constitutes that part of income that gets respent; in this model we subtract in the denominator the marginal propensity to spend on services out of disposable income multiplied by the ratio of disposable to total income, that is, again that fraction of income that will stay in the domestic spending stream and be spent on domestic goods.

To make empirical applications of the formula more readily understandable, it is useful to standardize the increase in value added with regard to the initial levels of GNP. This can be done by dividing both sides of Equation (11–14) by the initial GNP level, yielding the following:

$$\frac{V}{\overline{V}} = \frac{1}{1 - e_S(1 - t_1)} \frac{\overline{V}_I}{\overline{V}} \cdot S \qquad (11\text{–}15)$$

Table 11–6 shows the parameters necessary for empirical evaluation of the once and for all growth potential for six Latin American countries. It is interesting to note the range of variation that exists for the marginal propensities to spend, particularly for agriculture. Evidently the classification of processed foods as industrial output is a factor reducing the agricultural coefficient; however, other factors are surely at work too. The levels of domestic taxation and the shares of industry also differ by large amounts. It is not surprising, therefore, that the income multipliers vary as well.

Table 11–7 shows the increases in GNP obtainable by raising shift work to two and three shifts in each of the six countries and compares these increases to recent per capita growth rates. It appears that for these countries moving to two shifts is equivalent to between one-half and five years of per capita growth, whereas moving to three

Table 11–6. Parameters Entering Estimation of GNP Increases from Multiple Shifting

1. *Marginal Propensities to Spend:*

	e_A	e_I	e_S
Brazil	0.17	0.32	0.51
Chile	0.128	0.4059	0.4658
Colombia	0.16	0.28	0.55
Costa Rica	0.15	0.36	0.48
Peru	0.14	0.40	0.46
Venezuela	0.18	0.32	0.50

2. *Domestic Taxation, Share of Industry, Average Shift Work.*

	t_1	$\overline{V}_I/\overline{V}$	S
Brazil	0.1707	0.24	2.01
Chile	0.181	0.28	1.69
Colombia	0.0848	0.225	1.67
Costa Rica	0.156	0.19	1.55*
Peru	0.1063	0.239	1.69
Venezuela	0.045	0.171	1.84

*Production increases possible without additional shifting imply an equivalence of 1.33 shifts worked on average.

Table 11-7. Estimated GNP Increases from Multiple Shifting

	Brazil		Chile		Colombia		Costa Rica		Peru		Venezuela	
Shift Basis:	2	3	2	3	2	3	2	3	2	3	2	3
Absolute Increases:												
Industrial VA	14562.	87060	6603.5	22942.8	15340.8	33293.5	768.1	1935.7	11.705	40.755	2388.2	7572.4
Service VA	10673.9	63814	4073.0	14151.1	15555.5	33759.6	523.1	1318.2	8.170	28.447	2182.8	6921.6
Total VA	25235.9	150874	10676.5	37093.9	30896.3	67053.1	1291.3	3253.9	19.875	69.202	4571.0	14493.6
Percentage Increases:												
Industrial VA	2.07	12.42	7.13	24.76	8.27	17.94	9.34	23.55	4.43	15.41	4.29	13.60
Service VA	1.52	9.1	4.40	15.27	8.38	18.20	6.37	16.04	3.09	10.76	3.92	12.43
Total VA	3.6	21.52	11.53	40.03	16.65	36.14	15.71	39.59	7.52	26.17	8.21	26.03
Recent per capita growth rate	7.8		-3.1		4.1		3.6		3.0		2.3	
Memorandum:												
Average shifts worked	2.01		1.60		1.67		1.55*		1.69		1.84	
Δ Shift: equivalent to raising all firms to at least 2(3) shifts	0.16	0.99	0.40	1.40	0.61	1.33	0.5	1.67	0.31	1.31	0.46	1.16
Income multiplier	1.7330		1.6168		2.014		1.681		1.698		1.914	
Units in millions of	Cruceiros		Escudos		Pesos		Colones		Soles		Bolivares	
Base year	1974		1970		1972		1972		1971		1971	

*See footnote to Table 11-6.

shifts would imply an equivalent of between three and eleven years of growth.

It should be remembered that the foregoing analysis and numerical evaluation refer only to the once and for all impact of utilization. Naturally this once and for all change will raise the base from which future growth will take place and thus will provide a lasting absolute effect throughout time. A further growth effect is obtained, however, through the impact that the full utilization of newly installed machinery will have on the marginal capital/output ratio. The precise impact of such changes depends naturally on the extent of availability of cooperating factors, on the elasticity of substitution between capital and such factors, and on the relative price changes of capital and labor that might accompany the process.

An upper bound of this effect on the growth rate can be obtained by assuming that there is no substitution between capital and labor and that even after all existing capital is fully utilized, unemployed labor will continue to exist, that is, by adopting strict Harrod-Domar assumptions. Under these assumptions, the increase in the growth rate is directly proportional to the change in the capital output ratio resulting from multiple shifting and to the proportion of economic activity affected by such an increase. This can be seen from Equations (11–16) through (11–21), where g signifies the rate of growth, s signifies the average savings rate, k stands for the output/capital ratio, the subscripts represent before and after, p is the share of industrial value added in total value added, w is the proportional change in the output/capital ratio in industry, and the superscripts refer to nonindustrial (nI) and industrial (I) output/capital ratios, respectively. Moreover, w is also the proportionate increase in shift work.

$$g_0 = s_0 k_0 = s_0 [k_0^{nI}(1 - p) + k_0^I(p)] \qquad (11\text{–}16)$$

$$g_1 = s_0 [k_0^{nI}(1 - p) + k_0^I(p)(1 + w)] \qquad (11\text{–}17)$$

$$g_1 = s_0 [k_0^{nI}(1 - p) + k_0^I(p) + k_0^I pw] \qquad (11\text{–}17a)$$

$$g_1 = s_0 k_0 + s_0 k_0^I pw = g_0 + s_0 k_0^I pw \qquad (11\text{–}17b)$$

$$g_1 - g_0 = s_0 k_0^I pw \qquad (11\text{–}18)$$

$$w = S \qquad (11\text{–}19)$$

$$g_1 - g_0 = s_0 k_0^I p\, S \qquad (11\text{–}20)$$

$$\frac{g_1 - g_0}{g_0} = \frac{k_0^I}{k_0} p S \qquad (11-21)$$

An evaluation of the value of the maximum growth effect for the six countries previously mentioned is shown in Table 11-8. It is clear that the relative size of the indsutrial sector in the various countries significantly affects the growth impact. Were it to be ascertained that excess capacity exists also in services, as most likely is the case in view of the extensive underutilization of transportation systems, restaurants, and recreation facilities during the night hours, it might well be that this growth effect would rise. On the other hand, if substitution exists in the production function, the fall in the capital output ratio would be less, and if most or all unemployment were absorbed by the utilization of already existing capital, then evidently the growth effect would be even lower.

It should also be borne in mind that the static and dynamic effects interact in view of the change of the base of growth. Table 11-9 shows the income levels at the year 2000 for growth at the current levels of shifting at two and at three shifts under the assumptions made in Tables 11-2 and 11-3. It will be noted that the income level after twenty-five years of growth is more than doubled by triple shifting in five out of six of the countries and rises by 90 percent in the remaining one.

5. THE EMPLOYMENT POTENTIAL OF CAPITAL UTILIZATION

As is the case with the effects on growth, capital utilization provides two types of effects on employment. There is a once and for all employment effect arising from the utilization of existing installed capacity, and there is a continuous cumulative effect associated with the change in the growth path resulting from higher utilization of newly invested capital.

The first of these effects is distributed between the industrial and the service sectors. In industry, employment increases as a direct effect of increased shift work. This effect may be proportional with no economies of scale with regard to labor; it may be less than proportional where economies of factor inputs are possible such as in administration and supervision; or it may be more than proportional where the expansion of output requires greater complexity of tasks. Evidently productivity differences in different shifts will also affect the employment generated.

Table 11-8. Increases in the Growth Rate due to Multiple Shifting

	Brazil	Chile	Colombia	Costa Rica	Peru	Venezuela
Share of industry	0.24	0.28	0.225	0.19	0.239	0.171
Ratio of industrial to total output/capital ratio (assumed)	2	2	2	2	2	2
Proportionate shift increase to two shifts	0.16	0.40	0.61	0.5	0.31	0.46
Proportionate increase in growth rate at two shifts	0.08	0.22	0.275	0.19	0.148	0.157
Absolute increase in growth rate at two shifts	0.83%	0.35%	2.01%	1.3%	0.90%	0.82%
Proportionate shift increase to three shifts	0.99	1.40	1.33	1.67	1.31	1.16
Proportionate increase in growth rate at three shifts	0.48	0.78	0.599	0.635	0.63	0.40
Absolute increase in growth rate at three shifts	4.99%	1.25%	4.37%	4.32%	3.84%	2.08%

Table 11-9.   Growth 1976-2000 under Single and Multiple Shifts

	Index of Per Capita Income, Year 2000		
	Current Shifts Pattern	Two Shifts	Three Shifts
Brazil	654	821	2463
Chile*	149	181	283
Colombia	273	514	1039
Costa Rica	242	383	938
Peru	209	280	660
Venezuela	177	233	368

*Based on 1965-1970 per capita growth = 1.6%; 1976 = 100.

New employment will be generated in the service sector as a result of the increased output called forth in this sector by the higher level of income generated in industry. This increase in service employment may accompany more intensive utilization of existing capital in these sectors (e.g., transportation, restaurants, banks, commerce) or may imply expansion of capital stock (e.g., energy). Since the service sector is generally more labor-intensive than industry, the importance of the derived employment generated in services should not be underrated.

The effect on employment of a new "multiple shift" growth path is a composite result of several factors. The first of these is a lowering of the capital stock to employment ratio, which occurs as a simple result of the more intensive use of capital. This ratio is to be distinguished from the ratio of capital services to employment, commonly referred to as a capital/labor ratio, which may well be invariant to shift work, and which is related to the capital stock/employment ratio by the coefficient of shift work. A second element affecting the growth of employment originates in the higher absolute and possibly relative level of investment. A third element affecting the demand for labor arises from the change in the marginal product mix. Whereas under current shift work arrangements economic growth is inward looking, under a multiple shift policy the pattern of growth is export led; the attendant trade policy allows growth to correspond more closely to the comparative advantage of the country. This will naturally imply the more intensive use of the plentiful factors and hence a better demand for labor. Finally, the outward looking policy required by a multiple shift strategy will simultaneously attract more foreign private investment and make it more acceptable to the host country,[19] thus raising the level of investment and employment even further.

The projection of the employment effects arising from the utilization of the existing capital are best done on a sector by sector basis. For each branch of industry, the following relation will hold:

$$E_2 = E_1(1 + \lambda)$$

$$E_3 = E_1(1 + 2\lambda)$$

where E stands for employment, the subscripts refer to the number of shifts worked, and λ is the coefficient of increased employment in an additional shift with regard to the first shift.

In turn, actual employment, E_A, can be defined as follows:

$$E_A = E_1[1 + \lambda(n - 1)]$$

where n is the number of shifts actually worked.

Increases in employment can now be defined by combining the previous formulae as follows:

$$E_i = \frac{1 + \lambda(i - 1)}{1 + \lambda(n - 1)} E_A \qquad \begin{matrix} i = 2, 3 \\ i \geqslant n \end{matrix}$$

Information on λ, the employment coefficient of increased shifting, is not easy to come by. Observations on existing relative size of different shifts is not a fully reliable estimator since, under existing conditions, it is often profitable to work with less than full crews in the second and third shift. Furthermore, different capital intensity of different processes often makes it optimal for the entrepreneur under current institutional arrangements to operate some sections of the plant for a single shift but at a larger scale in order to process the second- and third-shift output of other sections. This is particularly the case in finishing and/or packaging, where the day shift often packages production that has taken place during the afternoon or night shift. Under such circumstances, a comparison of day and night shift is obviously a misleading guide to what would happen if multiple shifting were widely applied. A further source of information is observed productivity of second- and third-shift workers as opposed to first-shift workers. Again, existing practice is not a fully reliable guide to what would occur if multiple shifting were more widely practiced; furthermore, productivity differentials between shifts vary significantly across industries with most industries showing lower productivity on the second and third shift but some showing higher productivity as well.

Table 11-10 shows a projection of increases in industrial employment for six Latin American countries on the assumption that blue
collar labor has an expansion coefficient of 1. The values of the
estimated employment creation are staggering. For the medium-sized
countries a full second shift is worth one hundred thousand new industrial jobs. Full two shift operation of only industry increases employment by a proportion ranging from about 1.5 percent in large
Brazil to about 4 percent in Peru and Chile. Three shifts imply
employment expansion of from 4.5 percent in Colombia to almost
15 percent in Peru.

The projection of increased employment in the service sector is
much more difficult since only an aggregated output projection is
usually available. It is necessary therefore to use a single marginal
output/labor ratio for the whole service sector taken together and to
apply that to the increased output projected as a result of multiple
shifting. The respective projections are also shown in Table 11-5. It
is interesting to note that the volume of employment generated in
services is very considerable, in some cases exceeding our estimates
for expansion of employment in industry.

6. CAPITAL UTILIZATION AND
BALANCE OF PAYMENTS AND
PRICE STABILIZATION POLICY

When, for whatever reason, the balance of payments situation is not
satisfactory or prices are rising too rapidly, policy typically focuses
on the demand side. It either depresses aggregate demand to simultaneously reduce imports and demand-pull on domestic goods or
raises the price of imports to choke off the outflow of foreign exchange. This policy occurs even if it is at the price of a once and for
all rise in domestic prices.

It is remarkable, by contrast, that the supply side has received
little or no attention. Yet recognition of the supply potential inherent in underutilized capital makes a supply-oriented balance-of-
payments policy or price stabilization policy feasible. To counter a
balance-of-payments deficit, the whole of the industrial supply that
can be produced with the existing installed capacity is potentially
exportable. For a small country that takes its terms of trade as given,
exporting then becomes largely a matter of meeting the world price
for goods of the respective quality.[20] To stabilize domestic prices,
the additional output can be used to offset existing demand. It is
important to assure, however, that the additional income created
through the mobilization of existing capital not increase the demand

Table 11-10. Estimated Increases in Employment due to Multiple Shifting

	Brazil	Chile	Costa Rica	Colombia	Peru	Venezuela
Two-Shift Operation:						
Increase in industrial employment	591,942	111,400	18,424	103,700	151,467	78,990
% of present employment	1.4	2.7	2.6	2.1	4.7	2.6
Increase in service employment	423,090	94,371	30,607	278,000	114,135	100,692
% of present employment	1.1	3.2	4.3	5.5	3.5	3.3
Total	965,032	205,771	49,031	381,700	265,602	179,682
% of present employment	2.5	6.9	6.9	7.6	8.2	5.9
Three-Shift Operation:						
Increase in industrial employment	2,751,432	343,400	45,891	225,100	463,334	227,999
% of present employment	7.2	11.5	6.4	4.5	14.3	7.6
Increase in service employment	2,529,447	327,881	77,115	603,400	397,405	319,275
% of present employment	6.6	11.0	10.9	11.9	12.3	10.6
Total	5,280,879	671,281	123,006	828,500	860,739	547,274
% of present employment	13.8	22.5	17.3	16.4	26.6	18.2

Industrial Employment: Country study estimates adjusted to standard size shifts and National Accounts level of industrial output.

Service Employment: Based on following employment/value added coefficients Brazil 104.31 per million Cr. in 1969 prices; Chile 23.17 per million Esc. in 1970 prices; Costa Rica 58.5 per million Col. in 1972 prices; Colombia 76.3 per million Pesos at 1958 prices; Peru 13.97 per million Soles at 1971 prices; Venezuela 46.13 per million Bolivares at 1971 prices.

for goods to an extent that negates the effect of the additional supply. Monetary and fiscal policy has an important role in preventing such an outcome.

It is apparent that a supply-oriented balance of payments or price stabilization policy is significantly less painful and costly in welfare terms than a demand-oriented policy. Whereas the latter implies deflation and unemployment, the former implies expansion and employment. Whereas the latter requires an addition to savings out of a reduced income, the supply policy at best requires an increased rate of savings out of new income.

From the quantitative point of view, the relationship between additional output, additional expenditure, additional exports, and new import demand is of the essence. We will therefore extend the GNP generation model developed in Section 4 to explore the implications for the balance-of-payments and domestic inflationary pressures.

Consider first the balance-of-payments effects of shift work. Imports of two different kinds will increase: complementary imports (M_1), which are inputs needed for production to go forward, and competitive imports (M_2), which will supply the excess demand of domestically produced import competing goods. Increase in complementary imports in turn depends on the import intensity of industrial (M_I) and service (M_s) production and increases in the value added in these sectors (V_I, V_S). Competitive imports are composed of competitive agricultural imports (M_A) and competitive industrial imports (M_I). All these relationships are symbolically shown in the following equations:

$$M = M_1 + M_2 \qquad (11\text{--}22)$$

$$M_1 = m_I V_I + m_s V_s \qquad (11\text{--}23)$$

$$M_2 = M_A + M_I \qquad (11\text{--}24)$$

Note that since by assumption there is no increase in the production of the agricultural sector, the total increase in agricultural demand (E_A) must come from imports. That is shown by Equation (11-25). On the other hand, the situation in industry is more complex. In those industrial sectors in which the new supply exceeds the new demand, which will be typically those sectors in which output has gone up the most, there will be export supply. Under our small country assumption and an export policy appropriate to allow domestic producers to meet the going world market price, this export supply will be equal to new realized exports. At the same time, those sectors in which the new demand exceeds the new supply, which will typically be those sectors in which supply increases were low, there will be new imports. At the aggregate level it is possible to define directly the increase in the balance of trade that results from the newly generated industrial value added as well as from the new derived demand that results from the increased shifting. This is shown in Equation (11-26). Note that the new supply of industrial goods is greater than domestic industrial value added in view of the existence of an import component in industrial goods. Recall also that all variables are defined at domestic prices:

$$M_A = E_A \qquad (11\text{-}25)$$

$$(X - M_I) = V_I(1 + m_I) - E_I \qquad (11\text{-}26)$$

The total change in the balance of trade at domestic prices can be derived by appropriately consolidating Equations (11-22) to (11-26) and using (11-25). The procedure is shown in Equation (11-27) through (11-27d). As one can see from the last of these equations, the balance of trade at domestic prices is equal to the difference between the new income generated as a result of the use of shifts (new value added) and the resulting new private expenditure. This difference in turn is approximated here solely by the internal taxes collected on that value added.

$$X - M = V_I(1 + m_I) - E_I - E_A - m_I V_I - m_S V_S \qquad (11\text{-}27)$$

$$= V_I - E_I - E_A - E_S + E_S - m_S V_S \qquad (11\text{-}27\text{a})$$

$$= V_I - E + E_S - m_S V_S \qquad (11\text{-}27\text{b})$$

$$= V_I - E + V_S(1 + m_S) - m_S V_S \qquad (11\text{-}27\text{c})$$

$$X - M = V_I + V_S - E = V - E = t_1 V \qquad (11\text{-}27\text{d})$$

To calculate the balance of trade at world prices, it is obviously necessary to deflate exports and imports to their international values by the appropriate subsidy or tariff:

$$(X - M)_{INTL} = \frac{X}{1 + d} - \frac{M}{1 + t_2} \qquad (11\text{-}28)$$

$$= \frac{X}{1 + d} - \frac{M_1}{1 + t_{12}} - \frac{M_2}{1 + t_{22}} \qquad (11\text{-}28\text{a})$$

$$= \frac{X}{1 + d} - \frac{M_I}{1 + t_I} - \frac{M_A}{1 + t_A} - \frac{m_I V_I}{1 + tm_I} - \frac{m_S V_S}{1 + tm_S} \qquad (11\text{-}28\text{b})$$

where t_{12} is the average import tariff on complementary imports, t_{22} is the average tariff on competitive imports, t_I is the average tariff on competitive industrial imports, t_A is the average tariff on competitive agricultural imports, tm_I is the average tariff on complementary imports of industrial inputs, and tm_s is the average tariff on complementary imports of service inputs.

Since the model does not separately generate the absolute value of the new exports nor the new imports, it is necessary to derive an approximation to Equation (11-28b) by using the balance of trade at domestic prices and converting it directly to international prices on the assumption that the subsidy to new exports will on the average be equal to the import duty on the new imports. The appropriateness of the assumption depends on the particular mix of exports and imports and the ratio of domestic to world prices reflected by the tariffs or subsidies on the flows involved. For example, if the relatively more competitive products are exported and the less competitive imported, export subsidies will be lower on average than import duties; on the other hand, if FOB values are much below CIF values, a contrary effect will result. The following equations make use of the assumption of equality in the averages of export subsidies and import duties on industrial goods:

$$(X - M)_{INTL} \sim \frac{X - M_I}{1 + t_I} - \frac{M_A}{1 + t_A} - \frac{m_I V_I}{1 + tm_I} - \frac{m_S V_S}{1 + tm_S} \qquad (11\text{-}29)$$

$$\sim \frac{V_I(1 + m_I) - E_I}{1 + t_I} - \frac{E_A}{1 + t_A} - \frac{m_I V_I}{1 + tm_I} - \frac{m_S V_S}{1 + m_S} \qquad (11\text{-}29\text{a})$$

The empirical use of Equation (11-29a) presents the difficulty that it is usually very hard to distinguish complementary from competitive imports. Unfortunately, the usual classification of imports into finished, intermediate, and capital goods is not adequate for our purposes whenever the country produces intermediate goods domestically, because in this case it is necessary to be able to distinguish between imported inputs that compete with domestic production of inputs and imported inputs that do not compete with such domestic production. The inability to disaggregate inputs in this fashion loses importance if one is willing to assume that the average tariff on imports on noncompetitive industrial goods is equal to the average tariff on competitive industrial goods and if additionally one assumes the service sector has no imported inputs.[21] Under these assumptions $t_I = tm_I$ and $m_s = 0$; (10-29a) then simplifies to:

$$(X - M)_{INTL} \approx \frac{V_I - E_I}{1 + t_I} - \frac{E_A}{1 + t_A} \qquad (11\text{-}29b)$$

We can now make use of the relevant equations from the income-generating model to derive an expression in terms of the increase in shifts worked and the initial value added of industry.

$$(X - M)_{INTL} \approx \frac{V_I}{1 + t_I} - \frac{(1 - t_1)e_I V}{1 + t_I} - \frac{(1 - t_1)e_A V}{1 + t_A} \qquad (11\text{-}30)$$

$$\approx \left[\frac{1}{1 + t_I} - \frac{1 - t_1}{1 - e_S(1 - t_1)} \left(\frac{e_I}{1 + t_I} + \frac{e_A}{1 + t_A} \right) \right] \overline{V}_I S \qquad (11\text{-}30a)$$

Whether the balance of payments effect as derived in these equations is positive or negative obviously depends on the respective parameters. Tables (11-11) and (11-12) show the values of the parameters for Brazil, Chile, Colombia, Costa Rica, and Peru and derived annual balance of payments consequences of going to two and three shifts.

The absolute values of the balance of payments effects are of an interesting size in all countries except Venezuela; the same holds true in comparison to foreign exchange reserves. Indeed the surpluses for Brazil, Chile, Colombia, Costa Rica, and Peru are of a size that would justify multiple shifting on pure balance-of-payments grounds. It should also be noted that these figures are conservative since they assume that no effort is made to raise the tax take on the new income generated. Were the domestic fiscal slice larger, the surplus would be higher too.

Consider now the domestic income-expenditure balance. There are two domestic actors in our model: the private sector and the government. The private sector is assumed to spend its disposable income either for consumption or for investment (see Equation 11-27). Monetary savings have been excluded on the assumption that they are offset by new credit creation. The government, however, is not constrained to spend its income; it merely pays out export subsidies

Table 11-11. Parameters Entering Estimation of Balance of Payments

	e_A	e_I	e_S		t_1	t_A^*	t_I	BOP Multiplier
				Effects of Multiple Shifting				
Brazil	0.17	0.32	0.51		0.1707	0.02	0.115	0.2449
Chile	0.128	0.40	0.46		0.181	0.02	0.22	0.2236
Colombia	0.16	0.28	0.55		0.0848	0.02	0.176	0.1222
Costa Rica	0.15	0.36	0.48		0.156	0.02	0.09	0.2397
Peru	0.14	0.40	0.46		0.1063	0.02	0.291	0.096
Venezuela	0.18	0.32	0.50		0.045	0.02	0.0525	0.0719

*Assumed value.

Table 11-12. Estimated Annual Surpluses from Multiple Shifting
($ Millions)

	Full 2 Shifts	*Full 3 Shifts*	*International Reserves 9/31/74*
Brazil (1974)	525.1	3139.9	6516
Chile (1970)	127.8	444.2	-769.22*
Colombia (1972)	104.7	227.3	429
Costa Rica (1972)	21.7	54.4	13.81
Peru (1971)	29.0	101.1	550.7
Venezuela (1971)	38.67	122.5	6415

*1973/December.
Source: *International Financial Statistics*, I.M.F.

when needed to bridge the gap between domestic and foreign prices. Whenever the government runs a surplus as a result of shift work, therefore, capital utilization will have an anti-inflationary effect; when there is a deficit, then the effect will be inflationary. The behavior of the two sectors as described above makes it intuitively plausible for the fiscal surplus/deficit to be the domestic counterpart to the surplus/deficit on the balance of payments. It is useful, however, to formally set out the equivalent.

We can rewrite Equation (11-28) by defining the balance of payments at international prices as the difference between domestic priced exports minus the export subsidy and the domestic priced imports minus the import duty collections:

$$(X - M)_{INTL} = (X - G) - (M - T_2) \qquad (11\text{-}31)$$

Collecting terms and recalling that the balance of trade at domestic prices is equal to the collection of domestic taxes (11-27d), it becomes readily apparent that the balance of payments and fiscal surpluses (or deficits) must be equal.

$$(X - M)_{INTL} = (X - M) + T_2 - G = t_1 V + T_2 G \qquad (11\text{-}32)$$

$$(X - M)_{INTL} = T_1 + T_2 - G = T - G \qquad (11\text{-}32a)$$

Some sense of the potential contribution of capital utilization to stabilization can be derived by comparing the excess supply implicit in the continuous fiscal surplus with the level of GNP. This is done for six Latin American countries in Table 11-13. Evidently these magnitudes are the local currency equivalents of the annual FOB surpluses of Table 11-12. In addition to the annual BOP and disinflationary effects of shift work noted so far, there is a further one time effect resulting from the increase in the demand for money occurring in the transaction period during which income rises to its multiple shift level and additional cash balances are needed to finance the higher level of transactions in the economy. This additional demand for money represents savings that will depress expenditure temporarily, thus causing a one-time increase in international reserves and, by the same token, one-time deflationary pressure.

Table 11-13 shows the once and for all effects arising from the increased demand for transaction balances on the assumptions of a constant velocity of money in the respective economies and on the further assumption that no attempt whatsoever is made to either tax new income more heavily or to otherwise bring about the sterilization of part of the new income. As can be seen, the magnitudes are by no means inconsiderable.

7. INTEGRATED CAPITAL UTILIZATION POLICY

The discussion on the overcausation of underutilization of capital contained in Section 2 as well as the discussion on the necessary conditions for the full utilization of installed capacity contained in Section 3 lead directly to the conclusion that to be effective, capital utilization policy must be an integrated combination of measures with broad coverage. It is not very useful to aim its impact at a single or a few of the causes of underutilization. Unless most or all of them are tackled simultaneously, utilization may not be made privately attractive. Similarly, unless all the necessary macroeconomic conditions for full utilization are put in place, one or another constraint will make achievement of the goal impossible.

Our proposals for an integrated capital utilization policy fall into five areas: (a) trade policy, (b) domestic tax policy, (c) monetary policy, (d) wage policy, and (e) nonmonetary incentives. The policies suggested will be found to be mutually reinforcing and in some instances overlapping. In some cases it is possible to point to alternatives within these categories or between them. In most cases, at least one variant within each category must be implemented for the package to be complete. This does not imply "going for broke" since in most cases it is possible to link the effects of the policy directly to the actual utilization of shifts. Hence to the extent that no increase in shifting takes place, no cost is incurred. Furthermore, as will be

Table 11–13. Stabilization Potential of Capital Utilization

	Annual Excess Supply				One-Time Effect			
	Absolute (Millions)		% of GNP		Absolute (Millions)		% of GNP	
	2 Shifts	3 Shifts	2 Shifts	3 Shifts	2 Shifts	3 Shifts	2 Shifts	3 Shifts
(1974) Brazil	3566	21320.	0.5	3.04	5301	31696.	0.8	4.5
(1970) Chile	1476.5	5130.0	1.6	5.5	1494.7	5193.1	1.6	5.6
(1972) Colombia	1874.6	4068.5	1.1	2.2	5254.5	11403.6	2.8	6.2
(1972) Costa Rica	184.1	463.9	2.2	5.6	258.3	650.8	3.1	7.9
(1971) Peru	1123.7	3912.5	0.4	1.5	3577.5	12456.4	1.4	4.7
(1971) Venezuela	171.71	544.5	0.3	1.0	685.7	2174.0	1.2	3.9

seen, most of these policies are desirable on other grounds as well, thus their benefits far exceed their impact on shifting. Let us examine the direct policy categories one by one:

7.1 Trade Policy

The fundamental goals to be achieved by trade policy are (i) export promotion, to make the relevant part of the increased output saleable abroad, and (ii) import liberalization, to allow in the required inputs and the finished goods essential to absorb the excess demand that will arise in some sectors. In addition, it is desirable to provide stability in the real level of incentives on both sides of the trade balance.

Export promotion can be achieved by a variety of mechanisms. One very simple mechanism is an export subsidy equal to the difference between the domestic and the foreign prices. This type of subsidy is incorporated in the model used for calculations in the preceding sections. It is administratively simple and in a wide range of circumstances it is self-financing.[22] It has the drawback, however, of infringing GATT rules and of provoking retaliation on the part of trading partners under national antidumping regulations.

An effect essentially equivalent to the provision of an export subsidy can be achieved by adopting a "compensated devaluation," consisting of a devaluation of the financial exchange rate, and the concurrent adoption of a downward adjustment of import duties and of the imposition of an export tax on those exports that are not to be promoted. In essence this mechanism allows only the exchange rates affecting nontraditional exports and financial transactions to be devalued since the nominal change in exchange rates for the remainder of the foreign transactions is offset by changes in trade taxation of equal size and opposite direction.[23] This is again a policy that is fairly easy to implement; furthermore, it is in accord with all international agreements currently in force. It may run into opposition from traditional exporting sectors, however, who would now perceive themselves as paying an export tax that they were not previously subjected to despite the fact that they are in reality getting precisely the same amount of units of domestic currency per unit of foreign exchange.

Import liberalization is technically necessary only in countries using quantitative import controls to regulate their foreign trade. Where tariffs are used, no action on the import side is necessary since at the margin imports are the residual supplier, albeit at a higher price than under free trade. Where quantitative restrictions are in use, liberalization can take the form of relaxing these restrictions or alternatively of linking the export and import sides of the balance of payments.[24]

The real stability in incentives is best achieved by a crawling or trotting peg, based on the goal of maintaining a constant cost parity between domestic production and imports.[25]

7.2 Tax Policy

The policy goals under this heading again are two: (i) to remove disincentives to multiple shifting and instead provide incentives to do so; and (ii) to eliminate the subsidy to the use of capital and replace it if at all possible by a tax.

The instruments to achieve these goals are several. In the first place, the price of capital goods can be affected directly by abolishing import exemptions for capital goods and instead raising the tariff on imports of such goods and/or putting an excise tax on them. Second, a specific disincentive to multiple shifting is constituted by the lack of relationship between the rate of depreciation and the intensity of use of the equipment. Direct proportionality between shifting and the depreciation rate allowable for the income tax calculation would be a simple and effective reform. Third, the availability of tax deductions from corporate income tax whenever new investment takes place, provided the investment is documented by the purchase of fixed assets, is a further incentive to expand the capital stock in preference of utilizing what already exists. Such measures should either be repealed, or if they are regarded as important to promote corporate savings, should be redrafted so as to count as equivalent to the expansion of capacity the more intensive use of existing capital. Or put differently, the same benefits should accrue to the firm that adds a new shift of production on existing machines as accrues to the firm that expands production with new machines.

Beyond these policies very direct carrot and stick alternatives exist to promote multiple shifting. For example, the basic corporate tax rate can go down for multiple shifters or it can go up for single shifters. Special deductions connected to second-shift or third-shift wage bills can be introduced, double or triple depreciation for double or triple shifters can be legislated, and so on. To what extent these direct measures are desirable depends in part on what can be done on wage policy and to what extent tax tools must be used to offset the differential between market and shadow wage and between the day and the night shift.

7.3 Credit Policy

The policy goal in this case is to offset the strong biases that currently exist both in interest rate and availability of credit for loans connected with the purchase of fixed assets. Indeed, loans for working capital are used essentially to finance inventories of goods in process and of finished goods, be they unsold or sold on credit.[26] These goods consist of embodied raw material, labor, and capital, with only the first two items requiring financing for the period of production and sale. Since the market price of labor is above the shadow wage, it follows that for production from already installed capital, the marginal social cost of goods in process is below the marginal private cost. Hence an argument for the subsidization of credit for working capital can be made. The same argument does not apply to working capital necessary to cooperate with new investments; the relationship between the market and shadow cost of goods in process in this case depends on the relative intensity of capital and labor and on the differences between the respective shadow and market prices of these factors.

Since in the short run the major demand for working capital would arise from utilization of existing investment, it would seem appropriate to have a vigorous lending policy for borrowers who wish to increase the utilization of installed capital. One simple policy measure would be to extend to those who "invest in the utilization of capital" the same facilities now available to those who wish to invest in additional real assets. Such loans might well have to require a commitment on the part of borrowers to indeed increase the number of shifts worked by a certain amount within a given period. The policing of such commitments should not be much more difficult than the verification that the appropriate machinery has been bought for new investment projects. Indeed, faced with the certain loss of all credit for nonfulfillment of a commitment to multiple shift, it is unlikely that firms would deliberately default on their obligation.

7.4 Wage Policy

The policy goal here again is very clear—to minimize the excess of the market cost of labor over the shadow price and particularly of the cost of second- and third-shift labor with regard to its shadow price. Since some reduction in wages is involved, any policy that can be suggested under this heading will encounter significant opposition.

The most promising approach is to make any reduction in benefits accruing to workers only applicable to those not already employed that is, to have the changes apply only to the new jobs created by the multiple shift policy. The policing aspects of such marginal policies are not unconsiderable, however. Another alternative is to suspend some or all of the social legislation that raises the cost of labor for a limited period of time and only for new second and third shifters.

Finally, the line of least resistence is to transfer the cost of social security and other fringe benefits to the government.

A prime candidate for some type of action is the explicit wage premium, which raises the night wage above the day wage and thus serves to widen the difference between the market and shadow prices of labor even further than during normal working hours. A second and no less important target is the implementation of special tenure rules for second and third shifts to allow the experimental adoption of shifts. In some countries, it is illegal to fire a worker after the first three months of employment. Under such circumstances, experiments at more intensive utilization of capital are perceived as being risky by the entrepreneur since he is often not certain that the additional shift will be a lasting one. Thus he may find himself in the disagreeable situation of having to cut output but not being able to fire the laborers hired for the new shift.

7.5 Nonmonetary Incentives

The response elasticity of entrepreneurs to the monetary incentives discussed above is to a large extent determined by the general atmosphere prevailing toward multiple shifting. It is in the creation of that atmosphere that the nonmonetary incentives have a major role to play. These incentives may range from preferential access to government services and processing for multiple shifters, through award of decorations for full use of capacity, to lower preference rating on government contracts for single shifters. As a transitory measure, compulsory double shifting can also be considered, certainly on all new investments, but very possibly on existing investment as well. Whereas such a requirement would violate entrepreneurial freedom of choice, a welfare cost would be incurred by the economy only in those cases where single shifting is optimal, which are assuredly quite few. If in addition, compulsory double shifting were not the only measure adopted but were used to reinforce a package of the kind discussed above, the welfare cost of operating under very distorted factor prices and hence wrong factor proportions would be avoided.

8. SUMMARY AND CONCLUSION

Underutilized capital coexists with idle labor in Latin America. It takes the form of low shift work, a few days worked, and under-production within the hours worked. In shiftwork, only about two-thirds of the firms in six Latin American countries studied work only one shift. These single shift firms provide about half the industrial employment of the countries, own a quarter of the capital stock, and generate over a third of the value added.

Entrepreneurs who do not triple shift are rational. They respond to systematic distortions in the price and incentive systems that generate divergence between the private and social optimums. Labor legislation, tax legislation, lending rules and policies, and international trade policy all have elements favoring single shifting and the use of more machines rather than multiple shifting and economizing of capital stock. In addition, the objectives of the entrepreneur as well as nonprice factors are at work to reinforce the tendency to work few shifts.

The coexistence of idle installed capacity with unemployed labor offers a unique opportunity for Latin American countries to get something for almost nothing. A generalized two-shift operation is worth up to five years of per capita growth; three shifts is equivalent to up to eleven years of growth. The employment effect is in the hundreds of thousands of new jobs. Full double shifting raises employment by up to 5 percent, full triple shifting by up to 15 percent.

Mobilization of the idle capacity is not simple, for in addition to motivating the firm to work additional shifts, balance of payments and fiscal constraints need to be borne in mind. However, neither is this task exceedingly complicated. Essentially, policy must see to it that exports lead rather than follow the process of capacity utilization.

The policies appropriate to achieve stabilization, growth, and employment seem in part counterintuitive and often run against "conventional wisdom." Thus stabilization requires increased government subsidies and expansion of credit; balance of payments improvement is preceded by import liberalization; growth and employment are brought about by taxing capital goods, and so on. Yet these recommendations are no more revolutionary than Keynes's prescription to "spend one's way out of the recession." A world of idle factors is a world upside down and the sooner the potential gains of putting capital (and labor) to work are realized, the better.

NOTES

1. Early documentation on underutilization of capital can be found in various publications of ECLA, for example, ILPES/CELADE, *Elementos para la Elaboración de una Política de Desarrollo con Integración en América Latina, 1968, Ch. 3.* More recent data has been developed on Brazil, Chile, Colombia, Costa Rica, Peru, and Venezuela in the context of a collaborative research pro-

ject coordinated by the author at Boston University's Center for Latin American Development Studies. See Kogut (1975), Ramos (1974), Thoumi (1975), Schydlowsky (1975), Abusada (1975a,b), CORDIPLAN (1974), Abusada (1976).

2. For Chile, this breakdown has not been tabulated.

3. The greater incidence of shift work in Brazil may be due to the higher representation of large enterprise in the Brazilian sample.

4. Note, however, that the K/L ratio must be defined as the ratio of capital *services* to labor or a distorted measure will result.

5. See Abusada (1975a) and (1976).

6. Note, however, that in Costa Rica, the percentage of firms working only one shift rises as one goes to the highest size group.

7. See Abusada (1975a) and (1976).

8. See, for example, Abusada and Millán (1973), Betancourt and Clague (1975a,b,c), Baily (1972), Millán (1973), (1974), Schydlowsky (1974), Winston (1972).

9. Note that what is at issue is a comparison between the undistorted supply price of higher shift labor on the part of Latin America's unemployed and the market wage the regulations require paying.

10. For a detailed analysis of the role of working capital in utilization see Betancourt and Clague (1975c) and Schydlowsky (1974).

11. It could, of course, be argued that if governments have rigged market prices in Latin America they have good reasons for so doing and hence market prices are optimal. This writer's observation of the policies and how they are generated makes it impossible for him to accept such a view.

12. For a more extensive discussion of these problems see Schydlowsky (1973).

13. See Section 6 for a discussion and quantification of these effects.

14. Note that a constant ratio of inventories to the input of capital services translates to a higher ratio of inventories to capital stock when utilization is increased. Hence a higher ratio of working capital to fixed capital is a necessary feature of long-term higher utilization of fixed capital.

15. When the elasticity of substitution between capital and labor is greater than one a multiple shift plant will have a *higher* capital output ratio than a single shift plant *at the same factor prices*. See Betancourt and Clague (1975a) and Millán (1974). A change in the shift pattern usually requires a fall in the wage/rental ratio; hence on balance the capital/output ratio will ordinarily fall.

16. If industry is working currently at 1.25 shifts on the average and if the level of activity is projected to go to two shifts, the value of the shift coefficient will be 0.6.

17. Note that the model therefore excludes both monetary savings and credit. Both could easily be introduced; however, the simultaneous exclusion is unimportant as long as bank credit is neutral, that is, neither inflationary nor deflationary.

18. This assumption is equivalent to having the user "assemble" the domestic and imported components of services.

19. In the context of a higher growth rate and of a more broadly based export sector, foreign capital is less of a threat because the alternatives to it are more plentiful than under stagnation and balance of payments penury.

20. It is also essential that the exports have a positive value added at world prices, that is, that the direct and indirect foreign exchange costs do not exceed foreign exchange revenue.

21. This is equivalent to supposing that it is the final user who "assembles" the services and their imported input.

22. See Schydlowsky (1971) for a discussion of the conditions under which the "full capacity budget" is in surplus.

23. For a detailed discussion see Schydlowsky (1967).

24. Temporary import regimes such as Colombia's Plan Vallejo solve only the problem of direct complementary imports required for export production. Thus a broader instrument such as the "bonus voucher," in use for many years in Pakistan, seems more appropriate. See Bruton and Bose (1963) for discussion.

25. If such a solution is not acceptable for one reason or another, the import-export voucher link is a feasible alternative since the entitlement price will rise automatically as the domestic and world prices diverge, thus maintaining constant the incentives to trade for the goods included in the system.

26. A sale on credit is equivalent to moving the merchandise from the seller's to the buyer's warehouse. Until payment occurs, the goods are still in the seller's financial inventory.

REFERENCES

Abusada, R. "A Shift Choice Model of Capital Utilization," July 1975 (a) (mimeo).

——. "Utilización del Capital Instalado en el Sector Industrial Peruano," August 1975 (b) (mimeo).

——. "Capacity Utilization in Venezuela Industry," June 1976 (mimeo).

Abusada, R., and P. Millán. "Optima Utilización del Capital Instalado en Empresas con Participatión de los Trabajadores en la Gestión," December 1973 (mimeo).

Betancourt, R., and C. Clague. "An Economic Analysis of Capital Utilization." *Southern Economic Journal* (July 1975 [a]).

——. "The Determinants of Capital Utilization in Labor Managed Enterprises," June 1975 (b) (mimeo).

——. "The Profitability of Shift-Work in Imperfect Capital Markets," July 1975 (c) (mimeo).

Baily, M.A. "Capital Utilization in Kenya Manufacturing Industry." Ph.D. Dissertation, M.I.T., December 1972.

Bruton, H., and S. Bose. *The Pakistan Export Bonus Scheme.* Karachi: Institute of Development Economics, 1963.

CORDIPLAN. "Capacidad Utilizada de la Industria Manufacturera Fabril," May 1974.

Kogut, E.L. "Estudo Sobre o Uso de Turno de Trabalho na Industria de

Transformaçao do Brasil," 1975 (mimeo).

Millán, P., "Economic Analysis of Multiple Shifting in the Short Run," December 1973 (mimeo).

——. "Multiple Shifts in the Pure Investment Decision," December 1974 (mimeo).

Schydlowsky, D.M. "From Import Substitution to Export Promotion for Semi-Grown-Up Industries: A Policy Proposal." *Journal of Development Studies* III: 4 (July 1967).

——. "Short Run Policy in Semi-Industrial Economies." *Economic Development and Cultural Change* XIX:3 (April 1971).

——. "On Determining the Causality of Underutilization of Capacity: A Working Note," 1973 (mimeo).

——. "Influencia del Mercado de Capital Sobre la Utilización de Capacidad Instalada," *Desarrollo Económico* 54 (Julio-Set 1974).

——. "La Utilizacion de Capacidad Industrial Instalada Como Fuente de Empleo y Crecimiento en Costa Rica," 1975 (mimeo).

Ramos, Joseph. "La Ampliación de Turnos en la Industria Chilena: La Factibilidad de una Política de Empleo Productivo," PREALC, May 1974 (mimeo).

Thoumi, F. "Fixed Capital Utilization in Colombia Manufacture," April 1975 (mimeo).

Winston, G.C. "Capital Utilization, Employment and Investment: A Neo-classical Model of Optimal Shift Work," 1972 (mimeo).

Index

Aggregate demand. *See also* Demand
  equation, 134, 135–136
  and inflation, 227, 228–229, 233–234, 235–240
  models using in developing countries, 3
  and urban unemployment, 12
Aggregate supply. *See also* Supply
  for Argentina, 148–150
  for Brazil, 148–150
  equation, 134–136
Aggregation, in developing countries, 3–4
Agricultural sector
  and inflation, 230–231
    in Chile, 230, 234
    in Latin America, 240
  in Latin America, inelastic supply in, 227–228
  value added increase, 328
Agriculture, 11
  and demand, 238, 239, 240
  in Latin America, 230
  in Nicaragua, 85
  in Panama, 47–53
Ando, Albert, 4, 5, 22
Arboledo, H., 40
Argentina
  aggregate supply for, 148–150
  data for, 144–145
  economy of, and Phillips curve, 201–225
  and exchange rates, 221–222
  expectations for, 206–211, 218–222
  expected inflation in, and Phillips curve, 205–211
  expected prices for, 145–148
  and foreign sector, 15

Gelbard period in, 212–214, 218–220
incomes policy in, and Phillips curve, 211–215, 218–222
inflation dynamics for, 153–157, 159–163
Krieger-Vasena period in, 212–214, 218–220
model for, 144–163
nominal income, 150–153
output dynamics for, 153–157, 159–163
political trends in, 210–211
price dynamics for, 153–157, 159–163
unions in, and Phillips curve, 211–215, 219
Assets, 22–24
Autoregressive integrated average (ARIMA) process, 140, 154, 164n.2

Balance of payments
  and capital utilization, 338–346
  monetary model of, 258–278
  in Nicaragua, 97–98, 101
  and shocks, 259
  surplus, 24
Balboa, and U.S. dollar, 41, 67–68
Bananas, as exports, 43, 304–305
Banco de Mexico, 119
Banking system, of Nicaragua, 93–94, 99–100
Banks, central, 269–274
Barro, Robert J., 14
  on money and output in Mexico, Colombia, and Brazil, 177–199
Beans, 49

About the Editors

Jere R. Behrman is a Professor and Chairperson of Economics at the University of Pennsylvania. His primary research interest is in applied economic analysis of the domestic and international aspects of economic development. His secondary research interests include international trade, more generally and economic distribution in the United States. He has considerable international experience, particularly in Latin America. He has served as a consultant or research associate for the World Bank, Wharton Econometric Forecasting Associates, the National Bureau of Economic Research, SIECA, ILPES, UNDP, UNCTAD, INCAE, AID, ECIEL, NSF, ODC, HIID, the Ford Foundation, The Rockefeller Foundation, and Central Banks, Planning Agencies, and ministries for various governments. He is author or co-author of *Macroeconomic Policy in a Developing Country; The International Economic Order, Economic Development, and International Commodity Agreements; Econometric Modeling of World Commodity Policy; International Commodity Agreements: An Evaluation of the UNCTAD Integrated Programme; Socioeconomic Success: A Study of the Effects of Genetic Endowments, Family Environment and Schooling; Econometric Models of World Agricultural Commodity Markets; Foreign Trade Regimes and Economic Development; and Supply Response in Underdeveloped Agriculture.* He also has published in the *American Economic Review, Econometrica, The Journal of Political Economy, The International Economic Review, Cuadernos de Economía,* and other professional journals and collections of papers.

James A. Hanson is an associate professor of economics and chairman of the Latin American studies committee at Brown University. His experience in Latin America includes work in Venezuela under

367

the auspices of the Yale Growth Center, in Colombia and Panamá with the national planning agencies and as consultant to the BID, and the U.N. Economic Commission for Latin America, where he served as director of research for the Instituto Latino Americano de Planificación Económica y Social. He also has been a Fulbright lecturer in Ecuador and Uruguay. At present, he is editor of the *American Economic Association, Papers and Proceedings*. In addition to *Growth in Open Economies*, he has published articles in the *American Economic Review, Economic Inquiry, Economic Development and Cultural Change, Journal of Economic Studies, Cuadernos de Economia* and *Desarrollo Económico*.

About the Contributors

Robert Barro is professor of economics at the University of Rochester and was consultant to the Departmento Nacional de Planeación de Colombia. He has written extensively on money, hyperinflation, nonmarket clearing macroeconomic models, and most recently monetary effects in rational expectations models.

Abel Beltrán del Rio is director of the Wharton—DIEMEX project and has written extensively on econometric models of Latin American economies, especially Mexico.

George Borts is professor of economics at Brown University, editor of the *American Economic Review* and has written extensively on international finance, investment and trade.

Mario Brodersohn is a member of the Instituto Torcuato Di Tella in Buenos Aires, has served as a consultant for the ILO and PREALC, and written extensively on problems of employment and macroeconomic policy in Argentina and other Latin American economies.

Luis Duran Downing is a member of the Departamento de Estudios Económicos del Banco Central de Nicaragua.

Roque Fernandez was a staff member of ILPES and the IMF and has written extensively on econometric analysis and on inflation in Latin America. He is presently a member of the Centro de Estudios Macroeconomicos de Argentina in Buenos Aires.

Daniel Schydlowsky is professor of economics and associate director of the Center for Latin American Development Studies at Boston

University. He has written extensively on macroeconomic problems of Latin American countries and effective protection.

Gabriel Siri is director of the Study Unit for Integration and Development of the Permanent Secretariat of the General Treaty for Central American Integration (SIECA).

José Félix Solís is a member of the Departmento de Estudios Economicos del Banco Central de Nicaragua.

Juan Rafael Vargas is a staff member of the Study Unit for Integration and Development of the Permanent Secretariat of the General Treaty for Central American Integration (SIECA).

Susan Wachter is an associate professor of finance in the Wharton School of the University of Pennsylvania and has written extensively on structural inflation in Latin America.